Helck

Story and Art by
Nanaki Nanao

Contents

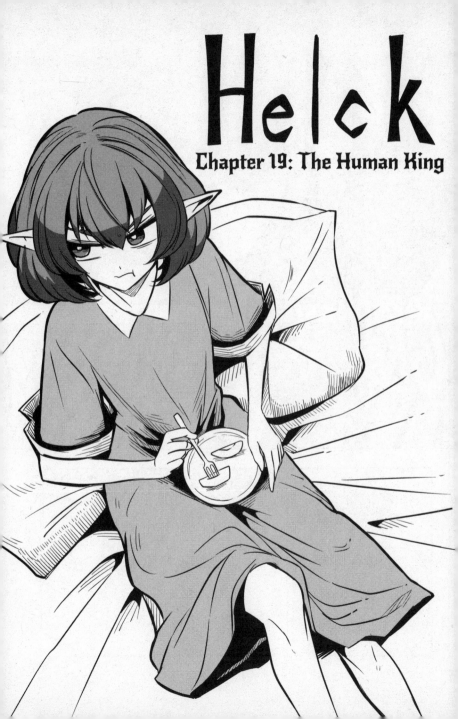

Helck
Chapter 19: The Human King

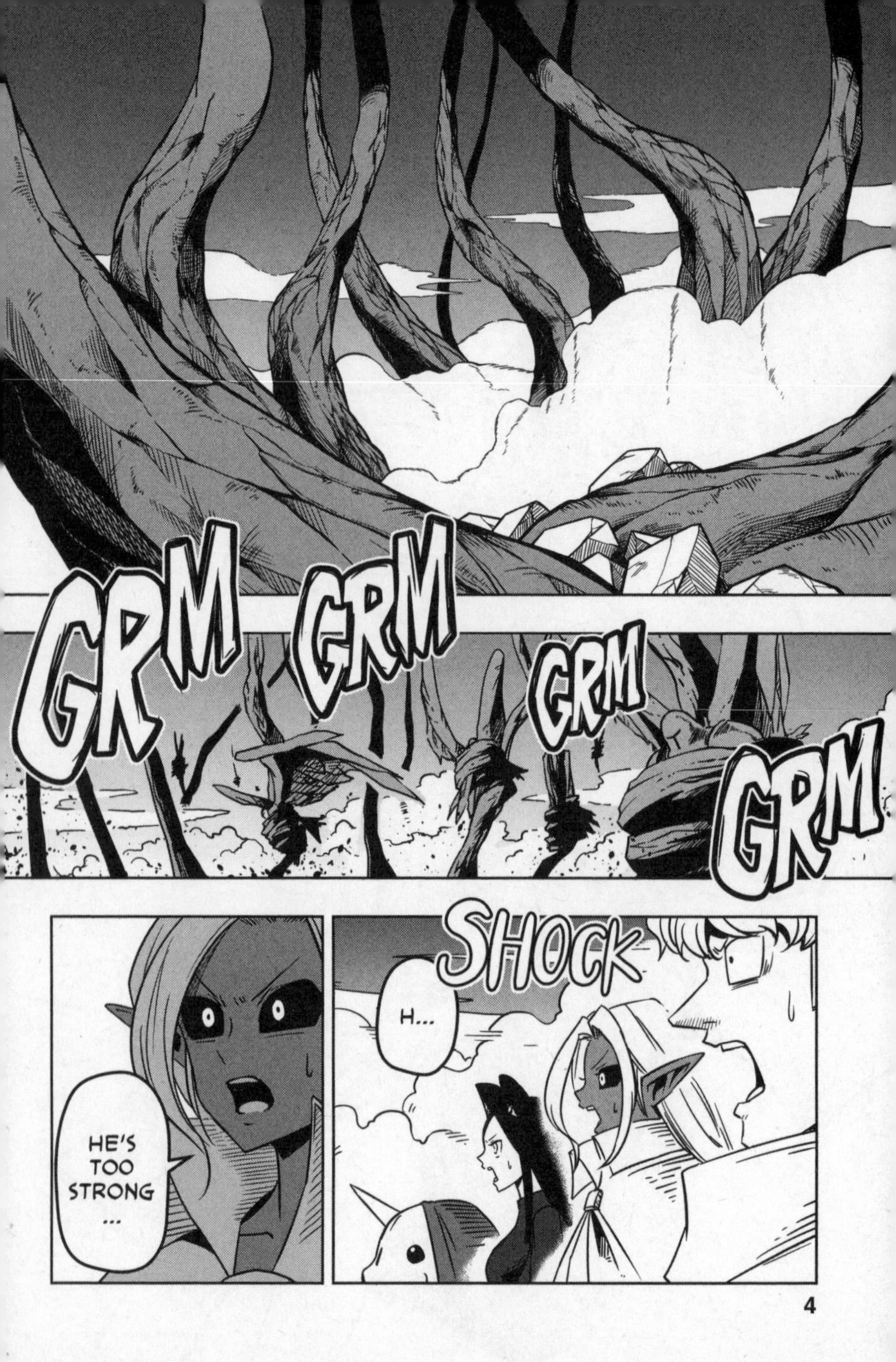
GRM
GRM
GRM
GRM
SHOCK
H...
HE'S TOO STRONG ...

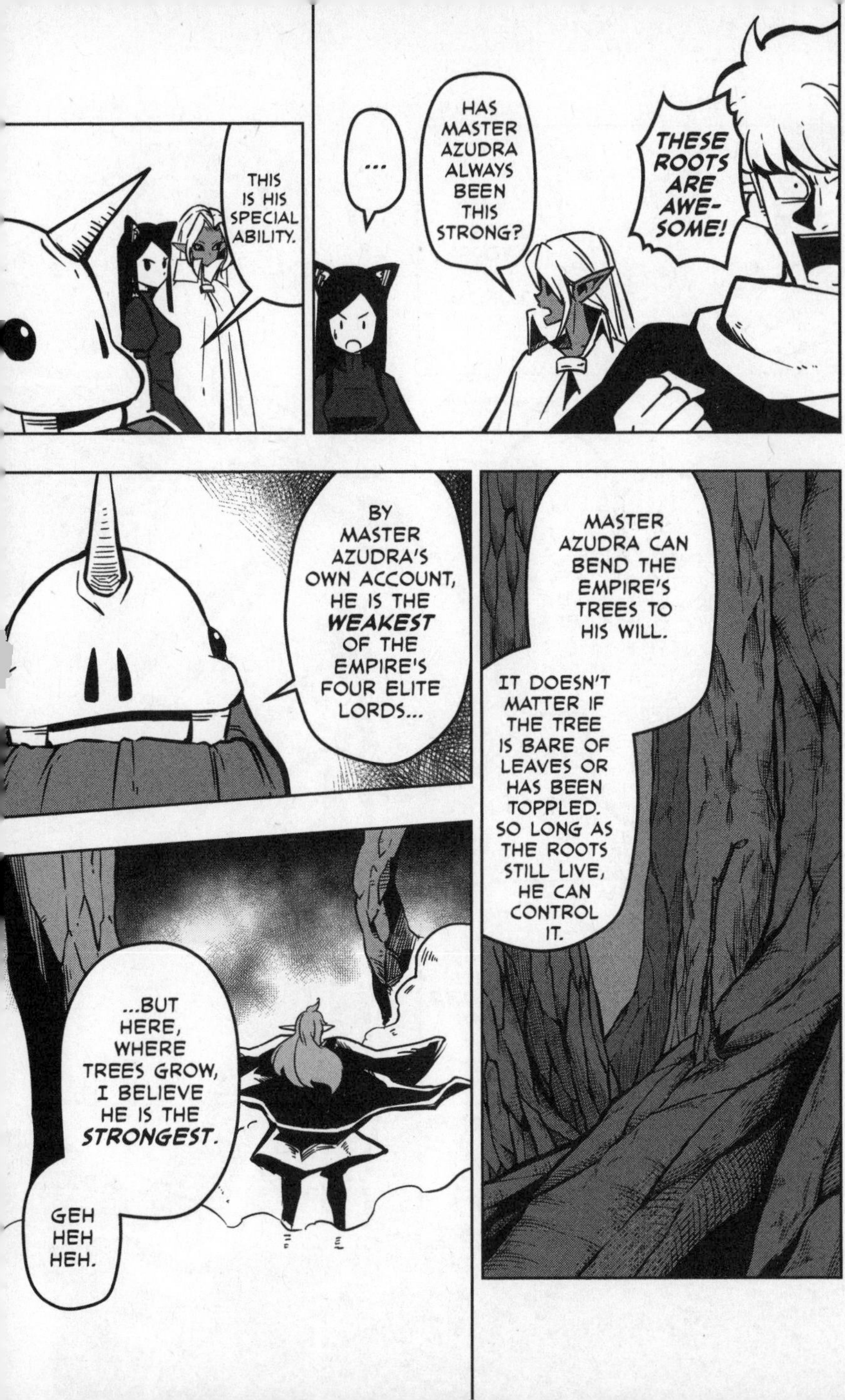

THESE ROOTS ARE AWE-SOME!
HAS MASTER AZUDRA ALWAYS BEEN THIS STRONG?
...
THIS IS HIS SPECIAL ABILITY.
MASTER AZUDRA CAN BEND THE EMPIRE'S TREES TO HIS WILL.
IT DOESN'T MATTER IF THE TREE IS BARE OF LEAVES OR HAS BEEN TOPPLED. SO LONG AS THE ROOTS STILL LIVE, HE CAN CONTROL IT.
BY MASTER AZUDRA'S OWN ACCOUNT, HE IS THE *WEAKEST* OF THE EMPIRE'S FOUR ELITE LORDS...
...BUT HERE, WHERE TREES GROW, I BELIEVE HE IS THE *STRONGEST*.
GEH HEH HEH.

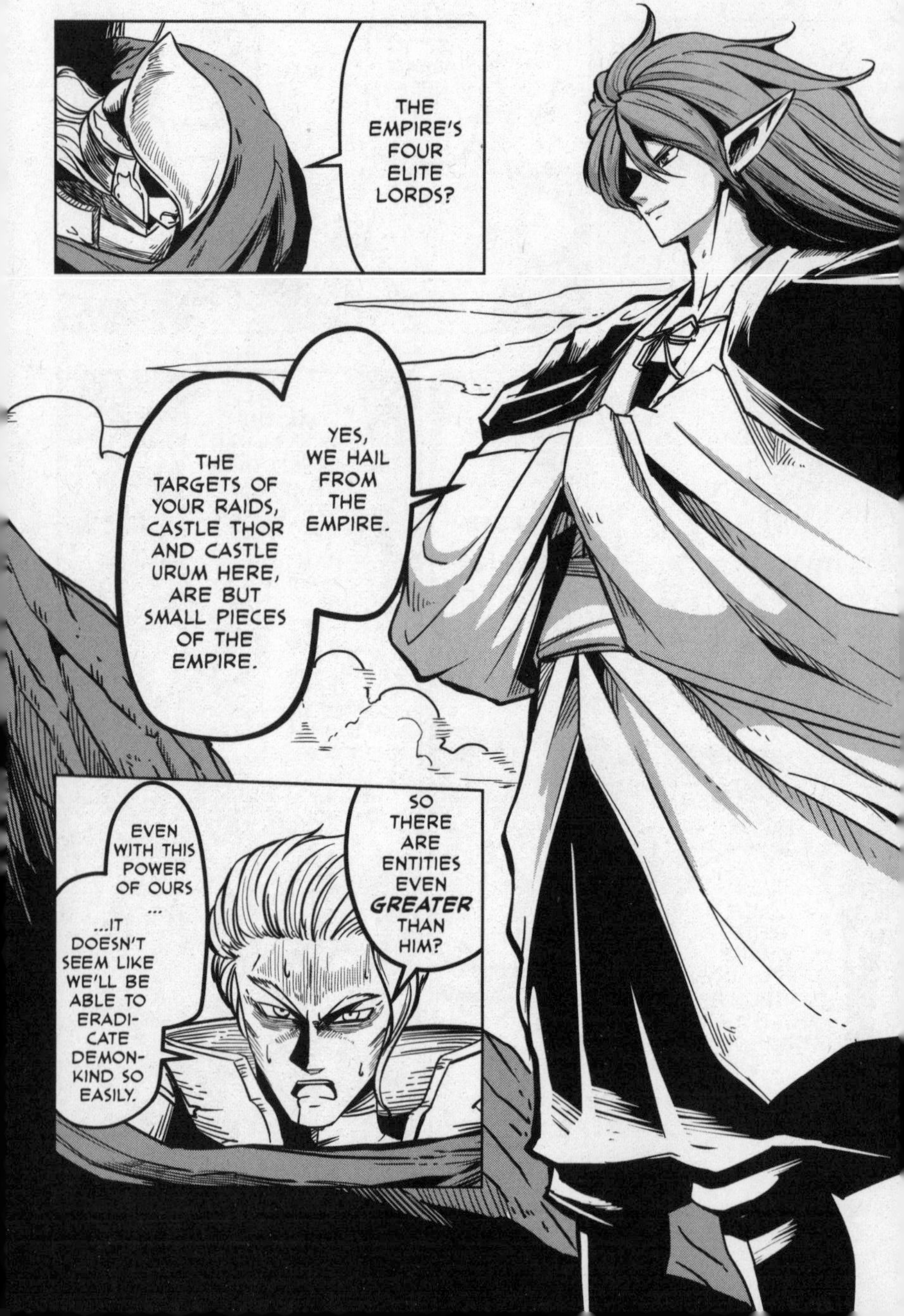
THE EMPIRE'S FOUR ELITE LORDS?
YES, WE HAIL FROM THE EMPIRE.
THE TARGETS OF YOUR RAIDS, CASTLE THOR AND CASTLE URUM HERE, ARE BUT SMALL PIECES OF THE EMPIRE.
SO THERE ARE ENTITIES EVEN *GREATER* THAN HIM?
EVEN WITH THIS POWER OF OURS ...
...IT DOESN'T SEEM LIKE WE'LL BE ABLE TO ERADI-CATE DEMON-KIND SO EASILY.

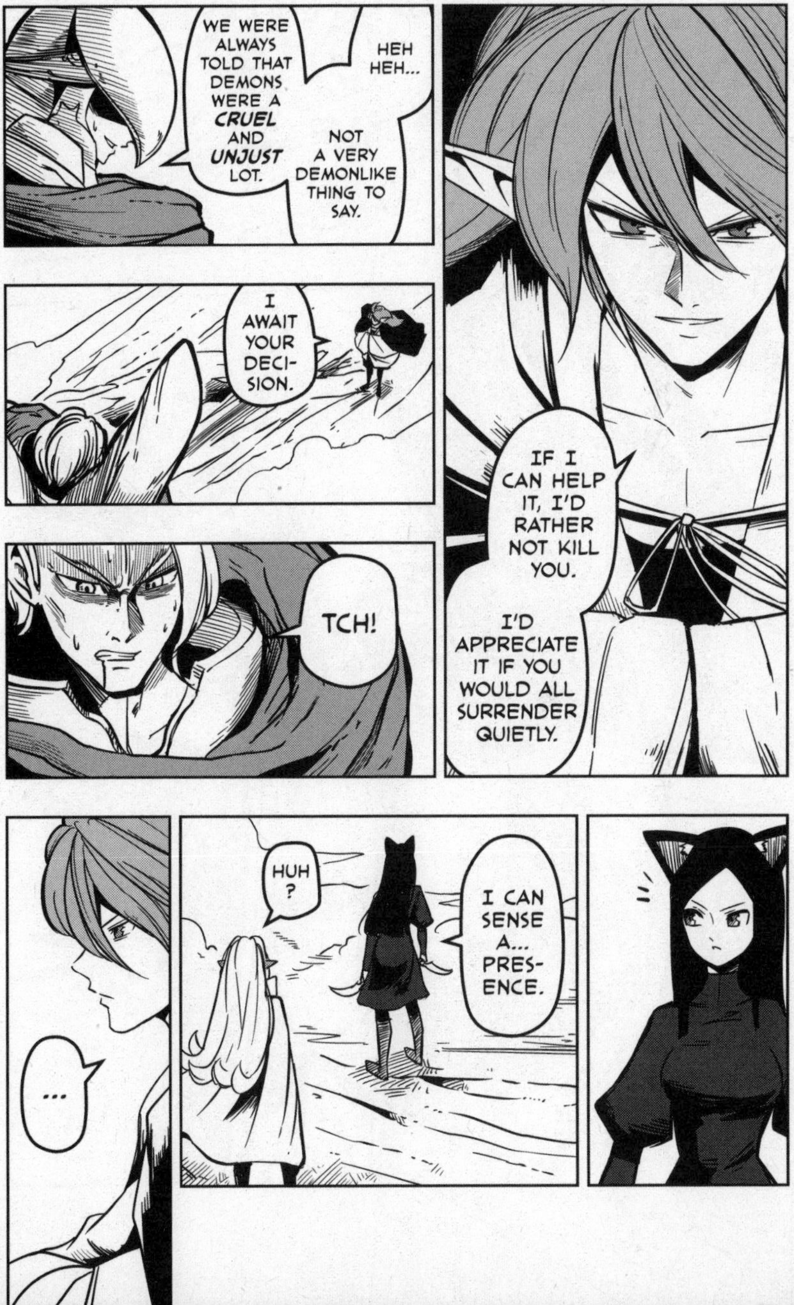
IF I CAN HELP IT, I'D RATHER NOT KILL YOU.
I'D APPRECIATE IT IF YOU WOULD ALL SURRENDER QUIETLY.
HEH HEH...
NOT A VERY DEMONLIKE THING TO SAY.
WE WERE ALWAYS TOLD THAT DEMONS WERE A *CRUEL* AND *UNJUST* LOT.
I AWAIT YOUR DECI-SION.
TCH!
I CAN SENSE A... PRES-ENCE.
HUH?
...

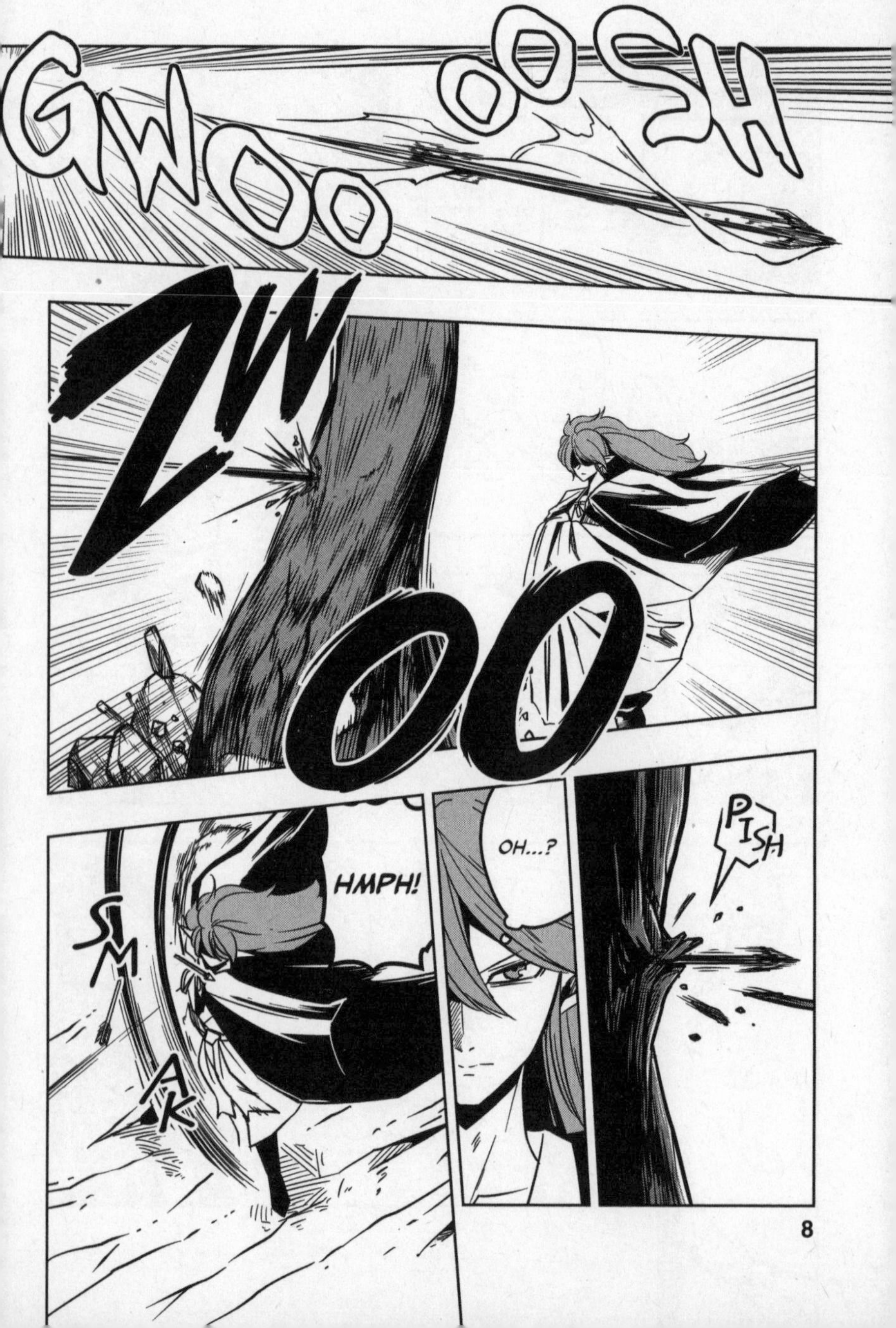
GWOOOOSH
ZWOOO
PISH
OH...?
HMPH!
SMAK

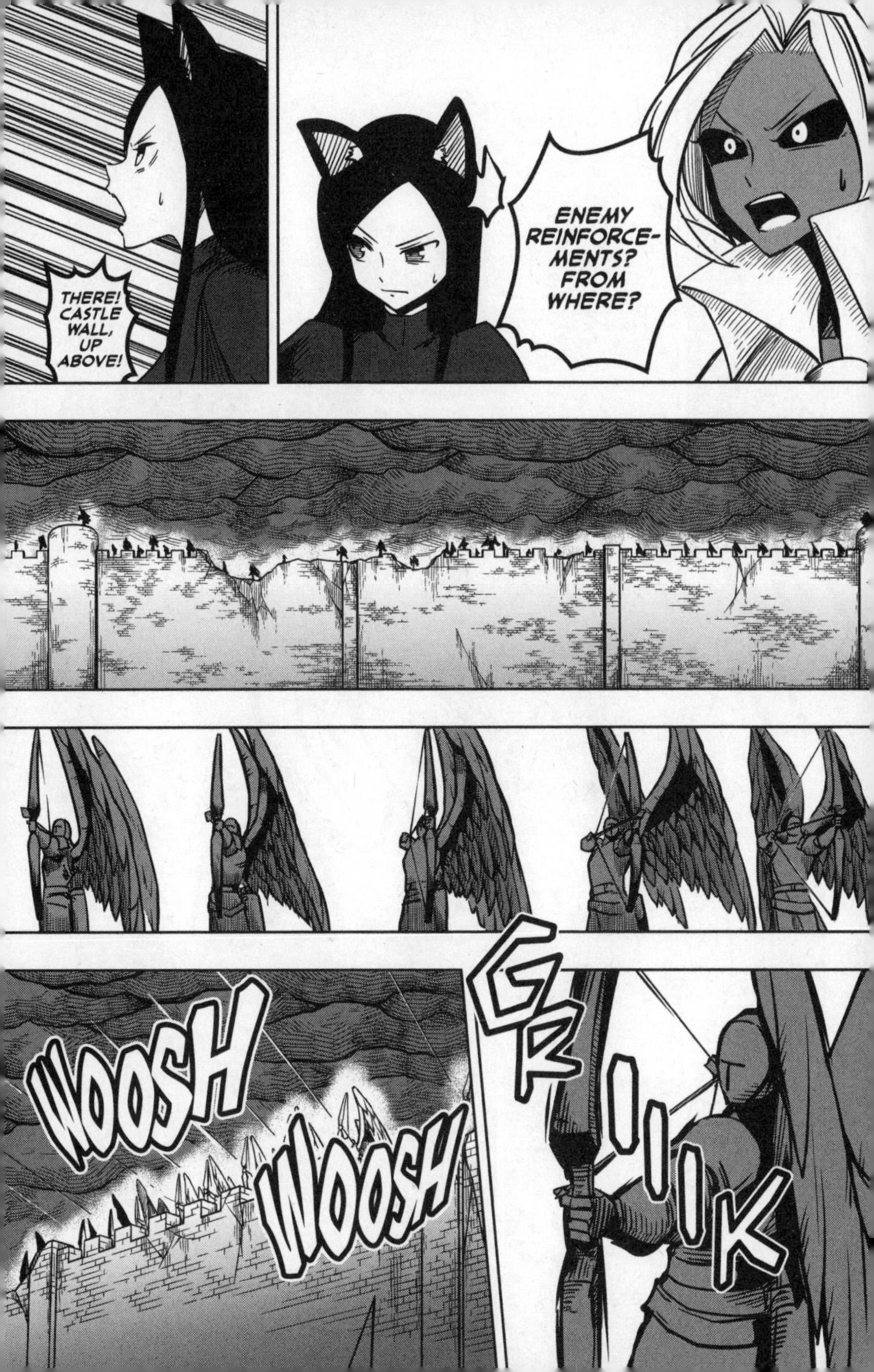
ENEMY REINFORCEMENTS? FROM WHERE?
THERE! CASTLE WALL, UP ABOVE!
GRIIIK
WOOSH
WOOSH

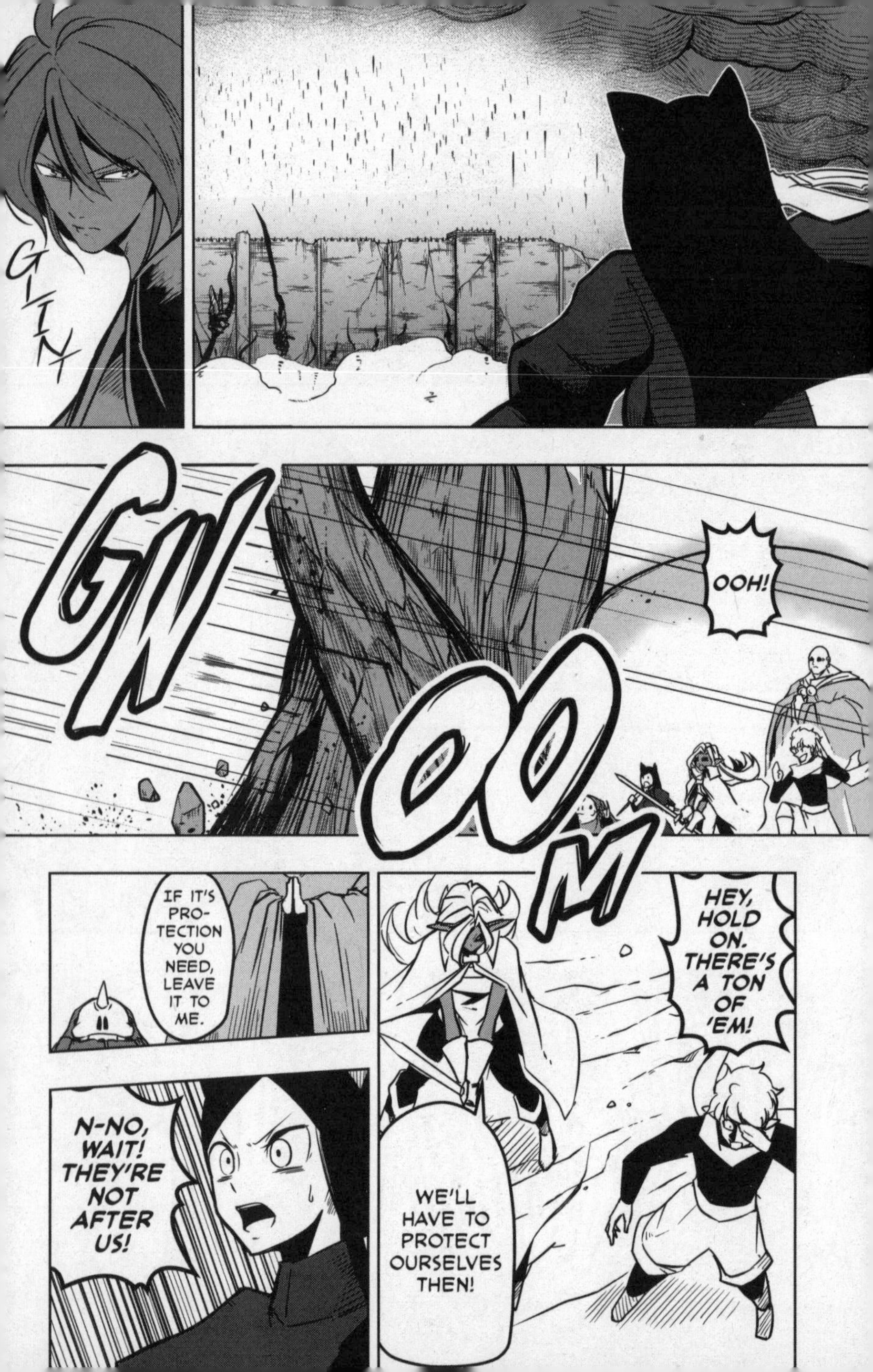
GLINT
GWOOM
OOH!
HEY, HOLD ON. THERE'S A TON OF 'EM!
WE'LL HAVE TO PROTECT OURSELVES THEN!
IF IT'S PRO-TECTION YOU NEED, LEAVE IT TO ME.
N-NO, WAIT! THEY'RE NOT AFTER US!

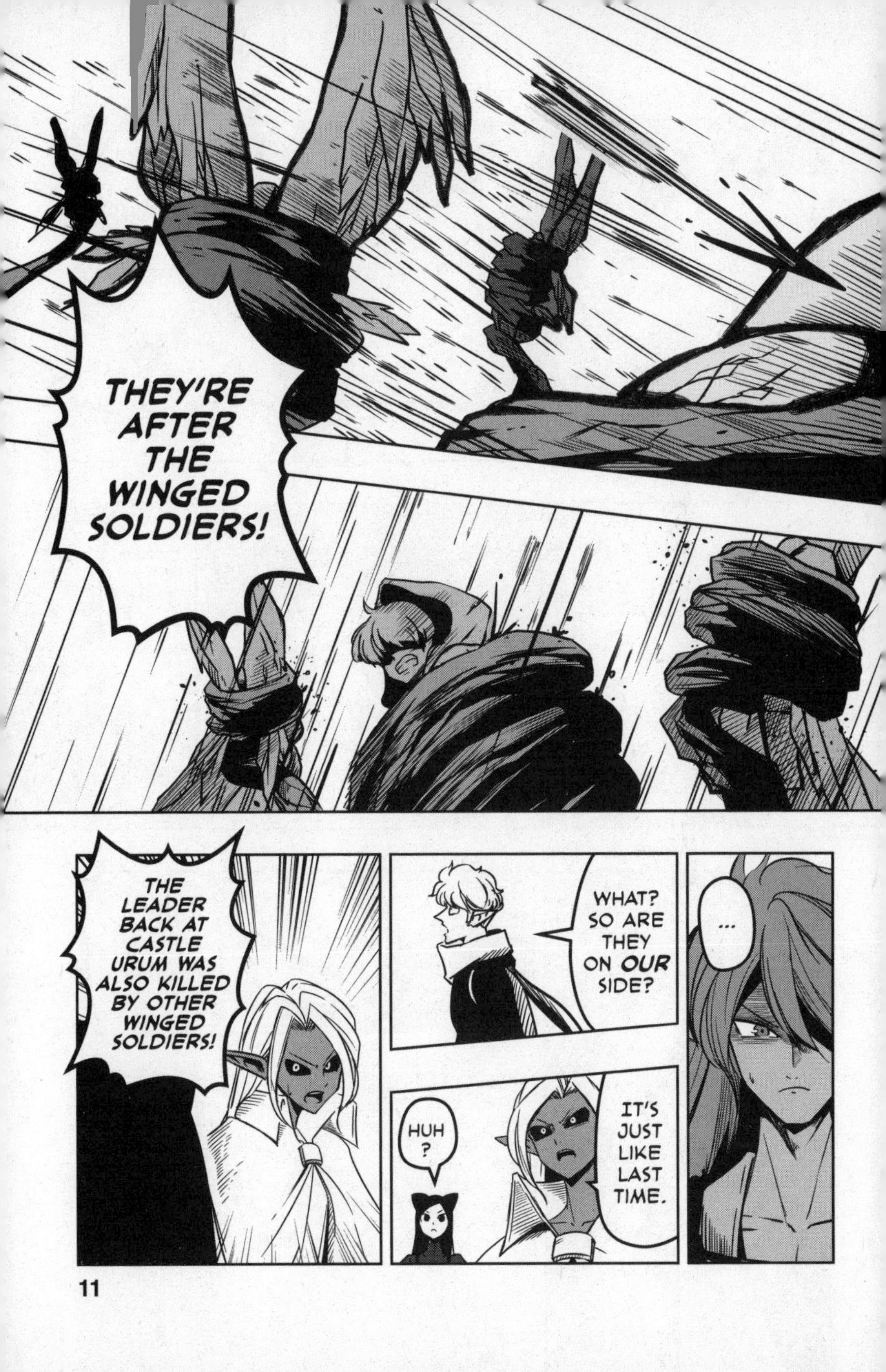
THEY'RE AFTER THE WINGED SOLDIERS!
...
WHAT? SO ARE THEY ON *OUR* SIDE?
IT'S JUST LIKE LAST TIME.
HUH?
THE LEADER BACK AT CASTLE URUM WAS ALSO KILLED BY OTHER WINGED SOLDIERS!

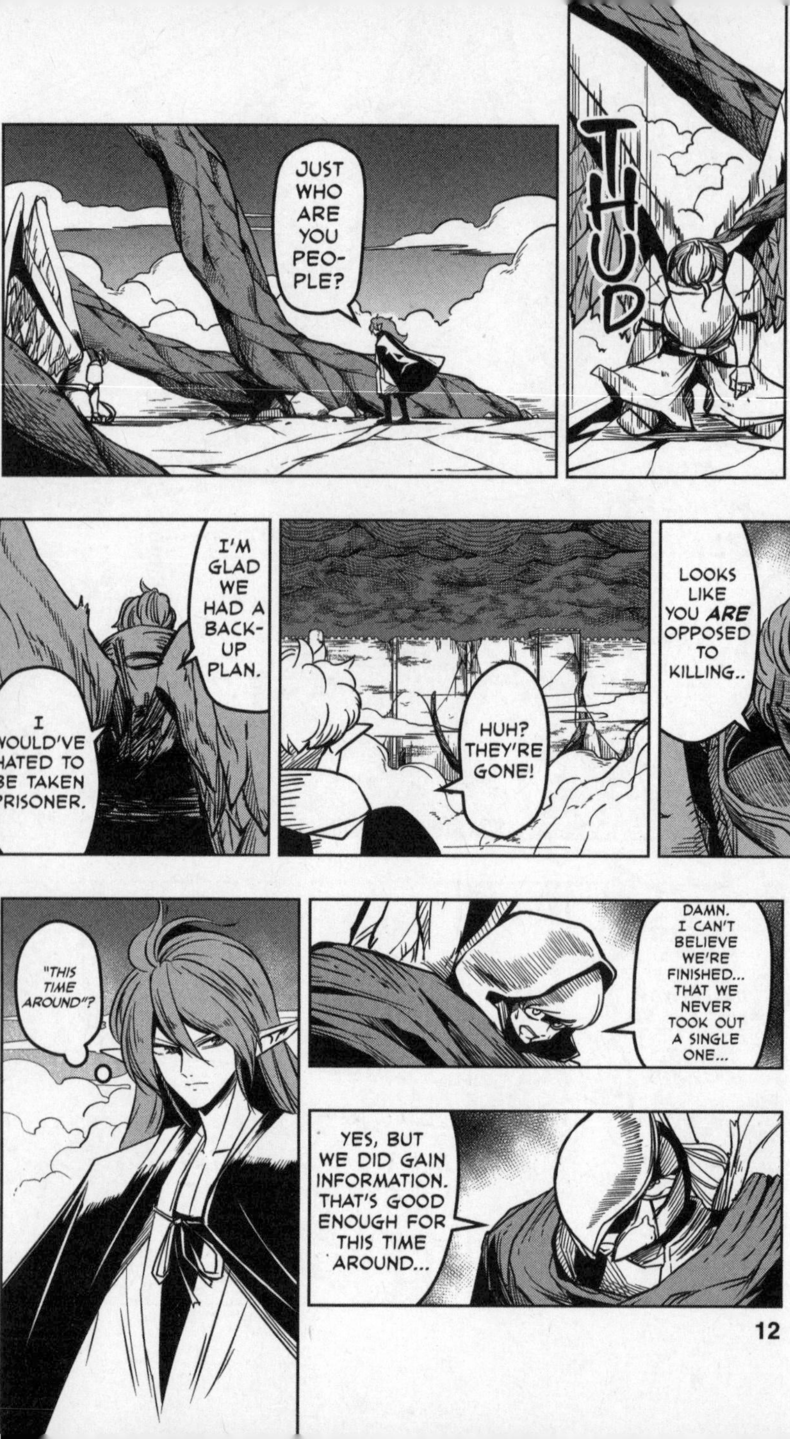
THUD
JUST WHO ARE YOU PEOPLE?
LOOKS LIKE YOU *ARE* OPPOSED TO KILLING..
HUH? THEY'RE GONE!
I'M GLAD WE HAD A BACK-UP PLAN.
I WOULD'VE HATED TO BE TAKEN PRISONER.
DAMN. I CAN'T BELIEVE WE'RE FINISHED... THAT WE NEVER TOOK OUT A SINGLE ONE...
YES, BUT WE DID GAIN INFORMATION. THAT'S GOOD ENOUGH FOR THIS TIME AROUND...
"THIS TIME AROUND"?

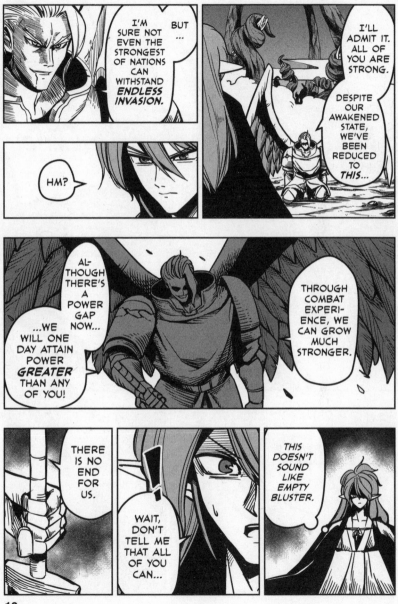

I'LL ADMIT IT. ALL OF YOU ARE STRONG.
DESPITE OUR AWAKENED STATE, WE'VE BEEN REDUCED TO *THIS*...
BUT ...
I'M SURE NOT EVEN THE STRONGEST OF NATIONS CAN WITHSTAND ***ENDLESS INVASION.***
HM?
THROUGH COMBAT EXPERI-ENCE, WE CAN GROW MUCH STRONGER.
AL-THOUGH THERE'S A POWER GAP NOW...
...WE WILL ONE DAY ATTAIN POWER ***GREATER*** THAN ANY OF YOU!
THIS DOESN'T SOUND LIKE EMPTY BLUSTER.
WAIT, DON'T TELL ME THAT ALL OF YOU CAN...
THERE IS NO END FOR US.

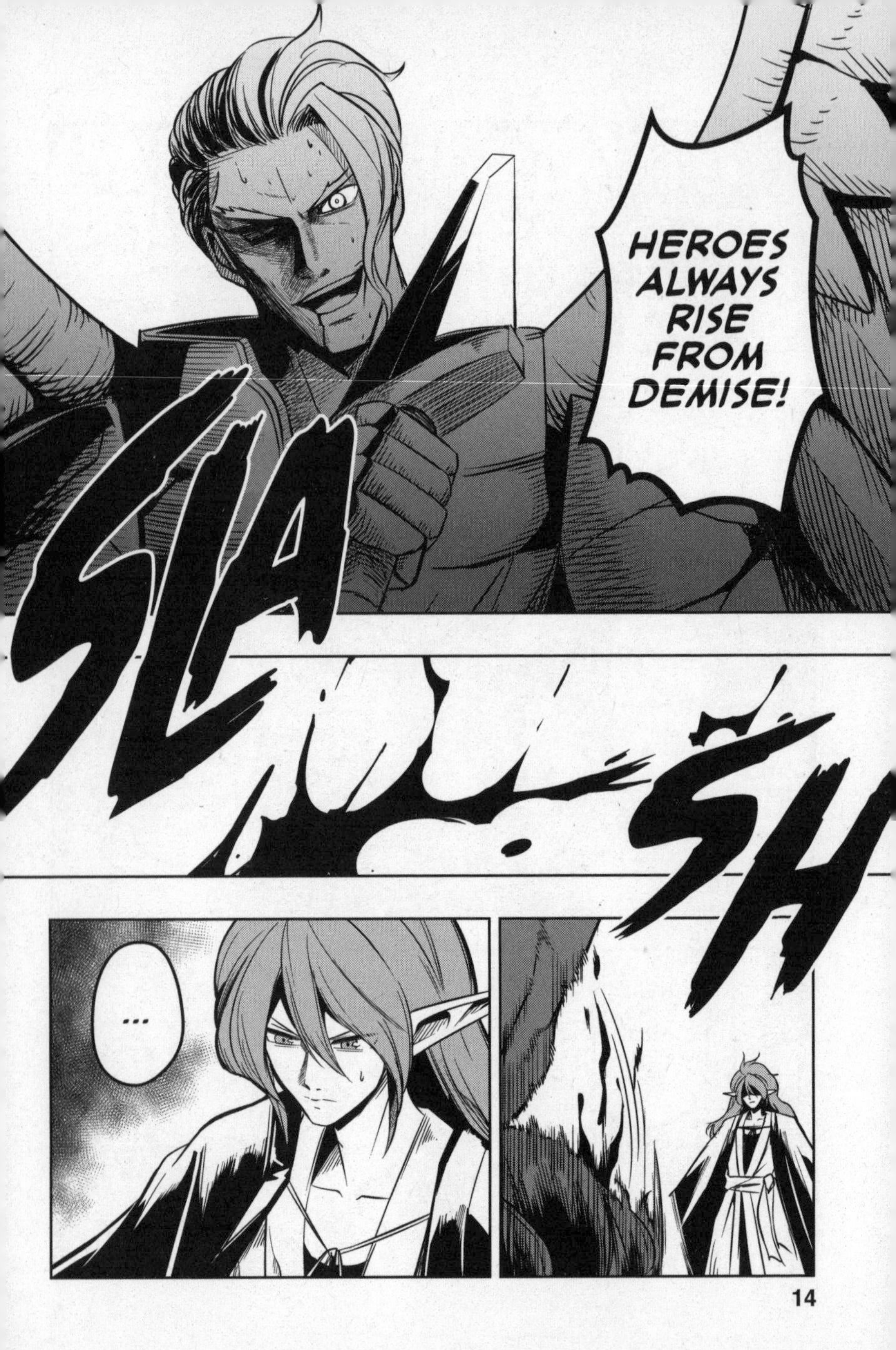
HEROES ALWAYS RISE FROM DEMISE!
SLASH
...

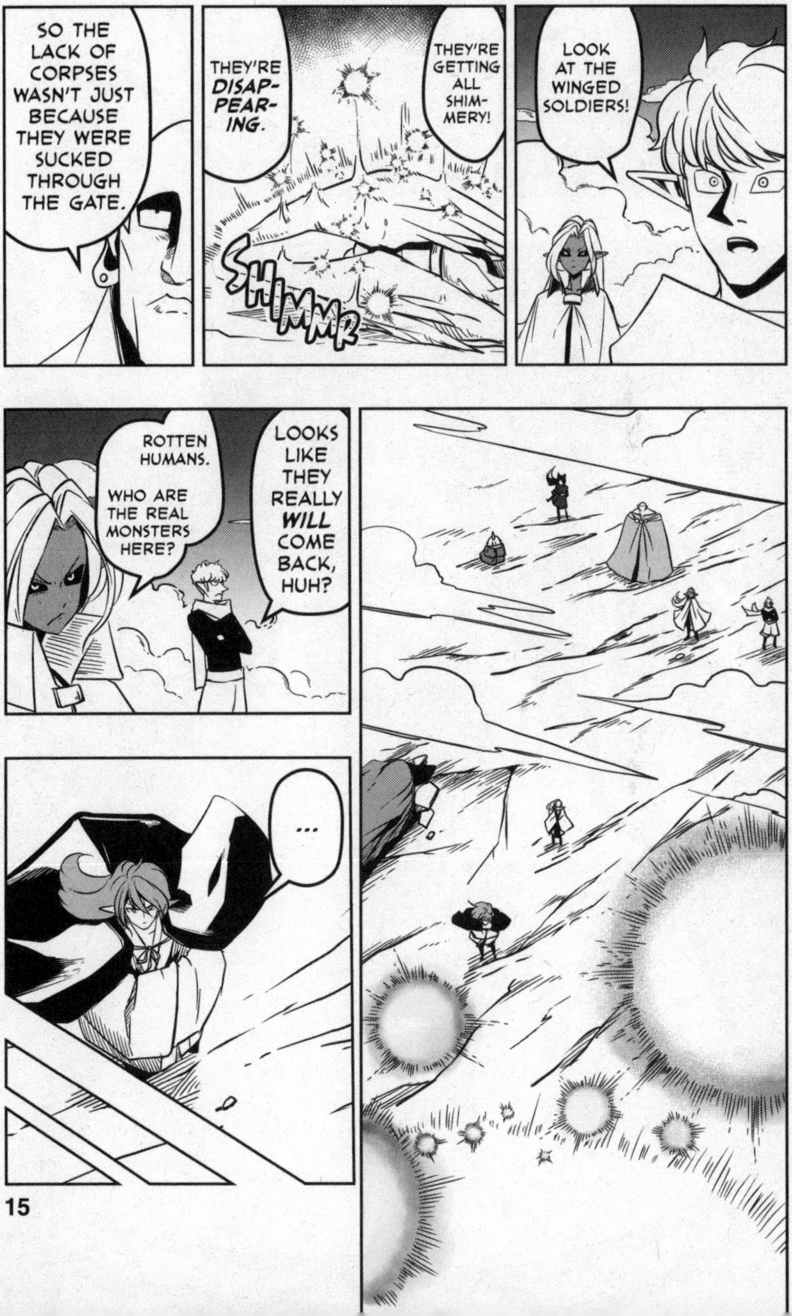
LOOK AT THE WINGED SOLDIERS!
THEY'RE GETTING ALL SHIMMERY!
THEY'RE *DISAPPEARING*.
SHIMMR
SO THE LACK OF CORPSES WASN'T JUST BECAUSE THEY WERE SUCKED THROUGH THE GATE.
LOOKS LIKE THEY REALLY *WILL* COME BACK, HUH?
ROTTEN HUMANS.
WHO ARE THE REAL MONSTERS HERE?
...

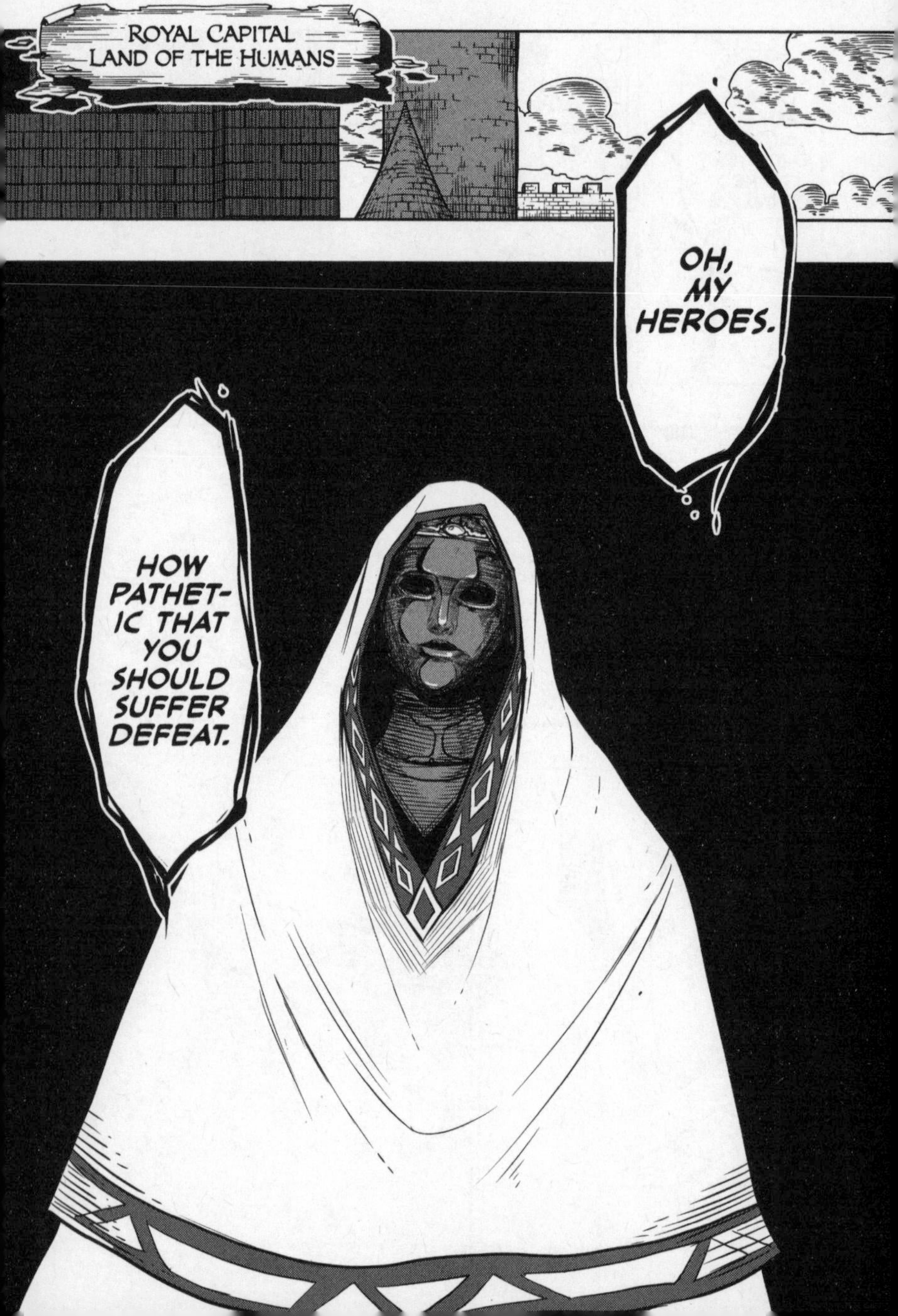
ROYAL CAPITAL LAND OF THE HUMANS
OH, MY HEROES.
HOW PATHET-IC THAT YOU SHOULD SUFFER DEFEAT.

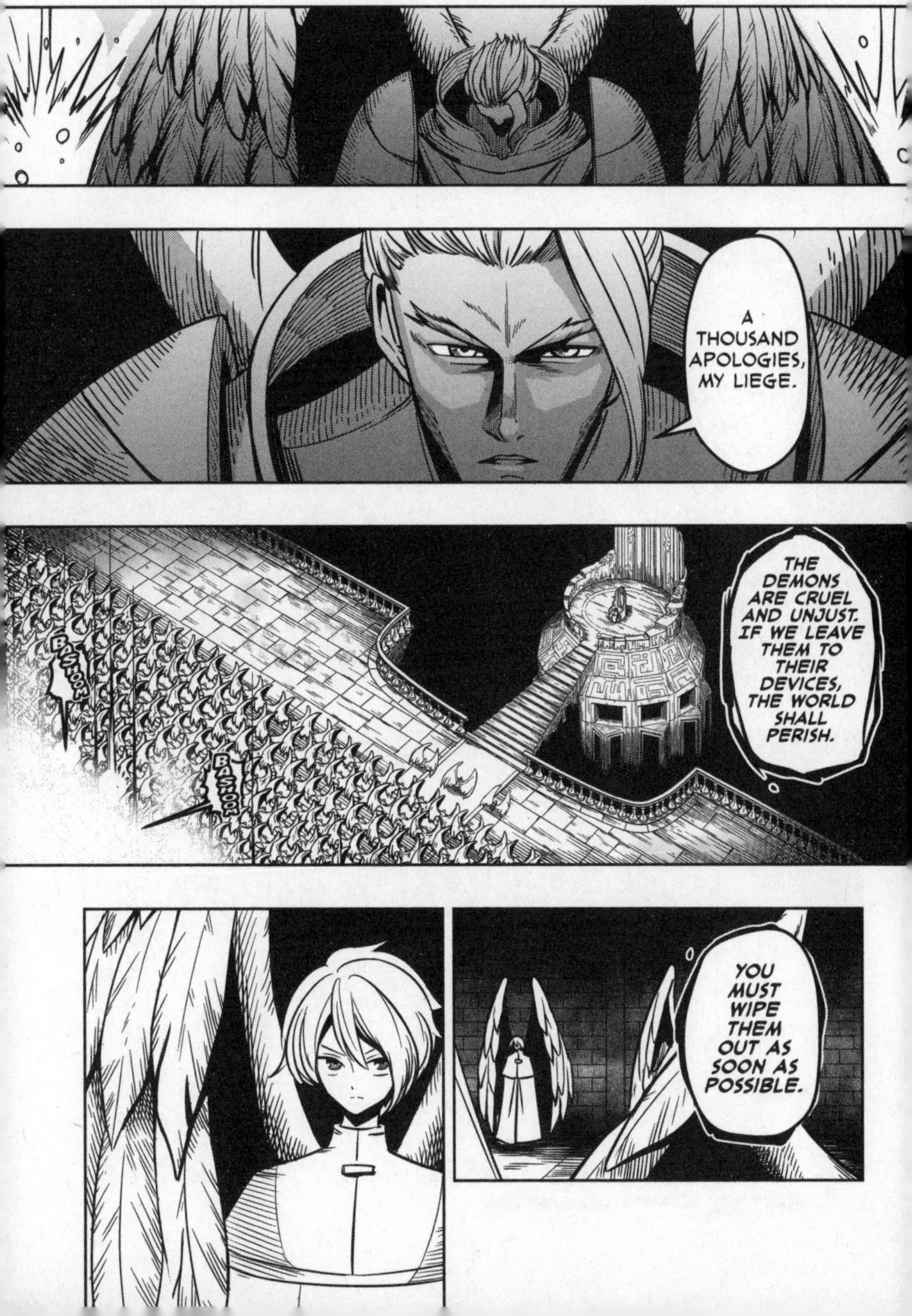
A THOUSAND APOLOGIES, MY LIEGE.
THE DEMONS ARE CRUEL AND UNJUST. IF WE LEAVE THEM TO THEIR DEVICES, THE WORLD SHALL PERISH.
BASHOOM
BASHOOM
YOU MUST WIPE THEM OUT AS SOON AS POSSIBLE.

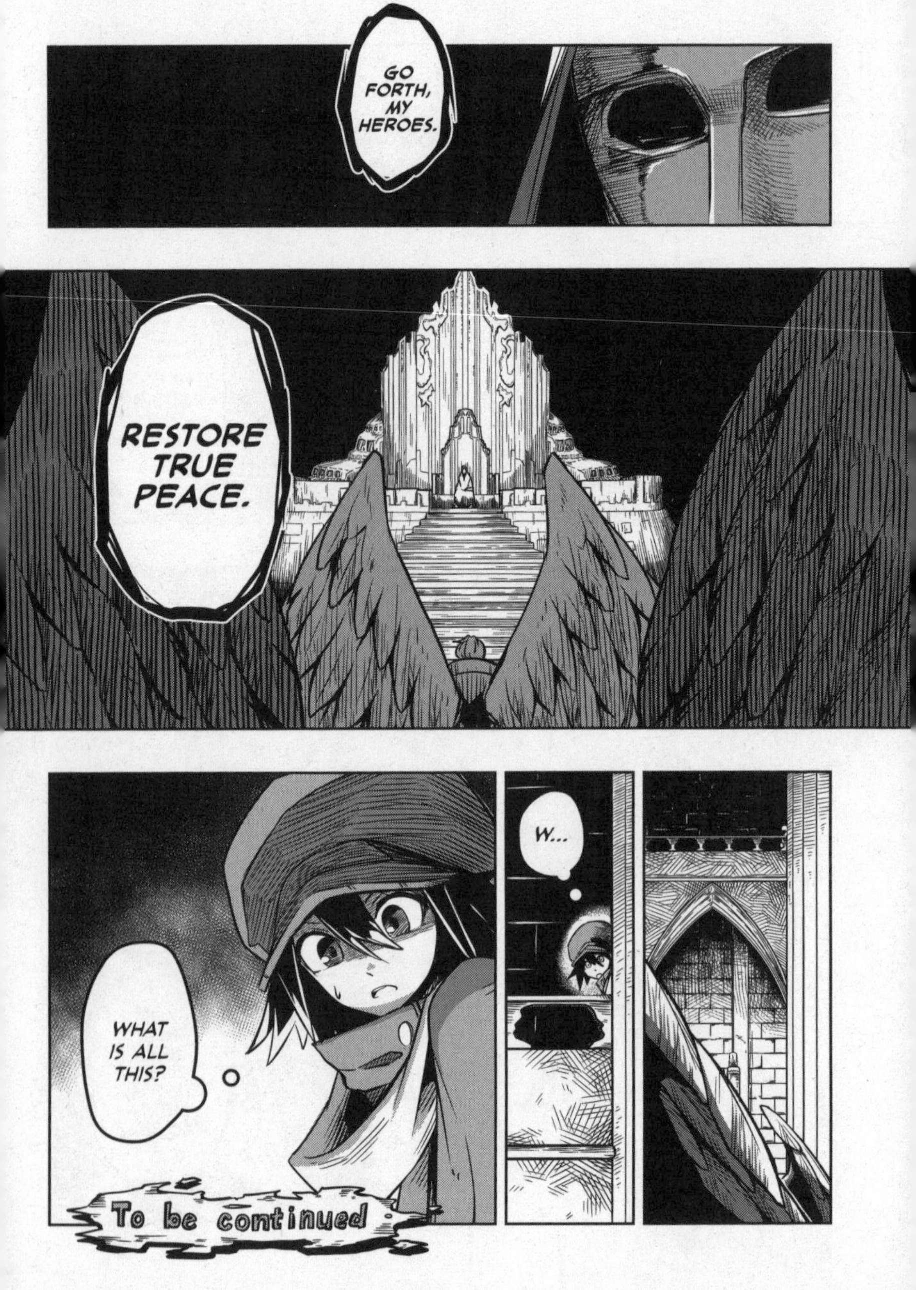
GO FORTH, MY HEROES.
RESTORE TRUE PEACE.
W...
WHAT IS ALL THIS?
To be continued

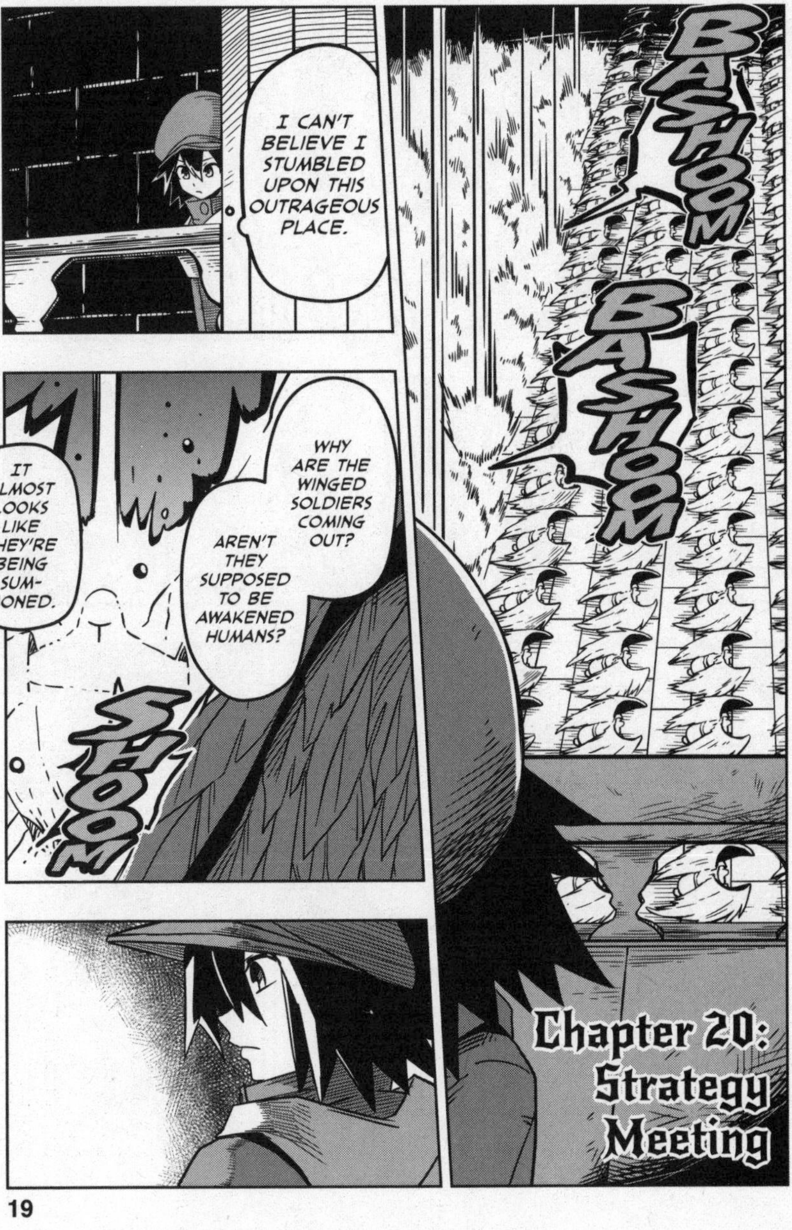
BASHOOM
BASHOOM
Chapter 20: Strategy Meeting
I CAN'T BELIEVE I STUMBLED UPON THIS OUTRAGEOUS PLACE.
WHY ARE THE WINGED SOLDIERS COMING OUT?
AREN'T THEY SUPPOSED TO BE AWAKENED HUMANS?
IT ALMOST LOOKS LIKE THEY'RE BEING SUM-MONED.
SHOOM

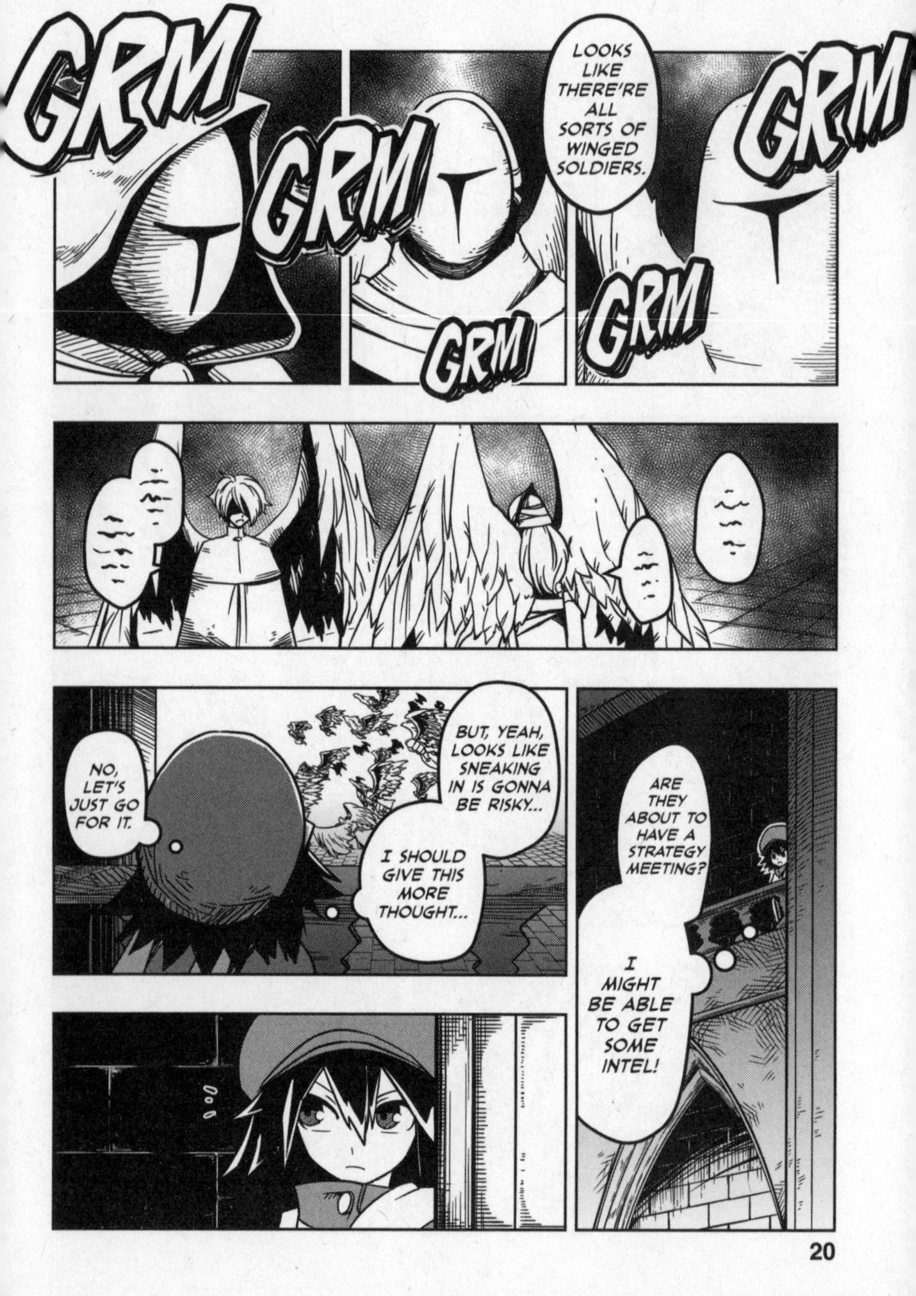
GRM
GRM
LOOKS LIKE THERE'RE ALL SORTS OF WINGED SOLDIERS.
GRM
GRM
GRM
ARE THEY ABOUT TO HAVE A STRATEGY MEETING?
I MIGHT BE ABLE TO GET SOME INTEL!
BUT, YEAH, LOOKS LIKE SNEAKING IN IS GONNA BE RISKY...
I SHOULD GIVE THIS MORE THOUGHT...
NO, LET'S JUST GO FOR IT.

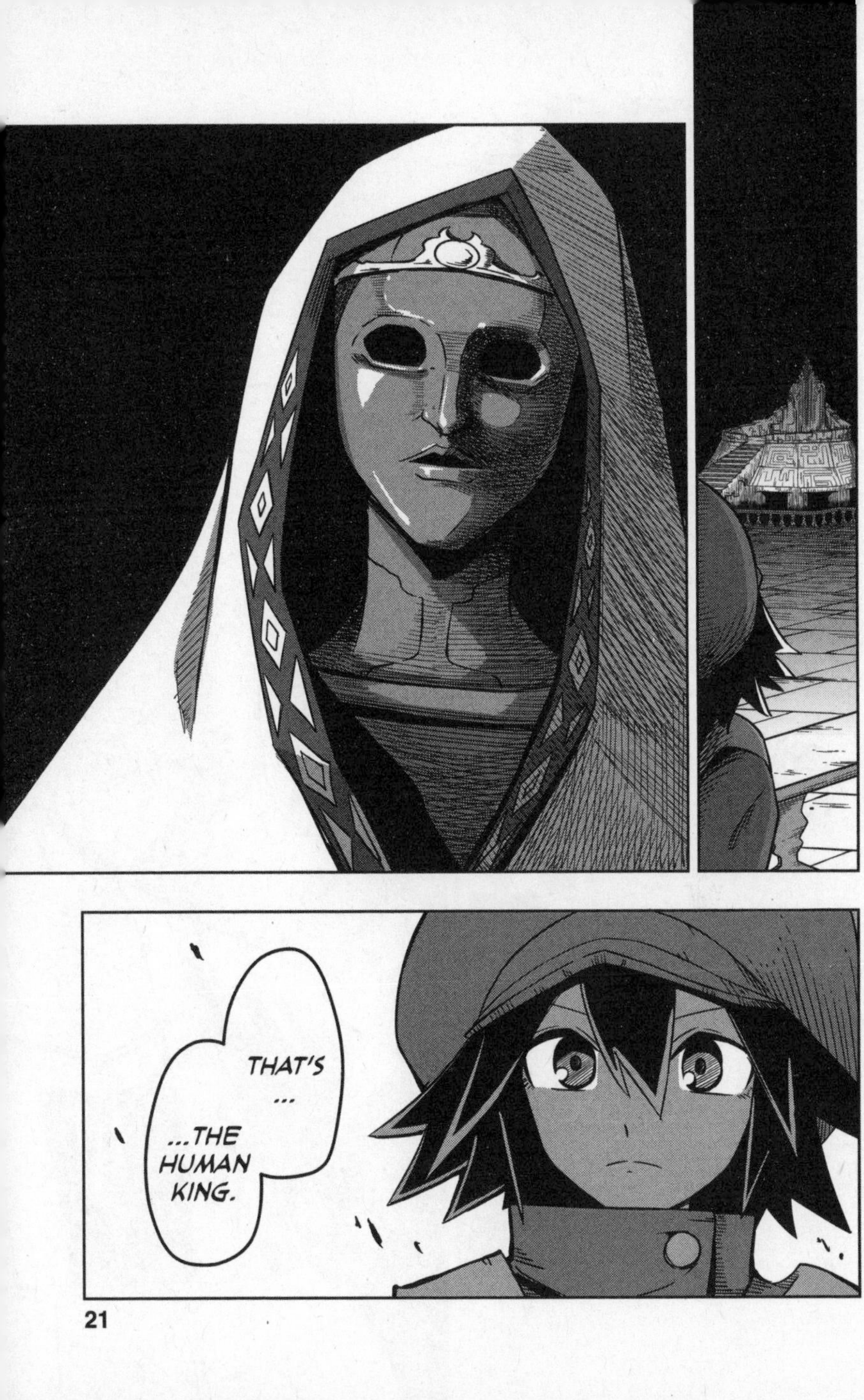
THAT'S ... ...THE HUMAN KING.

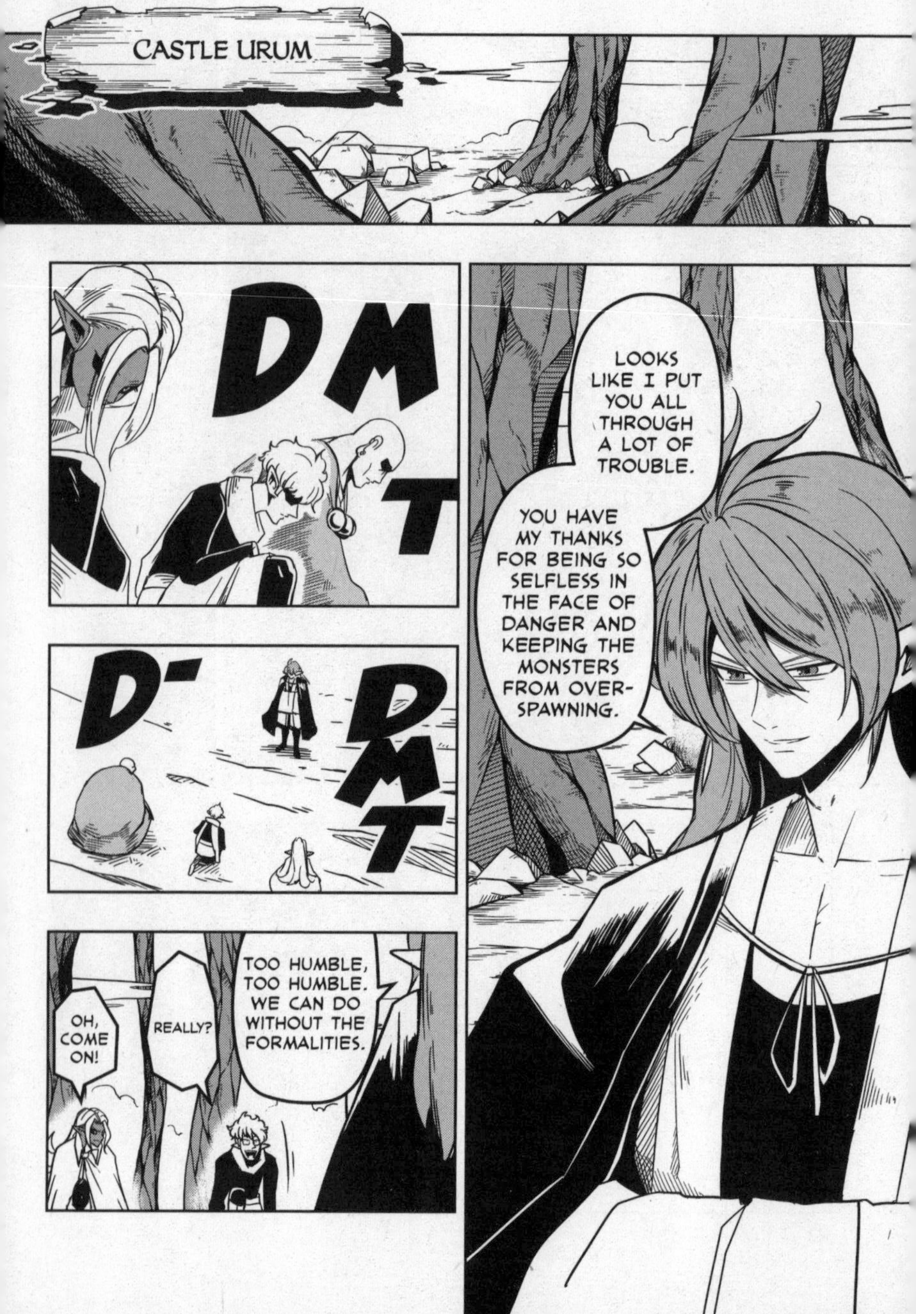
CASTLE URUM
LOOKS LIKE I PUT YOU ALL THROUGH A LOT OF TROUBLE.
YOU HAVE MY THANKS FOR BEING SO SELFLESS IN THE FACE OF DANGER AND KEEPING THE MONSTERS FROM OVER-SPAWNING.
DMT
D' DMT
TOO HUMBLE, TOO HUMBLE. WE CAN DO WITHOUT THE FORMALITIES.
REALLY?
OH, COME ON!

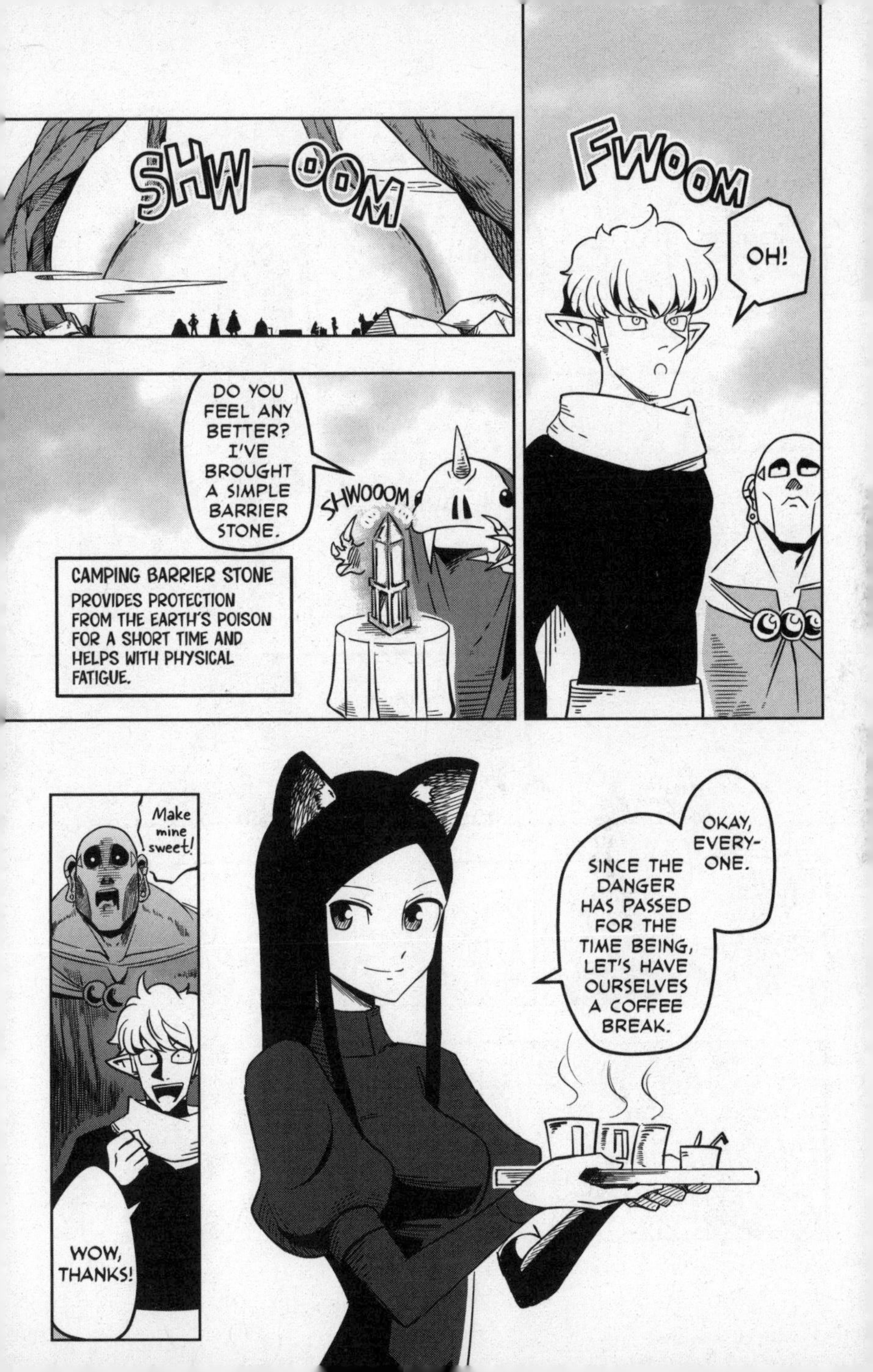
FWOOM
OH!
SHW OOM
DO YOU FEEL ANY BETTER? I'VE BROUGHT A SIMPLE BARRIER STONE.
SHWOOOM
CAMPING BARRIER STONE
PROVIDES PROTECTION FROM THE EARTH'S POISON FOR A SHORT TIME AND HELPS WITH PHYSICAL FATIGUE.
OKAY, EVERY-ONE.
SINCE THE DANGER HAS PASSED FOR THE TIME BEING, LET'S HAVE OURSELVES A COFFEE BREAK.
Make mine sweet!
WOW, THANKS!

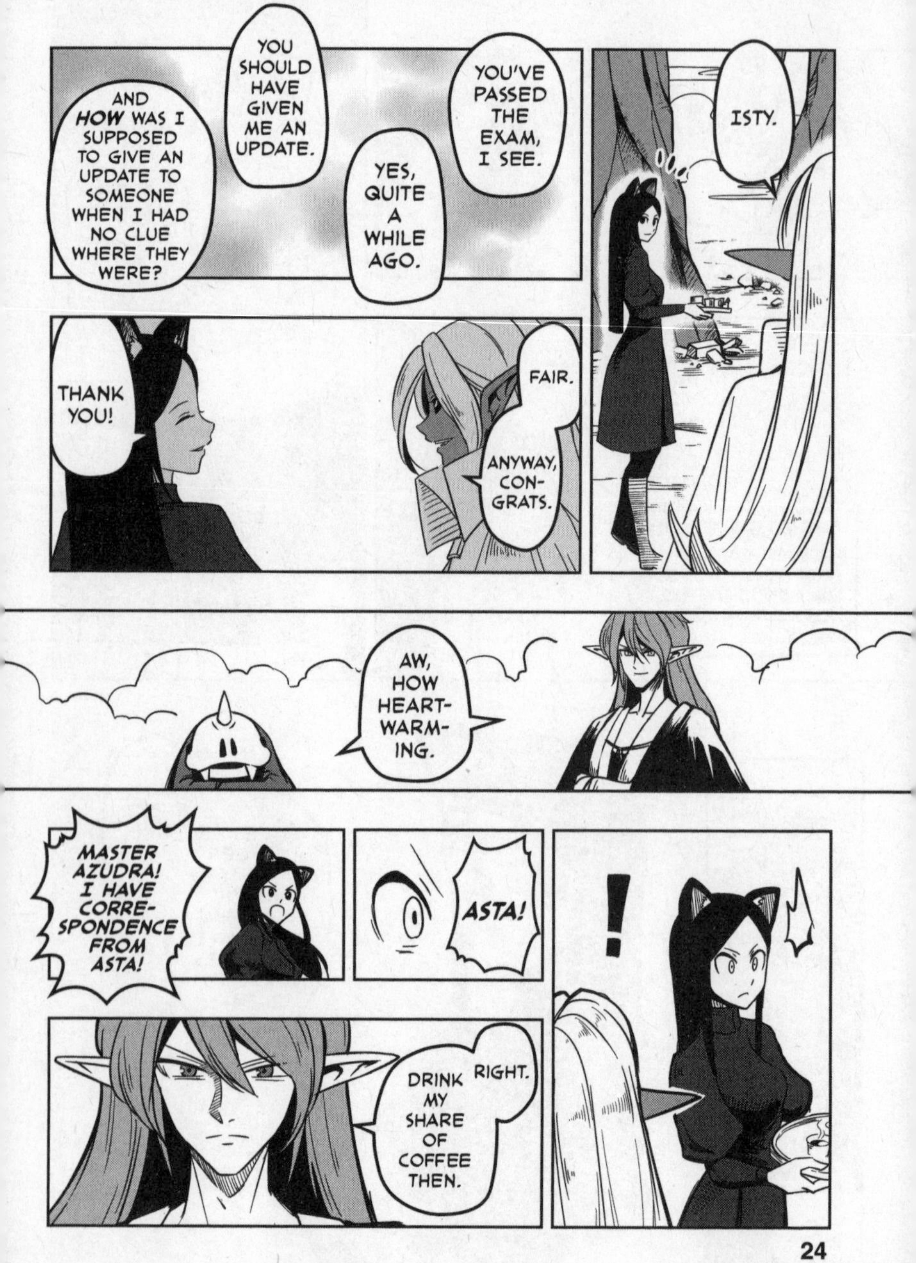
ISTY.
YOU'VE PASSED THE EXAM, I SEE.
YES, QUITE A WHILE AGO.
YOU SHOULD HAVE GIVEN ME AN UPDATE.
AND *HOW* WAS I SUPPOSED TO GIVE AN UPDATE TO SOMEONE WHEN I HAD NO CLUE WHERE THEY WERE?
FAIR.
ANYWAY, CON-GRATS.
THANK YOU!
AW, HOW HEART-WARM-ING.
!
ASTA!
MASTER AZUDRA! I HAVE CORRE-SPONDENCE FROM ASTA!
RIGHT.
DRINK MY SHARE OF COFFEE THEN.

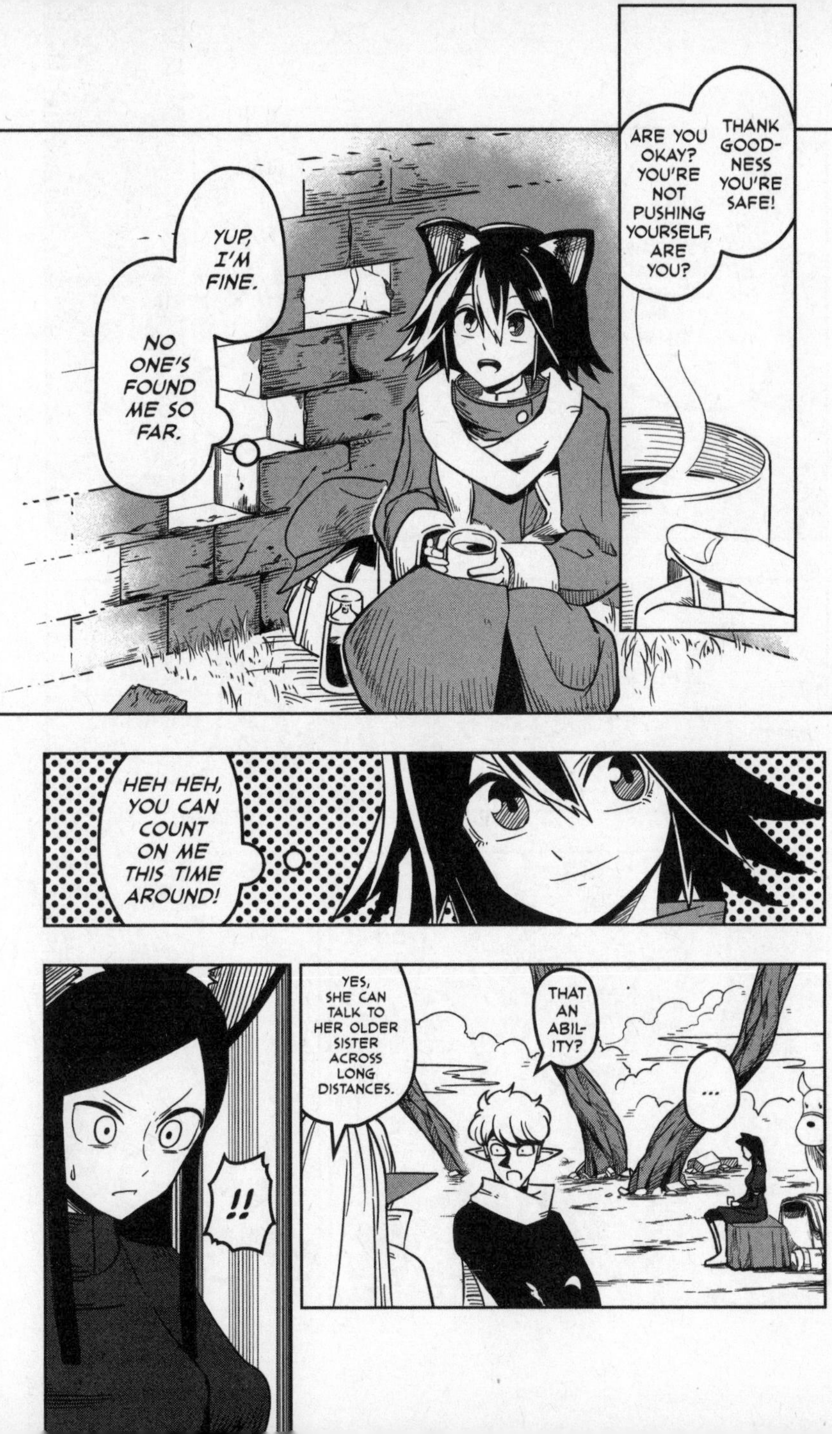
THANK GOODNESS YOU'RE SAFE!
ARE YOU OKAY? YOU'RE NOT PUSHING YOURSELF, ARE YOU?
YUP, I'M FINE.
NO ONE'S FOUND ME SO FAR.
HEH HEH, YOU CAN COUNT ON ME THIS TIME AROUND!
THAT AN ABILITY?
YES, SHE CAN TALK TO HER OLDER SISTER ACROSS LONG DISTANCES.
...
!!

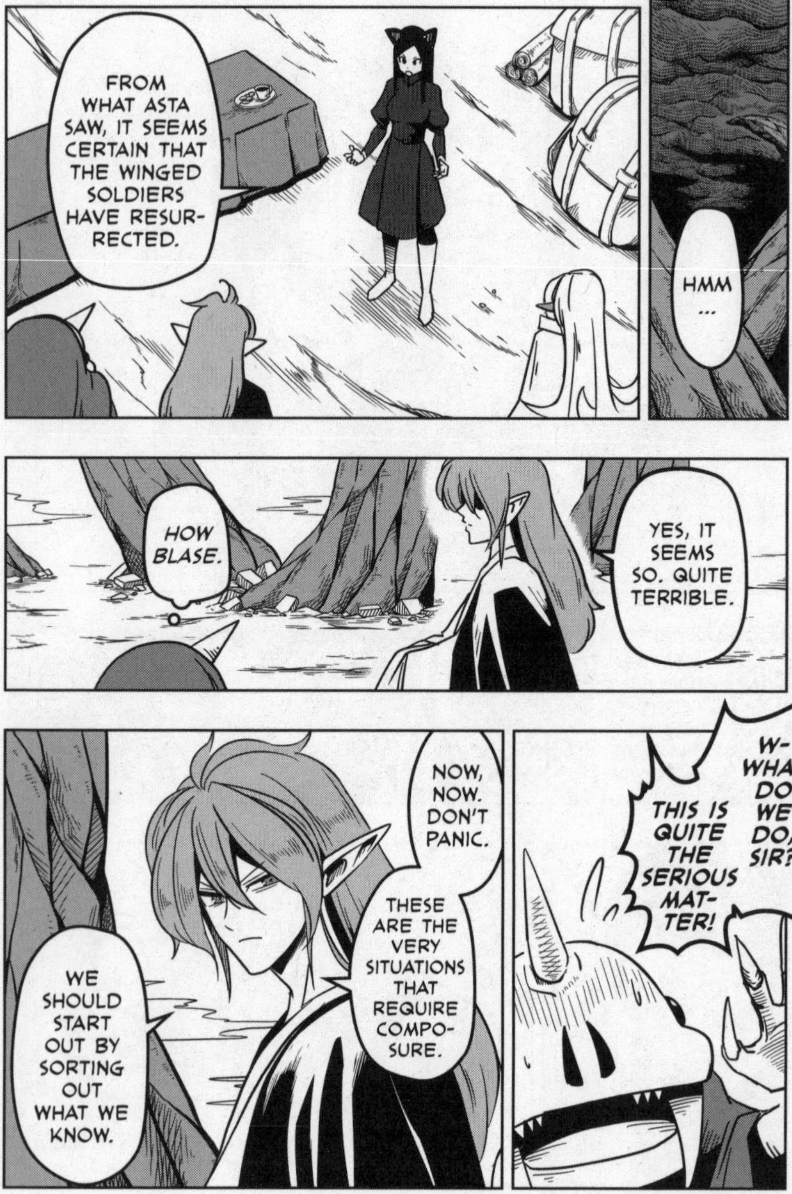
HMM...
FROM WHAT ASTA SAW, IT SEEMS CERTAIN THAT THE WINGED SOLDIERS HAVE RESUR-RECTED.
YES, IT SEEMS SO. QUITE TERRIBLE.
HOW BLASE.
W-WHAT DO WE DO, SIR?
THIS IS QUITE THE SERIOUS MAT-TER!
NOW, NOW. DON'T PANIC.
THESE ARE THE VERY SITUATIONS THAT REQUIRE COMPOSURE.
WE SHOULD START OUT BY SORTING OUT WHAT WE KNOW.

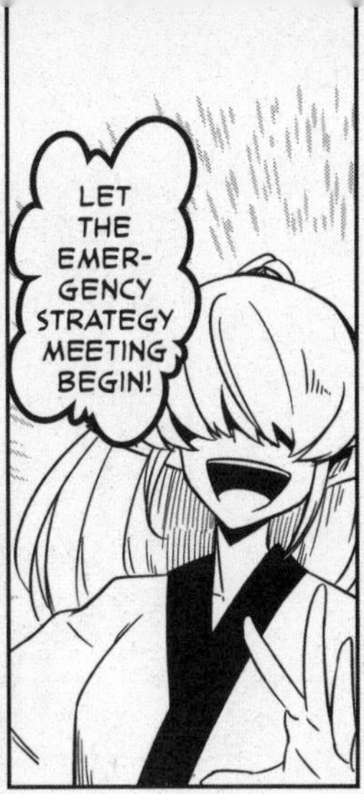
LET THE EMERGENCY STRATEGY MEETING BEGIN!

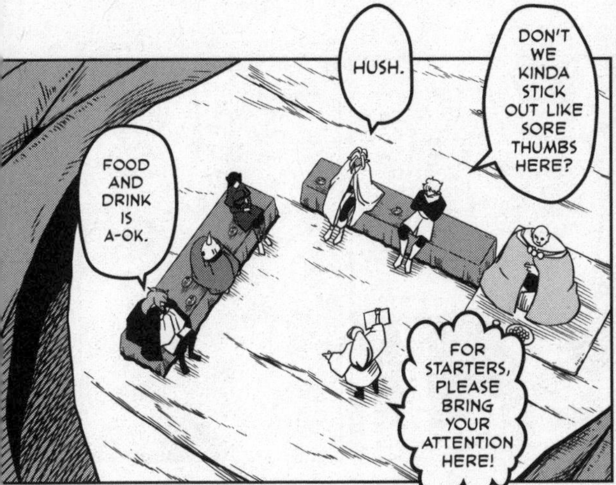
DON'T WE KINDA STICK OUT LIKE SORE THUMBS HERE?
HUSH.
FOOD AND DRINK IS A-OK.
FOR STARTERS, PLEASE BRING YOUR ATTENTION HERE!

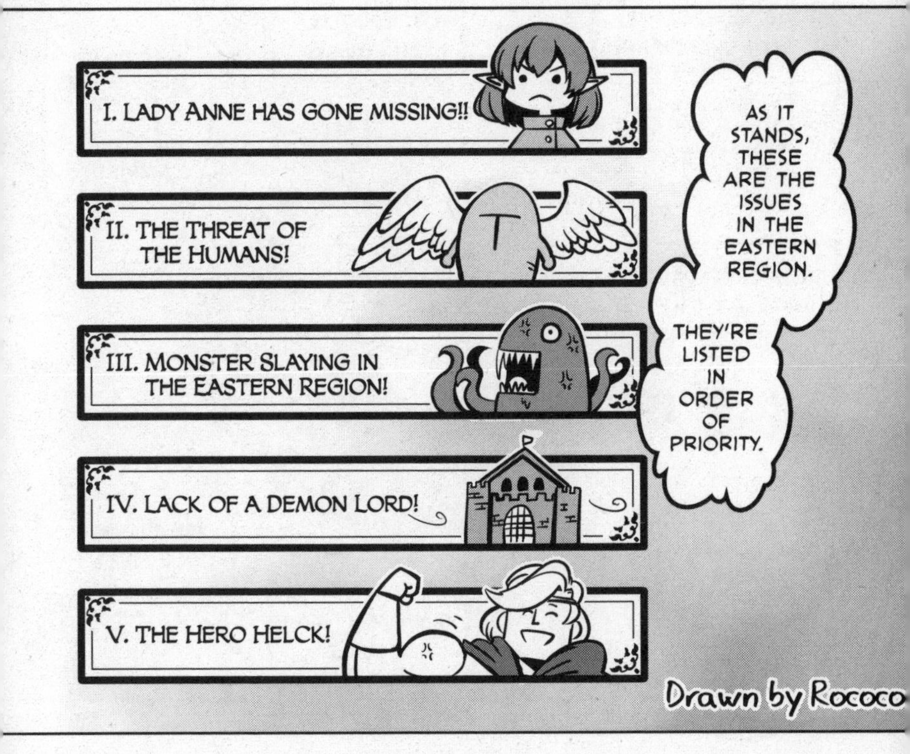
AS IT STANDS, THESE ARE THE ISSUES IN THE EASTERN REGION.
THEY'RE LISTED IN ORDER OF PRIORITY.
I. LADY ANNE HAS GONE MISSING!!
II. THE THREAT OF THE HUMANS!
III. MONSTER SLAYING IN THE EASTERN REGION!
IV. LACK OF A DEMON LORD!
V. THE HERO HELCK!
Drawn by Rococo

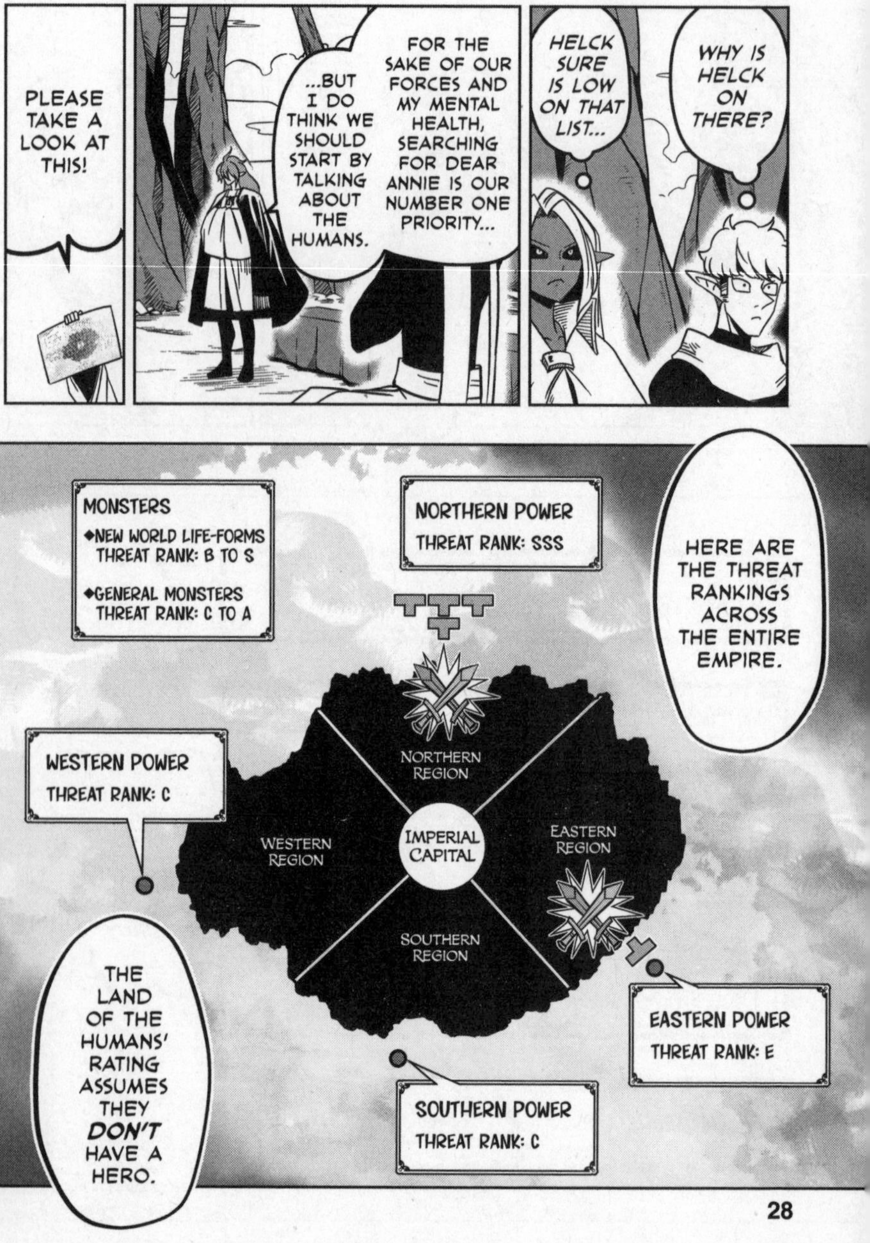
WHY IS HELCK ON THERE?
HELCK SURE IS LOW ON THAT LIST...
FOR THE SAKE OF OUR FORCES AND MY MENTAL HEALTH, SEARCHING FOR DEAR ANNIE IS OUR NUMBER ONE PRIORITY...
...BUT I DO THINK WE SHOULD START BY TALKING ABOUT THE HUMANS.
PLEASE TAKE A LOOK AT THIS!
HERE ARE THE THREAT RANKINGS ACROSS THE ENTIRE EMPIRE.
NORTHERN POWER THREAT RANK: SSS
MONSTERS
◆NEW WORLD LIFE-FORMS THREAT RANK: B TO S
◆GENERAL MONSTERS THREAT RANK: C TO A
NORTHERN REGION
WESTERN POWER THREAT RANK: C
WESTERN REGION
IMPERIAL CAPITAL
EASTERN REGION
SOUTHERN REGION
EASTERN POWER THREAT RANK: E
SOUTHERN POWER THREAT RANK: C
THE LAND OF THE HUMANS' RATING ASSUMES THEY DON'T HAVE A HERO.

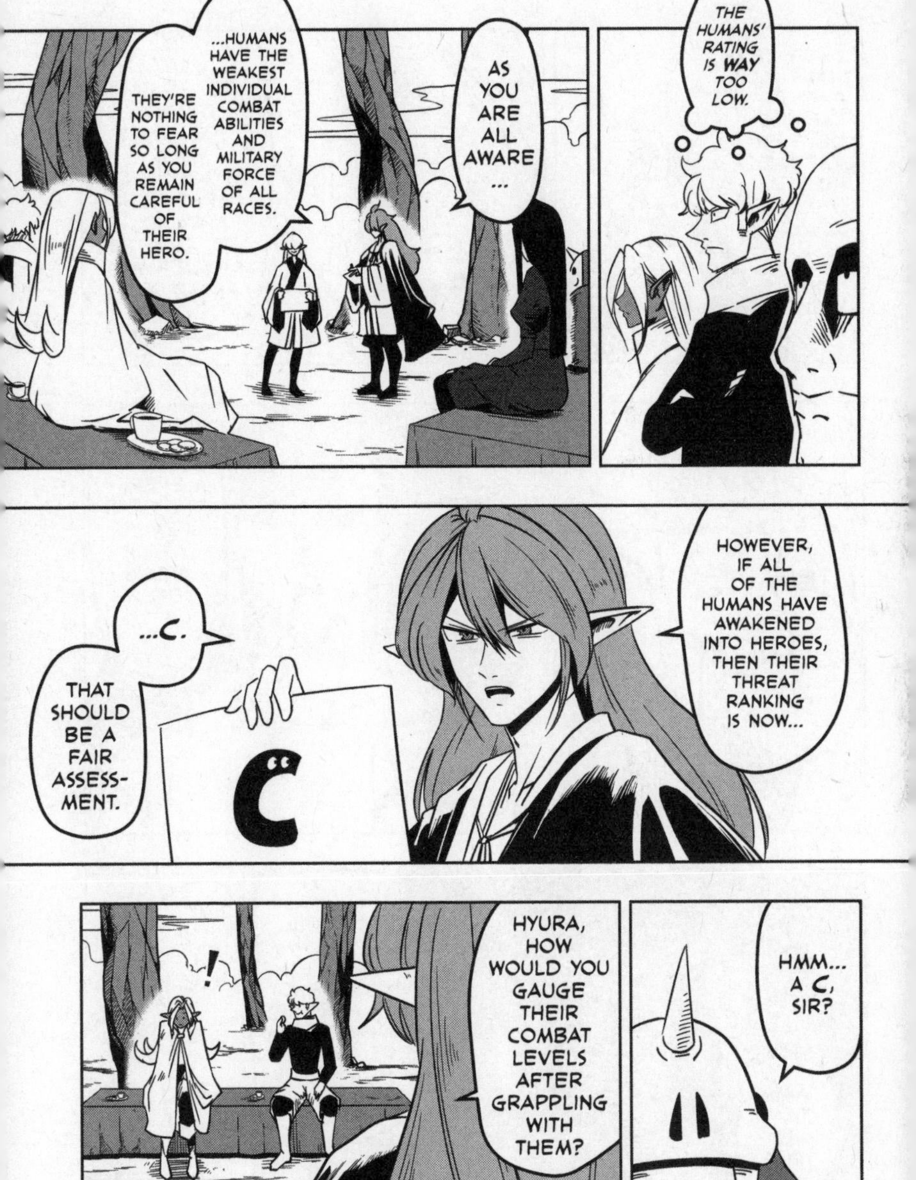
THE HUMANS' RATING IS WAY TOO LOW.
AS YOU ARE ALL AWARE...
...HUMANS HAVE THE WEAKEST INDIVIDUAL COMBAT ABILITIES AND MILITARY FORCE OF ALL RACES.
THEY'RE NOTHING TO FEAR SO LONG AS YOU REMAIN CAREFUL OF THEIR HERO.
HOWEVER, IF ALL OF THE HUMANS HAVE AWAKENED INTO HEROES, THEN THEIR THREAT RANKING IS NOW...
C
...C.
THAT SHOULD BE A FAIR ASSESS-MENT.
HMM... A C, SIR?
HYURA, HOW WOULD YOU GAUGE THEIR COMBAT LEVELS AFTER GRAPPLING WITH THEM?
!

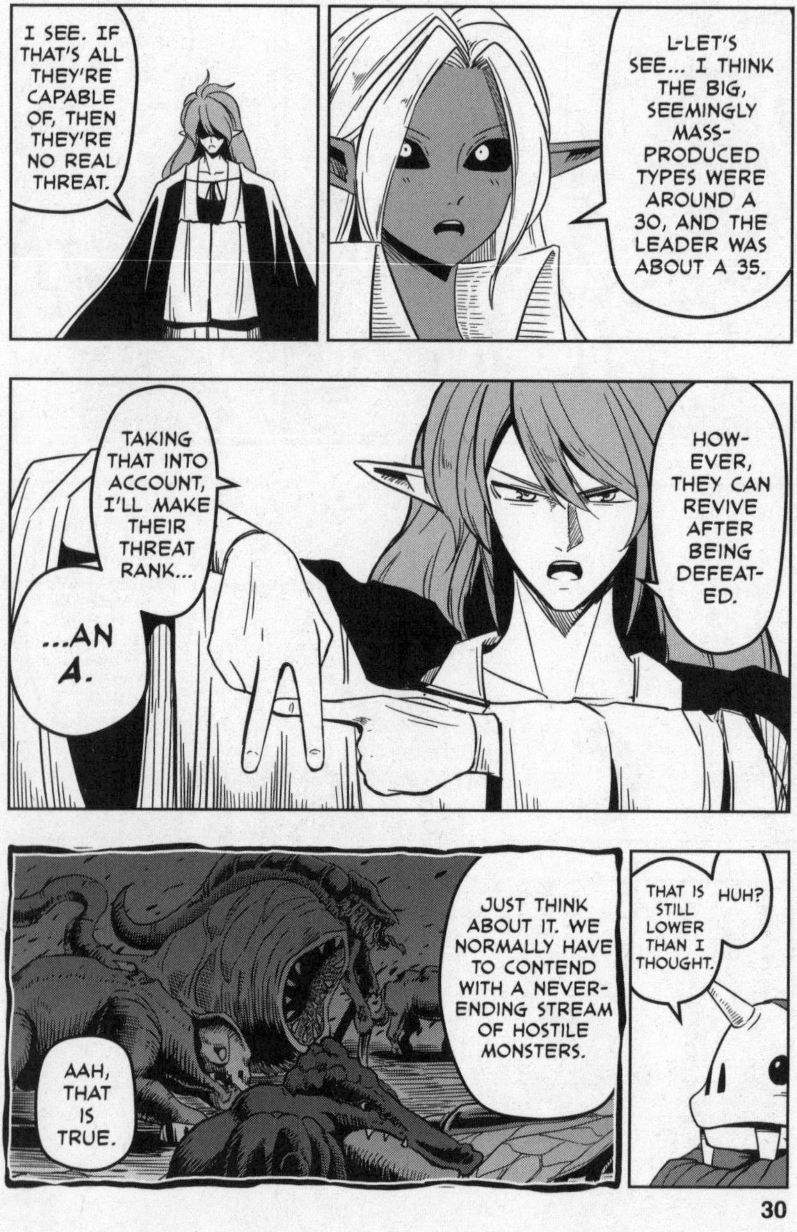
L-LET'S SEE... I THINK THE BIG, SEEMINGLY MASS-PRODUCED TYPES WERE AROUND A 30, AND THE LEADER WAS ABOUT A 35.
I SEE. IF THAT'S ALL THEY'RE CAPABLE OF, THEN THEY'RE NO REAL THREAT.
HOW-EVER, THEY CAN REVIVE AFTER BEING DEFEAT-ED.
TAKING THAT INTO ACCOUNT, I'LL MAKE THEIR THREAT RANK...
...AN A.
HUH?
THAT IS STILL LOWER THAN I THOUGHT.
JUST THINK ABOUT IT. WE NORMALLY HAVE TO CONTEND WITH A NEVER-ENDING STREAM OF HOSTILE MONSTERS.
AAH, THAT IS TRUE.

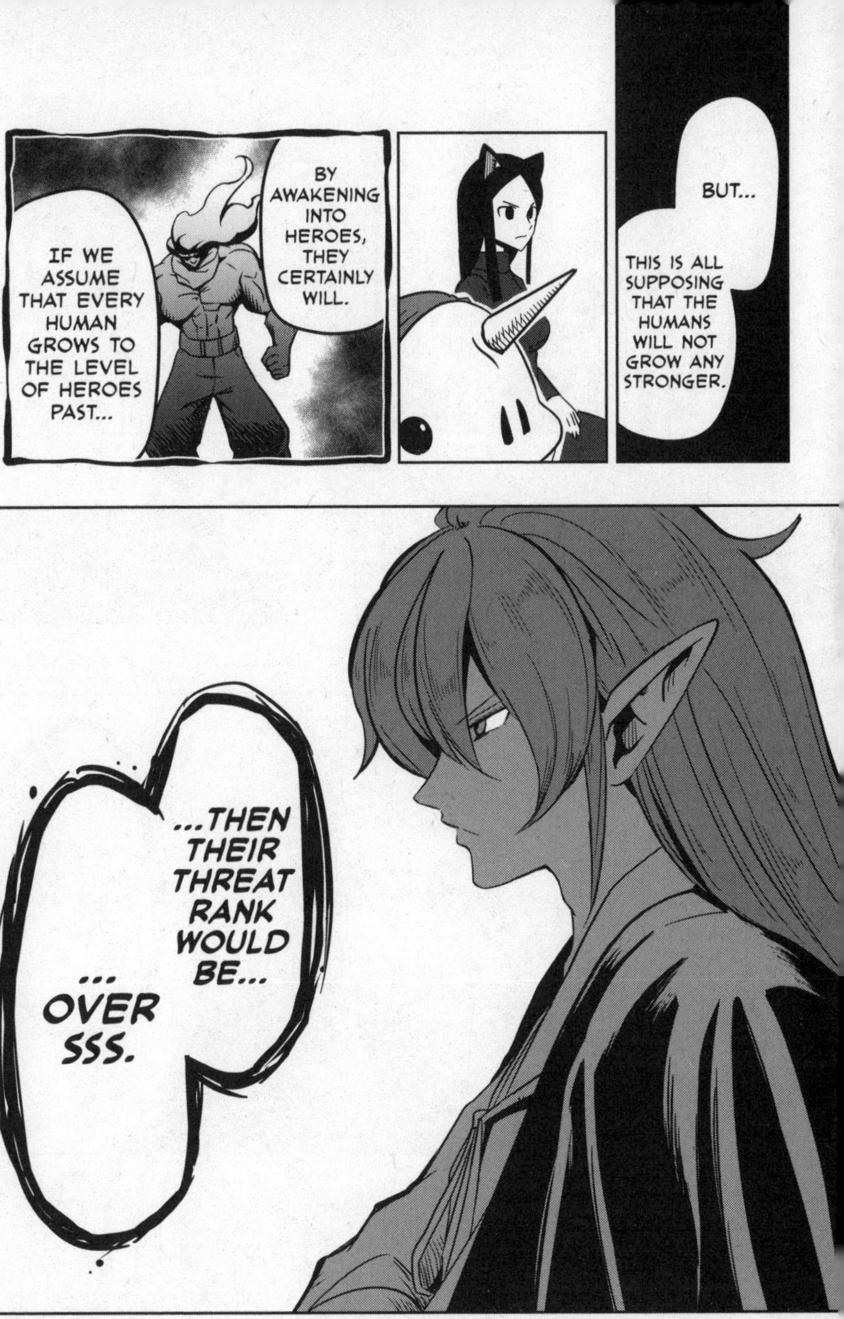
BUT...
THIS IS ALL SUPPOSING THAT THE HUMANS WILL NOT GROW ANY STRONGER.
BY AWAKENING INTO HEROES, THEY CERTAINLY WILL.
IF WE ASSUME THAT EVERY HUMAN GROWS TO THE LEVEL OF HEROES PAST...
...THEN THEIR THREAT RANK WOULD BE...
... OVER SSS.

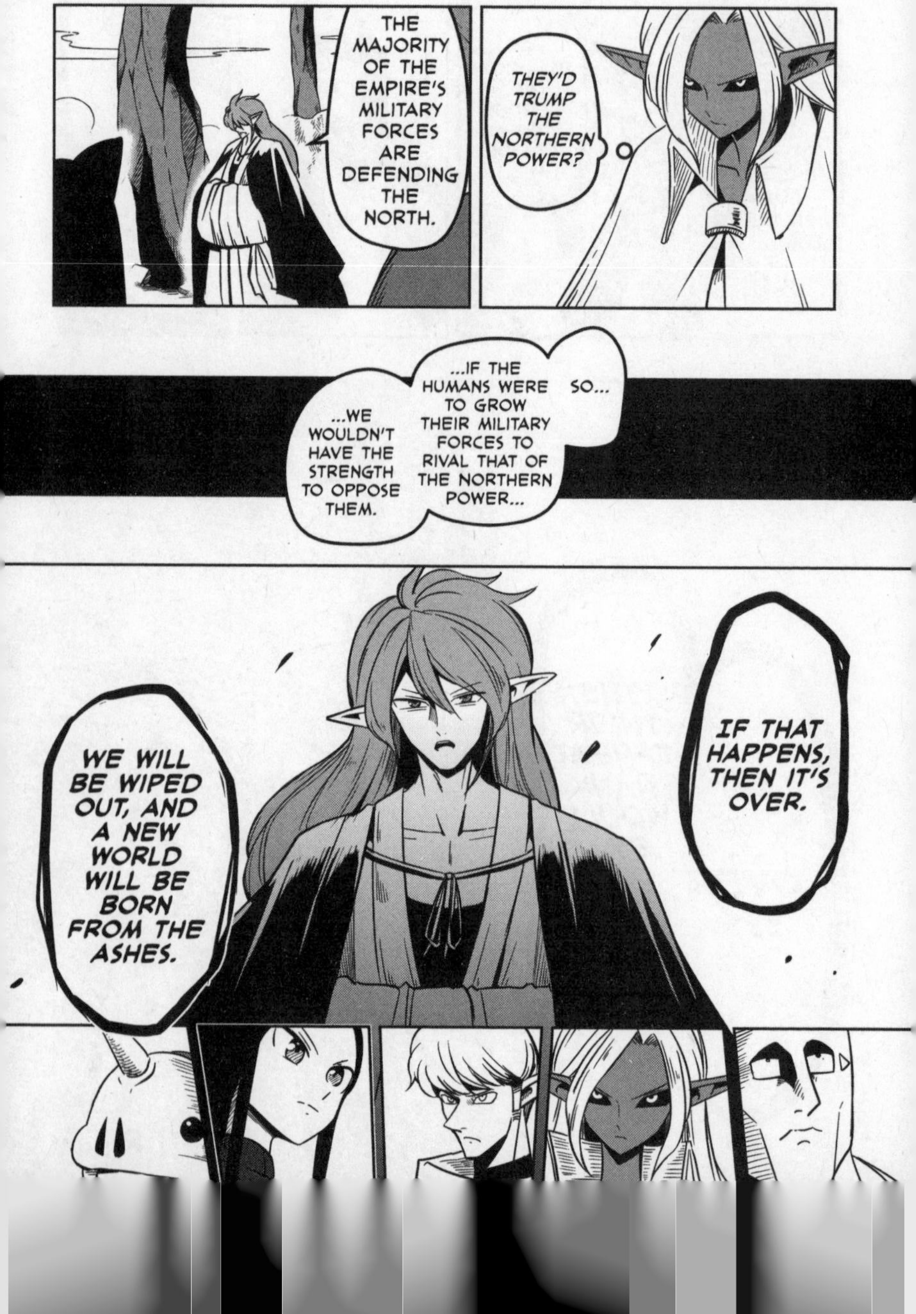
THEY'D TRUMP THE NORTHERN POWER?
THE MAJORITY OF THE EMPIRE'S MILITARY FORCES ARE DEFENDING THE NORTH.
SO...
...IF THE HUMANS WERE TO GROW THEIR MILITARY FORCES TO RIVAL THAT OF THE NORTHERN POWER...
...WE WOULDN'T HAVE THE STRENGTH TO OPPOSE THEM.
IF THAT HAPPENS, THEN IT'S OVER.
WE WILL BE WIPED OUT, AND A NEW WORLD WILL BE BORN FROM THE ASHES.

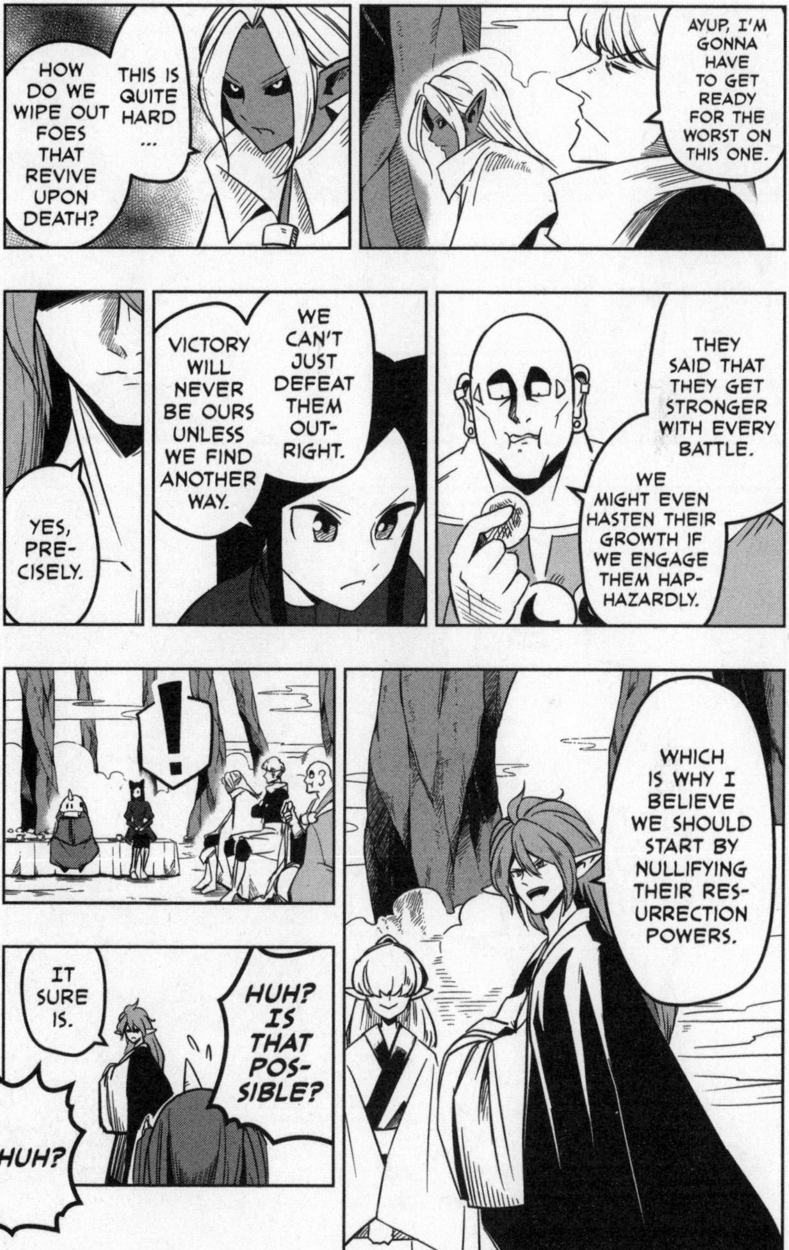
AYUP, I'M GONNA HAVE TO GET READY FOR THE WORST ON THIS ONE.
THIS IS QUITE HARD ...
HOW DO WE WIPE OUT FOES THAT REVIVE UPON DEATH?
THEY SAID THAT THEY GET STRONGER WITH EVERY BATTLE.
WE MIGHT EVEN HASTEN THEIR GROWTH IF WE ENGAGE THEM HAPHAZARDLY.
WE CAN'T JUST DEFEAT THEM OUTRIGHT.
VICTORY WILL NEVER BE OURS UNLESS WE FIND ANOTHER WAY.
YES, PRECISELY.
WHICH IS WHY I BELIEVE WE SHOULD START BY NULLIFYING THEIR RESURRECTION POWERS.
!
HUH? IS THAT POSSIBLE?
IT SURE IS.
WHUH?

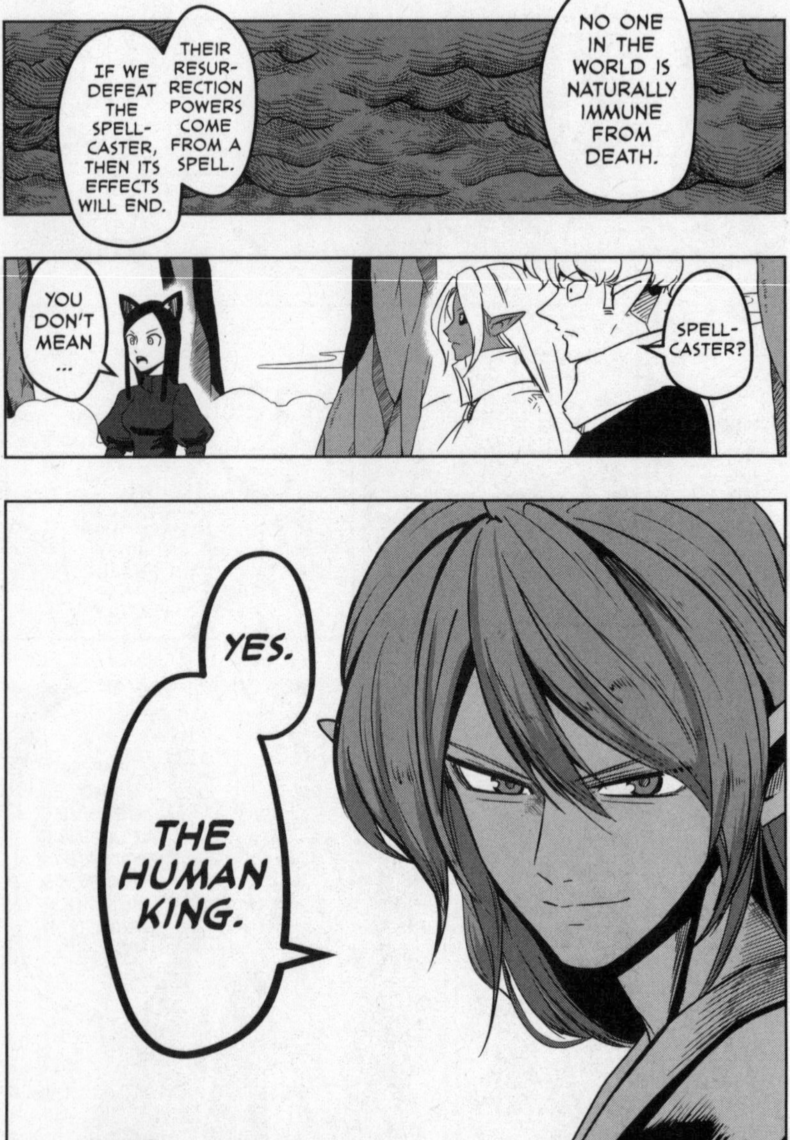
NO ONE IN THE WORLD IS NATURALLY IMMUNE FROM DEATH.
THEIR RESURRECTION POWERS COME FROM A SPELL.
IF WE DEFEAT THE SPELLCASTER, THEN ITS EFFECTS WILL END.
SPELLCASTER?
YOU DON'T MEAN ...
YES.
THE HUMAN KING.
To be continued

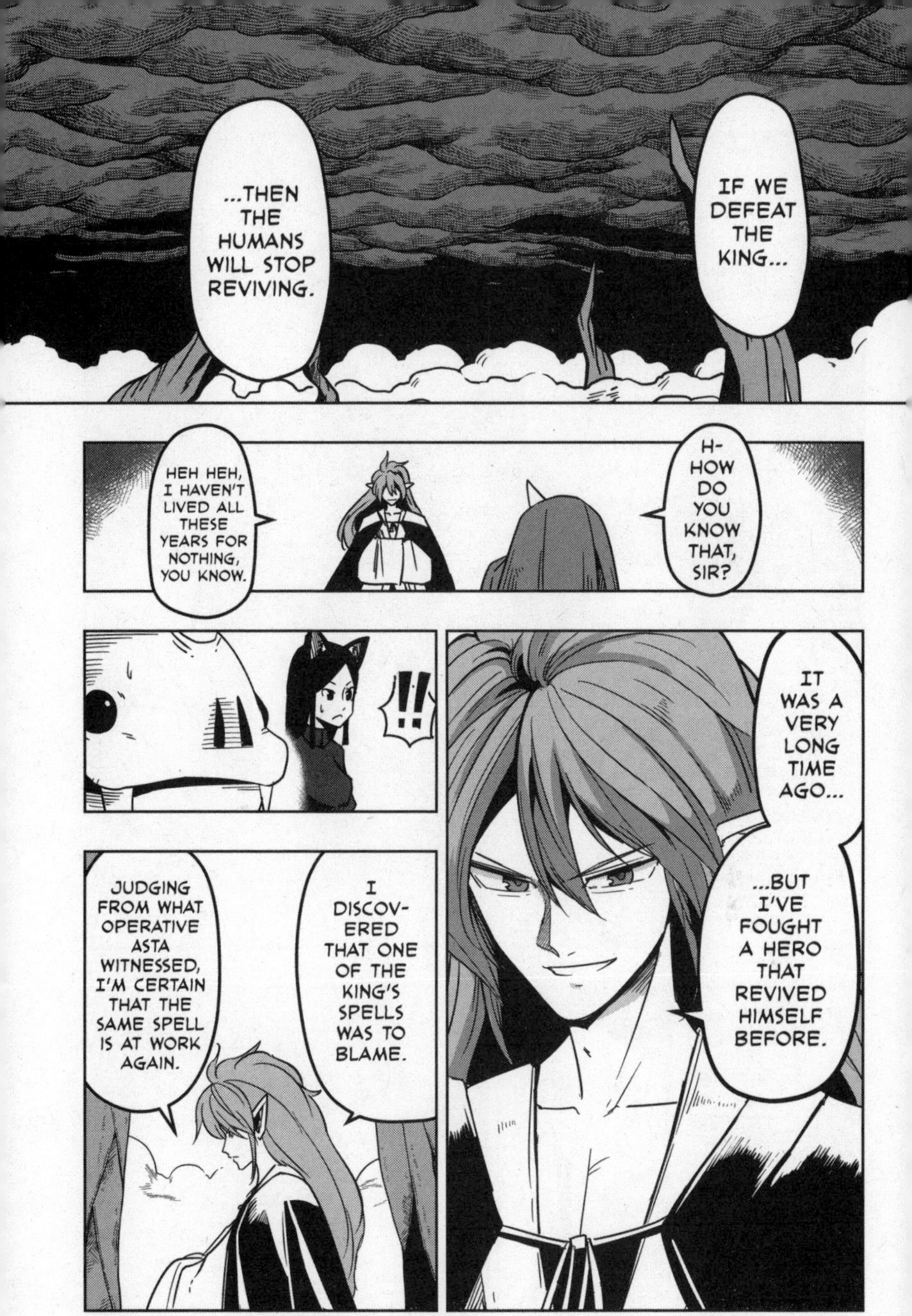
IF WE DEFEAT THE KING...
...THEN THE HUMANS WILL STOP REVIVING.
H-HOW DO YOU KNOW THAT, SIR?
HEH HEH, I HAVEN'T LIVED ALL THESE YEARS FOR NOTHING, YOU KNOW.
IT WAS A VERY LONG TIME AGO...
...BUT I'VE FOUGHT A HERO THAT REVIVED HIMSELF BEFORE.
!!
I DISCOVERED THAT ONE OF THE KING'S SPELLS WAS TO BLAME.
JUDGING FROM WHAT OPERATIVE ASTA WITNESSED, I'M CERTAIN THAT THE SAME SPELL IS AT WORK AGAIN.

Chapter 21: Efforts

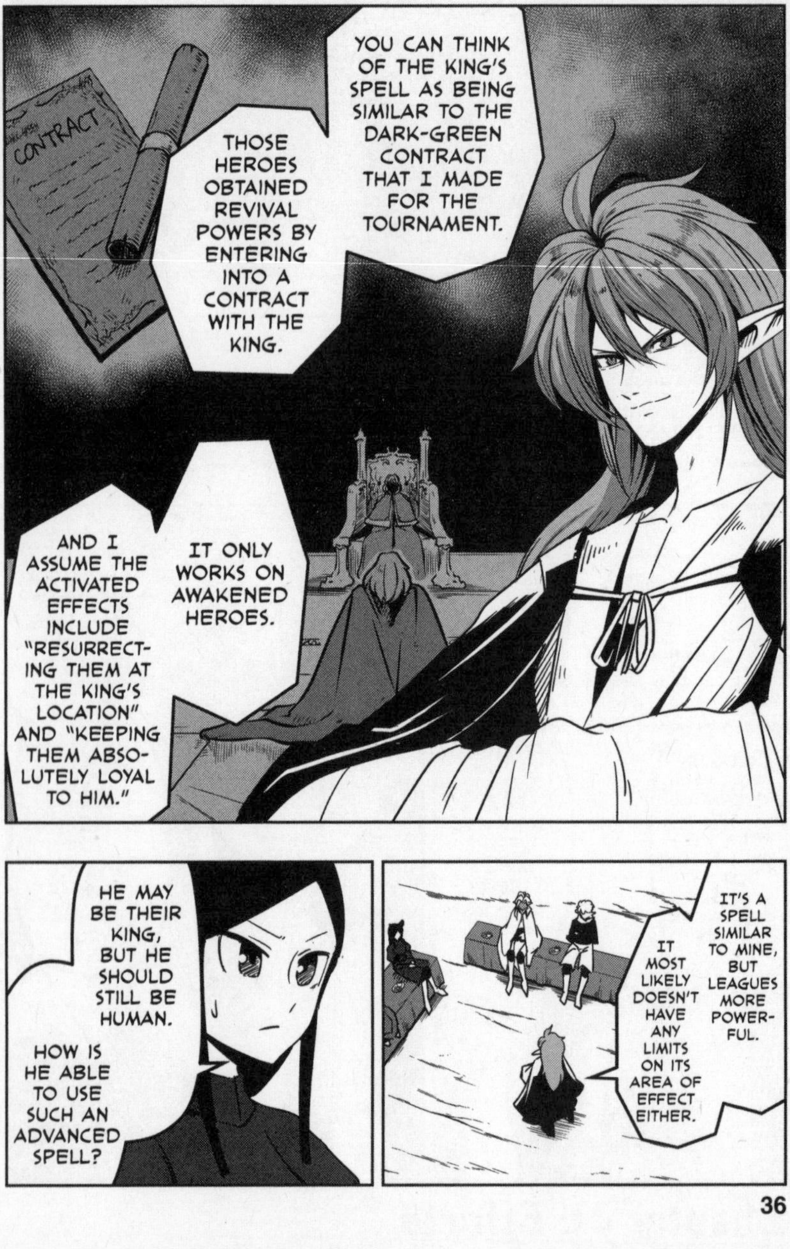
YOU CAN THINK OF THE KING'S SPELL AS BEING SIMILAR TO THE DARK-GREEN CONTRACT THAT I MADE FOR THE TOURNAMENT.
THOSE HEROES OBTAINED REVIVAL POWERS BY ENTERING INTO A CONTRACT WITH THE KING.
CONTRACT
IT ONLY WORKS ON AWAKENED HEROES.
AND I ASSUME THE ACTIVATED EFFECTS INCLUDE "RESURRECTING THEM AT THE KING'S LOCATION" AND "KEEPING THEM ABSOLUTELY LOYAL TO HIM."
IT'S A SPELL SIMILAR TO MINE, BUT LEAGUES MORE POWERFUL.
IT MOST LIKELY DOESN'T HAVE ANY LIMITS ON ITS AREA OF EFFECT EITHER.
HE MAY BE THEIR KING, BUT HE SHOULD STILL BE HUMAN.
HOW IS HE ABLE TO USE SUCH AN ADVANCED SPELL?

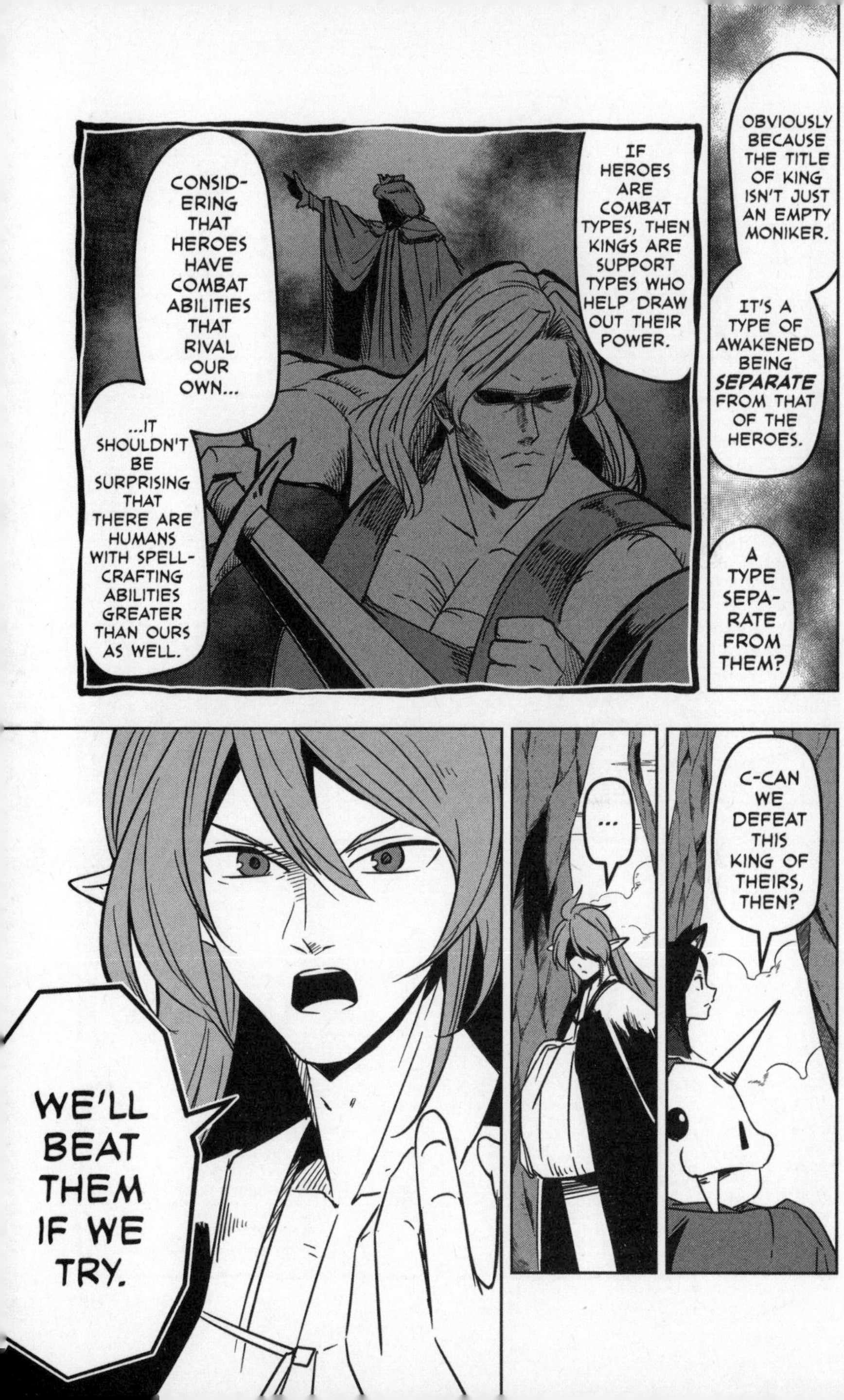
OBVIOUSLY BECAUSE THE TITLE OF KING ISN'T JUST AN EMPTY MONIKER.
IT'S A TYPE OF AWAKENED BEING *SEPARATE* FROM THAT OF THE HEROES.
A TYPE SEPARATE FROM THEM?
IF HEROES ARE COMBAT TYPES, THEN KINGS ARE SUPPORT TYPES WHO HELP DRAW OUT THEIR POWER.
CONSIDERING THAT HEROES HAVE COMBAT ABILITIES THAT RIVAL OUR OWN...
...IT SHOULDN'T BE SURPRISING THAT THERE ARE HUMANS WITH SPELL-CRAFTING ABILITIES GREATER THAN OURS AS WELL.
C-CAN WE DEFEAT THIS KING OF THEIRS, THEN?
...
WE'LL BEAT THEM IF WE TRY.

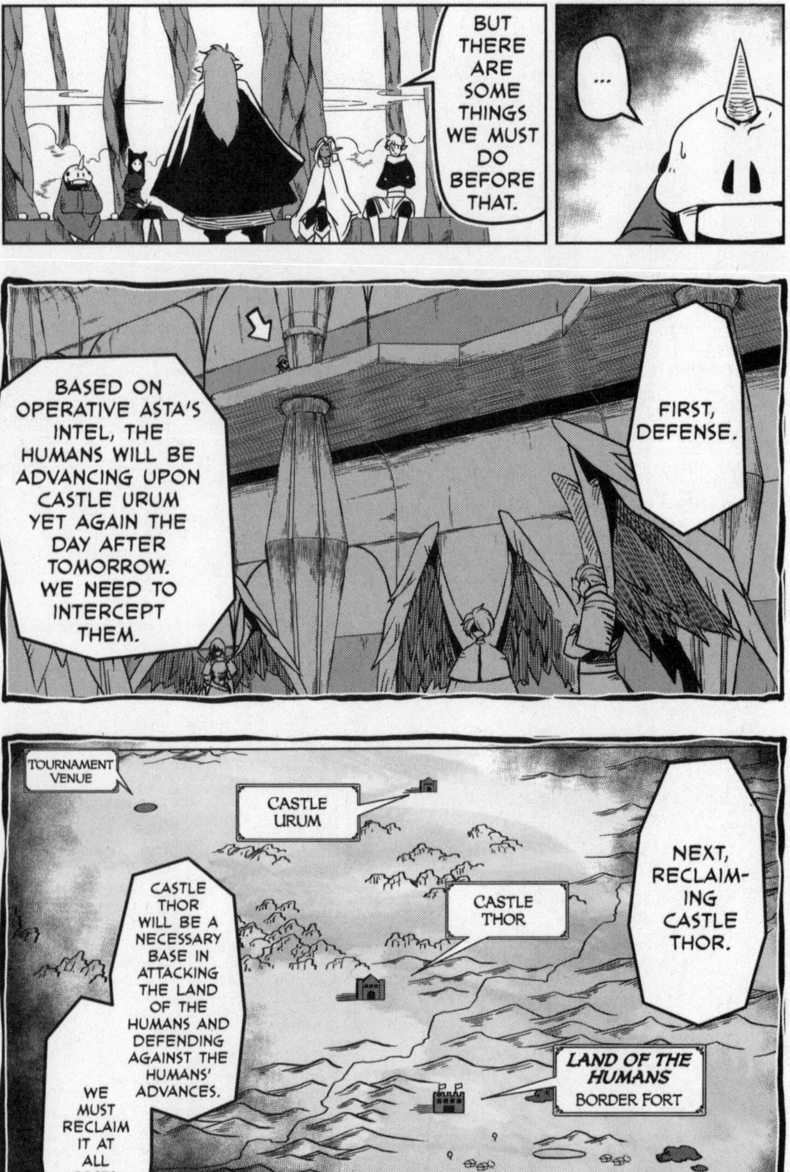
...
BUT THERE ARE SOME THINGS WE MUST DO BEFORE THAT.
FIRST, DEFENSE.
BASED ON OPERATIVE ASTA'S INTEL, THE HUMANS WILL BE ADVANCING UPON CASTLE URUM YET AGAIN THE DAY AFTER TOMORROW. WE NEED TO INTERCEPT THEM.
NEXT, RECLAIMING CASTLE THOR.
CASTLE URUM
TOURNAMENT VENUE
CASTLE THOR
LAND OF THE HUMANS
BORDER FORT
CASTLE THOR WILL BE A NECESSARY BASE IN ATTACKING THE LAND OF THE HUMANS AND DEFENDING AGAINST THE HUMANS' ADVANCES.
WE MUST RECLAIM IT AT ALL COSTS.

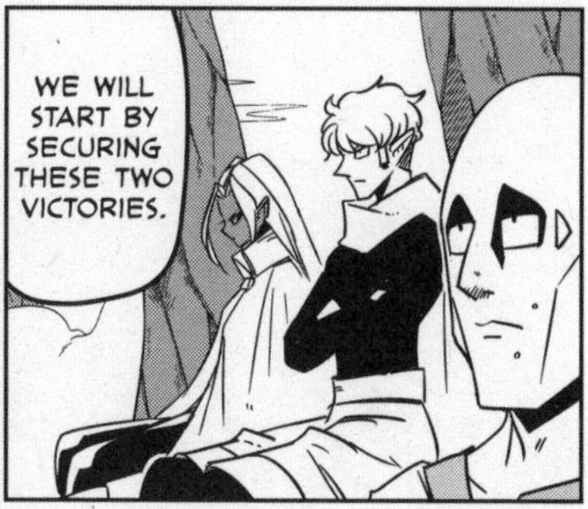
WE WILL START BY SECURING THESE TWO VICTORIES.

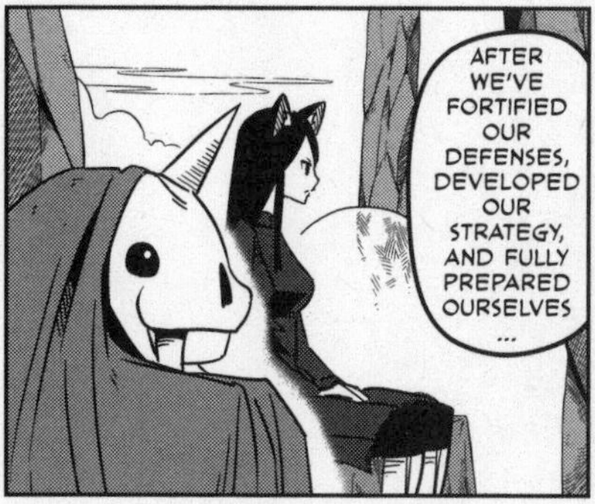
AFTER WE'VE FORTIFIED OUR DEFENSES, DEVELOPED OUR STRATEGY, AND FULLY PREPARED OURSELVES ...

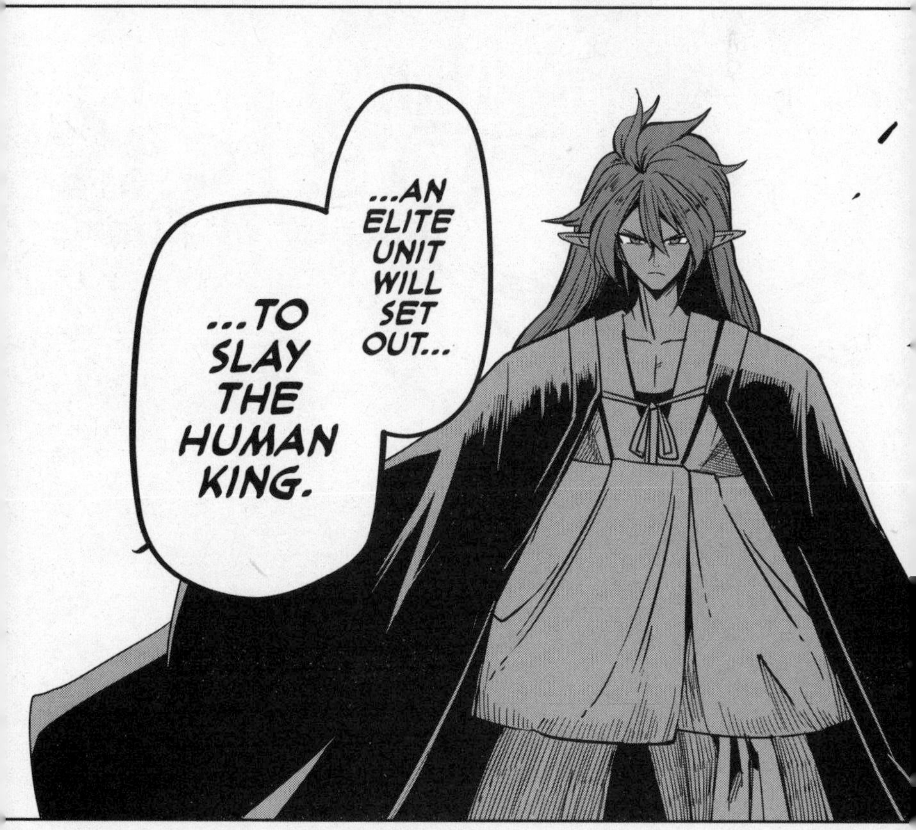
...AN ELITE UNIT WILL SET OUT...
...TO SLAY THE HUMAN KING.

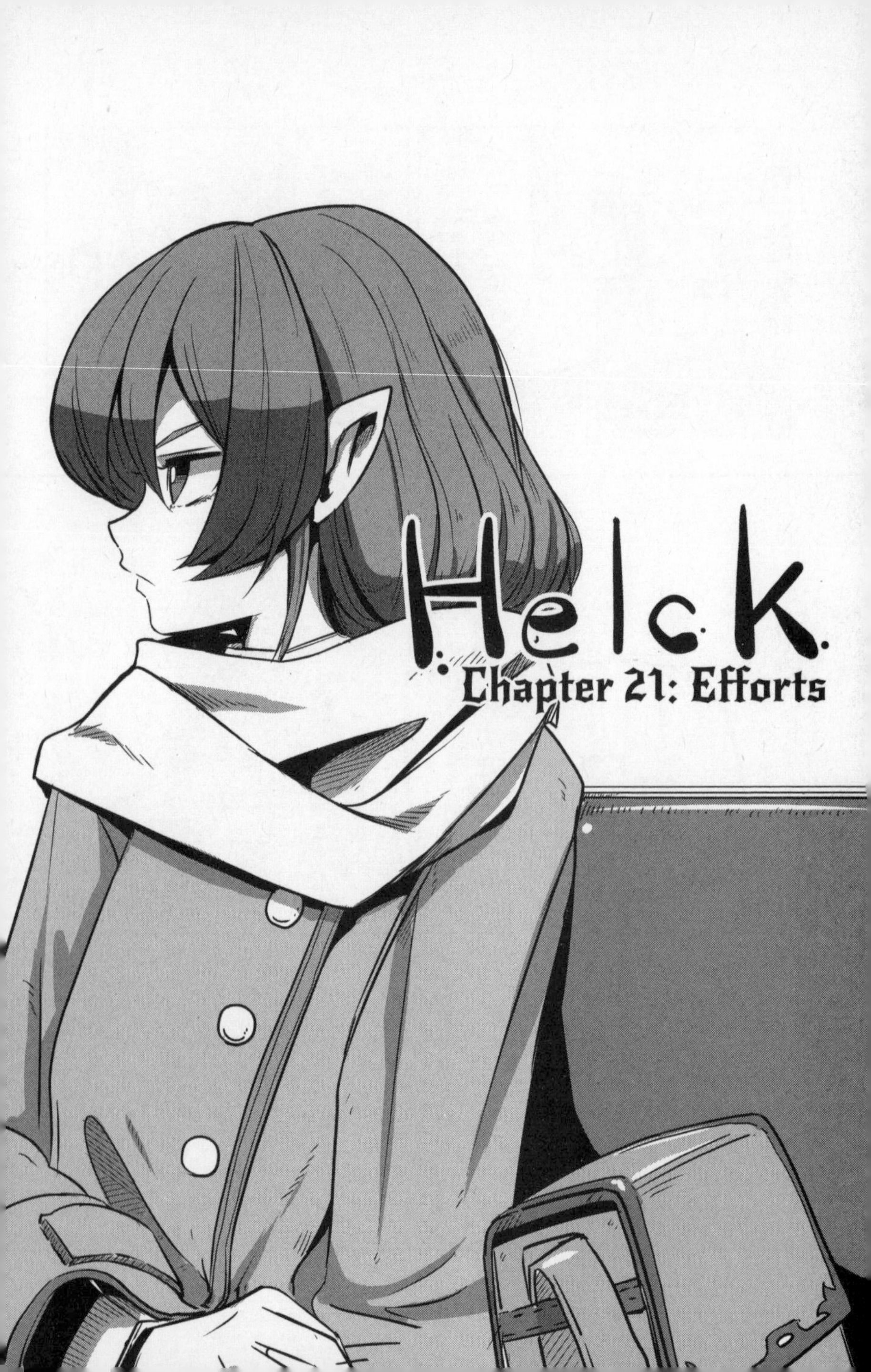
Helck
Chapter 21: Efforts

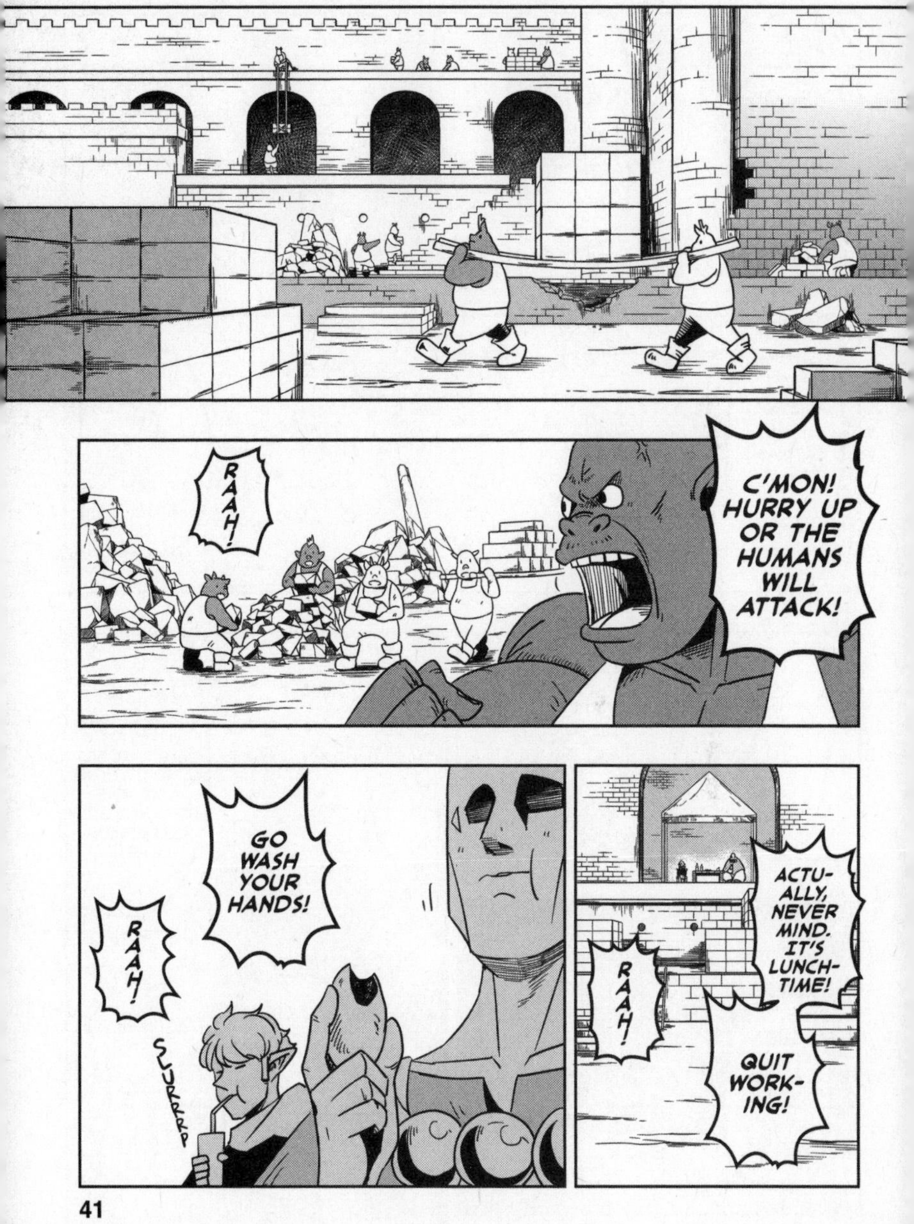
C'MON! HURRY UP OR THE HUMANS WILL ATTACK!
RAAH!
ACTUALLY, NEVER MIND. IT'S LUNCHTIME!
RAAH!
QUIT WORKING!
GO WASH YOUR HANDS!
RAAH!
SLURRRP

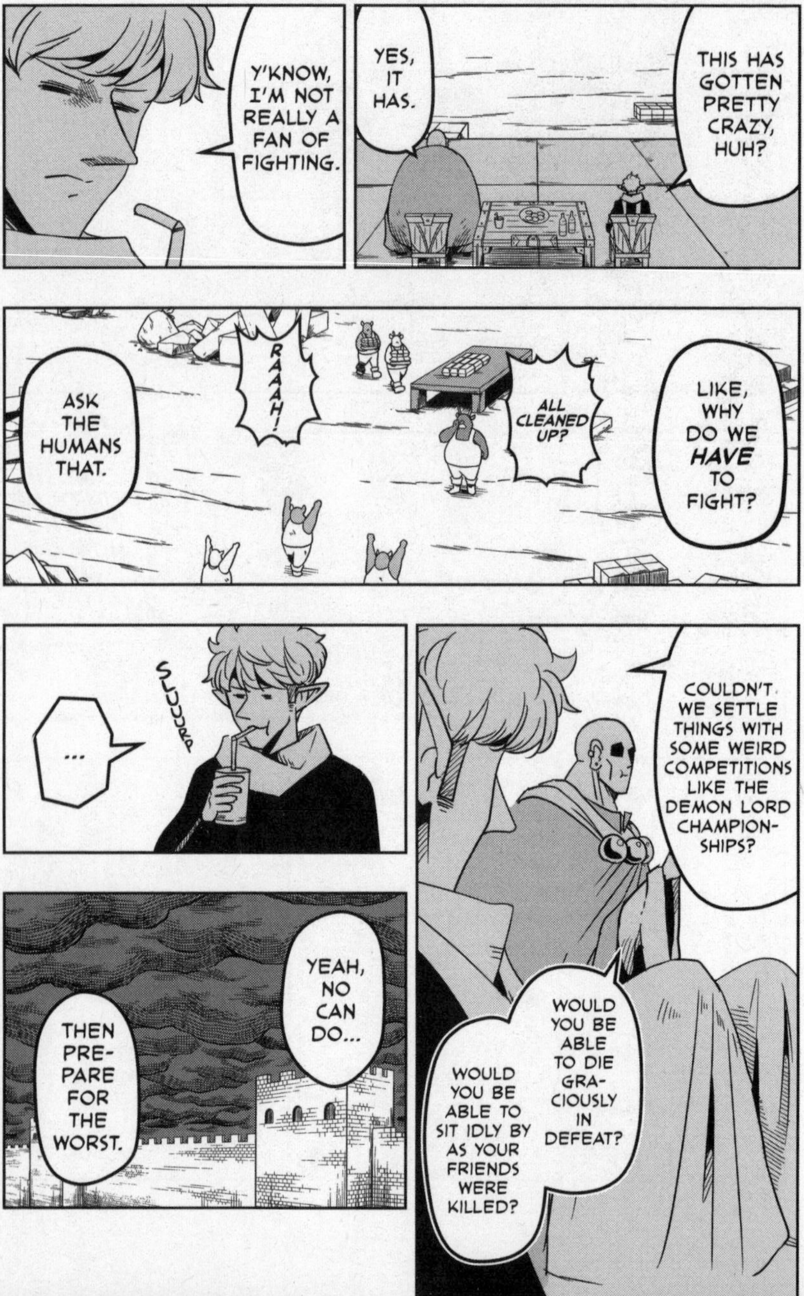
THIS HAS GOTTEN PRETTY CRAZY, HUH?
YES, IT HAS.
Y'KNOW, I'M NOT REALLY A FAN OF FIGHTING.
LIKE, WHY DO WE HAVE TO FIGHT?
ALL CLEANED UP?
RAAAAH!
ASK THE HUMANS THAT.
COULDN'T WE SETTLE THINGS WITH SOME WEIRD COMPETITIONS LIKE THE DEMON LORD CHAMPION-SHIPS?
WOULD YOU BE ABLE TO DIE GRA-CIOUSLY IN DEFEAT?
WOULD YOU BE ABLE TO SIT IDLY BY AS YOUR FRIENDS WERE KILLED?
SLUURP
...
YEAH, NO CAN DO...
THEN PRE-PARE FOR THE WORST.

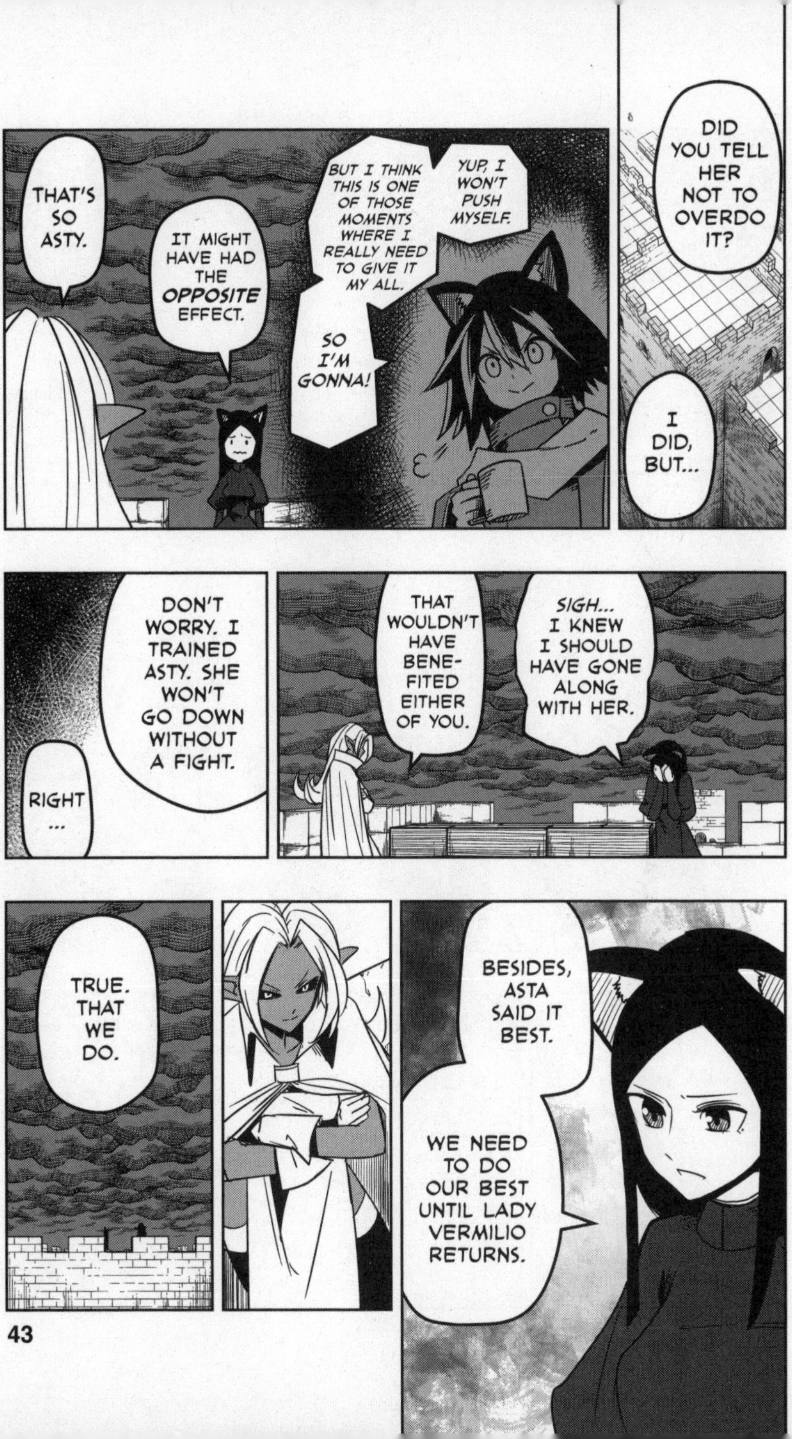
DID YOU TELL HER NOT TO OVERDO IT?
I DID, BUT...
YUP, I WON'T PUSH MYSELF.
BUT I THINK THIS IS ONE OF THOSE MOMENTS WHERE I REALLY NEED TO GIVE IT MY ALL.
SO I'M GONNA!
IT MIGHT HAVE HAD THE OPPOSITE EFFECT.
THAT'S SO ASTY.
SIGH... I KNEW I SHOULD HAVE GONE ALONG WITH HER.
THAT WOULDN'T HAVE BENE-FITED EITHER OF YOU.
DON'T WORRY. I TRAINED ASTY. SHE WON'T GO DOWN WITHOUT A FIGHT.
RIGHT...
BESIDES, ASTA SAID IT BEST.
WE NEED TO DO OUR BEST UNTIL LADY VERMILIO RETURNS.
TRUE. THAT WE DO.

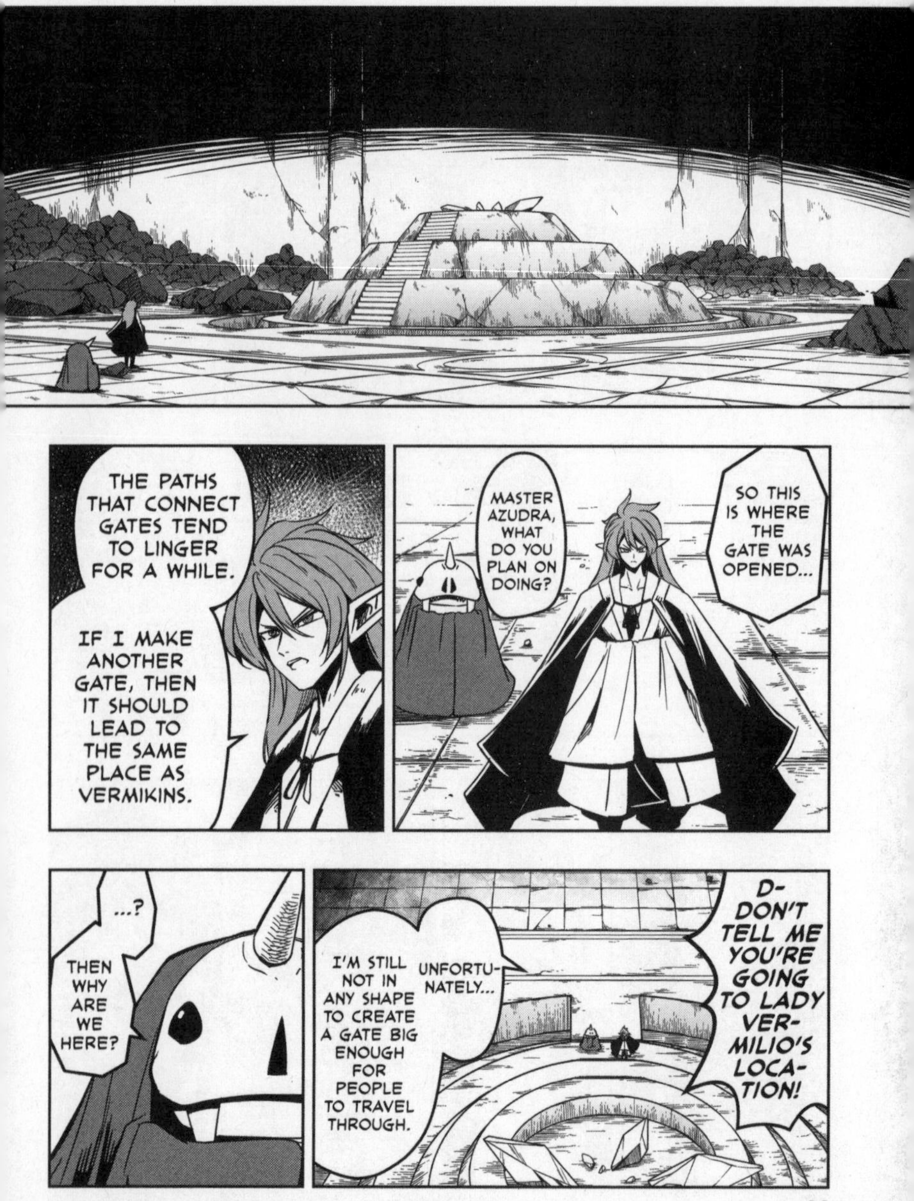
SO THIS IS WHERE THE GATE WAS OPENED...
MASTER AZUDRA, WHAT DO YOU PLAN ON DOING?
THE PATHS THAT CONNECT GATES TEND TO LINGER FOR A WHILE.
IF I MAKE ANOTHER GATE, THEN IT SHOULD LEAD TO THE SAME PLACE AS VERMIKINS.
D-DON'T TELL ME YOU'RE GOING TO LADY VER-MILIO'S LOCA-TION!
UNFORTU-NATELY...
I'M STILL NOT IN ANY SHAPE TO CREATE A GATE BIG ENOUGH FOR PEOPLE TO TRAVEL THROUGH.
...?
THEN WHY ARE WE HERE?

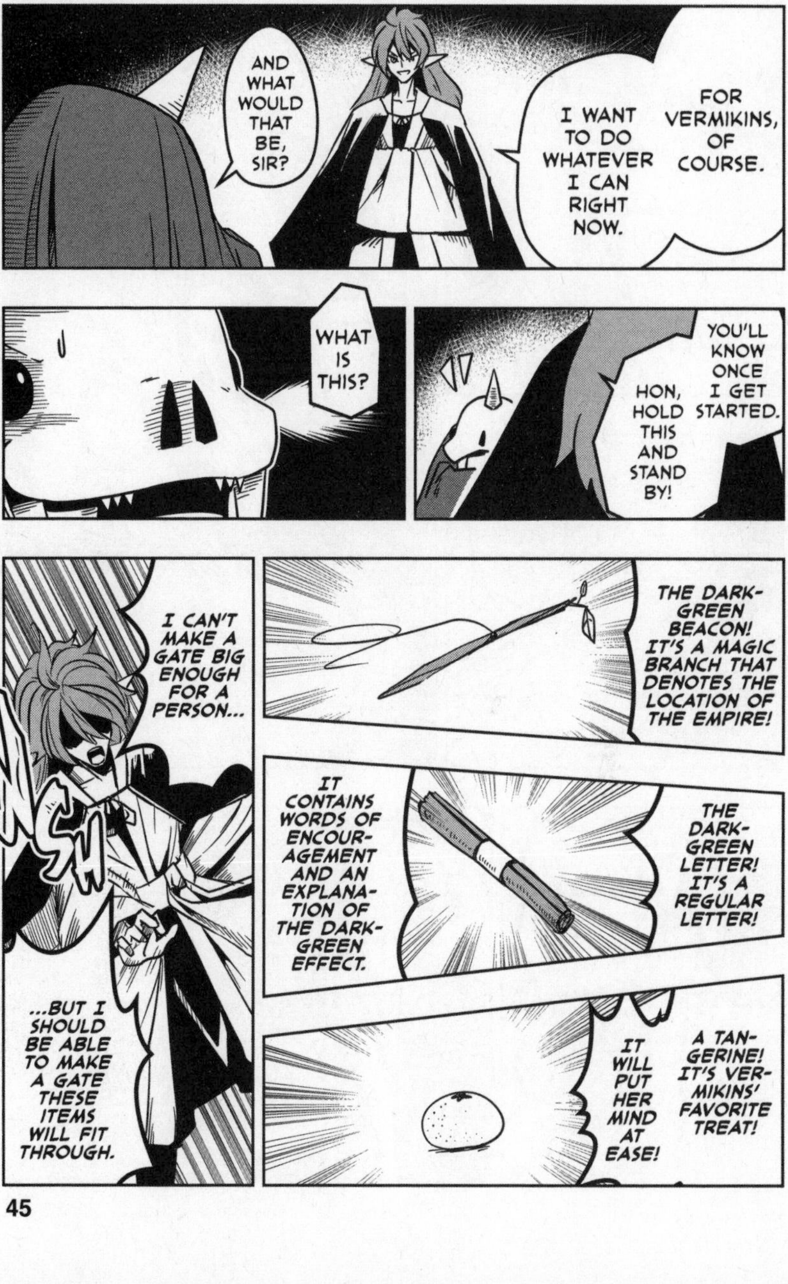
FOR VERMIKINS, OF COURSE.
I WANT TO DO WHATEVER I CAN RIGHT NOW.
AND WHAT WOULD THAT BE, SIR?
YOU'LL KNOW ONCE I GET STARTED.
HON, HOLD THIS AND STAND BY!
WHAT IS THIS?
THE DARK-GREEN BEACON! IT'S A MAGIC BRANCH THAT DENOTES THE LOCATION OF THE EMPIRE!
THE DARK-GREEN LETTER! IT'S A REGULAR LETTER!
IT CONTAINS WORDS OF ENCOURAGEMENT AND AN EXPLANATION OF THE DARK-GREEN EFFECT.
A TANGERINE! IT'S VERMIKINS' FAVORITE TREAT!
IT WILL PUT HER MIND AT EASE!
I CAN'T MAKE A GATE BIG ENOUGH FOR A PERSON...
WSSH
...BUT I SHOULD BE ABLE TO MAKE A GATE THESE ITEMS WILL FIT THROUGH.

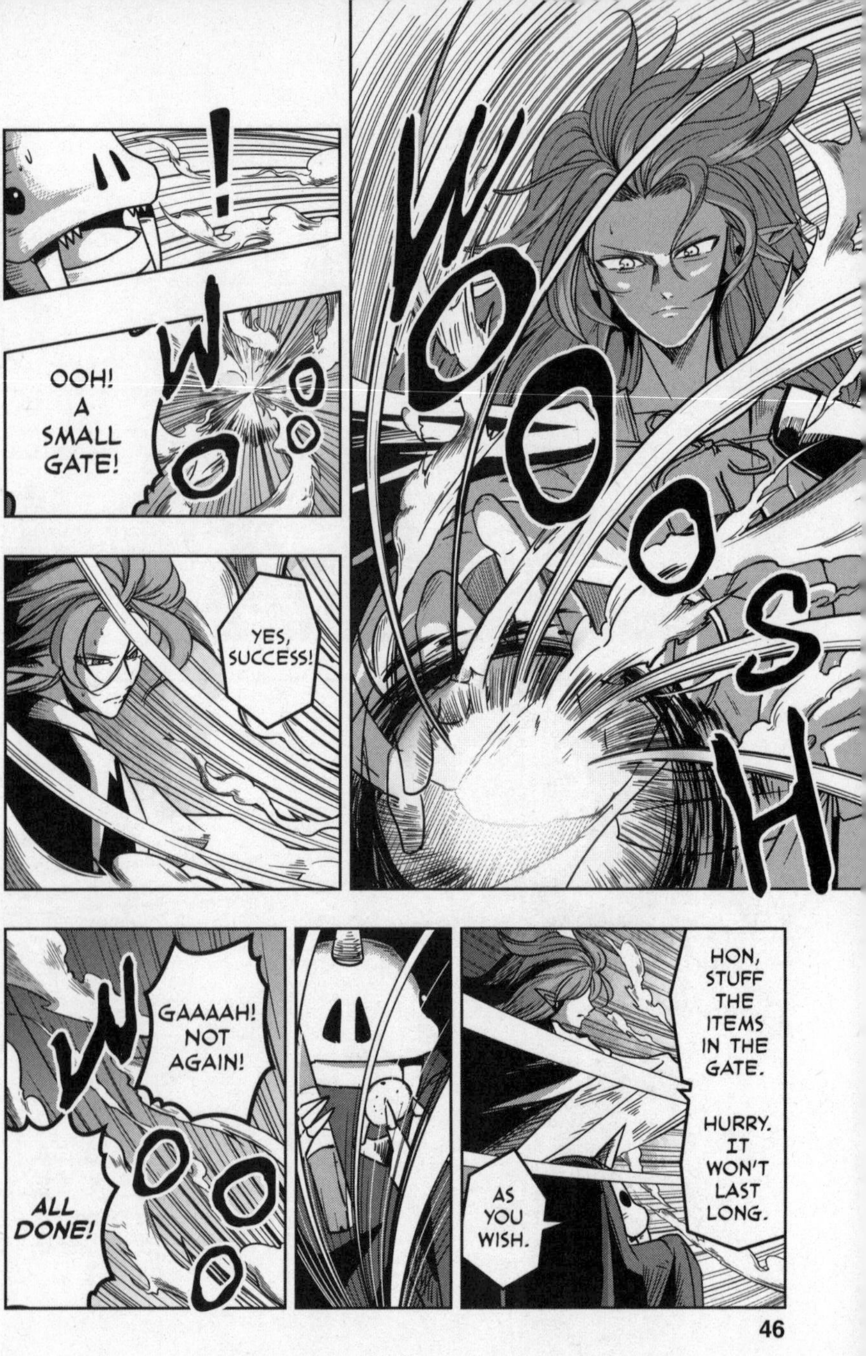
WOOOOSH
!
OOH! A SMALL GATE!
WOOO
YES, SUCCESS!
HON, STUFF THE ITEMS IN THE GATE.
HURRY. IT WON'T LAST LONG.
AS YOU WISH.
GAAAAH! NOT AGAIN!
WOOO
ALL DONE!

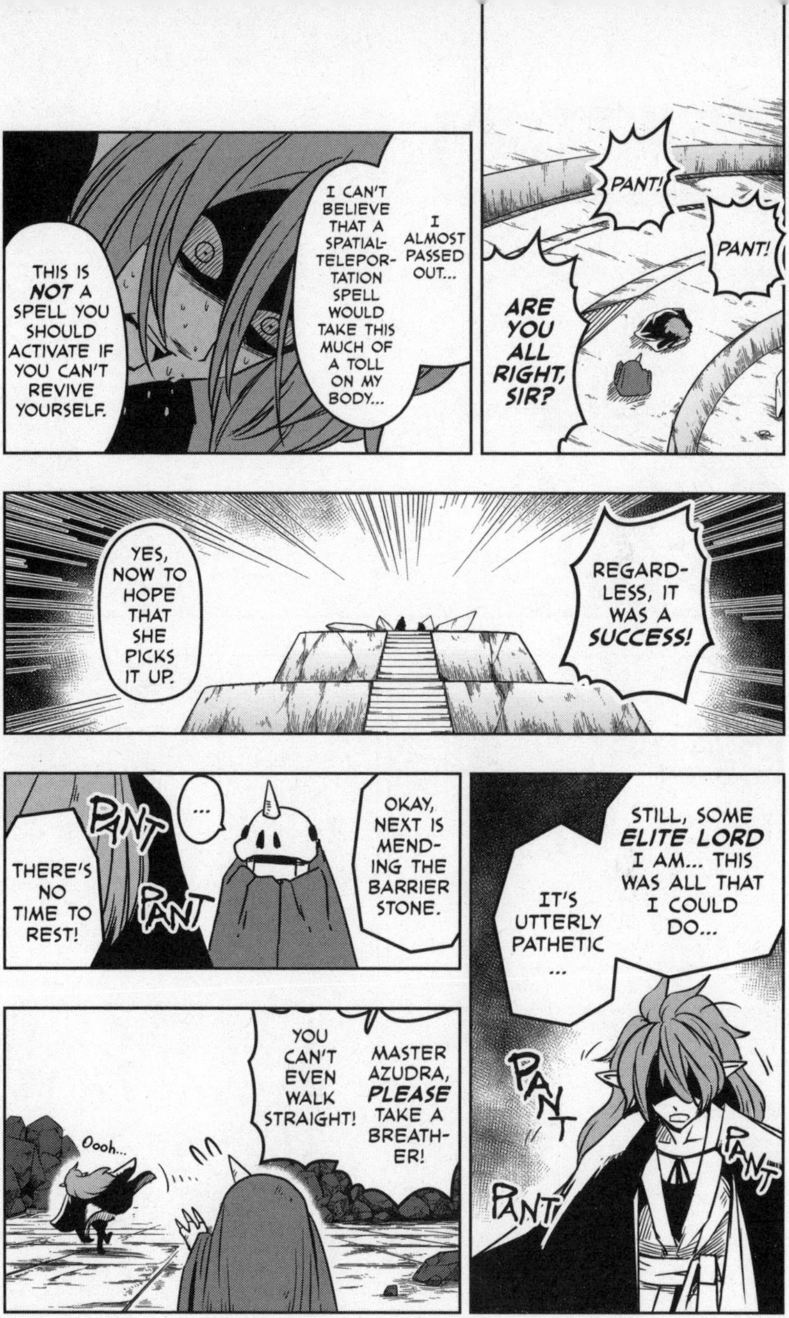
PANT!
PANT!
ARE YOU ALL RIGHT, SIR?
I ALMOST PASSED OUT...
I CAN'T BELIEVE THAT A SPATIAL-TELEPORTATION SPELL WOULD TAKE THIS MUCH OF A TOLL ON MY BODY...
THIS IS NOT A SPELL YOU SHOULD ACTIVATE IF YOU CAN'T REVIVE YOURSELF.
REGARDLESS, IT WAS A SUCCESS!
YES, NOW TO HOPE THAT SHE PICKS IT UP.
STILL, SOME ELITE LORD I AM... THIS WAS ALL THAT I COULD DO...
IT'S UTTERLY PATHETIC...
PANT
PANT
PANT
OKAY, NEXT IS MENDING THE BARRIER STONE.
...
PANT
PANT
THERE'S NO TIME TO REST!
MASTER AZUDRA, PLEASE TAKE A BREATHER!
YOU CAN'T EVEN WALK STRAIGHT!
Oooh...

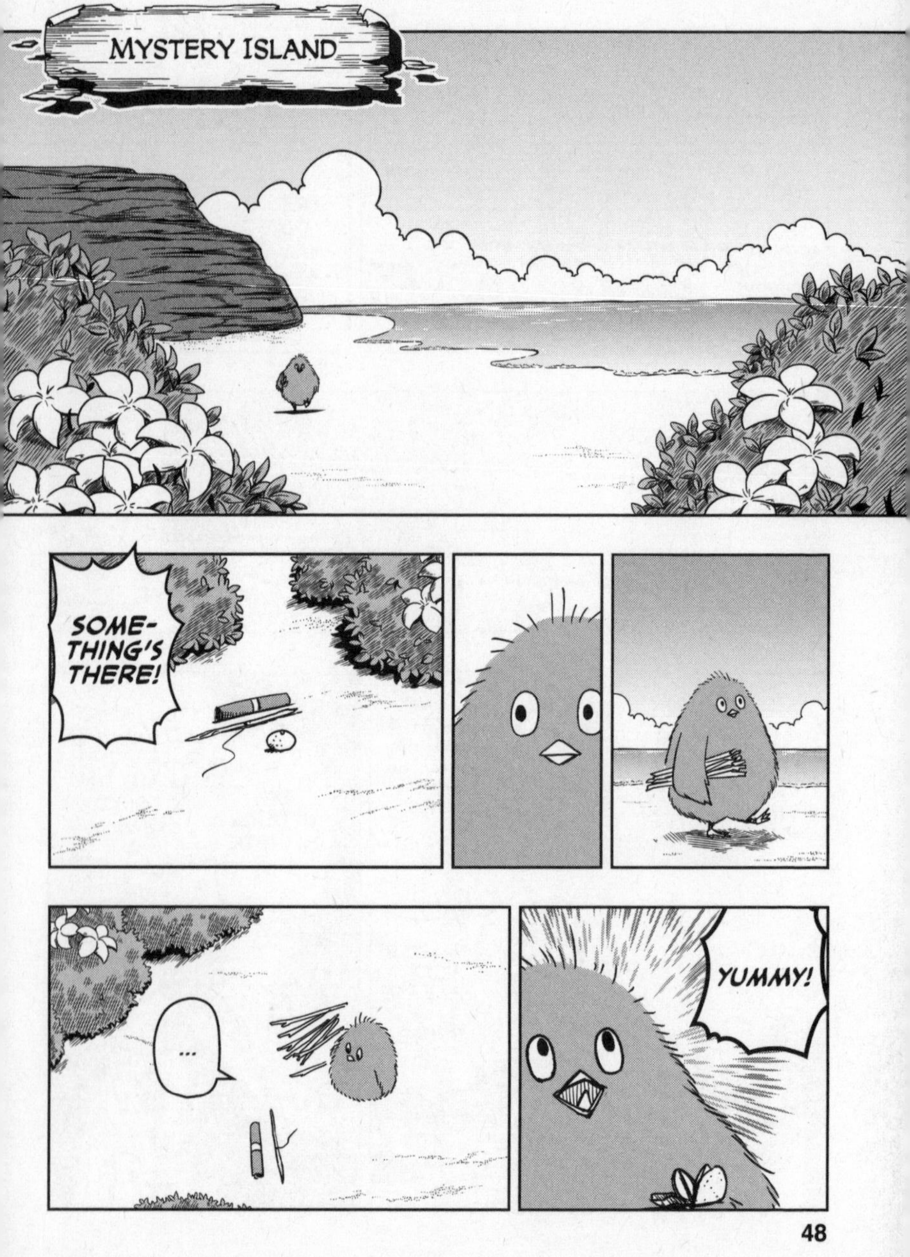
MYSTERY ISLAND
SOME-THING'S THERE!
YUMMY!
...

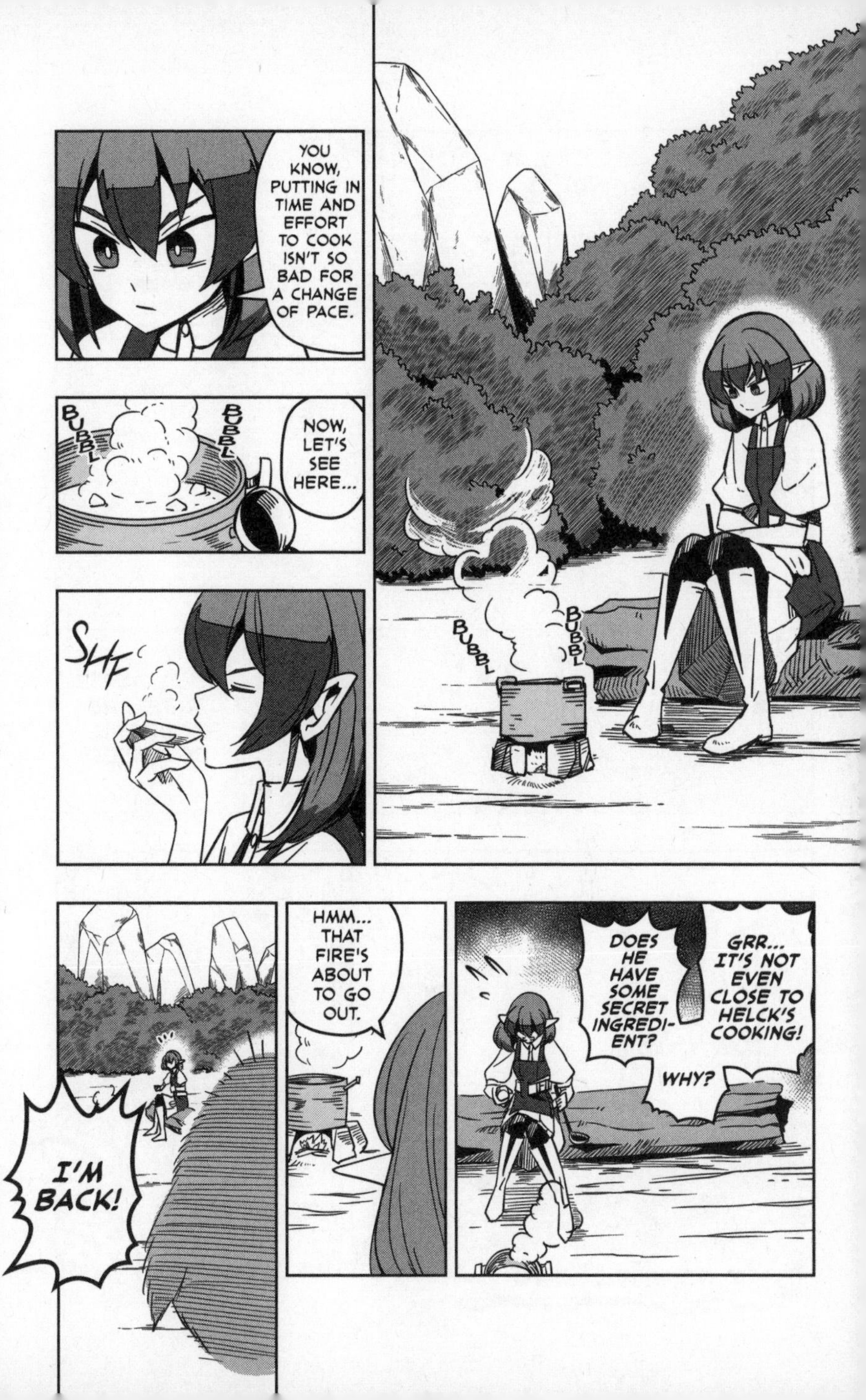
BUBBL
BUBBL
YOU KNOW, PUTTING IN TIME AND EFFORT TO COOK ISN'T SO BAD FOR A CHANGE OF PACE.
BUBBL
BUBBL
NOW, LET'S SEE HERE...
SHF
GRR... IT'S NOT EVEN CLOSE TO HELCK'S COOKING!
DOES HE HAVE SOME SECRET INGREDIENT?
WHY?
HMM... THAT FIRE'S ABOUT TO GO OUT.
I'M BACK!

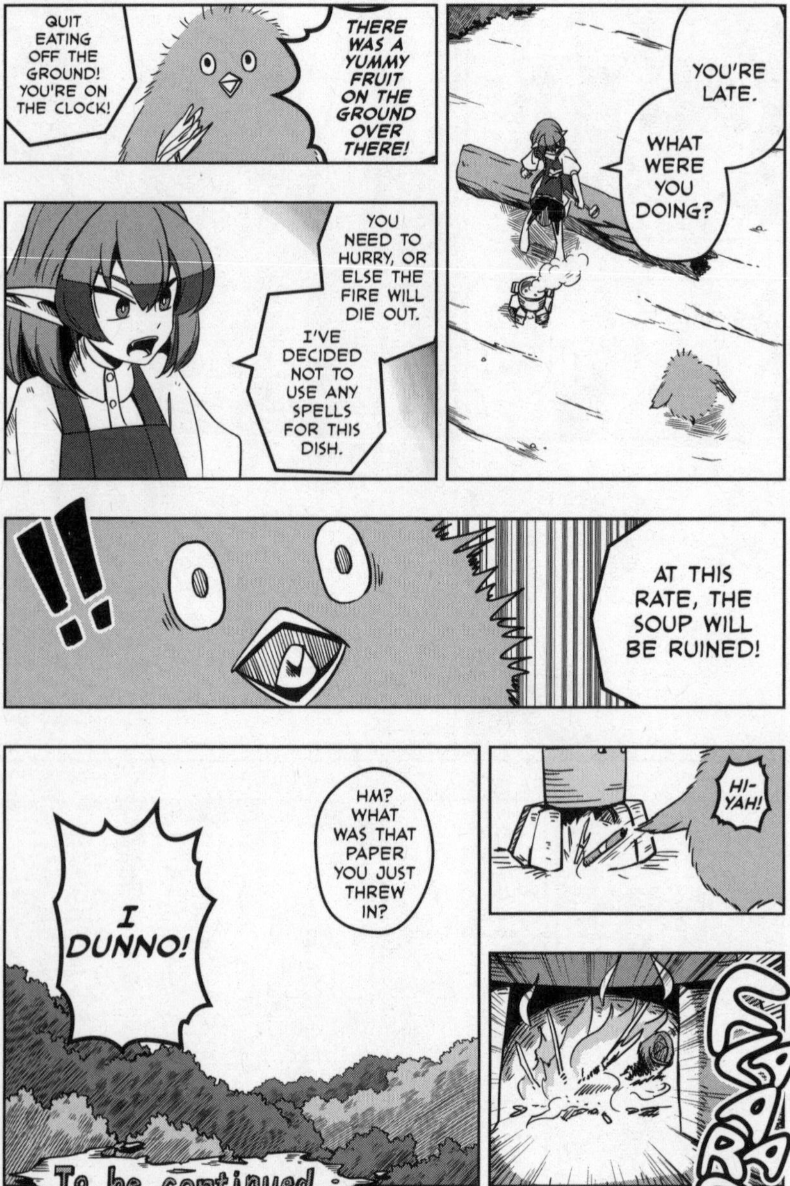
YOU'RE LATE.
WHAT WERE YOU DOING?
THERE WAS A YUMMY FRUIT ON THE GROUND OVER THERE!
QUIT EATING OFF THE GROUND! YOU'RE ON THE CLOCK!
YOU NEED TO HURRY, OR ELSE THE FIRE WILL DIE OUT.
I'VE DECIDED NOT TO USE ANY SPELLS FOR THIS DISH.
AT THIS RATE, THE SOUP WILL BE RUINED!
!!
HI-YAH!
HM? WHAT WAS THAT PAPER YOU JUST THREW IN?
I DUNNO!
To be continued

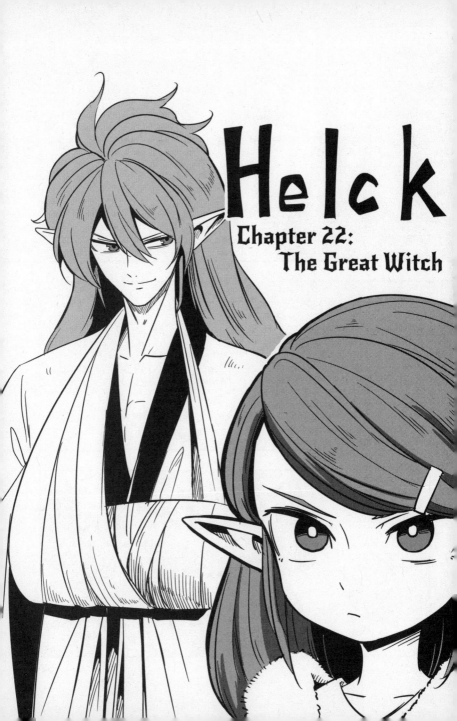

Helck

Chapter 22:
The Great Witch

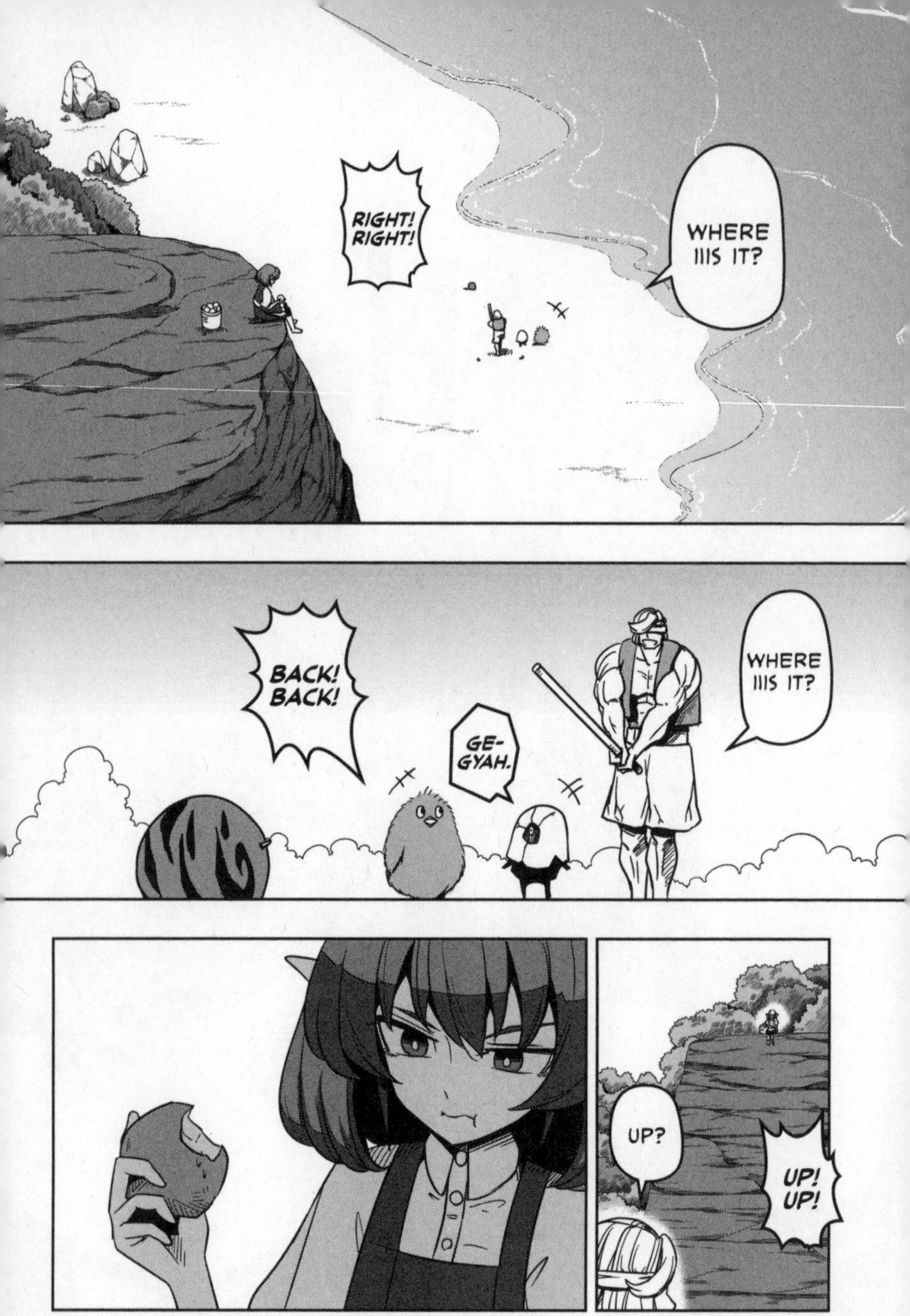
WHERE IIIS IT?
RIGHT! RIGHT!
WHERE IIIS IT?
GE-GYAH.
BACK! BACK!
UP?
UP! UP!

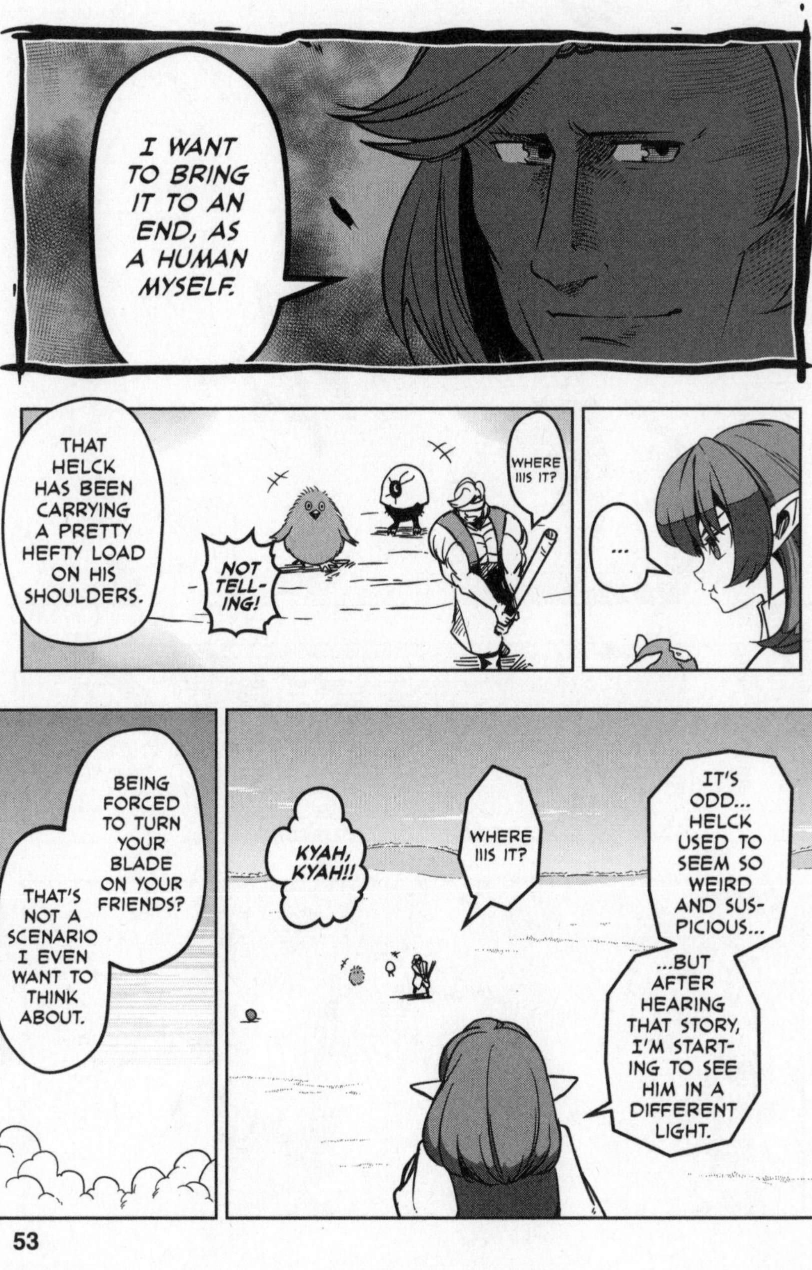
I WANT TO BRING IT TO AN END, AS A HUMAN MYSELF.
...
WHERE IIIS IT?
NOT TELLING!
THAT HELCK HAS BEEN CARRYING A PRETTY HEFTY LOAD ON HIS SHOULDERS.
IT'S ODD... HELCK USED TO SEEM SO WEIRD AND SUSPICIOUS...
...BUT AFTER HEARING THAT STORY, I'M STARTING TO SEE HIM IN A DIFFERENT LIGHT.
WHERE IIIS IT?
KYAH, KYAH!!
BEING FORCED TO TURN YOUR BLADE ON YOUR FRIENDS?
THAT'S NOT A SCENARIO I EVEN WANT TO THINK ABOUT.

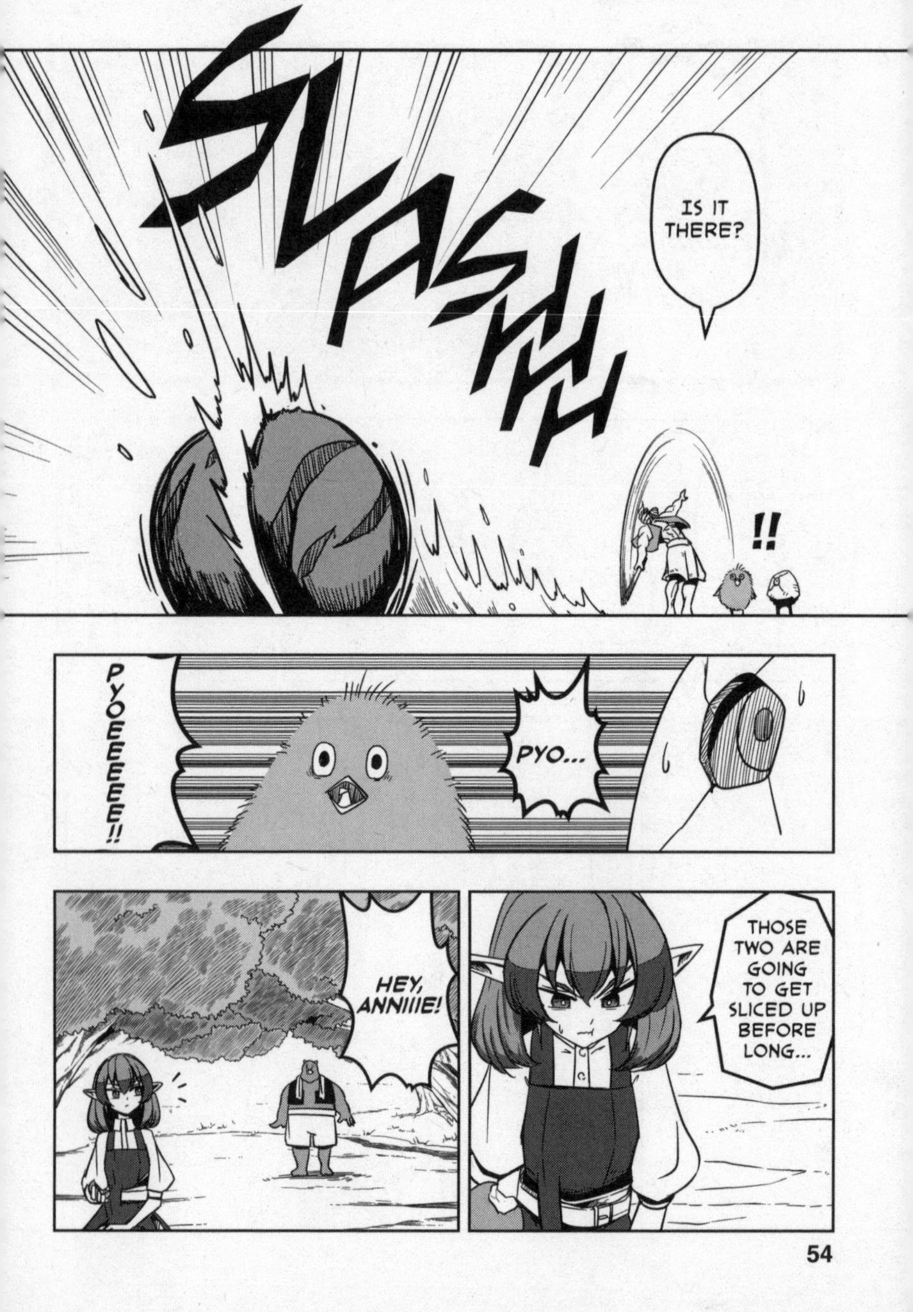
IS IT THERE?
SLASHHH
!!
PYO...
PYOEEEEE!!
THOSE TWO ARE GOING TO GET SLICED UP BEFORE LONG...
HEY, ANNIIIE!

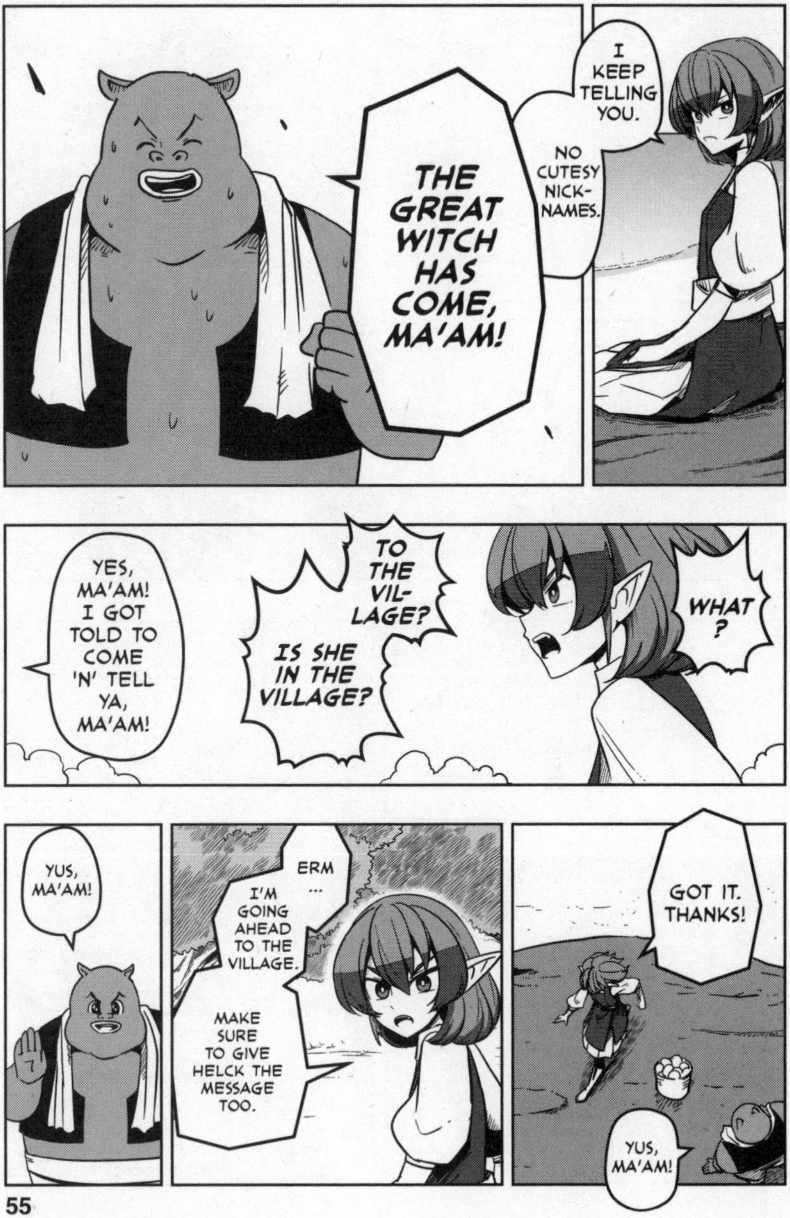
I KEEP TELLING YOU.
NO CUTESY NICK-NAMES.
THE GREAT WITCH HAS COME, MA'AM!
WHAT?
TO THE VIL-LAGE?
IS SHE IN THE VILLAGE?
YES, MA'AM! I GOT TOLD TO COME 'N' TELL YA, MA'AM!
GOT IT. THANKS!
YUS, MA'AM!
ERM ...
I'M GOING AHEAD TO THE VILLAGE.
MAKE SURE TO GIVE HELCK THE MESSAGE TOO.
YUS, MA'AM!

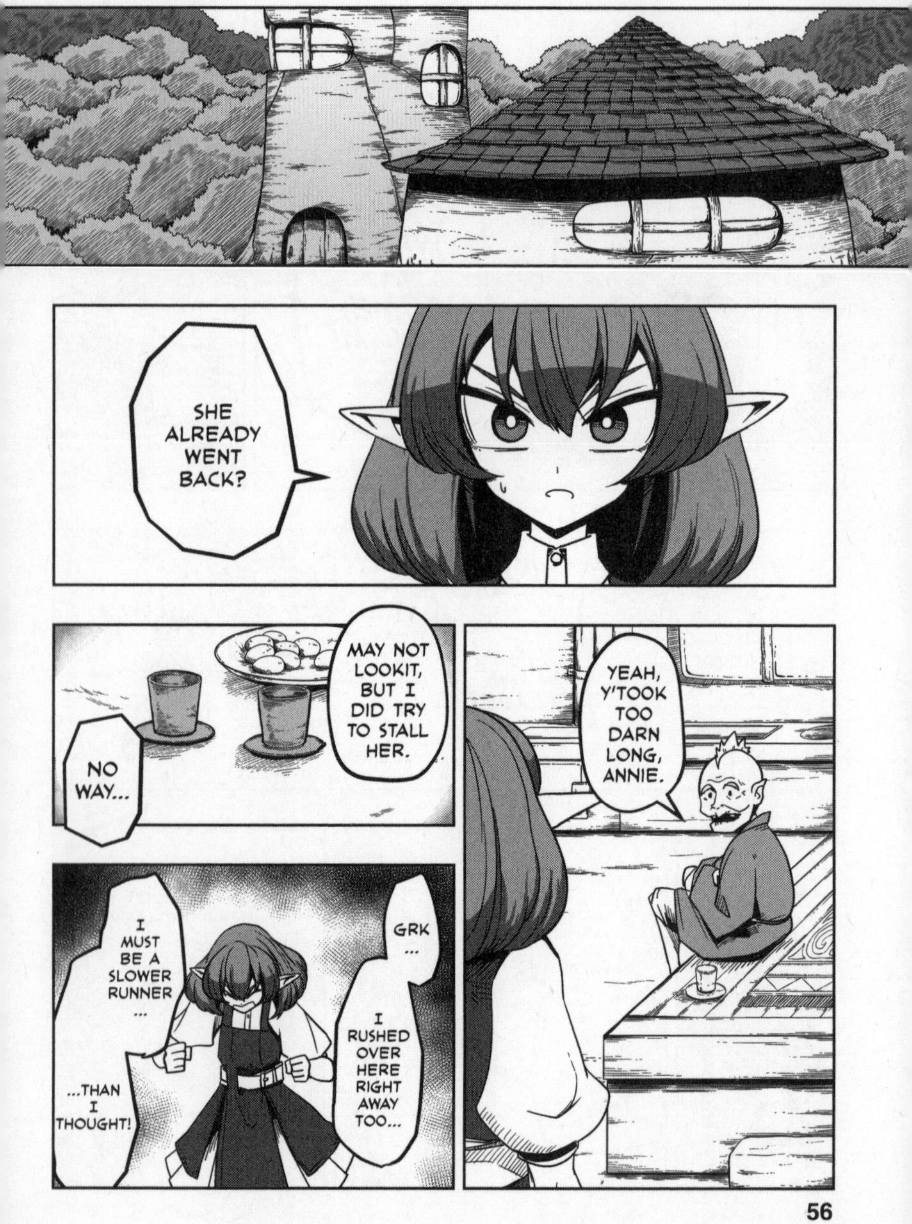
SHE ALREADY WENT BACK?
YEAH, Y'TOOK TOO DARN LONG, ANNIE.
MAY NOT LOOKIT, BUT I DID TRY TO STALL HER.
NO WAY...
GRK...
I RUSHED OVER HERE RIGHT AWAY TOO...
I MUST BE A SLOWER RUNNER...
...THAN I THOUGHT!

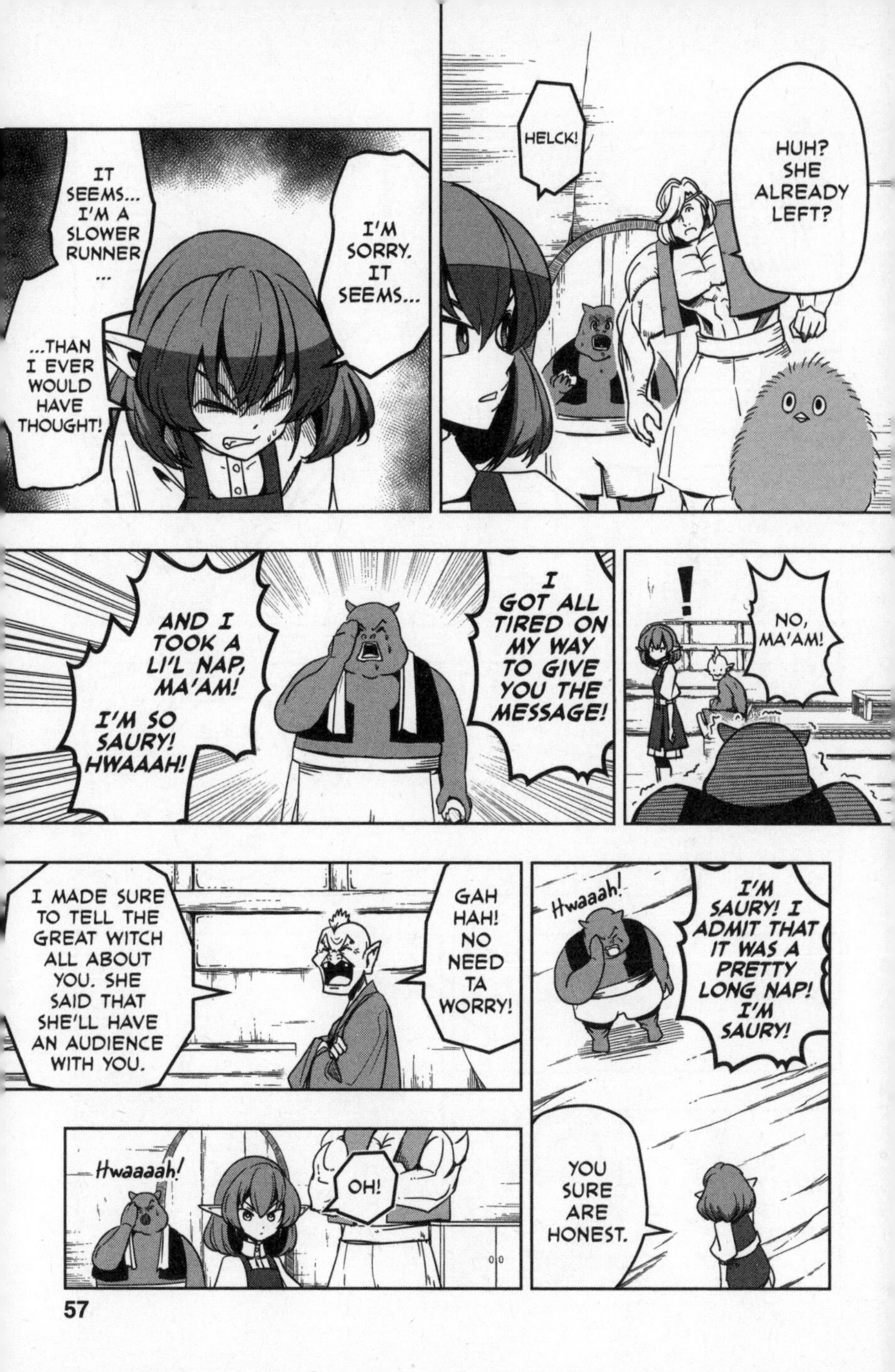
HUH? SHE ALREADY LEFT?
HELCK!
I'M SORRY. IT SEEMS...
IT SEEMS... I'M A SLOWER RUNNER ...
...THAN I EVER WOULD HAVE THOUGHT!
NO, MA'AM!
I GOT ALL TIRED ON MY WAY TO GIVE YOU THE MESSAGE!
AND I TOOK A LI'L NAP, MA'AM!
I'M SO SAURY! HWAAAH!
Hwaaah!
I'M SAURY! I ADMIT THAT IT WAS A PRETTY LONG NAP! I'M SAURY!
YOU SURE ARE HONEST.
GAH HAH! NO NEED TA WORRY!
I MADE SURE TO TELL THE GREAT WITCH ALL ABOUT YOU. SHE SAID THAT SHE'LL HAVE AN AUDIENCE WITH YOU.
OH!
Hwaaaah!

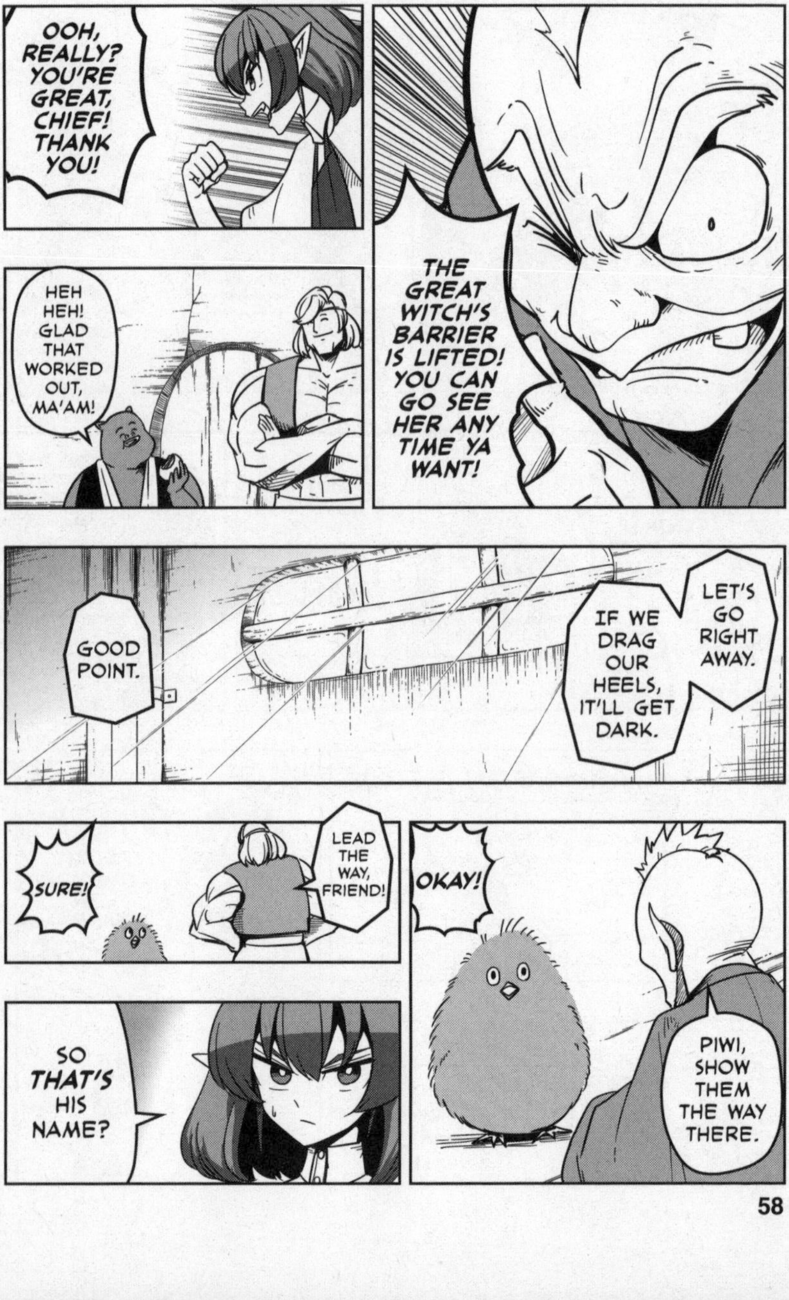
THE GREAT WITCH'S BARRIER IS LIFTED! YOU CAN GO SEE HER ANY TIME YA WANT!
OOH, REALLY? YOU'RE GREAT, CHIEF! THANK YOU!
HEH HEH! GLAD THAT WORKED OUT, MA'AM!
LET'S GO RIGHT AWAY.
IF WE DRAG OUR HEELS, IT'LL GET DARK.
GOOD POINT.
PIWI, SHOW THEM THE WAY THERE.
OKAY!
LEAD THE WAY, FRIEND!
SURE!
SO *THAT'S* HIS NAME?

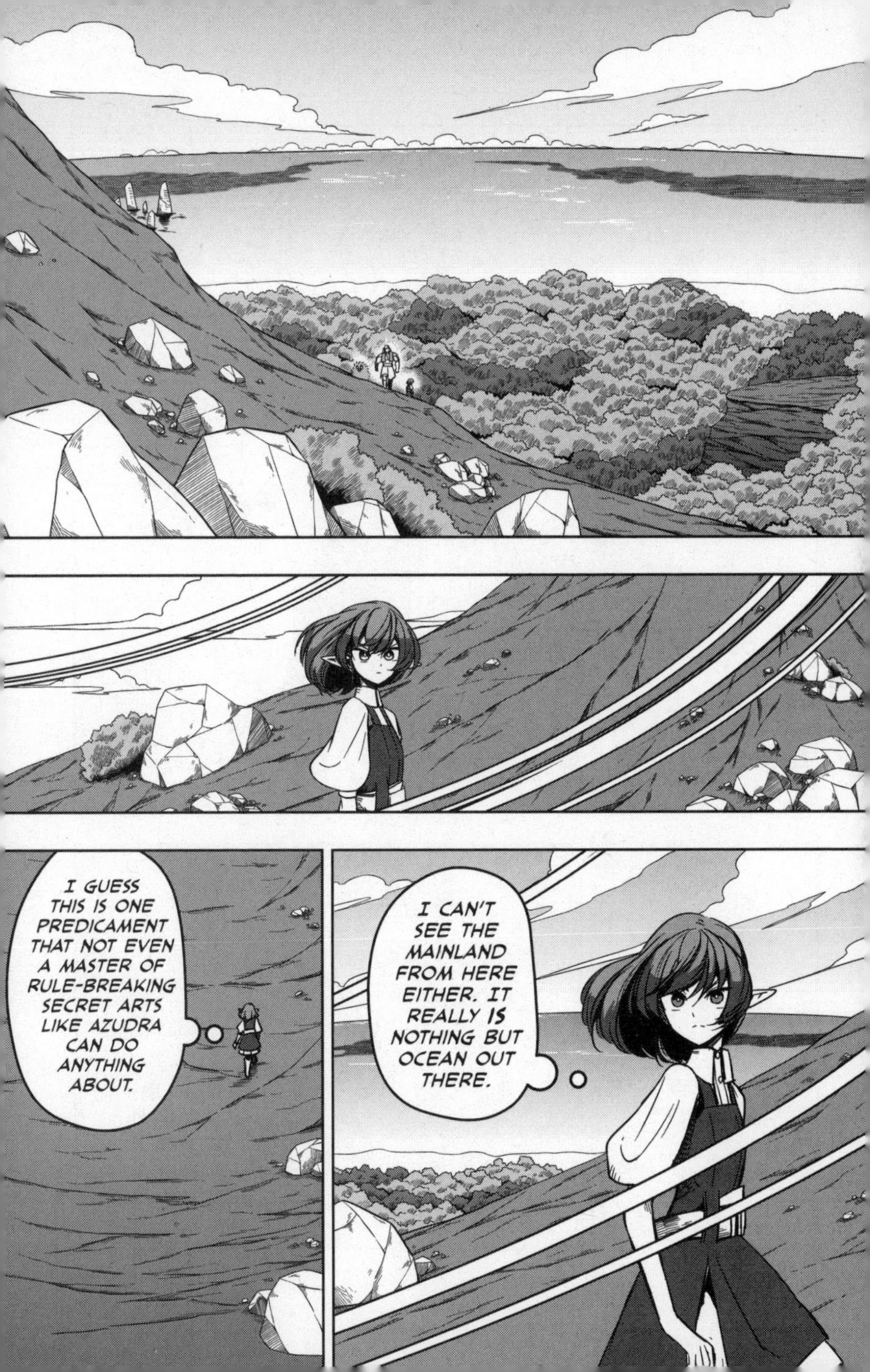
I CAN'T SEE THE MAINLAND FROM HERE EITHER. IT REALLY IS NOTHING BUT OCEAN OUT THERE.
I GUESS THIS IS ONE PREDICAMENT THAT NOT EVEN A MASTER OF RULE-BREAKING SECRET ARTS LIKE AZUDRA CAN DO ANYTHING ABOUT.

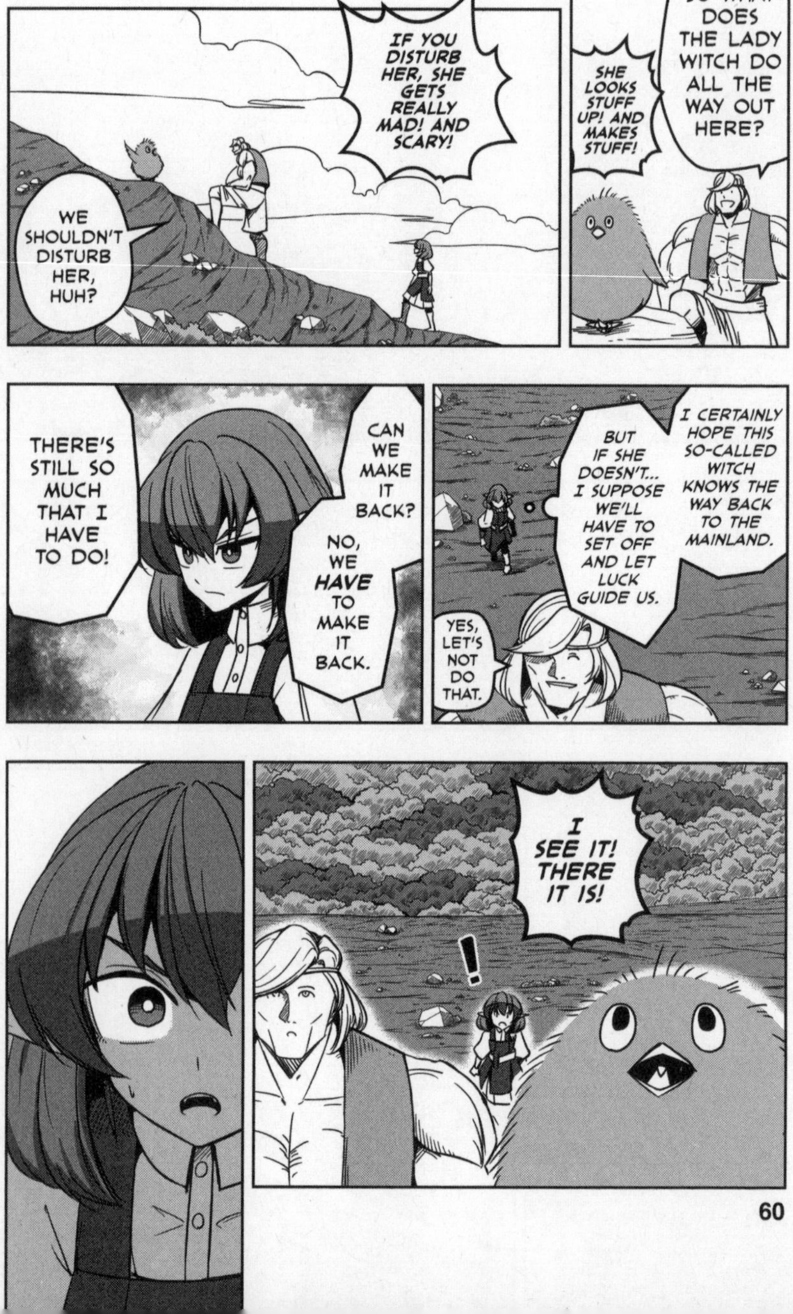
SO WHAT DOES THE LADY WITCH DO ALL THE WAY OUT HERE?
SHE LOOKS STUFF UP! AND MAKES STUFF!
IF YOU DISTURB HER, SHE GETS REALLY MAD! AND SCARY!
WE SHOULDN'T DISTURB HER, HUH?
I CERTAINLY HOPE THIS SO-CALLED WITCH KNOWS THE WAY BACK TO THE MAINLAND.
BUT IF SHE DOESN'T... I SUPPOSE WE'LL HAVE TO SET OFF AND LET LUCK GUIDE US.
YES, LET'S NOT DO THAT.
CAN WE MAKE IT BACK?
NO, WE *HAVE* TO MAKE IT BACK.
THERE'S STILL SO MUCH THAT I HAVE TO DO!
I SEE IT! THERE IT IS!
!

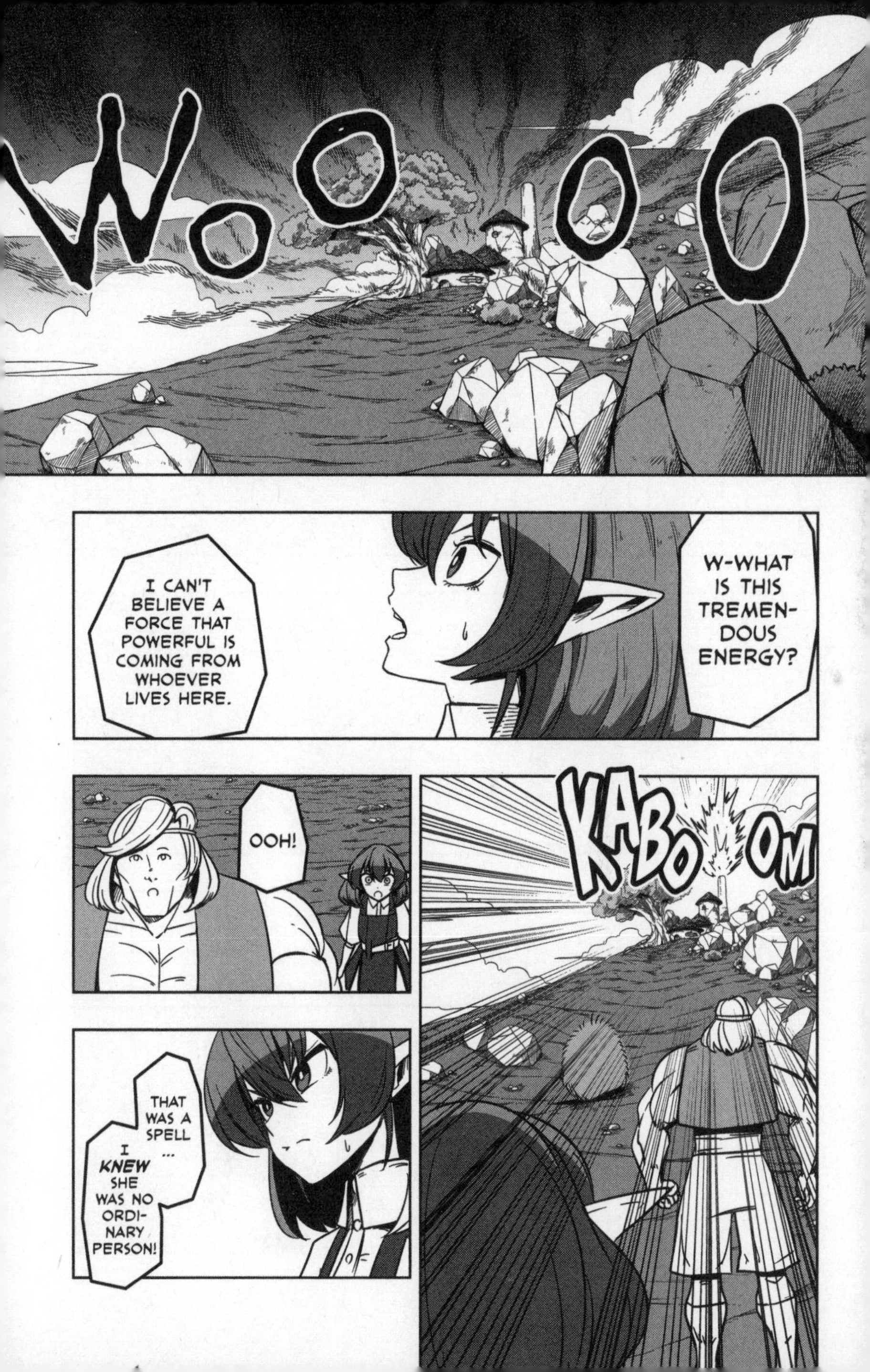
WOOOOO
W-WHAT IS THIS TREMENDOUS ENERGY?
I CAN'T BELIEVE A FORCE THAT POWERFUL IS COMING FROM WHOEVER LIVES HERE.
KABOOM
OOH!
THAT WAS A SPELL ...
I *KNEW* SHE WAS NO ORDINARY PERSON!

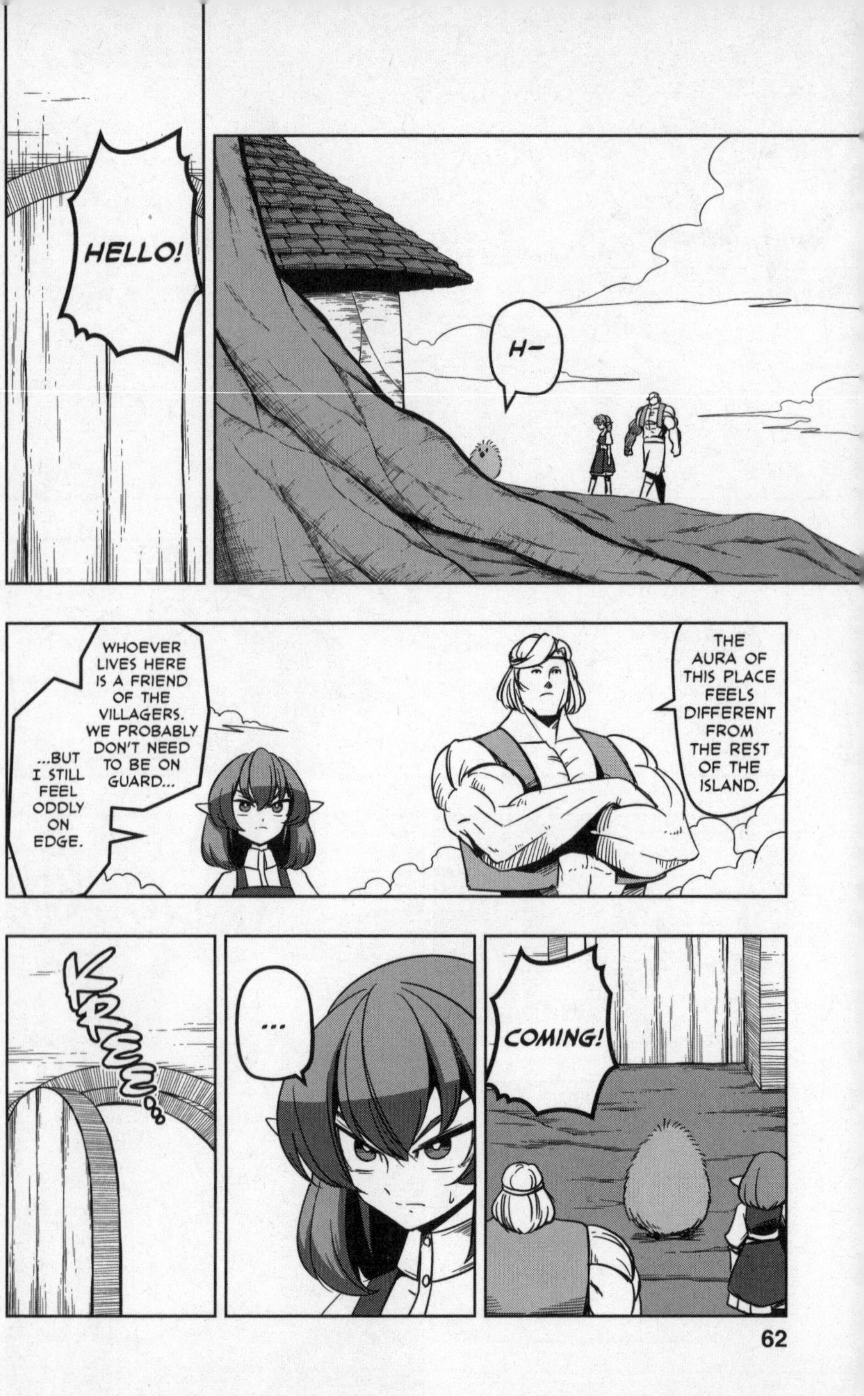
H-
HELLO!
THE AURA OF THIS PLACE FEELS DIFFERENT FROM THE REST OF THE ISLAND.
WHOEVER LIVES HERE IS A FRIEND OF THE VILLAGERS. WE PROBABLY DON'T NEED TO BE ON GUARD...
...BUT I STILL FEEL ODDLY ON EDGE.
COMING!
...
KREEE...

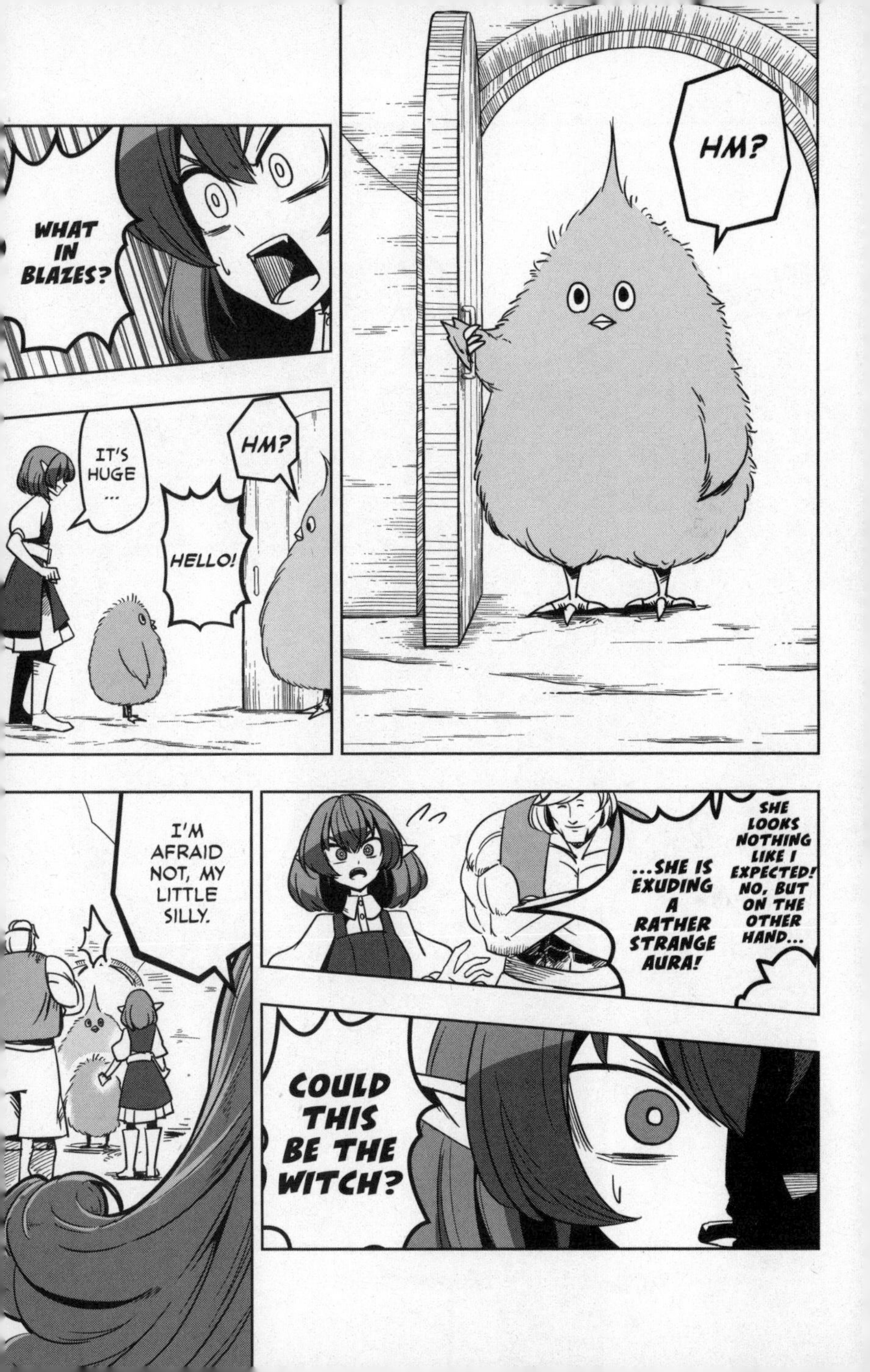
HM?
WHAT IN BLAZES?
HM?
HELLO!
IT'S HUGE ...
SHE LOOKS NOTHING LIKE I EXPECTED! NO, BUT ON THE OTHER HAND...
...SHE IS EXUDING A RATHER STRANGE AURA!
COULD THIS BE THE WITCH?
I'M AFRAID NOT, MY LITTLE SILLY.

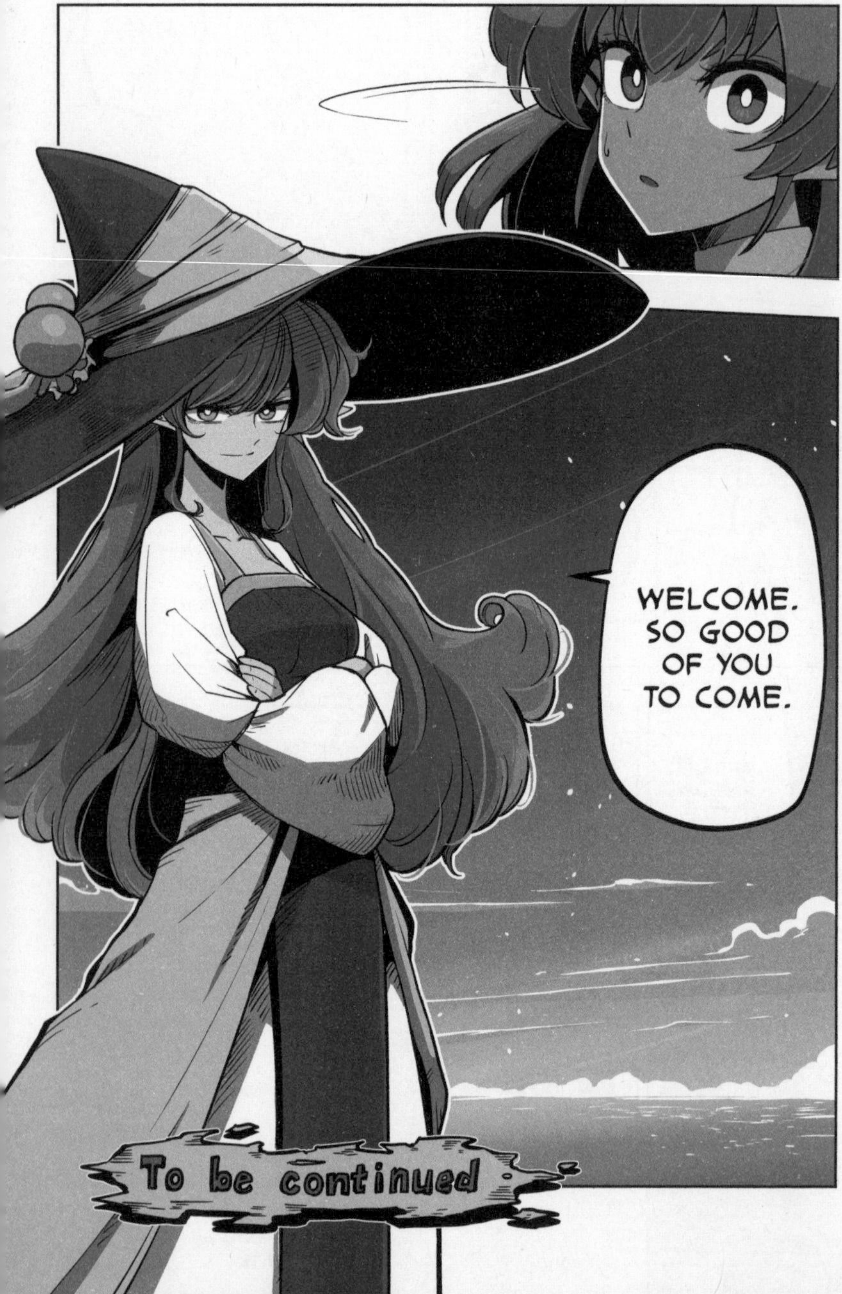
WELCOME. SO GOOD OF YOU TO COME.
To be continued

Chapter 23: To the Continent

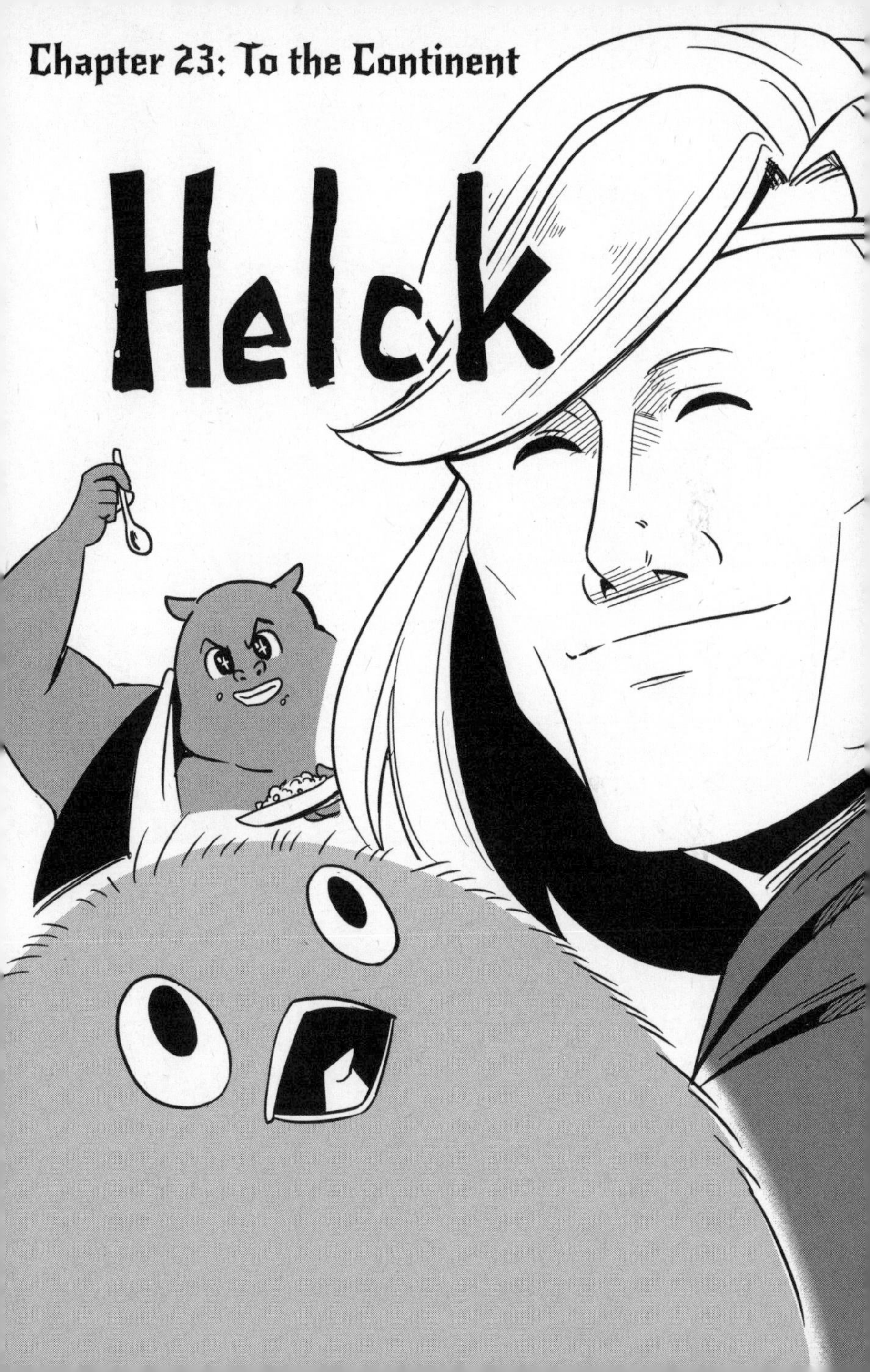
Helck

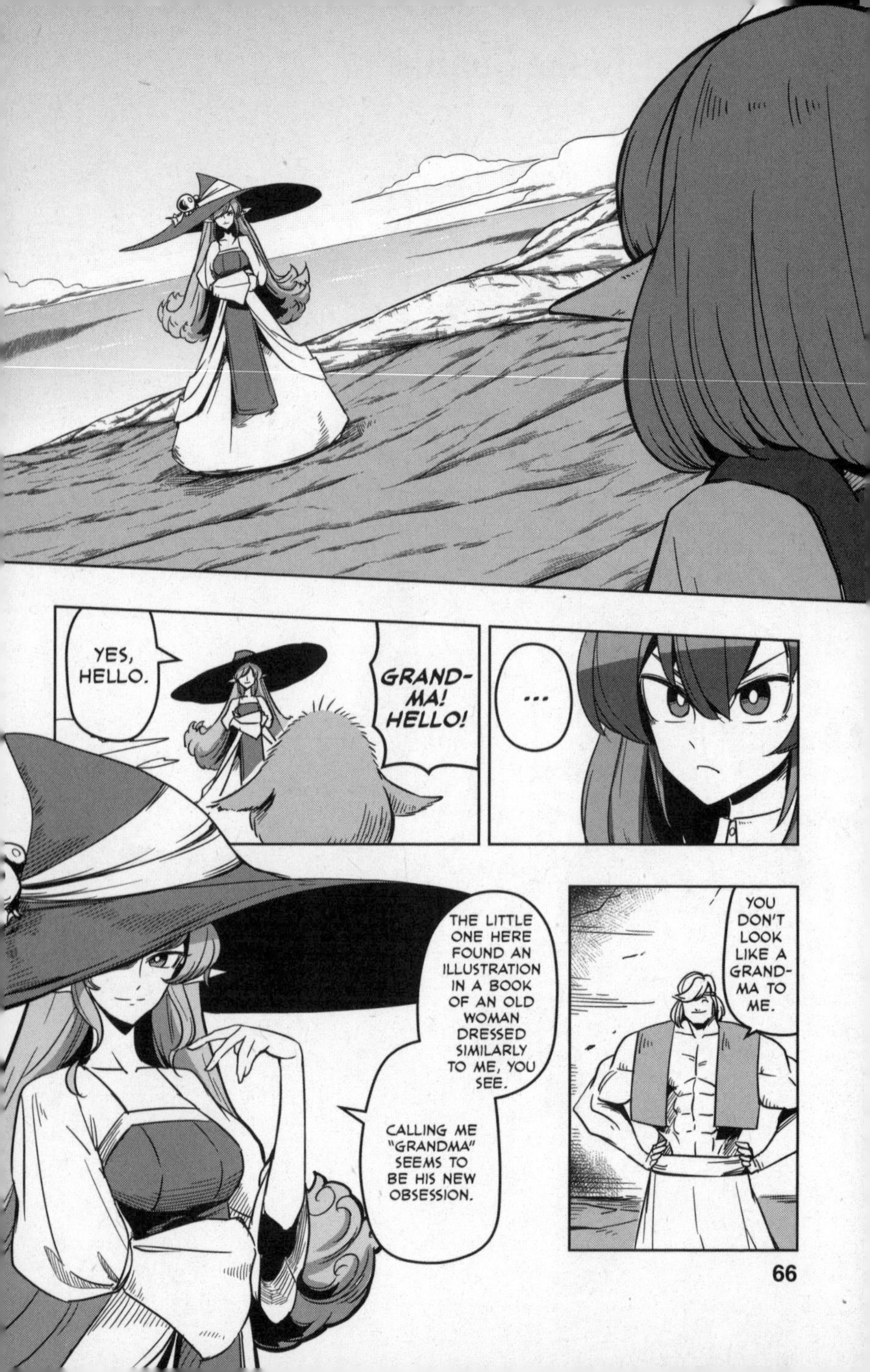
...
GRAND-MA! HELLO!
YES, HELLO.
YOU DON'T LOOK LIKE A GRAND-MA TO ME.
THE LITTLE ONE HERE FOUND AN ILLUSTRATION IN A BOOK OF AN OLD WOMAN DRESSED SIMILARLY TO ME, YOU SEE.
CALLING ME "GRANDMA" SEEMS TO BE HIS NEW OBSESSION.

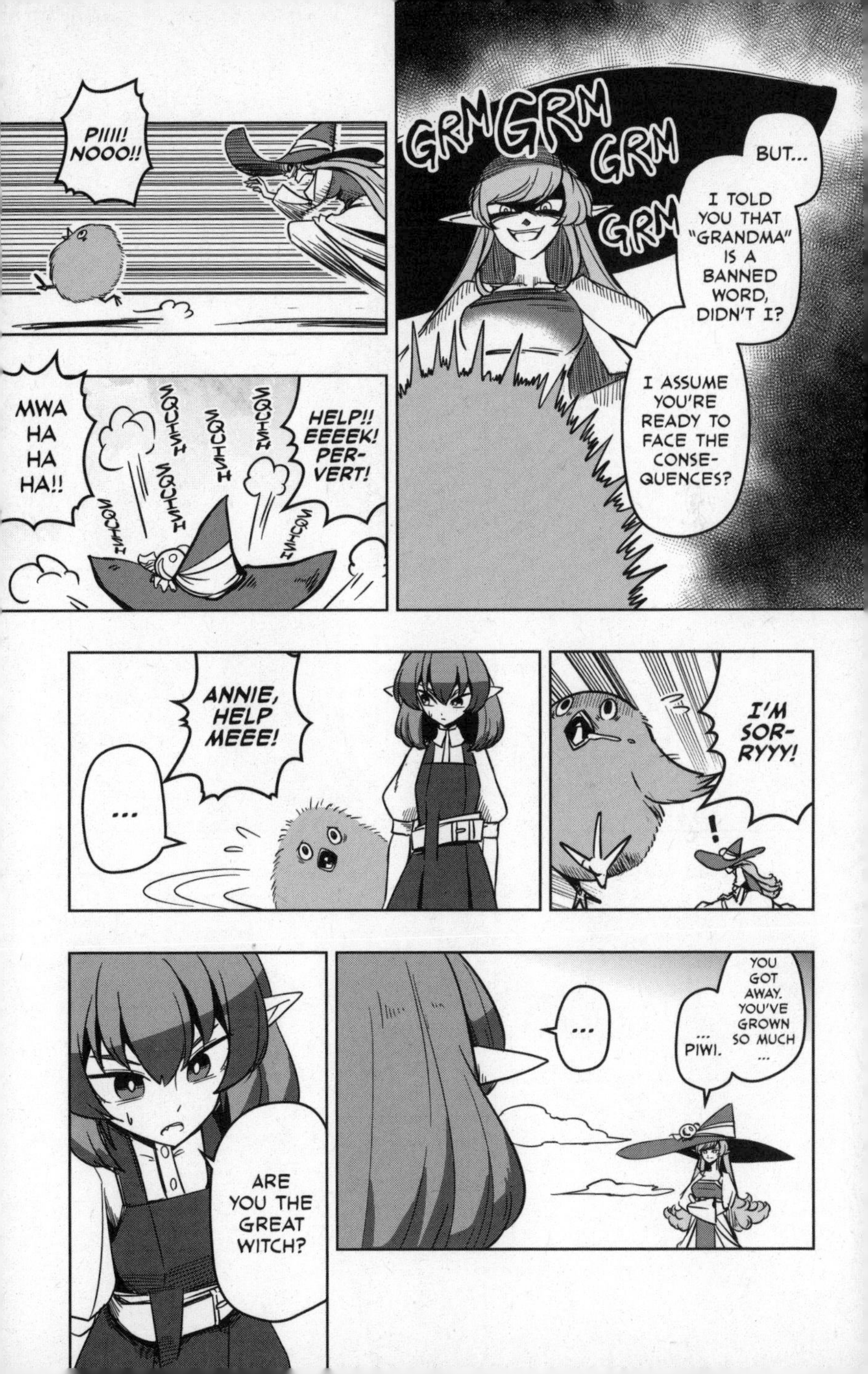
GRM GRM GRM GRM
BUT...
I TOLD YOU THAT "GRANDMA" IS A BANNED WORD, DIDN'T I?
I ASSUME YOU'RE READY TO FACE THE CONSE-QUENCES?
PIIII! NOOO!!
HELP!! EEEEK! PER-VERT!
SQUISH
SQUISH
SQUISH
SQUISH
SQUISH
MWA HA HA HA!!
I'M SOR-RYYY!
!
ANNIE, HELP MEEE!
...
YOU GOT AWAY. YOU'VE GROWN SO MUCH ...
... PIWI.
...
ARE YOU THE GREAT WITCH?

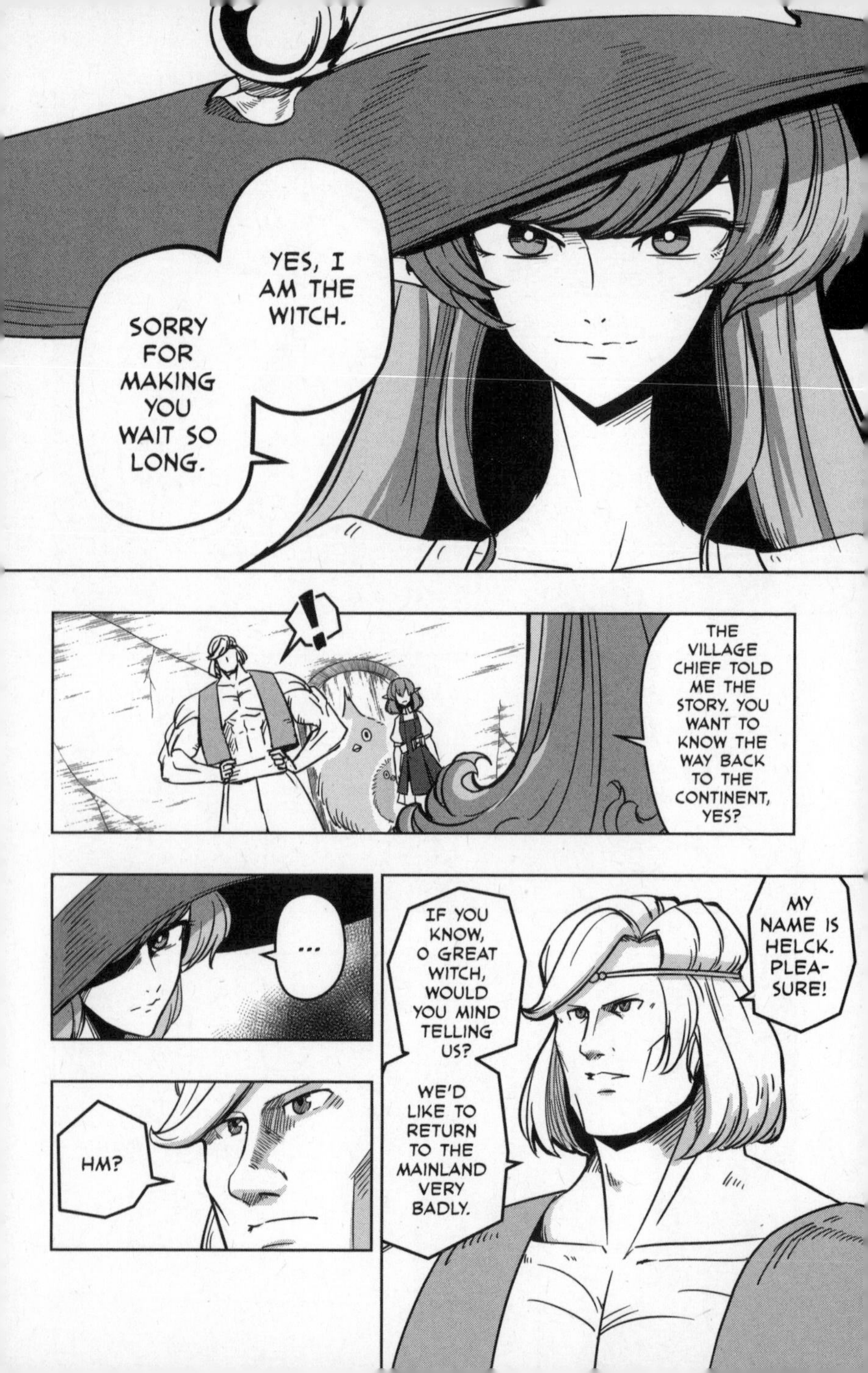
YES, I AM THE WITCH.
SORRY FOR MAKING YOU WAIT SO LONG.
THE VILLAGE CHIEF TOLD ME THE STORY. YOU WANT TO KNOW THE WAY BACK TO THE CONTINENT, YES?
!
MY NAME IS HELCK. PLEA-SURE!
IF YOU KNOW, O GREAT WITCH, WOULD YOU MIND TELLING US?
WE'D LIKE TO RETURN TO THE MAINLAND VERY BADLY.
...
HM?

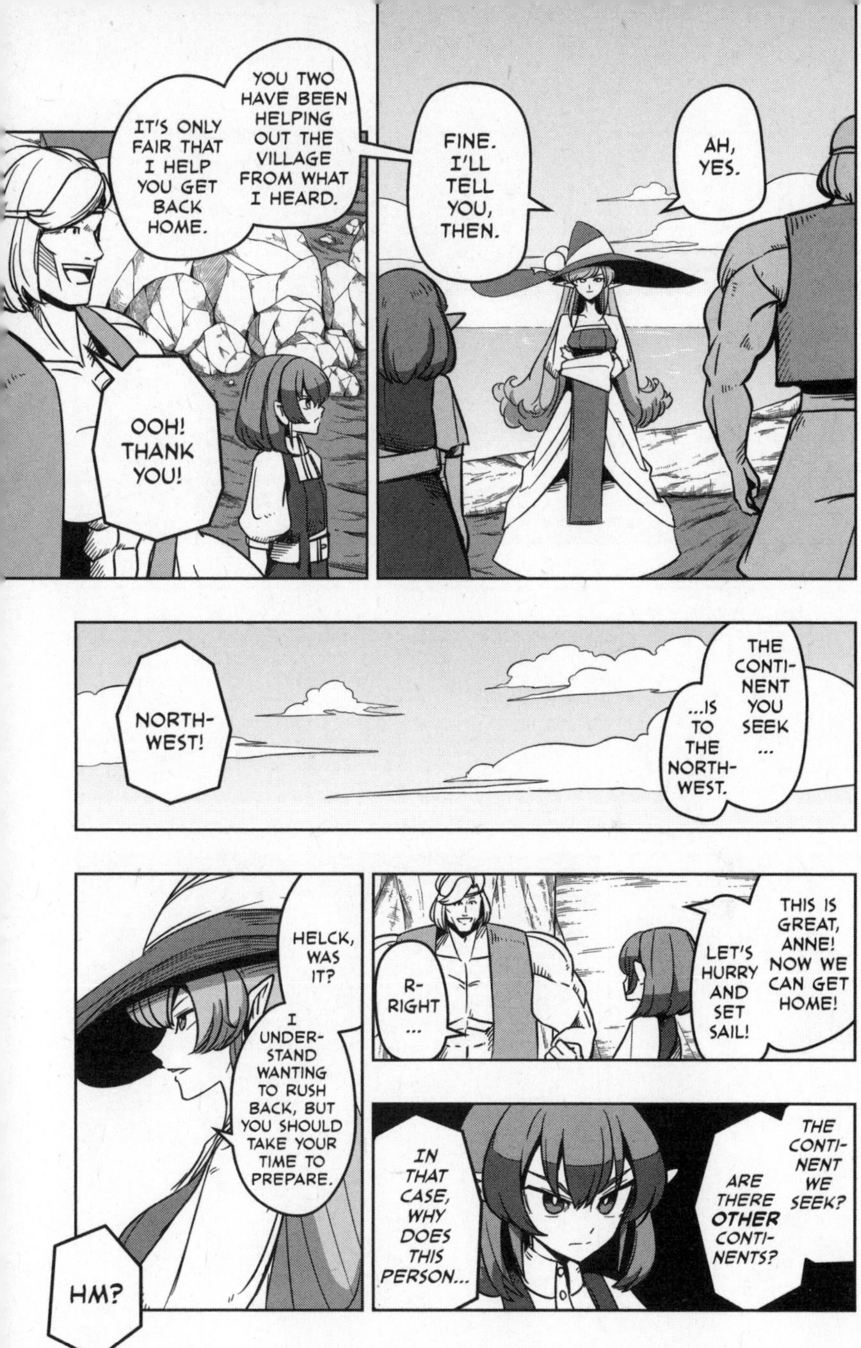
AH, YES.
FINE. I'LL TELL YOU, THEN.
YOU TWO HAVE BEEN HELPING OUT THE VILLAGE FROM WHAT I HEARD.
IT'S ONLY FAIR THAT I HELP YOU GET BACK HOME.
OOH! THANK YOU!
THE CONTI-NENT YOU SEEK...
...IS TO THE NORTH-WEST.
NORTH-WEST!
THIS IS GREAT, ANNE! NOW WE CAN GET HOME!
LET'S HURRY AND SET SAIL!
R-RIGHT...
THE CONTI-NENT WE SEEK?
ARE THERE **OTHER** CONTI-NENTS?
IN THAT CASE, WHY DOES THIS PERSON...
HELCK, WAS IT?
I UNDER-STAND WANTING TO RUSH BACK, BUT YOU SHOULD TAKE YOUR TIME TO PREPARE.
HM?

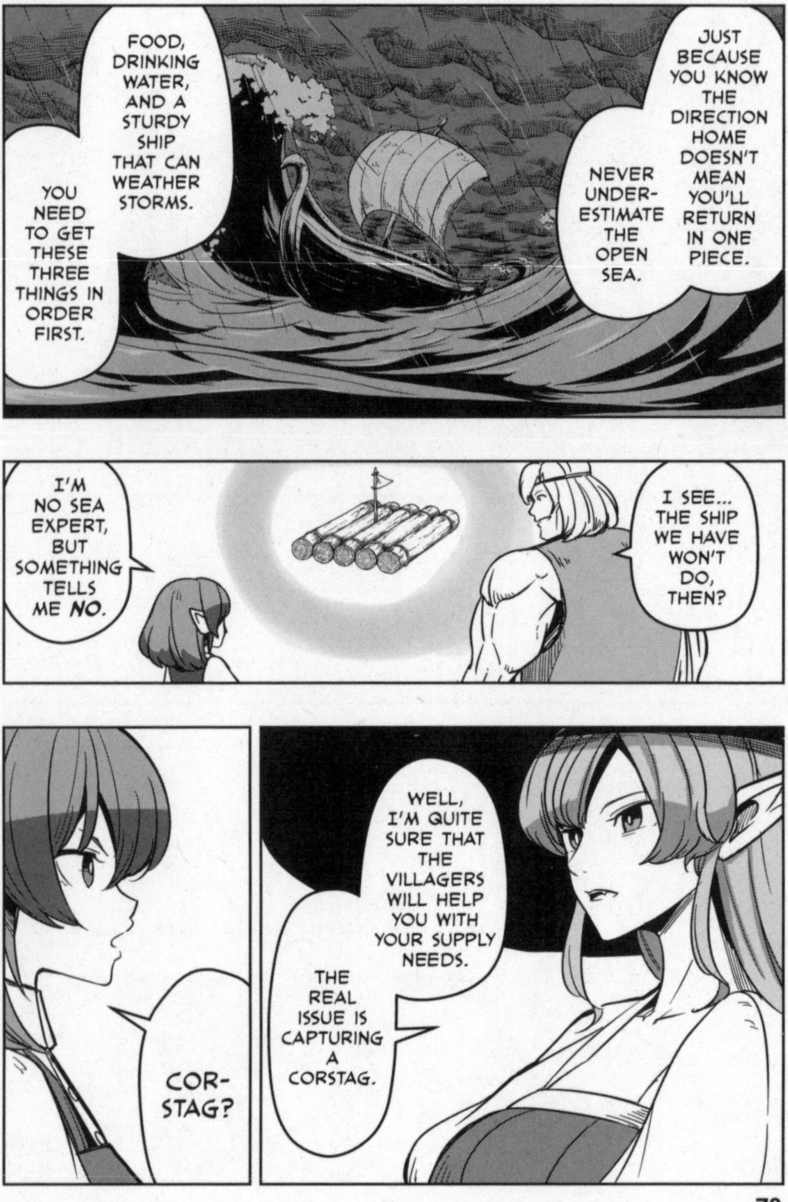
JUST BECAUSE YOU KNOW THE DIRECTION HOME DOESN'T MEAN YOU'LL RETURN IN ONE PIECE.
NEVER UNDER-ESTIMATE THE OPEN SEA.
FOOD, DRINKING WATER, AND A STURDY SHIP THAT CAN WEATHER STORMS.
YOU NEED TO GET THESE THREE THINGS IN ORDER FIRST.
I SEE... THE SHIP WE HAVE WON'T DO, THEN?
I'M NO SEA EXPERT, BUT SOMETHING TELLS ME ***NO***.
WELL, I'M QUITE SURE THAT THE VILLAGERS WILL HELP YOU WITH YOUR SUPPLY NEEDS.
THE REAL ISSUE IS CAPTURING A CORSTAG.
COR-STAG?

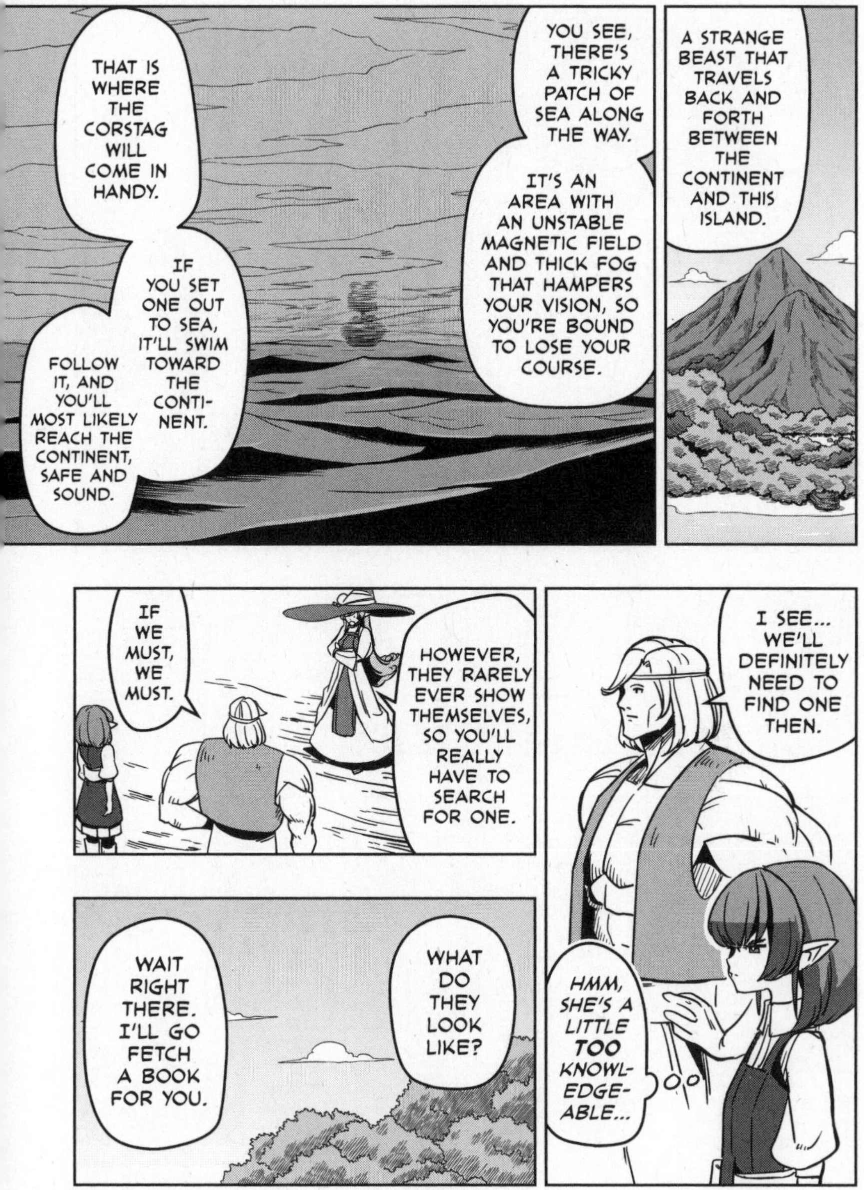

A STRANGE BEAST THAT TRAVELS BACK AND FORTH BETWEEN THE CONTINENT AND THIS ISLAND.
YOU SEE, THERE'S A TRICKY PATCH OF SEA ALONG THE WAY.
IT'S AN AREA WITH AN UNSTABLE MAGNETIC FIELD AND THICK FOG THAT HAMPERS YOUR VISION, SO YOU'RE BOUND TO LOSE YOUR COURSE.
THAT IS WHERE THE CORSTAG WILL COME IN HANDY.
IF YOU SET ONE OUT TO SEA, IT'LL SWIM TOWARD THE CONTI-NENT.
FOLLOW IT, AND YOU'LL MOST LIKELY REACH THE CONTINENT, SAFE AND SOUND.
I SEE... WE'LL DEFINITELY NEED TO FIND ONE THEN.
HMM, SHE'S A LITTLE TOO KNOWL-EDGE-ABLE...
HOWEVER, THEY RARELY EVER SHOW THEMSELVES, SO YOU'LL REALLY HAVE TO SEARCH FOR ONE.
IF WE MUST, WE MUST.
WHAT DO THEY LOOK LIKE?
WAIT RIGHT THERE. I'LL GO FETCH A BOOK FOR YOU.

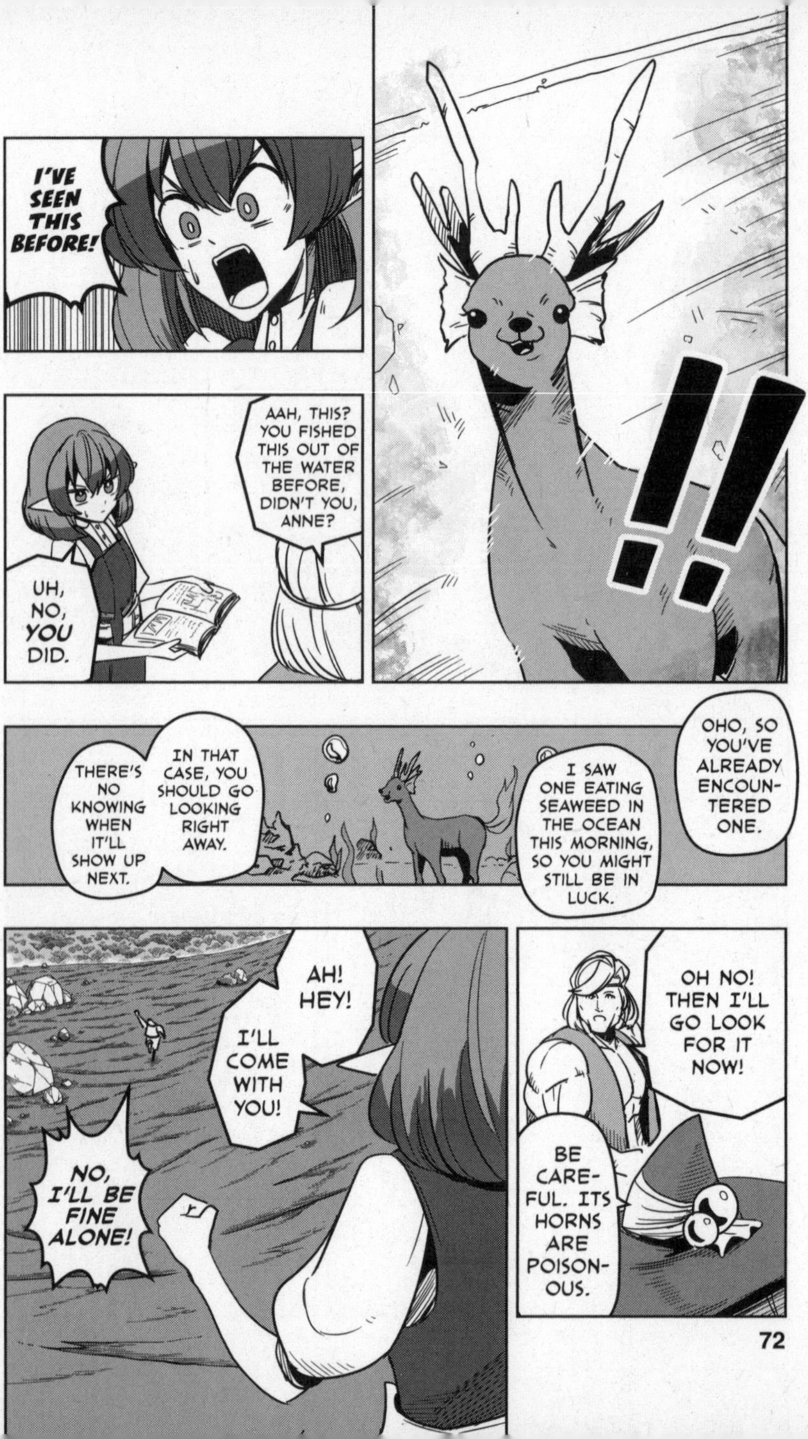
!!
I'VE SEEN THIS BEFORE!
AAH, THIS? YOU FISHED THIS OUT OF THE WATER BEFORE, DIDN'T YOU, ANNE?
UH, NO, YOU DID.
OHO, SO YOU'VE ALREADY ENCOUNTERED ONE.
I SAW ONE EATING SEAWEED IN THE OCEAN THIS MORNING, SO YOU MIGHT STILL BE IN LUCK.
IN THAT CASE, YOU SHOULD GO LOOKING RIGHT AWAY.
THERE'S NO KNOWING WHEN IT'LL SHOW UP NEXT.
OH NO! THEN I'LL GO LOOK FOR IT NOW!
BE CAREFUL. ITS HORNS ARE POISONOUS.
AH! HEY!
I'LL COME WITH YOU!
NO, I'LL BE FINE ALONE!

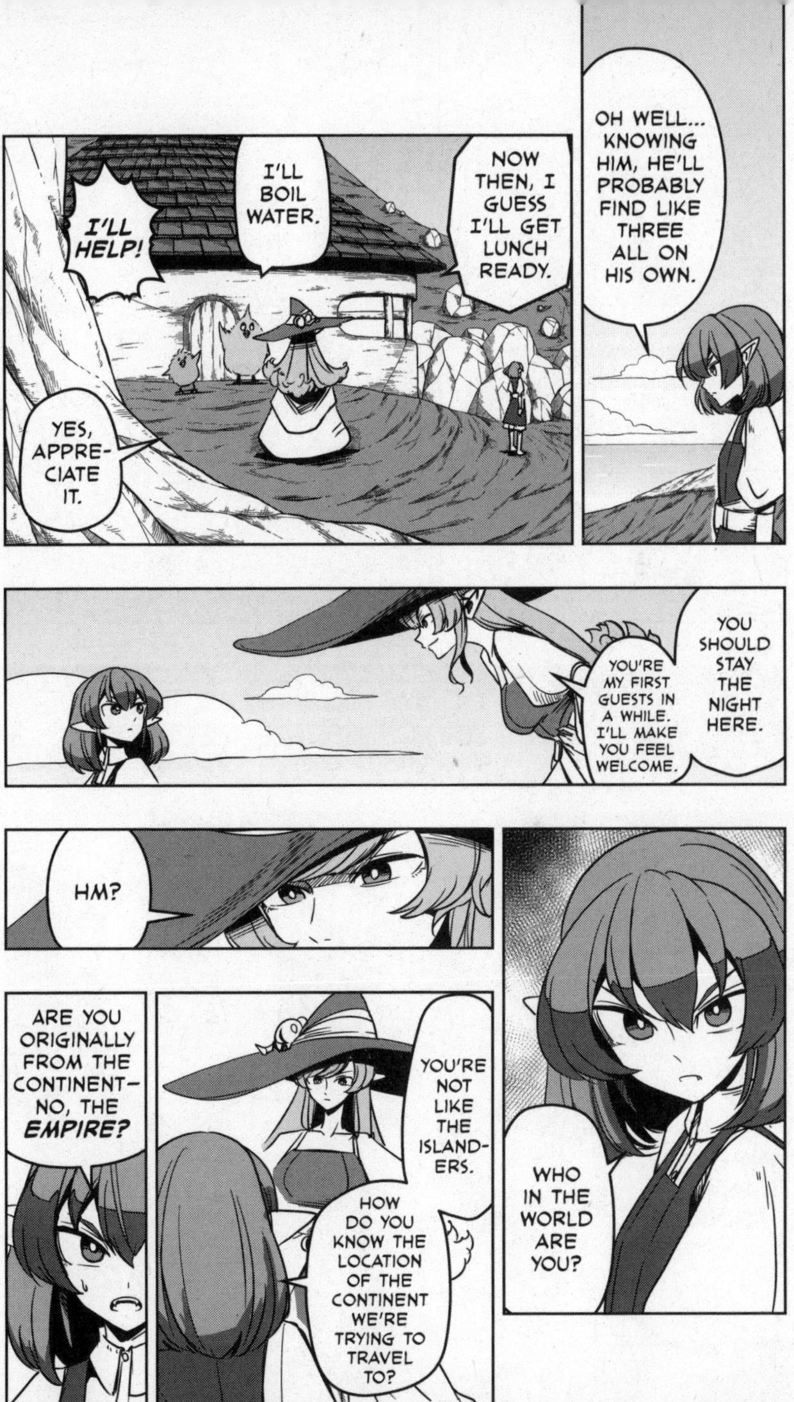
OH WELL... KNOWING HIM, HE'LL PROBABLY FIND LIKE THREE ALL ON HIS OWN.
NOW THEN, I GUESS I'LL GET LUNCH READY.
I'LL BOIL WATER.
I'LL HELP!
YES, APPRE-CIATE IT.
YOU SHOULD STAY THE NIGHT HERE.
YOU'RE MY FIRST GUESTS IN A WHILE. I'LL MAKE YOU FEEL WELCOME.
WHO IN THE WORLD ARE YOU?
HM?
YOU'RE NOT LIKE THE ISLAND-ERS.
HOW DO YOU KNOW THE LOCATION OF THE CONTINENT WE'RE TRYING TO TRAVEL TO?
ARE YOU ORIGINALLY FROM THE CONTINENT— NO, THE ***EMPIRE?***

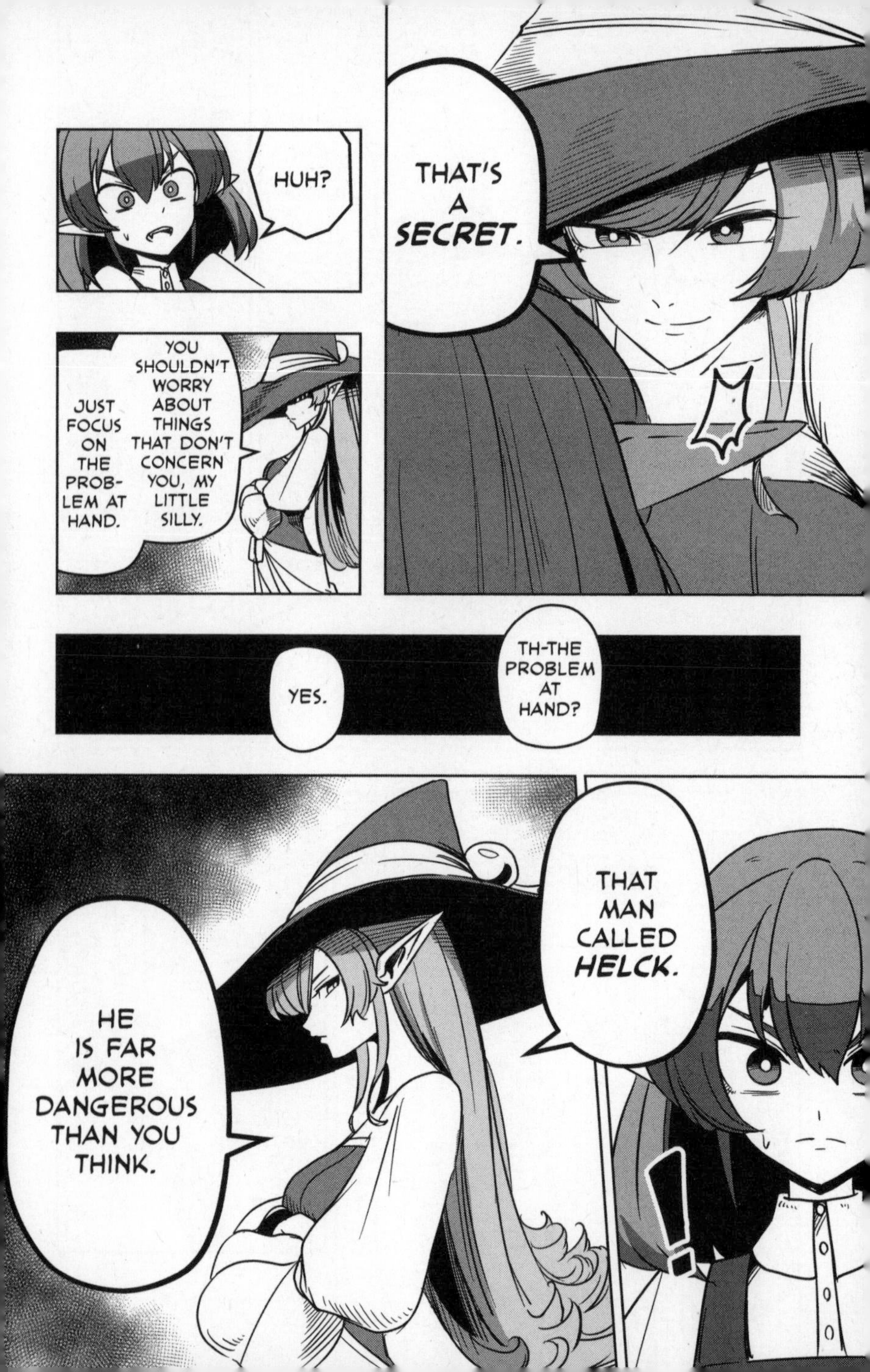
THAT'S A *SECRET*.
HUH?
YOU SHOULDN'T WORRY ABOUT THINGS THAT DON'T CONCERN YOU, MY LITTLE SILLY.
JUST FOCUS ON THE PROB-LEM AT HAND.
TH-THE PROBLEM AT HAND?
YES.
THAT MAN CALLED **HELCK**.
HE IS FAR MORE DANGEROUS THAN YOU THINK.

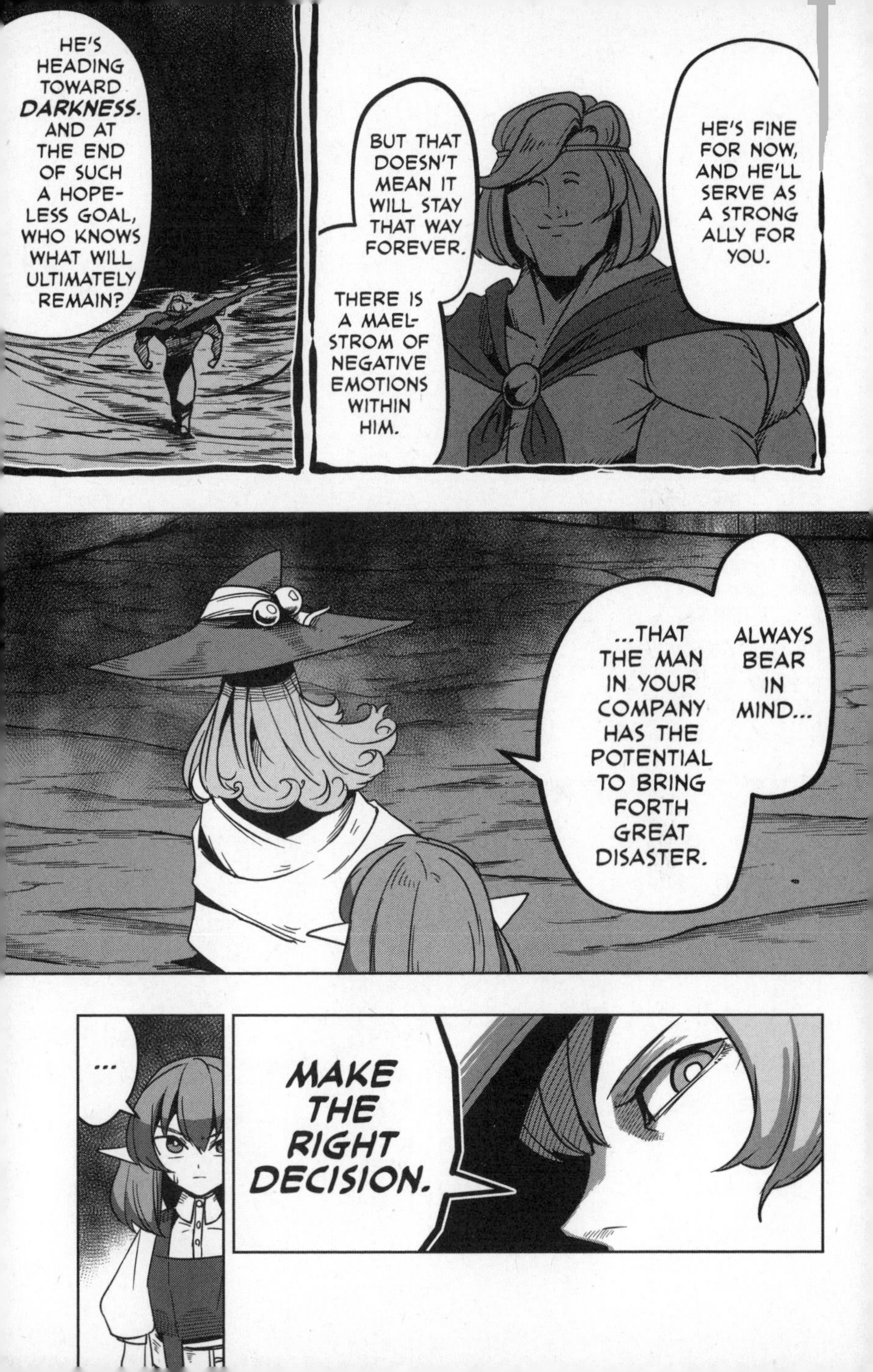
HE'S FINE FOR NOW, AND HE'LL SERVE AS A STRONG ALLY FOR YOU.
BUT THAT DOESN'T MEAN IT WILL STAY THAT WAY FOREVER.
THERE IS A MAEL-STROM OF NEGATIVE EMOTIONS WITHIN HIM.
HE'S HEADING TOWARD ***DARKNESS.*** AND AT THE END OF SUCH A HOPE-LESS GOAL, WHO KNOWS WHAT WILL ULTIMATELY REMAIN?
ALWAYS BEAR IN MIND...
...THAT THE MAN IN YOUR COMPANY HAS THE POTENTIAL TO BRING FORTH GREAT DISASTER.
MAKE THE RIGHT DECISION.
...

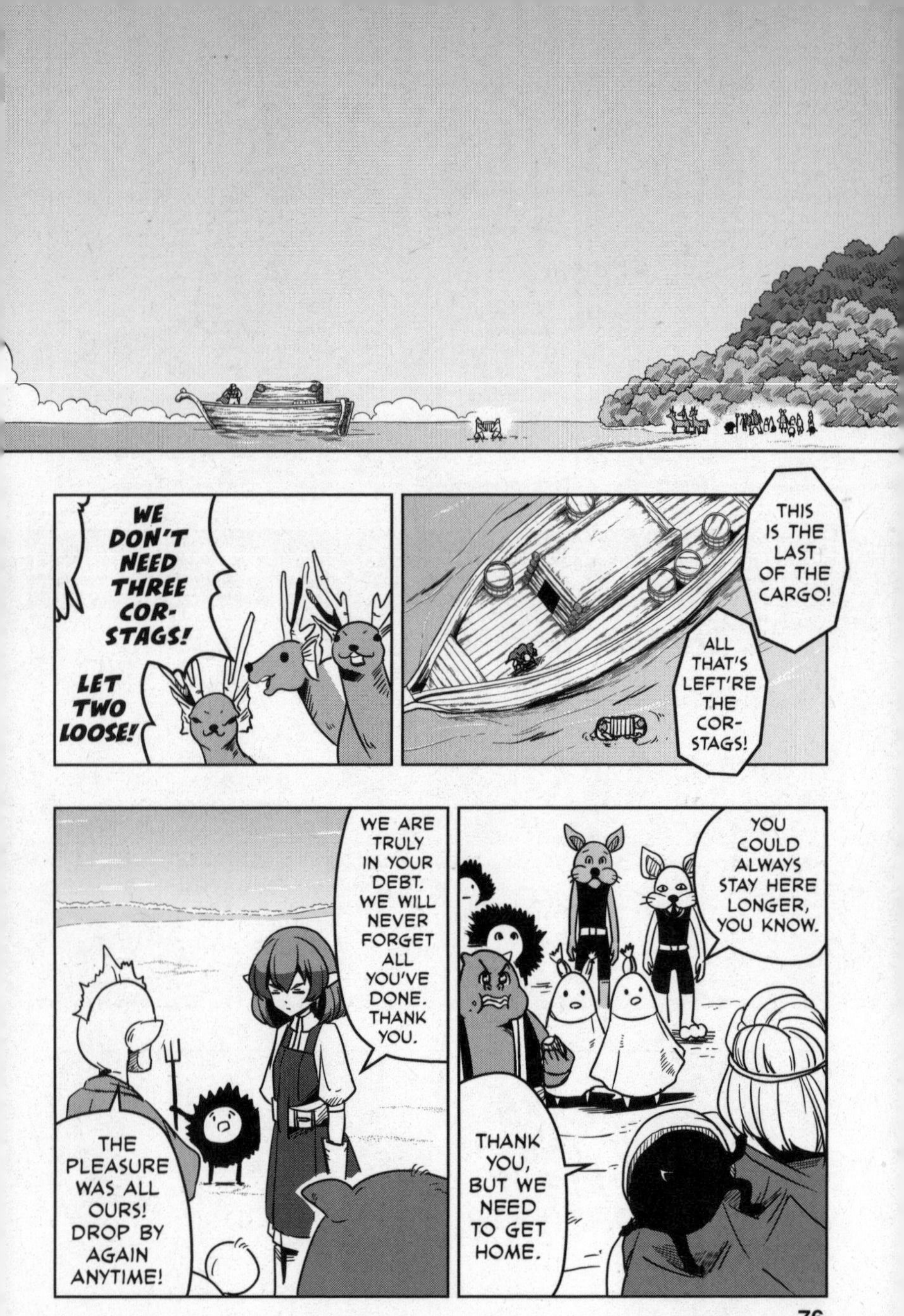
THIS IS THE LAST OF THE CARGO!
ALL THAT'S LEFT'RE THE COR-STAGS!
WE DON'T NEED THREE COR-STAGS!
LET TWO LOOSE!
YOU COULD ALWAYS STAY HERE LONGER, YOU KNOW.
THANK YOU, BUT WE NEED TO GET HOME.
WE ARE TRULY IN YOUR DEBT. WE WILL NEVER FORGET ALL YOU'VE DONE. THANK YOU.
THE PLEASURE WAS ALL OURS! DROP BY AGAIN ANYTIME!

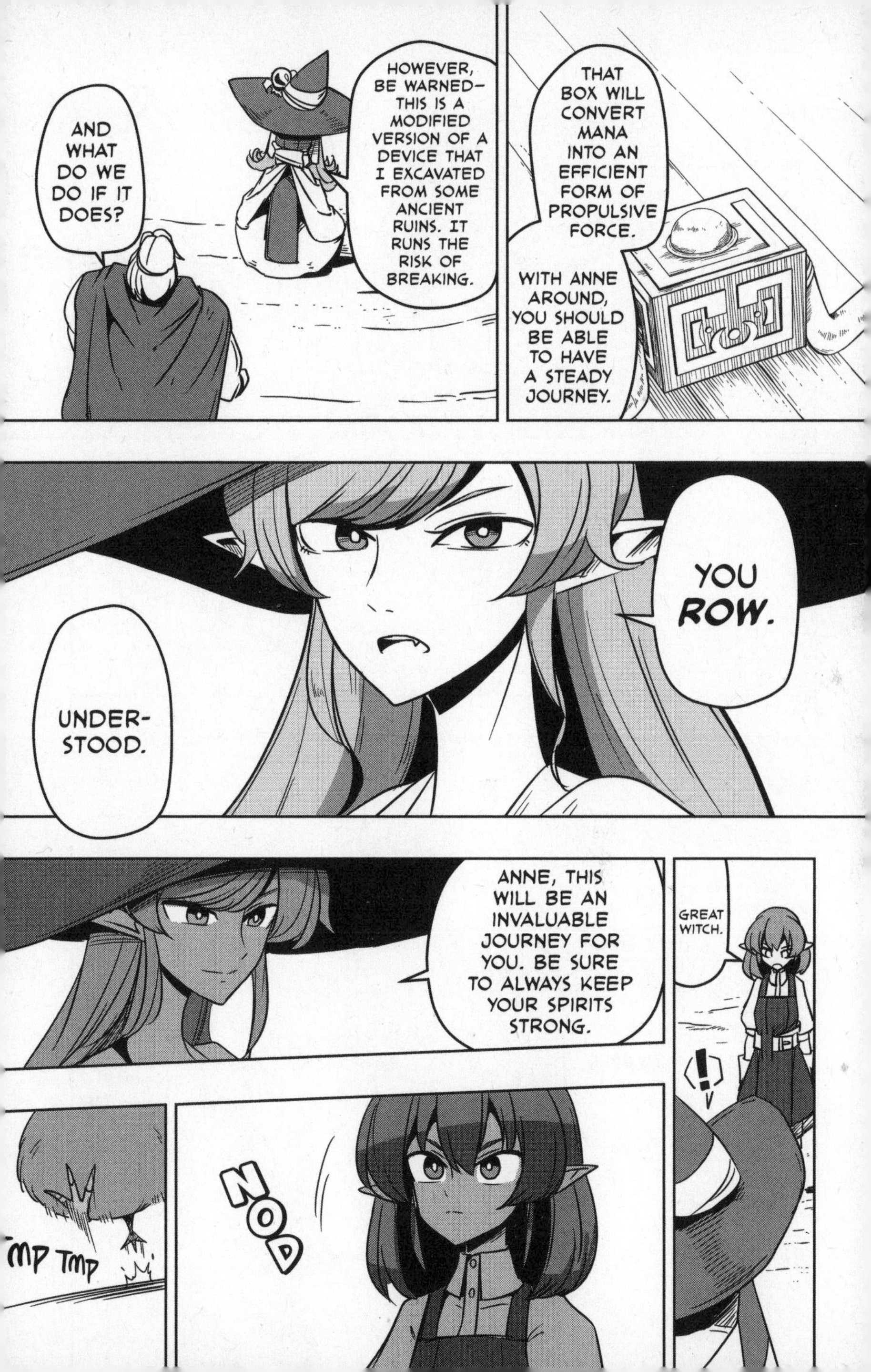
THAT BOX WILL CONVERT MANA INTO AN EFFICIENT FORM OF PROPULSIVE FORCE.
WITH ANNE AROUND, YOU SHOULD BE ABLE TO HAVE A STEADY JOURNEY.
HOWEVER, BE WARNED—THIS IS A MODIFIED VERSION OF A DEVICE THAT I EXCAVATED FROM SOME ANCIENT RUINS. IT RUNS THE RISK OF BREAKING.
AND WHAT DO WE DO IF IT DOES?
YOU ROW.
UNDER-STOOD.
GREAT WITCH.
!
ANNE, THIS WILL BE AN INVALUABLE JOURNEY FOR YOU. BE SURE TO ALWAYS KEEP YOUR SPIRITS STRONG.
NOD
TMP TMP

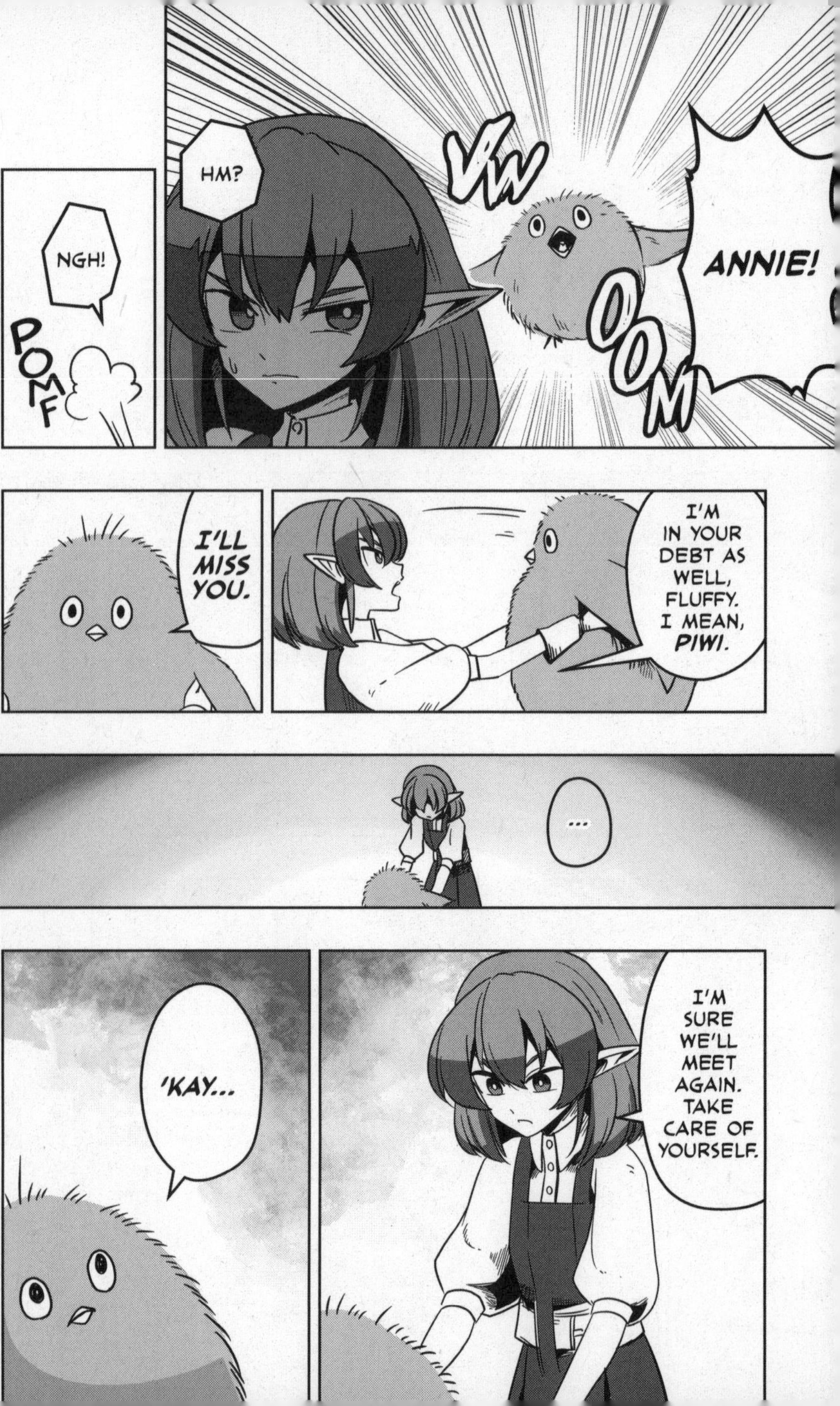
ANNIE!
VWOOM
HM?
NGH!
POMF
I'M IN YOUR DEBT AS WELL, FLUFFY. I MEAN, *PIWI.*
I'LL MISS YOU.
...
I'M SURE WE'LL MEET AGAIN. TAKE CARE OF YOURSELF.
'KAY...

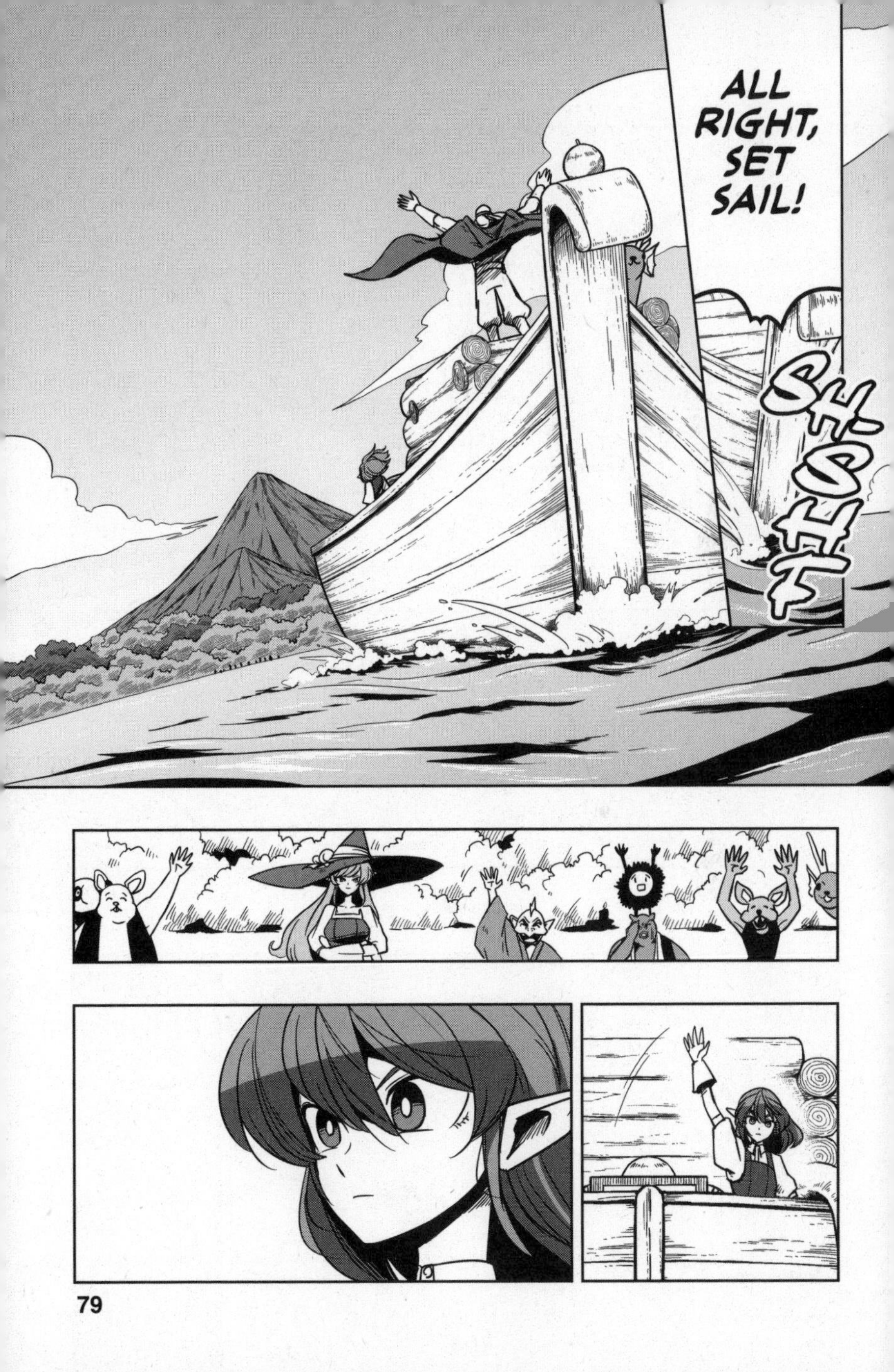
ALL RIGHT, SET SAIL!
SHSHT

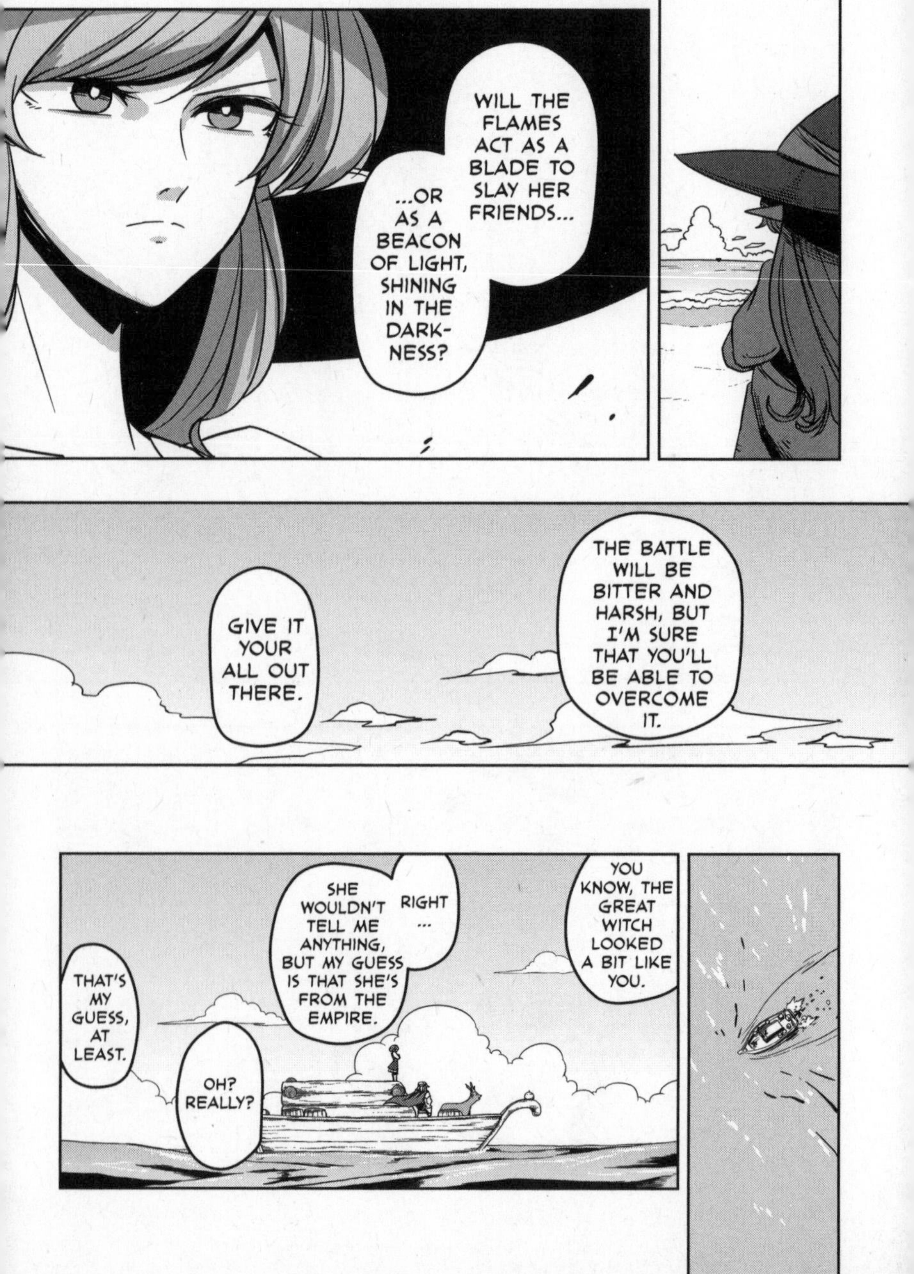
WILL THE FLAMES ACT AS A BLADE TO SLAY HER FRIENDS...
...OR AS A BEACON OF LIGHT, SHINING IN THE DARKNESS?
THE BATTLE WILL BE BITTER AND HARSH, BUT I'M SURE THAT YOU'LL BE ABLE TO OVERCOME IT.
GIVE IT YOUR ALL OUT THERE.
YOU KNOW, THE GREAT WITCH LOOKED A BIT LIKE YOU.
RIGHT...
SHE WOULDN'T TELL ME ANYTHING, BUT MY GUESS IS THAT SHE'S FROM THE EMPIRE.
THAT'S MY GUESS, AT LEAST.
OH? REALLY?

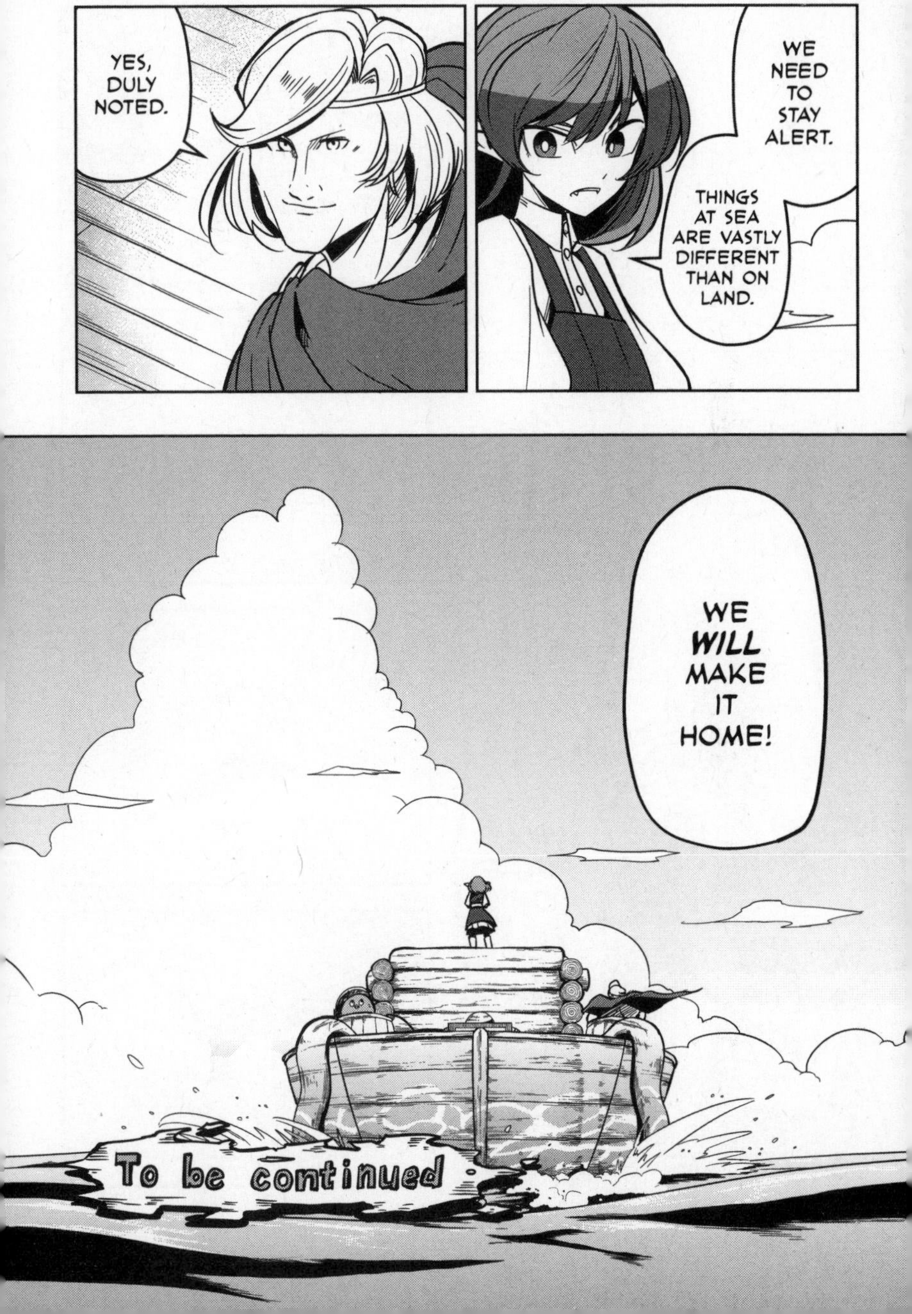
WE NEED TO STAY ALERT.
THINGS AT SEA ARE VASTLY DIFFERENT THAN ON LAND.
YES, DULY NOTED.
WE *WILL* MAKE IT HOME!
To be continued

I'M JUST FINE ①

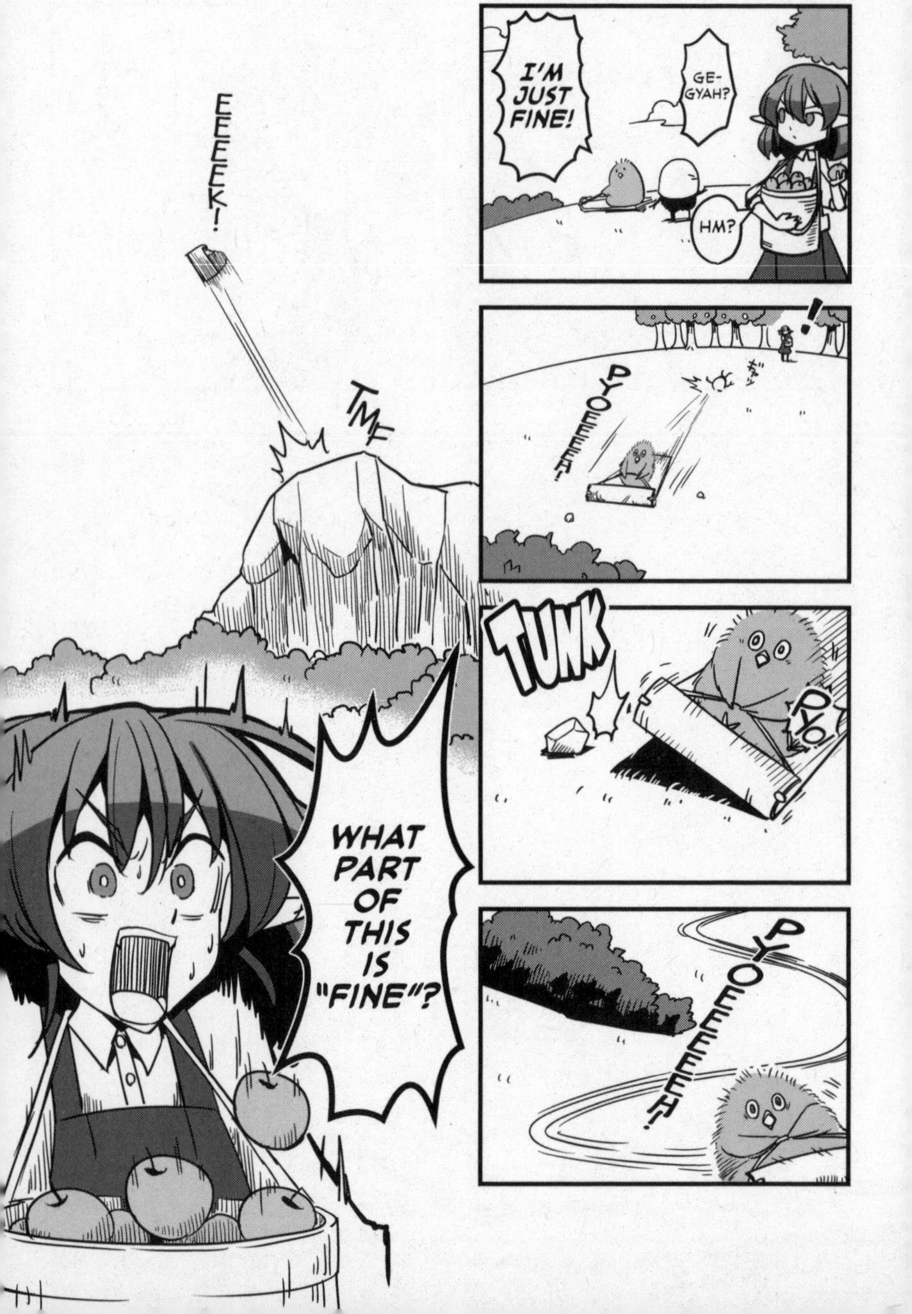
GE-GYAH?
I'M JUST FINE!
HM?
!
PYOEEEH!
TUNK
PYO
PYOEEEEEH!
EEEEEK!
TMF
WHAT PART OF THIS IS "FINE"?

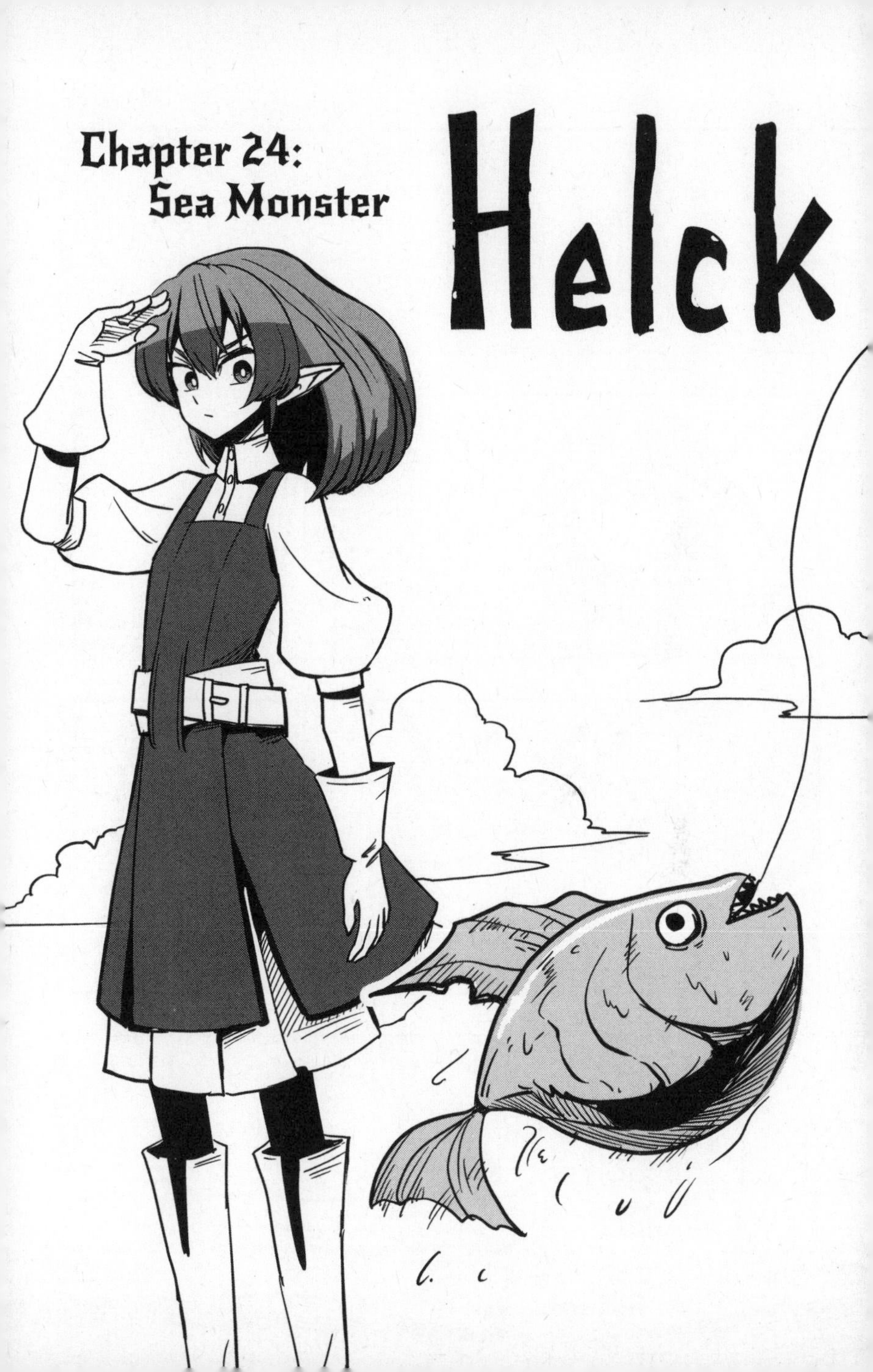
Chapter 24:
Sea Monster
Helck

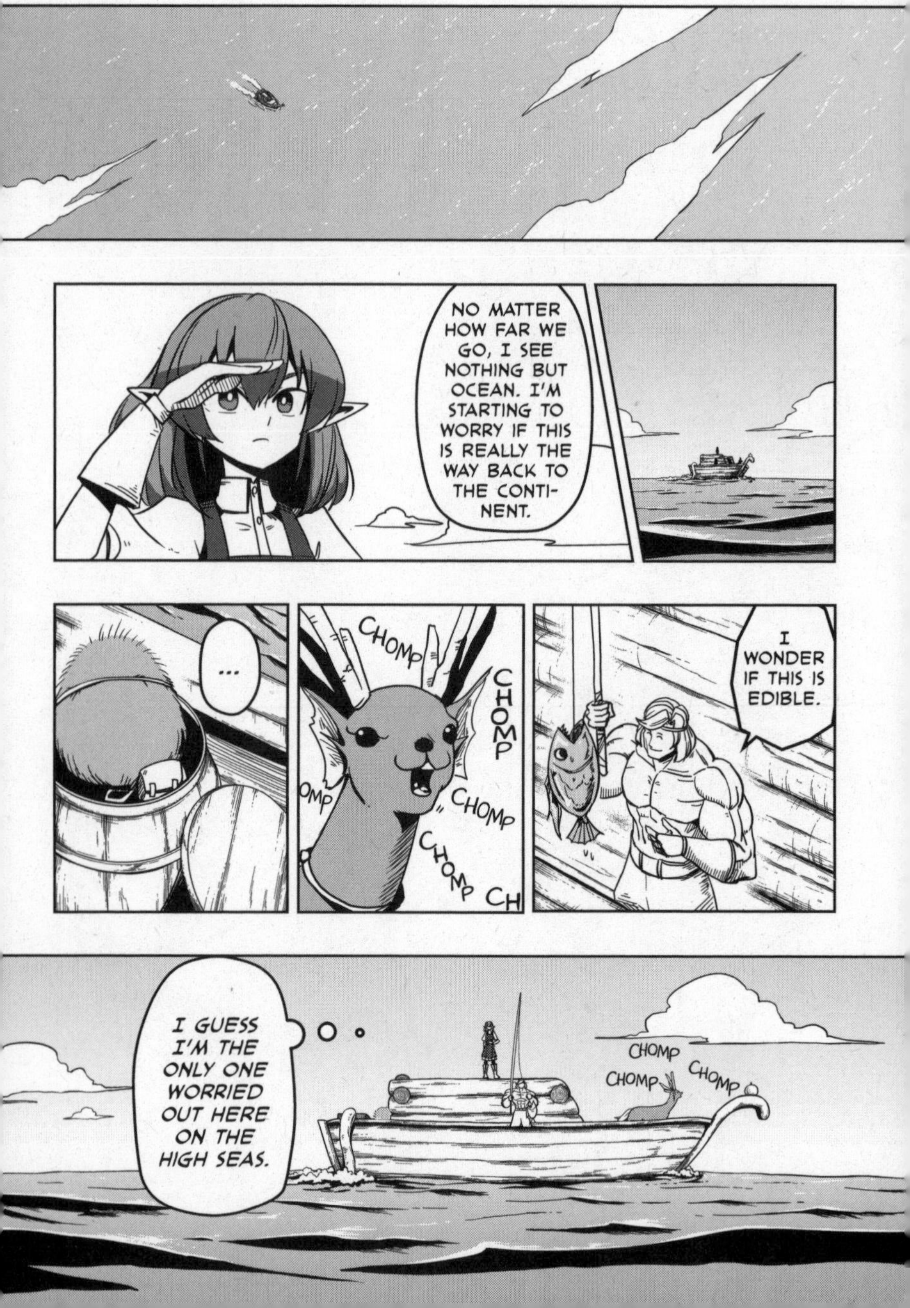
NO MATTER HOW FAR WE GO, I SEE NOTHING BUT OCEAN. I'M STARTING TO WORRY IF THIS IS REALLY THE WAY BACK TO THE CONTI-NENT.
I WONDER IF THIS IS EDIBLE.
CHOMP
CHOMP
OMP
CHOMP
CHOMP
CH
...
I GUESS I'M THE ONLY ONE WORRIED OUT HERE ON THE HIGH SEAS.
CHOMP
CHOMP
CHOMP

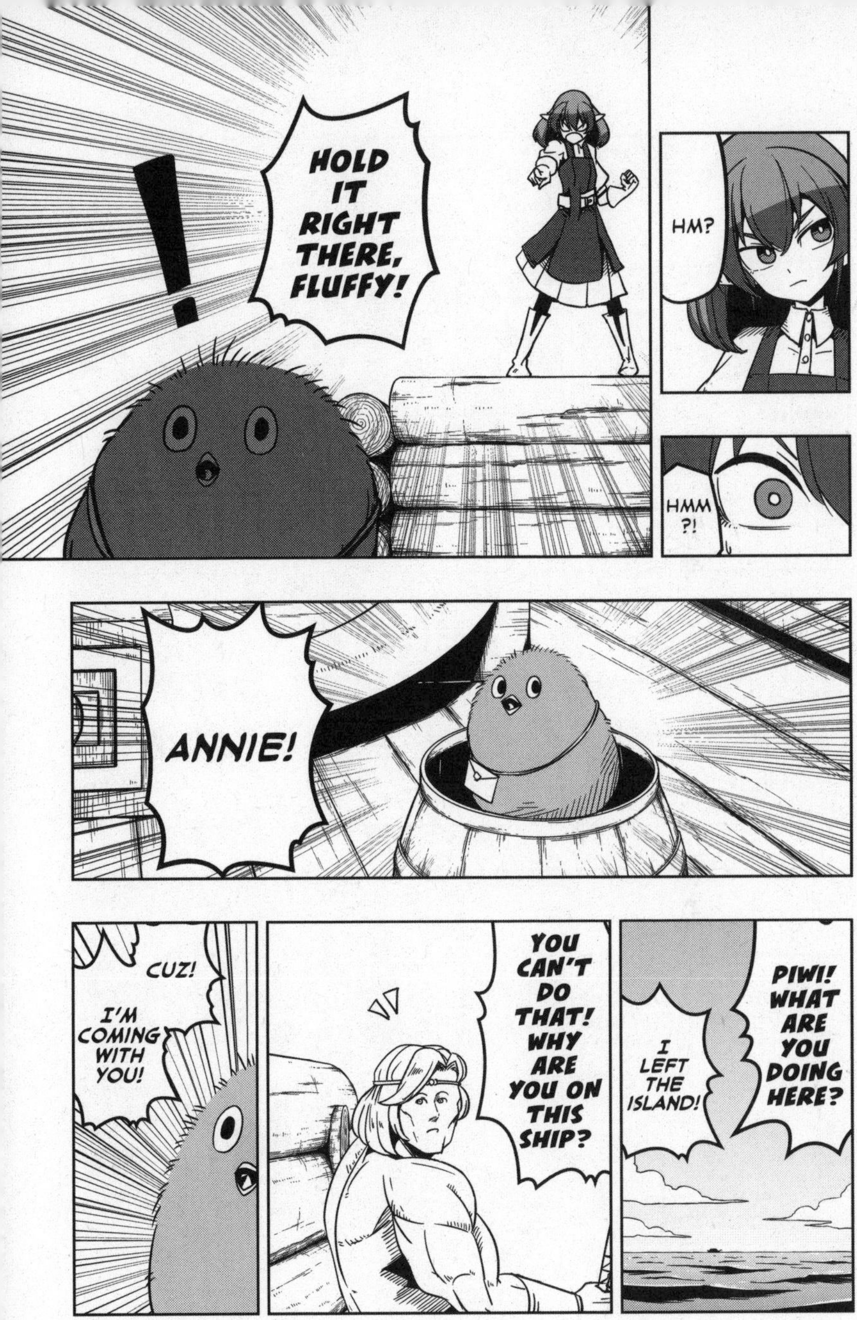
HM?
HMM ?!
HOLD IT RIGHT THERE, FLUFFY!
ANNIE!
PIWI! WHAT ARE YOU DOING HERE?
I LEFT THE ISLAND!
YOU CAN'T DO THAT! WHY ARE YOU ON THIS SHIP?
CUZ!
I'M COMING WITH YOU!

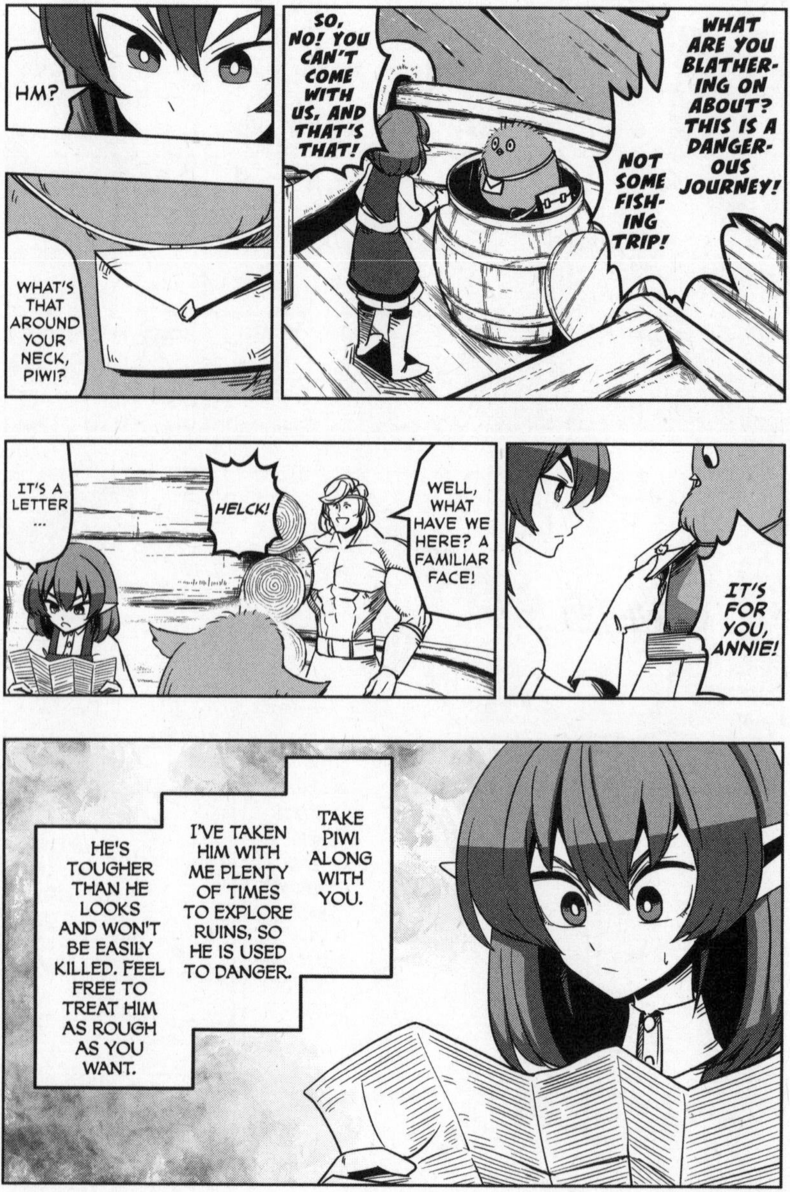
WHAT ARE YOU BLATHERING ON ABOUT? THIS IS A DANGEROUS JOURNEY!
NOT SOME FISHING TRIP!
SO, NO! YOU CAN'T COME WITH US, AND THAT'S THAT!
HM?
WHAT'S THAT AROUND YOUR NECK, PIWI?
IT'S FOR YOU, ANNIE!
WELL, WHAT HAVE WE HERE? A FAMILIAR FACE!
HELCK!
IT'S A LETTER ...
TAKE PIWI ALONG WITH YOU.
I'VE TAKEN HIM WITH ME PLENTY OF TIMES TO EXPLORE RUINS, SO HE IS USED TO DANGER.
HE'S TOUGHER THAN HE LOOKS AND WON'T BE EASILY KILLED. FEEL FREE TO TREAT HIM AS ROUGH AS YOU WANT.

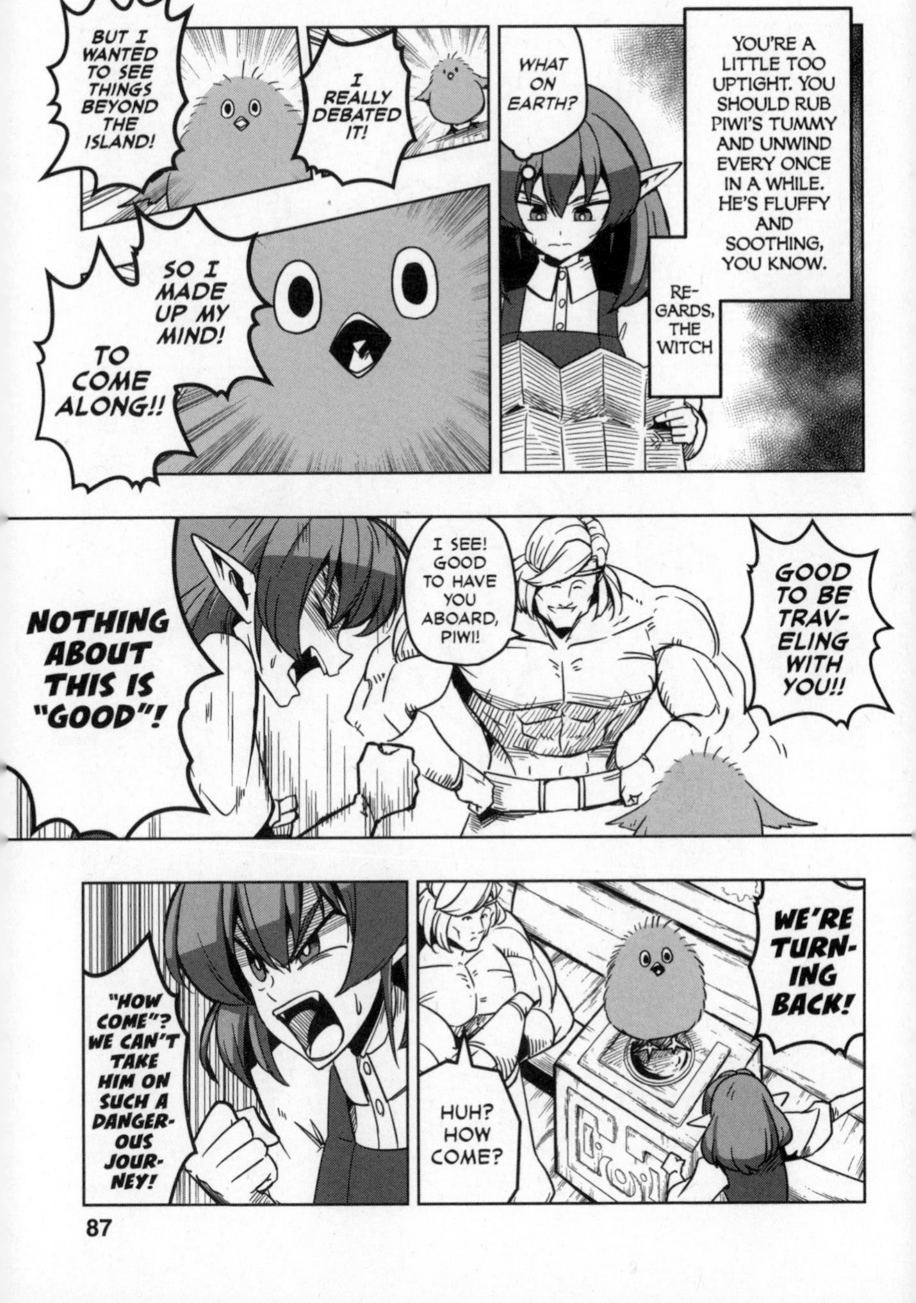
YOU'RE A LITTLE TOO UPTIGHT. YOU SHOULD RUB PIWI'S TUMMY AND UNWIND EVERY ONCE IN A WHILE. HE'S FLUFFY AND SOOTHING, YOU KNOW.
REGARDS, THE WITCH
WHAT ON EARTH?
I REALLY DEBATED IT!
BUT I WANTED TO SEE THINGS BEYOND THE ISLAND!
SO I MADE UP MY MIND!
TO COME ALONG!!
GOOD TO BE TRAVELING WITH YOU!!
I SEE! GOOD TO HAVE YOU ABOARD, PIWI!
NOTHING ABOUT THIS IS "GOOD"!
WE'RE TURNING BACK!
HUH? HOW COME?
"HOW COME"? WE CAN'T TAKE HIM ON SUCH A DANGEROUS JOURNEY!

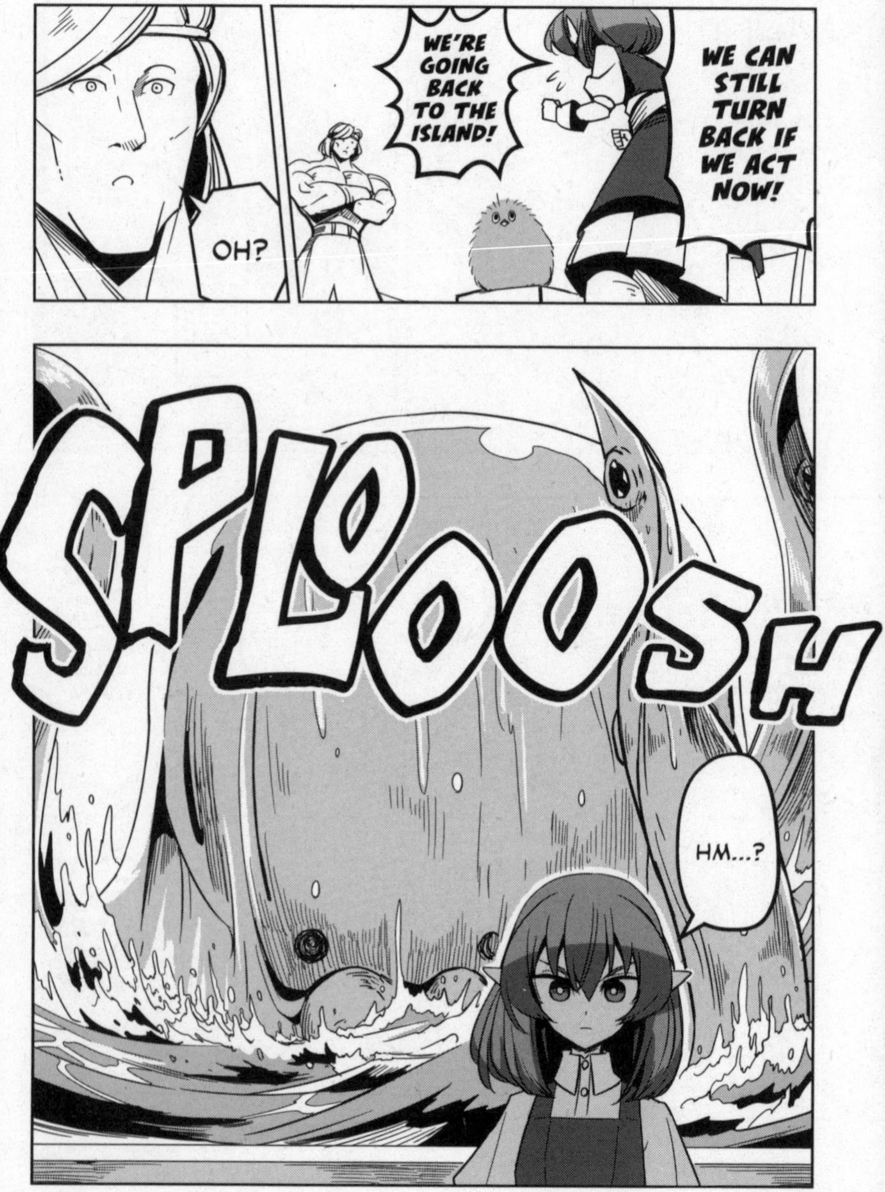
WE'RE GOING BACK TO THE ISLAND!
WE CAN STILL TURN BACK IF WE ACT NOW!
OH?
SPLOOSH
HM...?

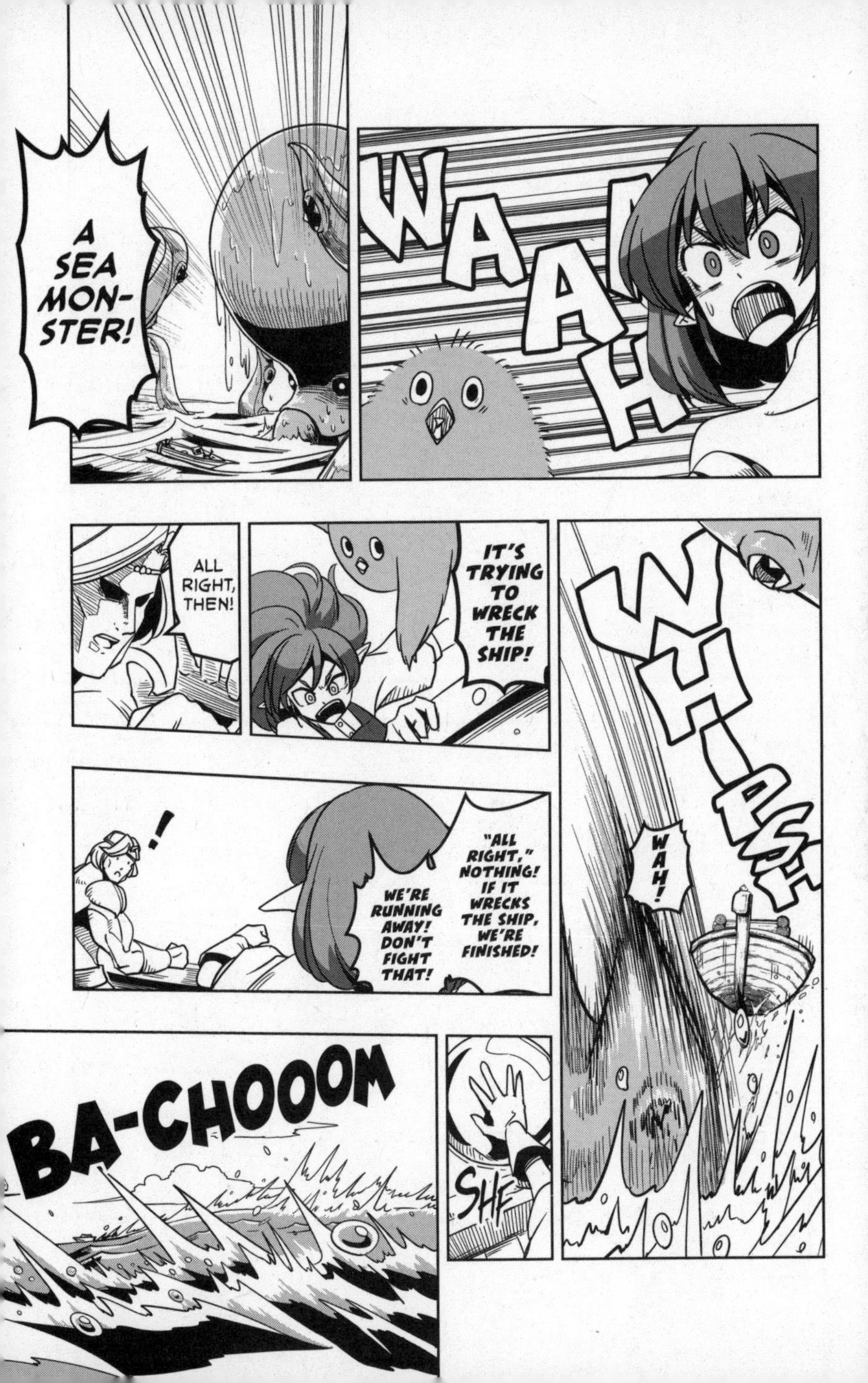
WAAAH
A SEA MONSTER!
WHIPSH
WAH!
IT'S TRYING TO WRECK THE SHIP!
ALL RIGHT, THEN!
"ALL RIGHT," NOTHING! IF IT WRECKS THE SHIP, WE'RE FINISHED!
WE'RE RUNNING AWAY! DON'T FIGHT THAT!
!
SHF
BA-CHOOOM

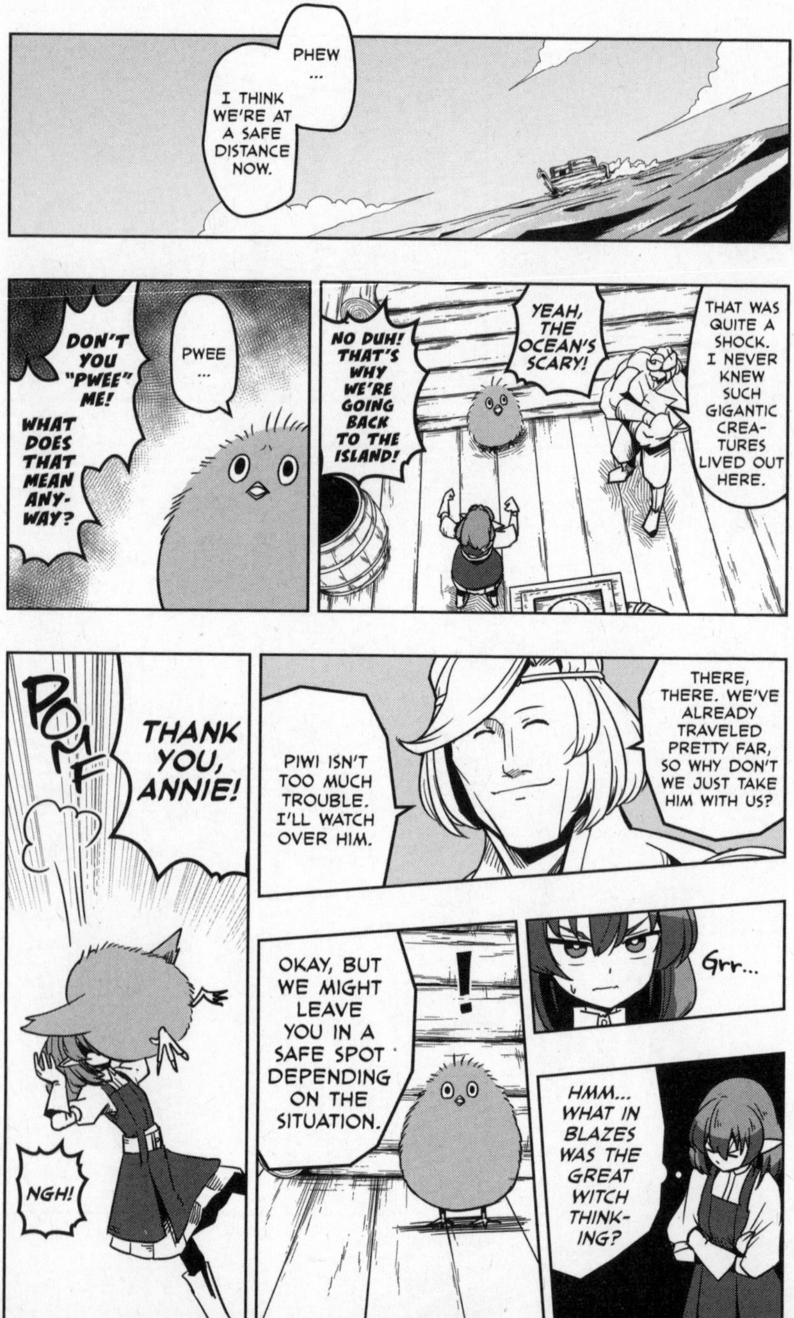
PHEW ... I THINK WE'RE AT A SAFE DISTANCE NOW.
THAT WAS QUITE A SHOCK. I NEVER KNEW SUCH GIGANTIC CREA-TURES LIVED OUT HERE.
YEAH, THE OCEAN'S SCARY!
NO DUH! THAT'S WHY WE'RE GOING BACK TO THE ISLAND!
PWEE ...
DON'T YOU "PWEE" ME!
WHAT DOES THAT MEAN ANY-WAY?
THERE, THERE. WE'VE ALREADY TRAVELED PRETTY FAR, SO WHY DON'T WE JUST TAKE HIM WITH US?
PIWI ISN'T TOO MUCH TROUBLE. I'LL WATCH OVER HIM.
Grr...
HMM... WHAT IN BLAZES WAS THE GREAT WITCH THINK-ING?
OKAY, BUT WE MIGHT LEAVE YOU IN A SAFE SPOT DEPENDING ON THE SITUATION.
!
THANK YOU, ANNIE!
POMF
NGH!

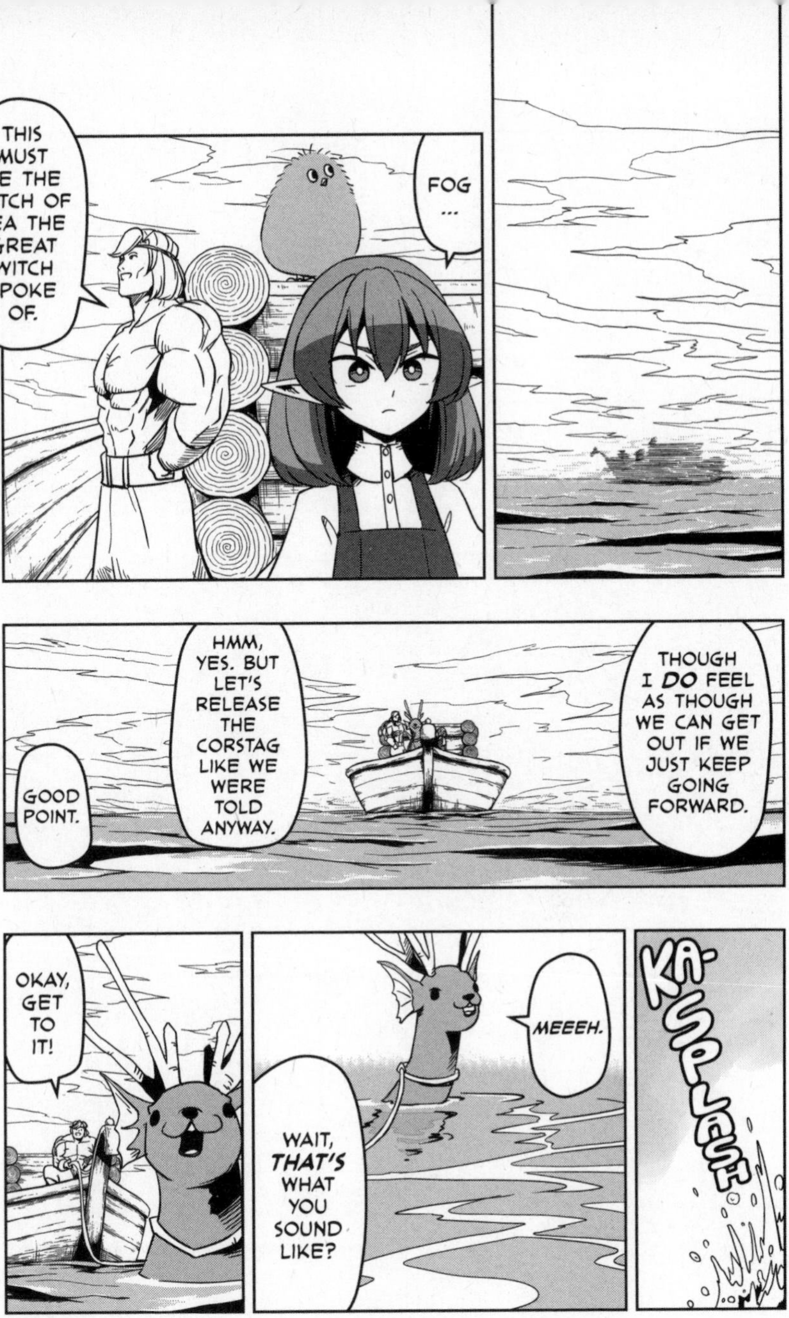
FOG ...
THIS MUST BE THE PATCH OF SEA THE GREAT WITCH SPOKE OF.
THOUGH I *DO* FEEL AS THOUGH WE CAN GET OUT IF WE JUST KEEP GOING FORWARD.
HMM, YES. BUT LET'S RELEASE THE CORSTAG LIKE WE WERE TOLD ANYWAY.
GOOD POINT.
KA-SPLASH
MEEEH.
WAIT, *THAT'S* WHAT YOU SOUND LIKE?
OKAY, GET TO IT!

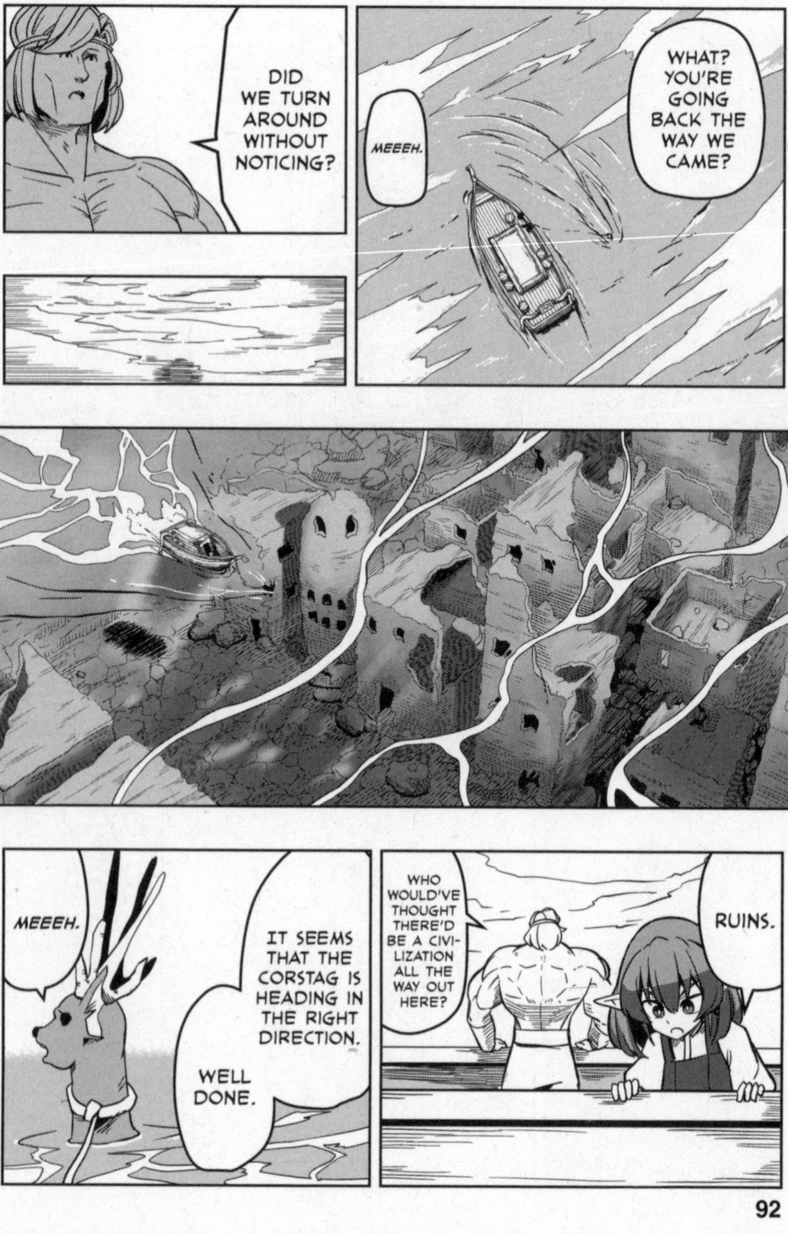
WHAT? YOU'RE GOING BACK THE WAY WE CAME?
MEEEH.
DID WE TURN AROUND WITHOUT NOTICING?
RUINS.
WHO WOULD'VE THOUGHT THERE'D BE A CIVI-LIZATION ALL THE WAY OUT HERE?
IT SEEMS THAT THE CORSTAG IS HEADING IN THE RIGHT DIRECTION.
WELL DONE.
MEEEH.

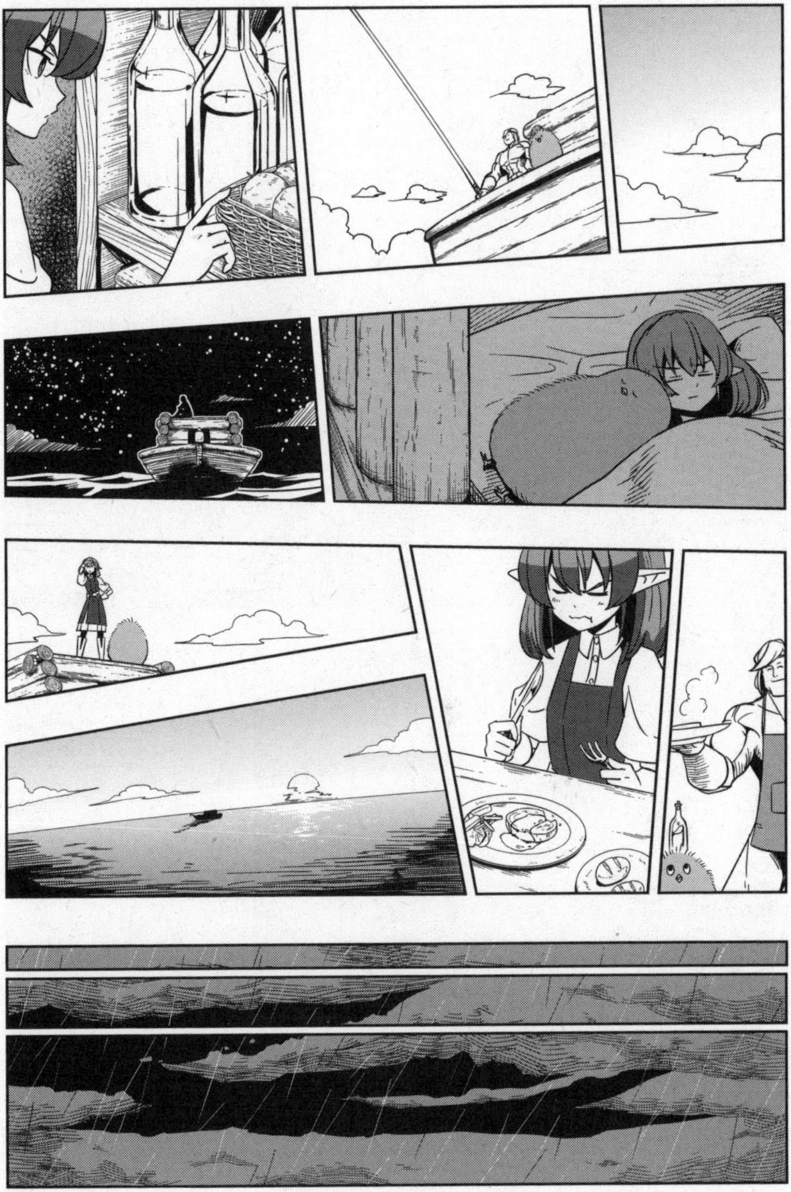

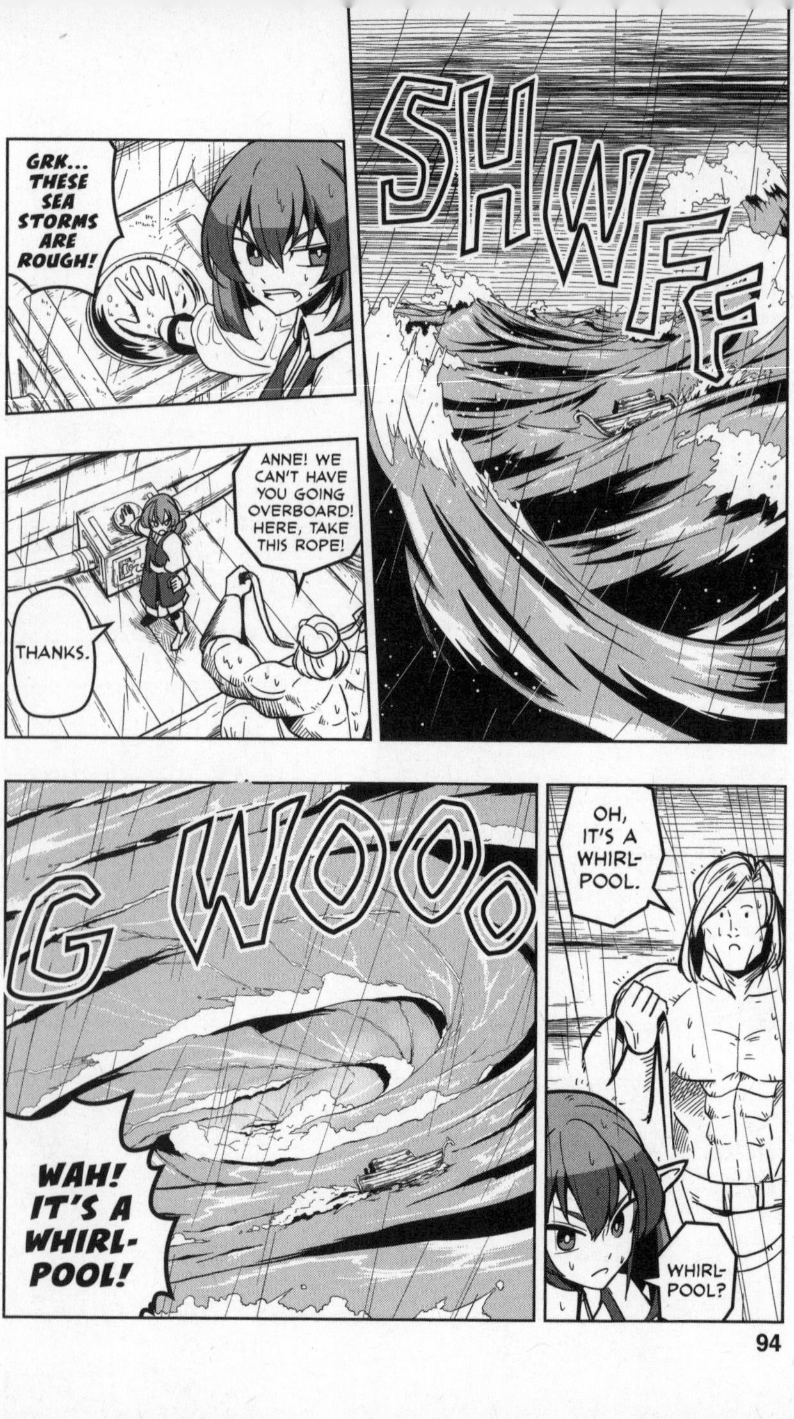
SHWFF
GRK... THESE SEA STORMS ARE ROUGH!
ANNE! WE CAN'T HAVE YOU GOING OVERBOARD! HERE, TAKE THIS ROPE!
THANKS.
OH, IT'S A WHIRL-POOL.
WHIRL-POOL?
GWOOO
WAH! IT'S A WHIRL-POOL!

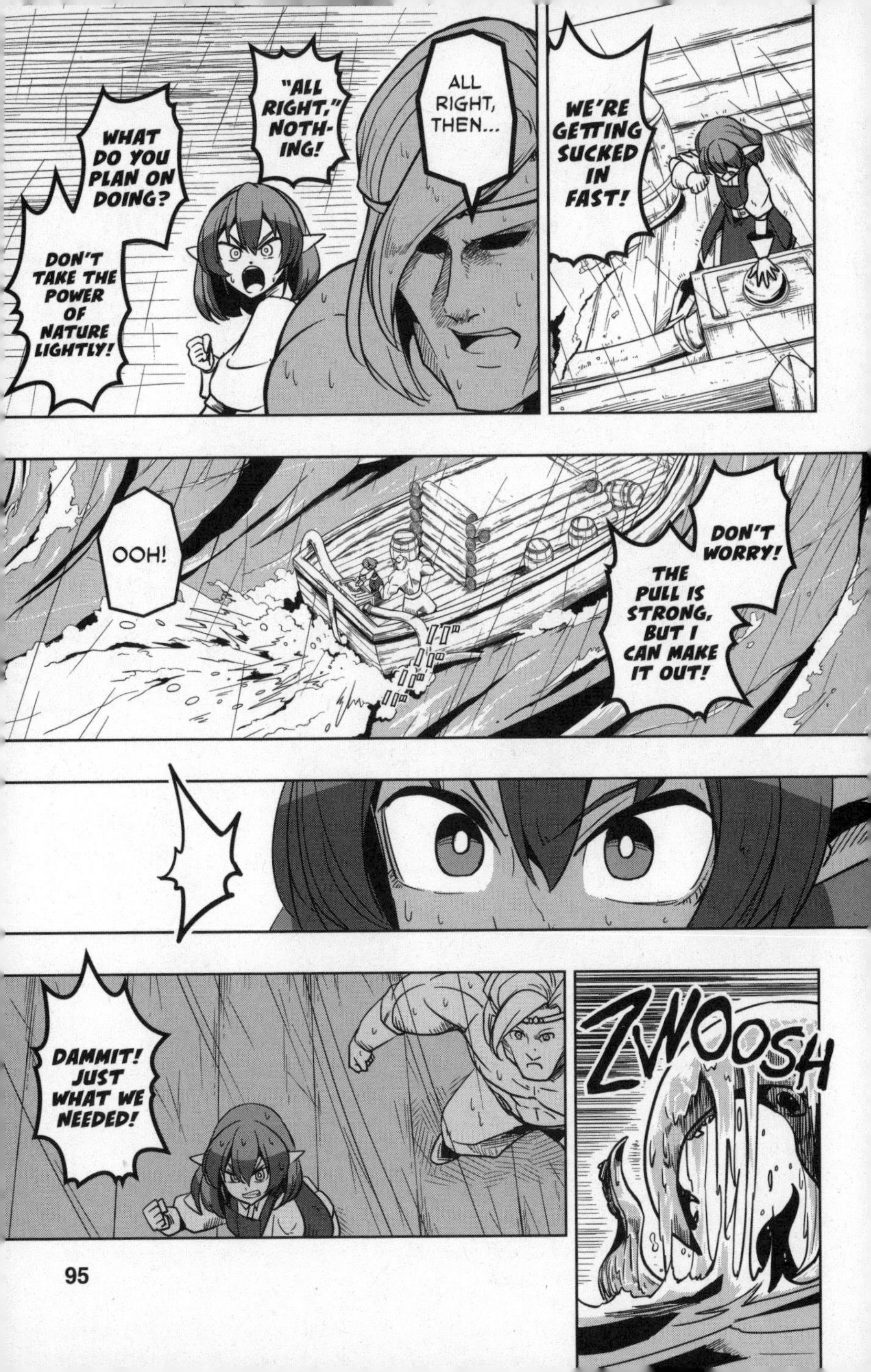
WE'RE GETTING SUCKED IN FAST!
ALL RIGHT, THEN...
"ALL RIGHT," NOTHING!
WHAT DO YOU PLAN ON DOING?
DON'T TAKE THE POWER OF NATURE LIGHTLY!
DON'T WORRY!
THE PULL IS STRONG, BUT I CAN MAKE IT OUT!
OOH!
ZWOOSH
DAMMIT! JUST WHAT WE NEEDED!

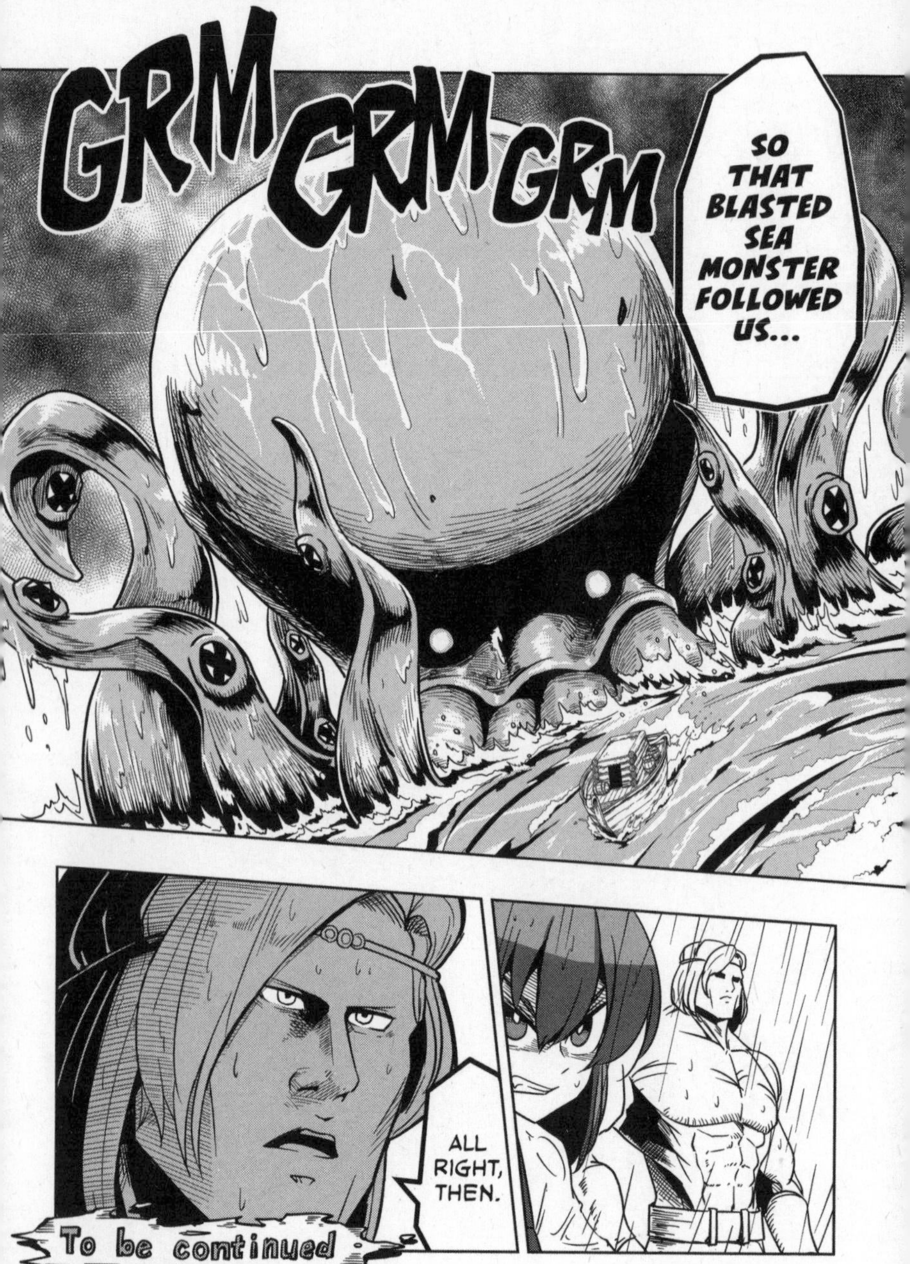
GRM GRM GRM
SO THAT BLASTED SEA MONSTER FOLLOWED US...
ALL RIGHT, THEN.
To be continued

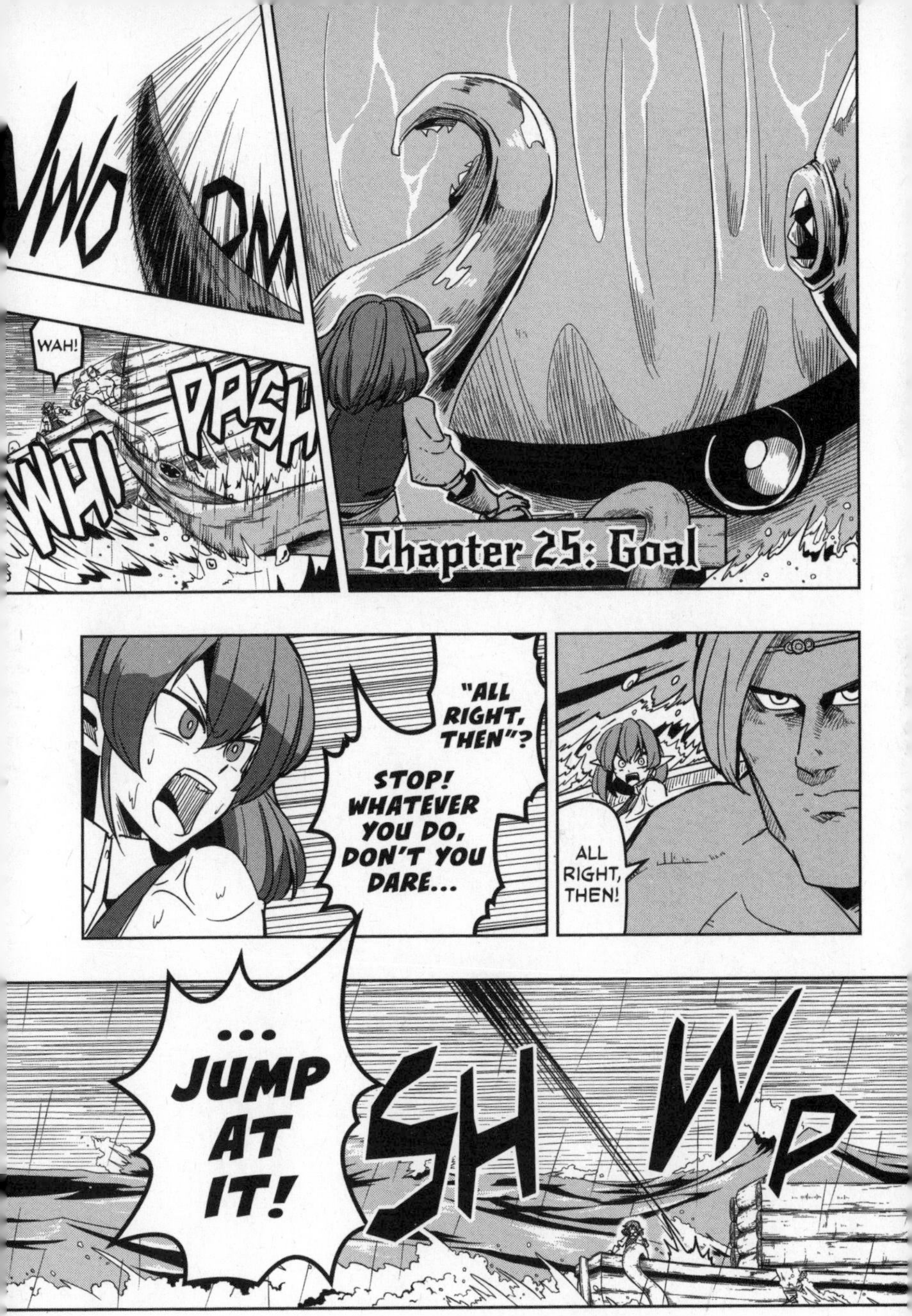
Chapter 25: Goal
WHOOM
WAH!
DASH
WHI
ALL RIGHT, THEN!
"ALL RIGHT, THEN"?
STOP! WHATEVER YOU DO, DON'T YOU DARE...
...JUMP AT IT!
SHWP

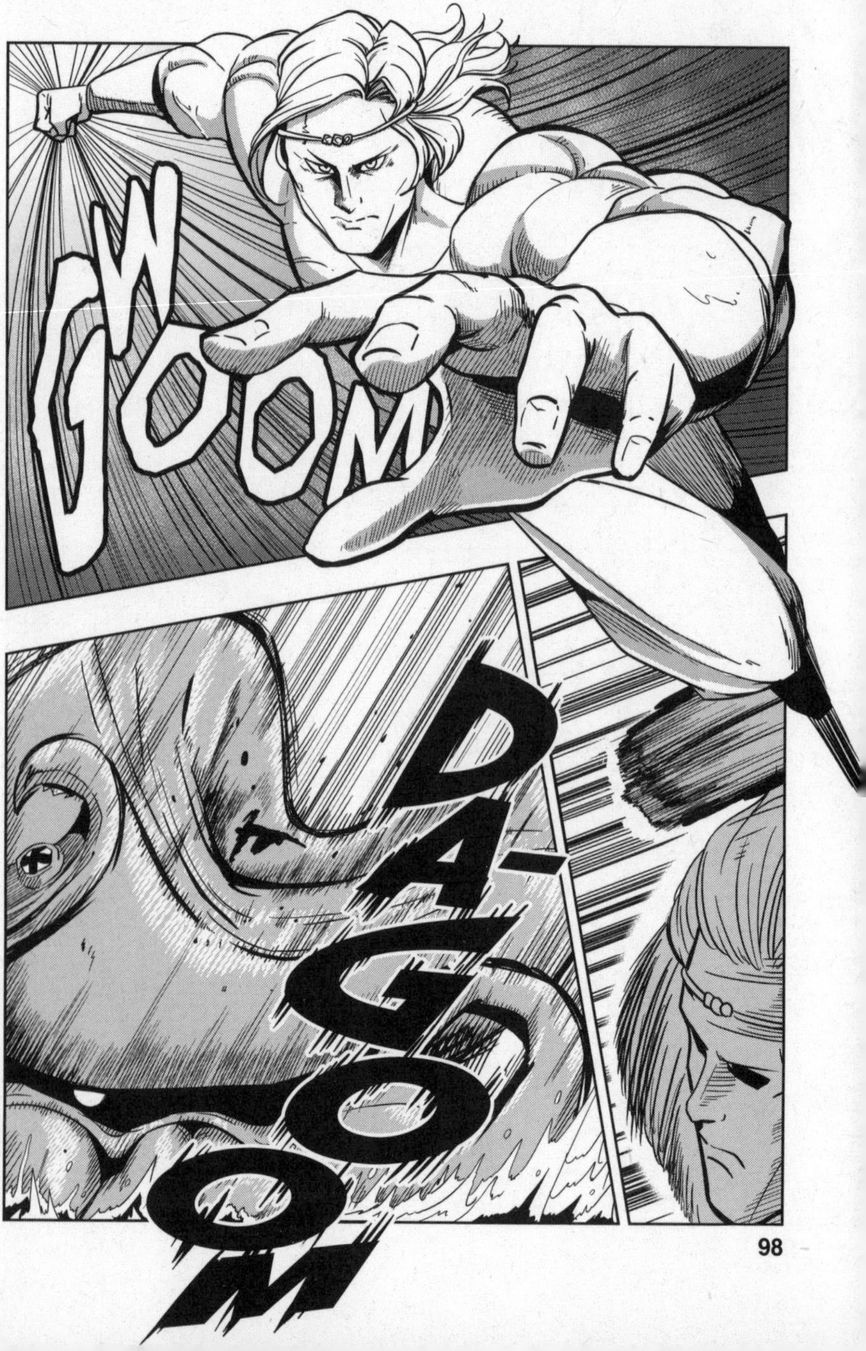
GWOOM
DA-GOOM

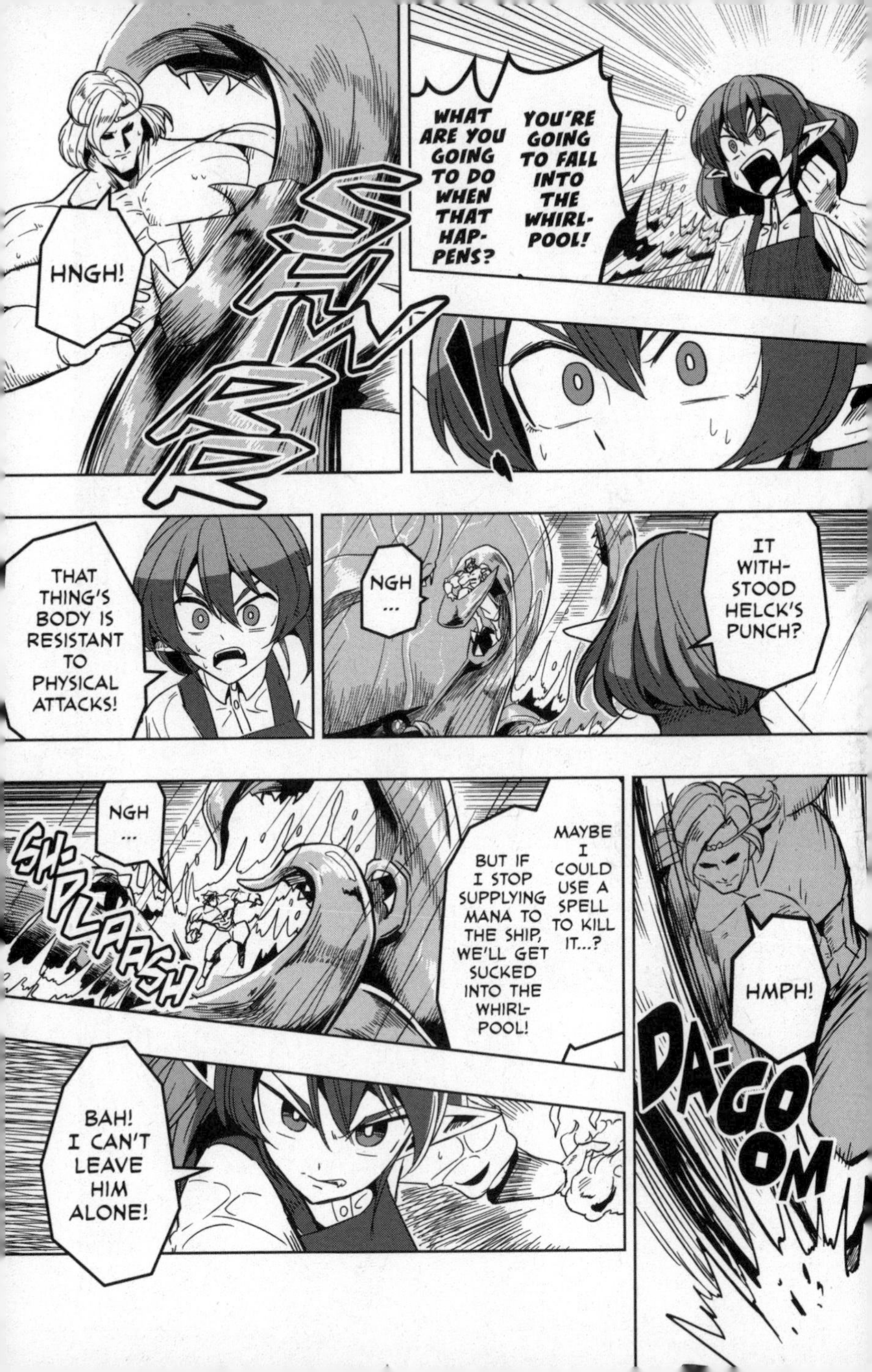
YOU'RE GOING TO FALL INTO THE WHIRL-POOL!
WHAT ARE YOU GOING TO DO WHEN THAT HAP-PENS?
HNGH!
IT WITH-STOOD HELCK'S PUNCH?
NGH ...
THAT THING'S BODY IS RESISTANT TO PHYSICAL ATTACKS!
HMPH!
DA-GOOM
MAYBE I COULD USE A SPELL TO KILL IT...?
BUT IF I STOP SUPPLYING MANA TO THE SHIP, WE'LL GET SUCKED INTO THE WHIRL-POOL!
NGH ...
SH-PLAASH
BAH! I CAN'T LEAVE HIM ALONE!

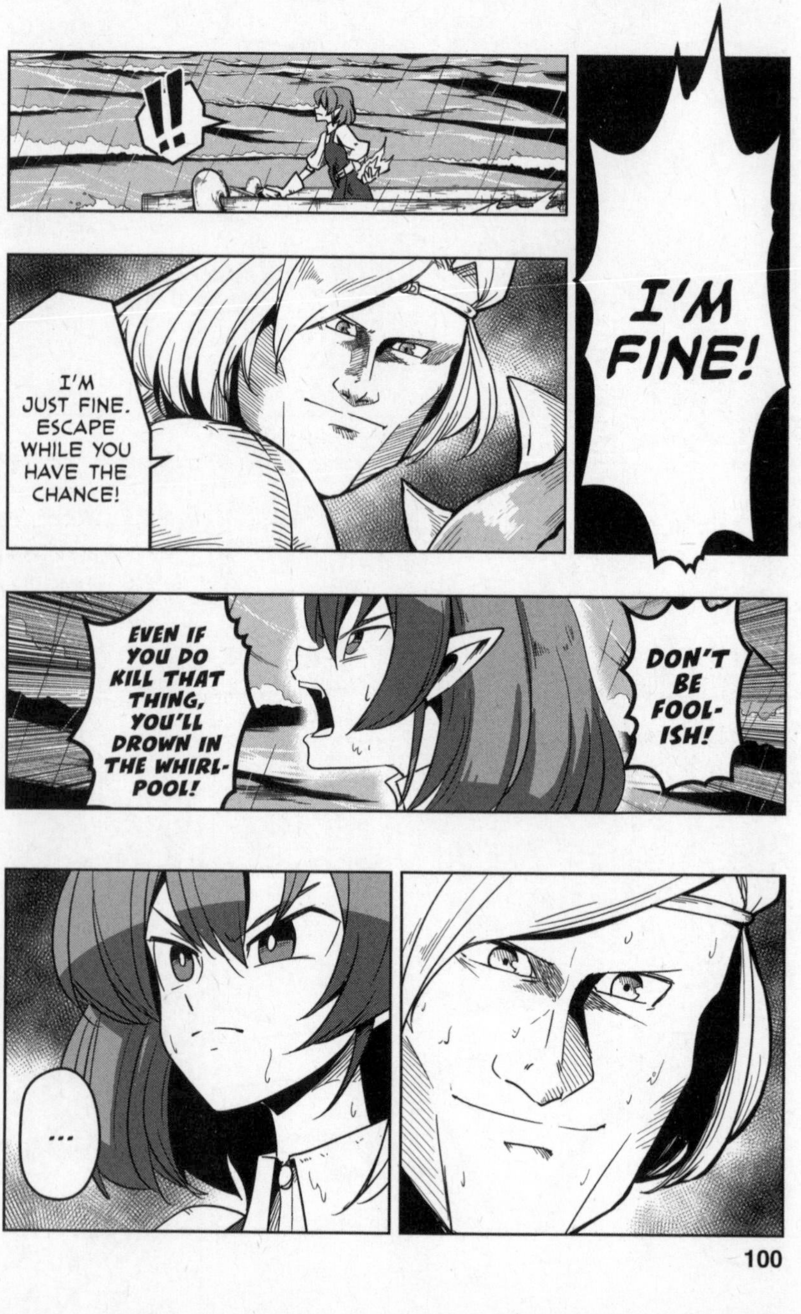

I'M FINE!
!!
I'M JUST FINE. ESCAPE WHILE YOU HAVE THE CHANCE!
DON'T BE FOOL-ISH!
EVEN IF YOU DO KILL THAT THING, YOU'LL DROWN IN THE WHIRL-POOL!
...

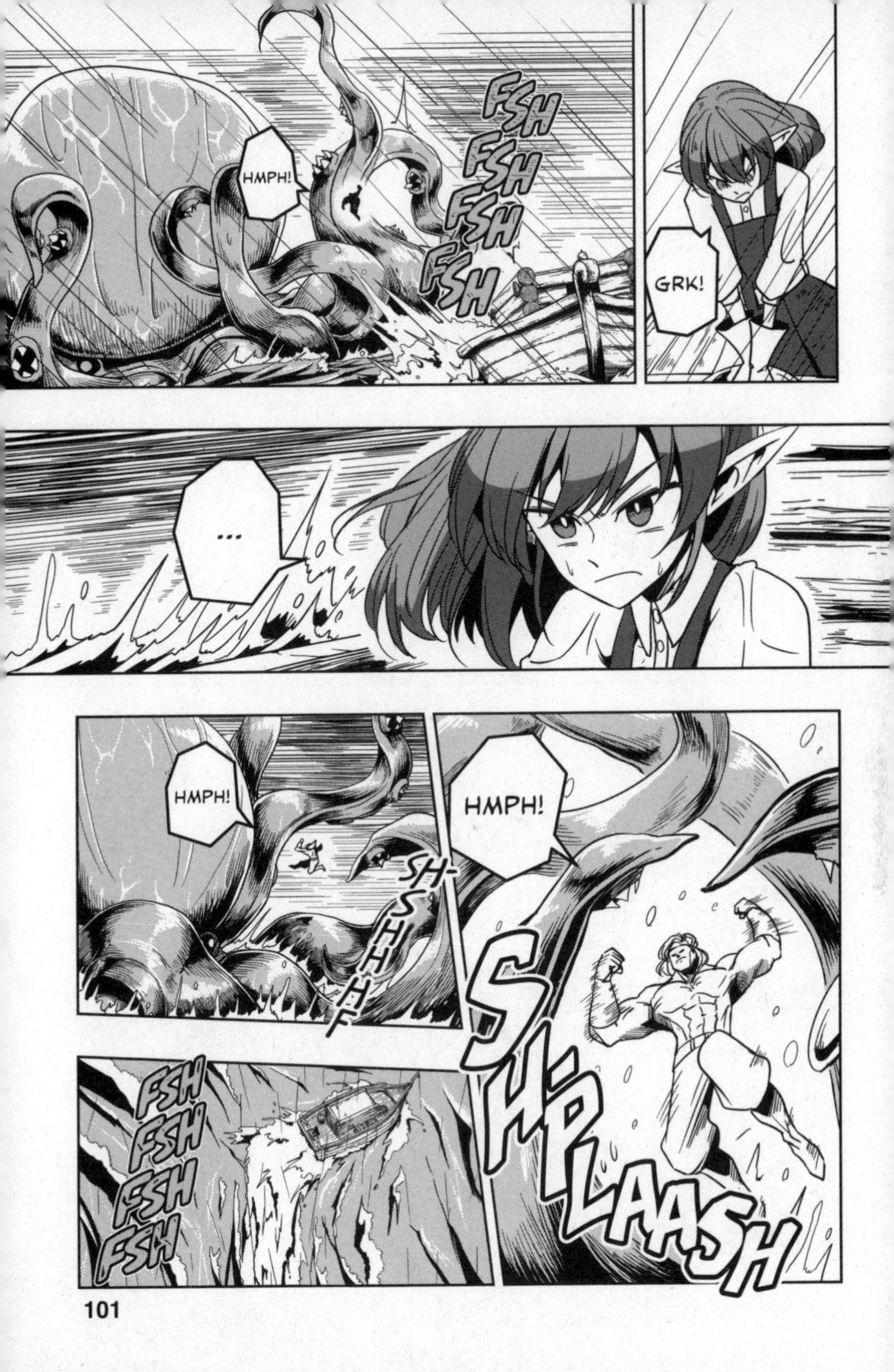
GRK!
HMPH!
FSH FSH FSH FSH
...
HMPH!
SH-PLAASH
HMPH!
SH-SHHHH
FSH FSH FSH FSH

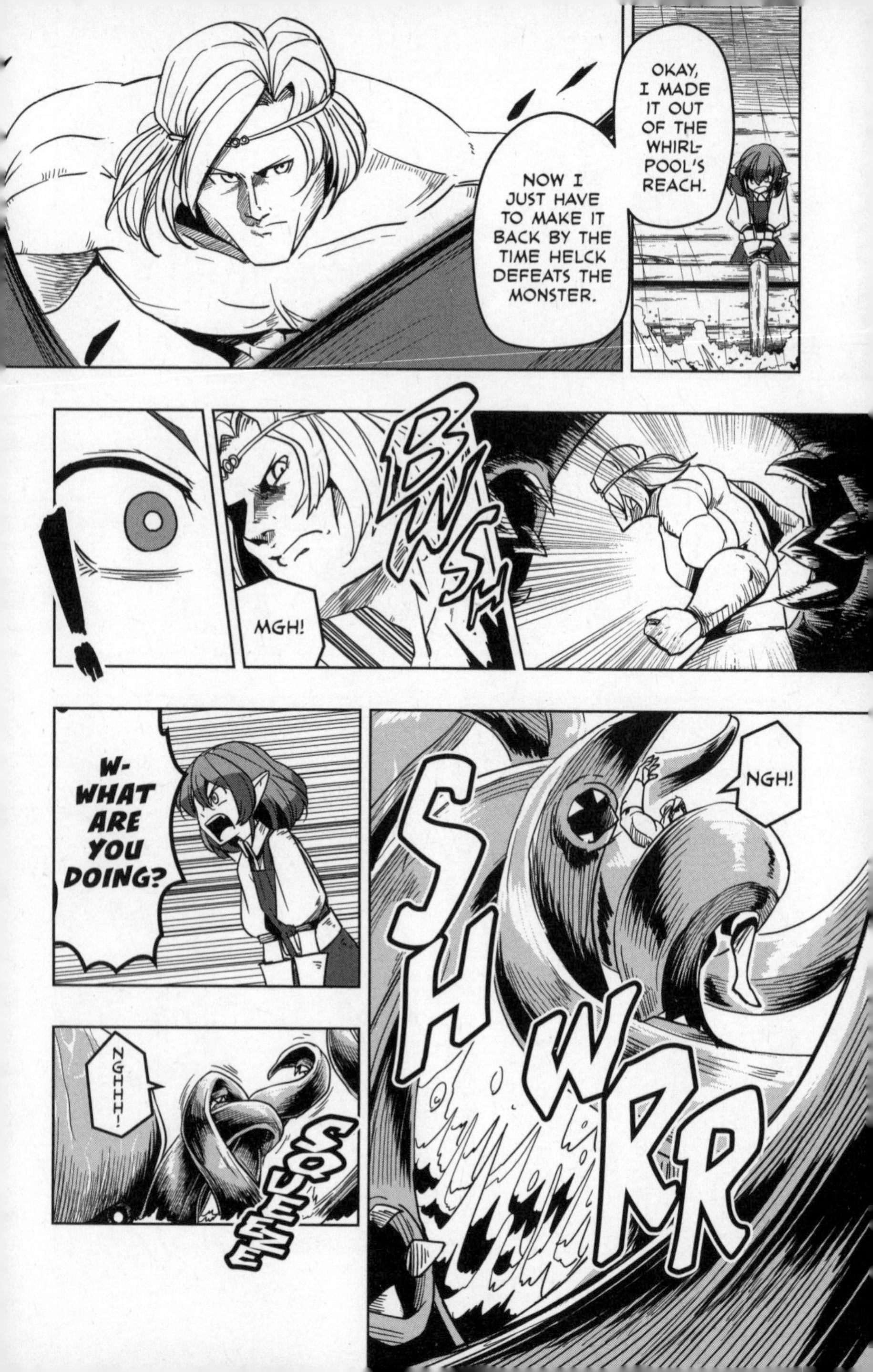
OKAY, I MADE IT OUT OF THE WHIRL-POOL'S REACH.
NOW I JUST HAVE TO MAKE IT BACK BY THE TIME HELCK DEFEATS THE MONSTER.
BWSH
MGH!
!
NGH!
SHWRR
W-WHAT ARE YOU DOING?
NGHHH!
SQUEEZE

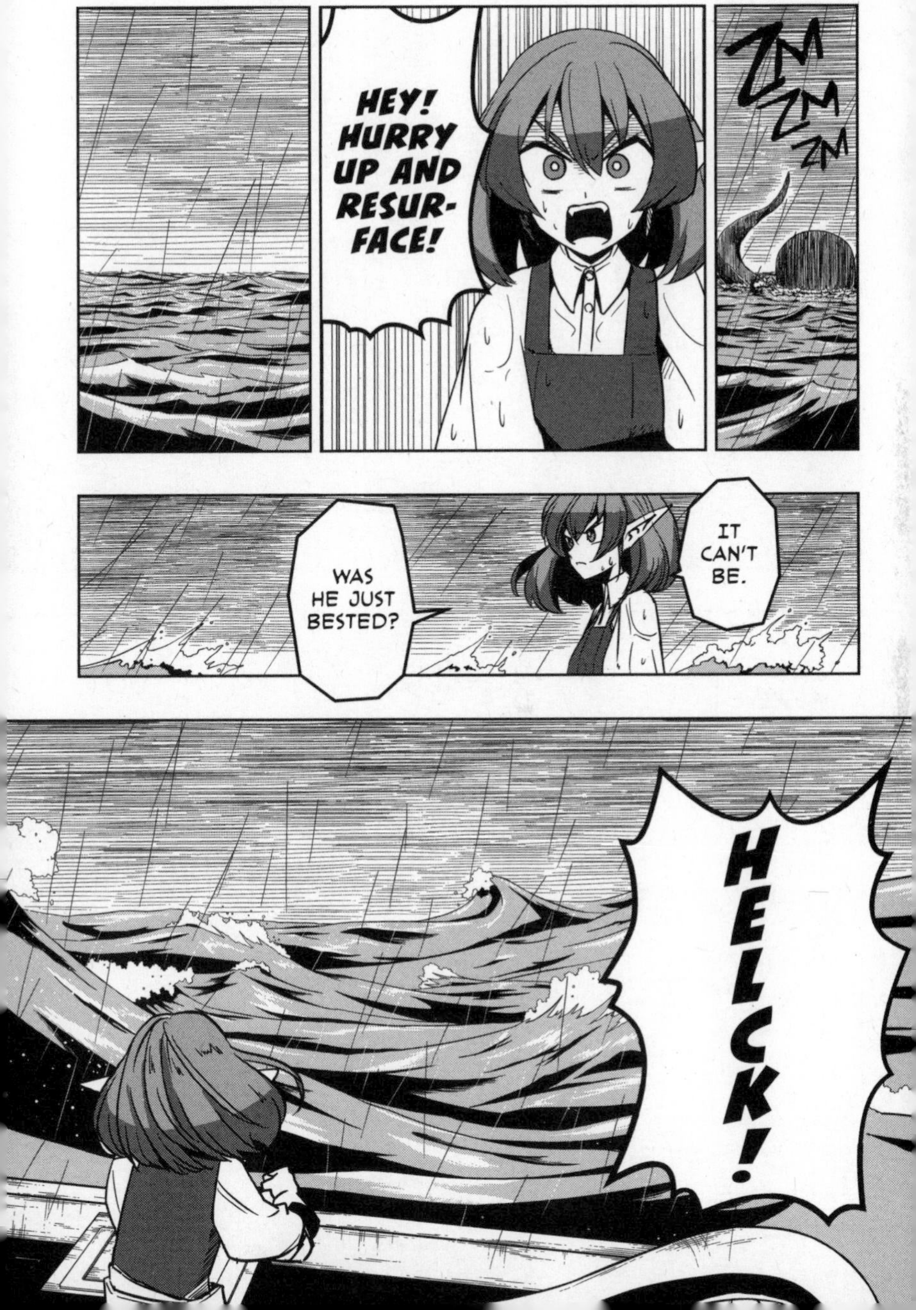
ZM ZM ZM ZM
HEY! HURRY UP AND RESUR-FACE!
IT CAN'T BE.
WAS HE JUST BESTED?
HELCK!

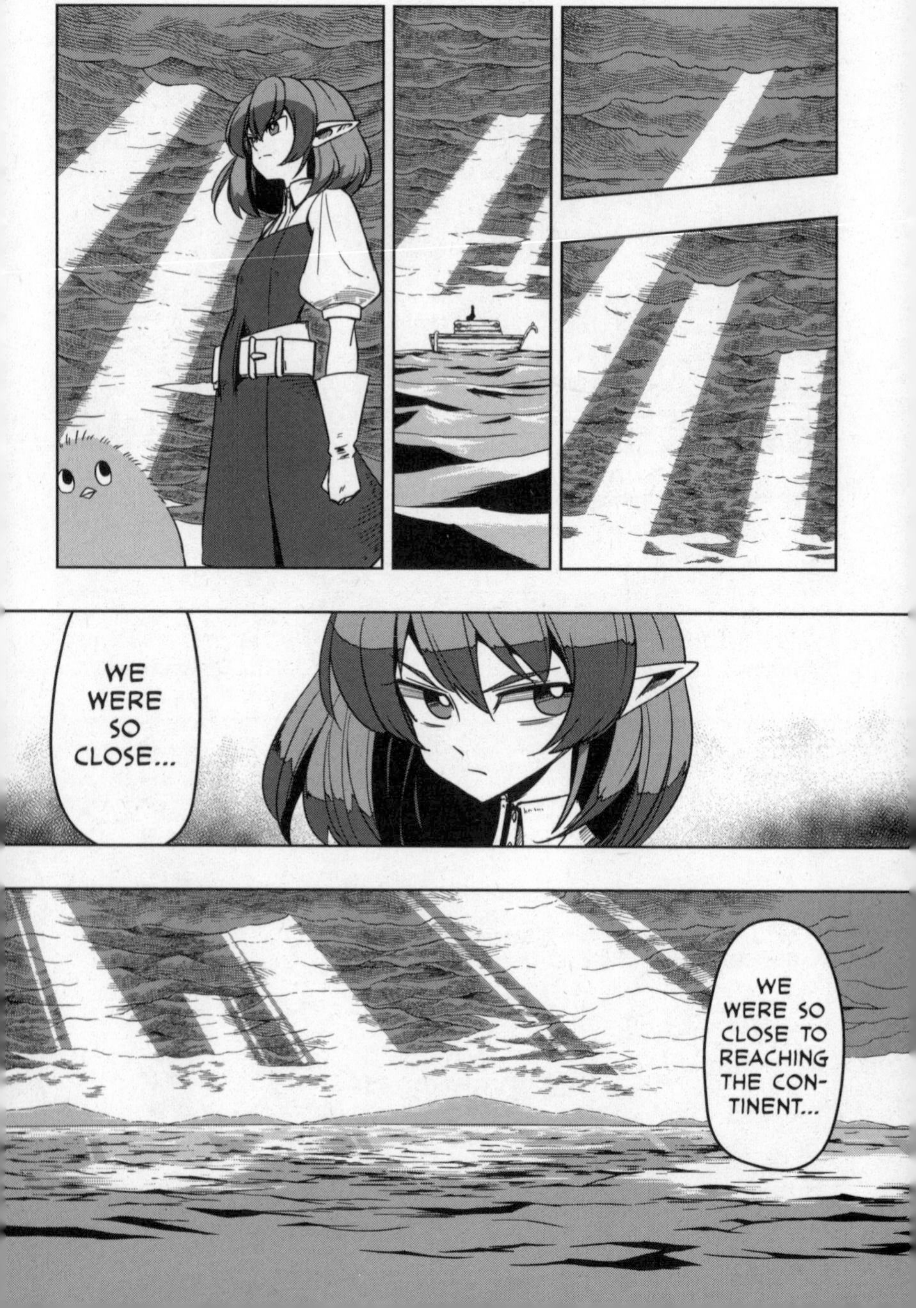
WE WERE SO CLOSE...
WE WERE SO CLOSE TO REACHING THE CON-TINENT...

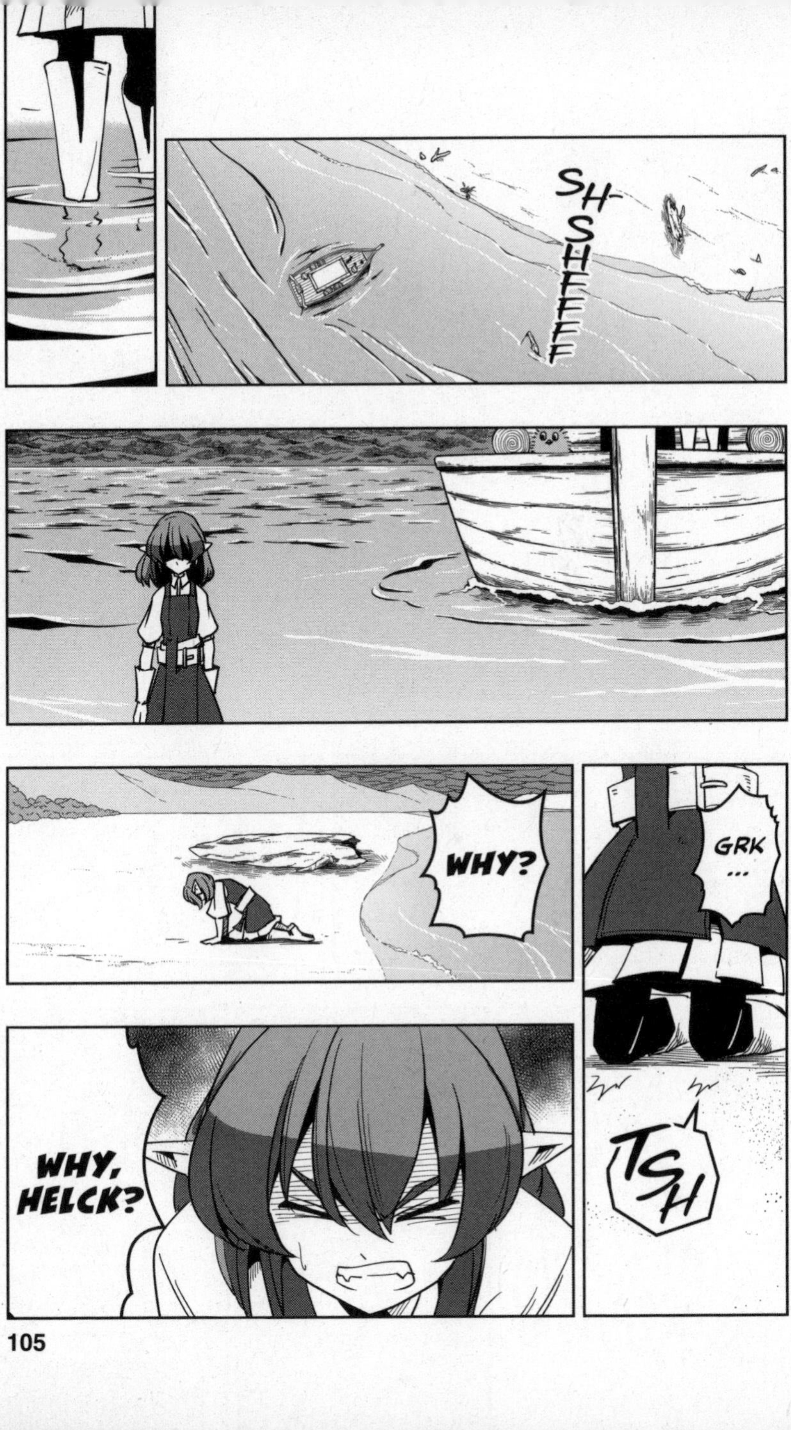
SH-SHFFFFF
GRK ...
TSH
WHY?
WHY, HELCK?

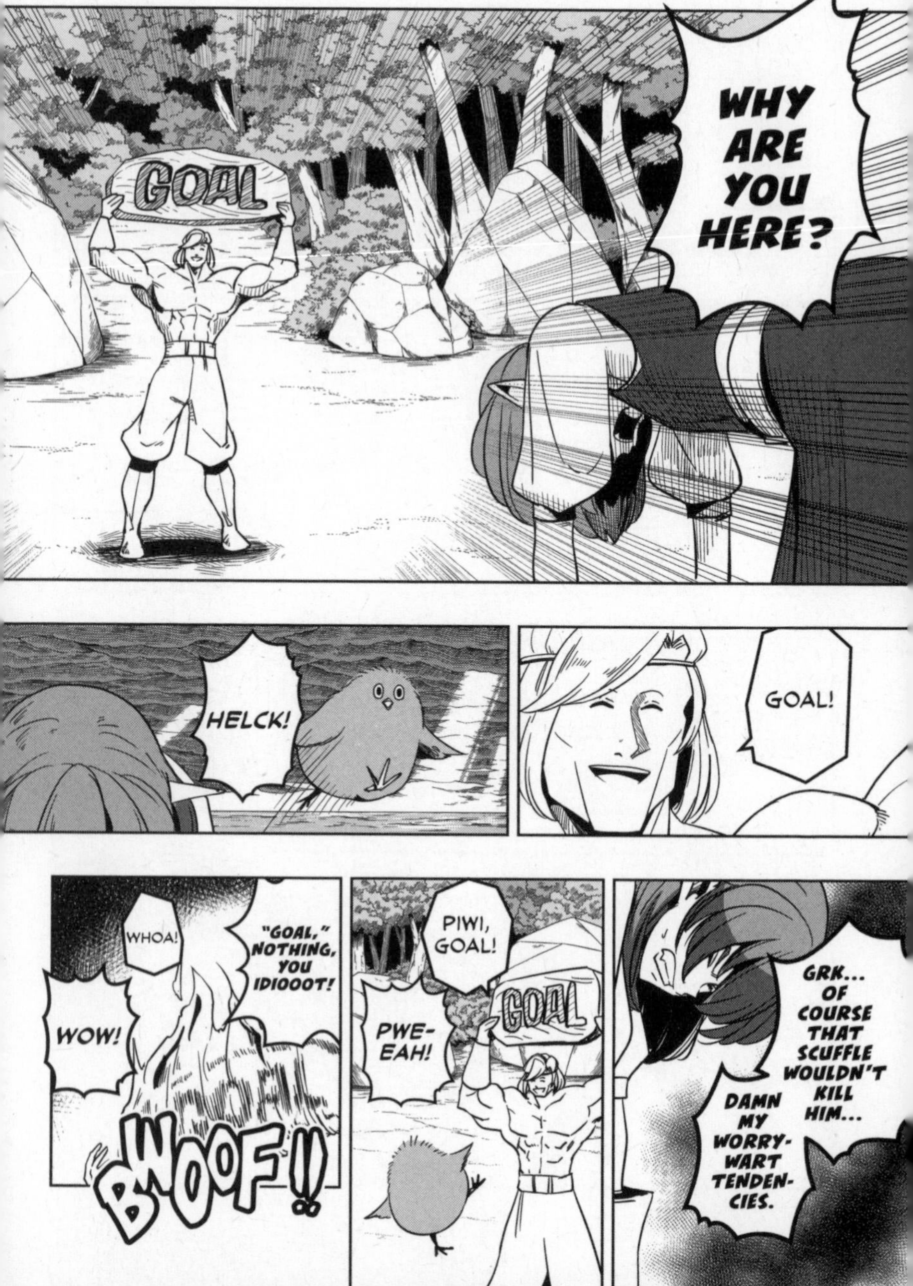
WHY ARE YOU HERE?
GOAL
GOAL!
HELCK!
GRK... OF COURSE THAT SCUFFLE WOULDN'T KILL HIM...
DAMN MY WORRY-WART TENDEN-CIES.
PIWI, GOAL!
PWE-EAH!
GOAL
"GOAL," NOTHING, YOU IDIOOOT!
WHOA!
WOW!
BWOOF!!

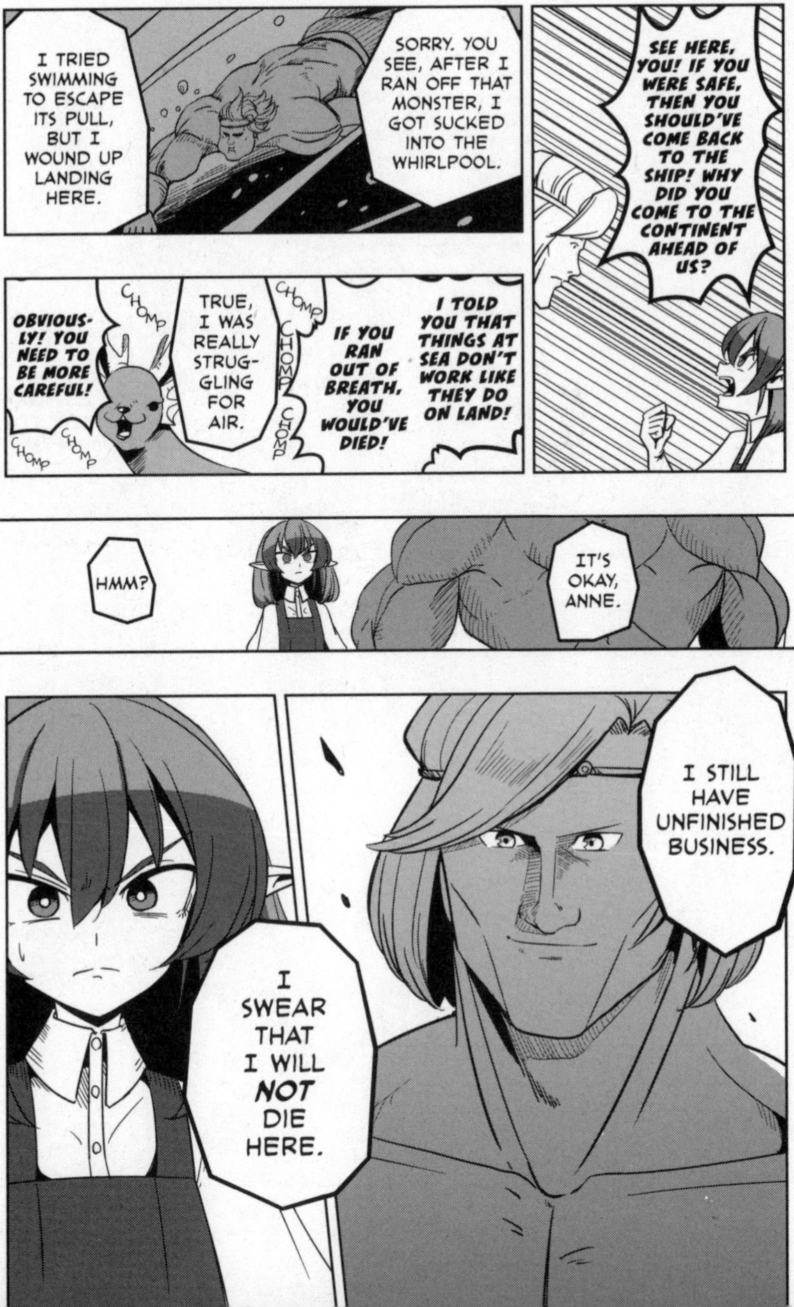
SEE HERE, YOU! IF YOU WERE SAFE, THEN YOU SHOULD'VE COME BACK TO THE SHIP! WHY DID YOU COME TO THE CONTINENT AHEAD OF US?
SORRY. YOU SEE, AFTER I RAN OFF THAT MONSTER, I GOT SUCKED INTO THE WHIRLPOOL.
I TRIED SWIMMING TO ESCAPE ITS PULL, BUT I WOUND UP LANDING HERE.
I TOLD YOU THAT THINGS AT SEA DON'T WORK LIKE THEY DO ON LAND!
IF YOU RAN OUT OF BREATH, YOU WOULD'VE DIED!
CHOMP CHOMP CHOMP
TRUE, I WAS REALLY STRUG-GLING FOR AIR.
CHOMP
OBVIOUS-LY! YOU NEED TO BE MORE CAREFUL!
CHOMP CHOMP
IT'S OKAY, ANNE.
HMM?
I STILL HAVE UNFINISHED BUSINESS.
I SWEAR THAT I WILL *NOT* DIE HERE.

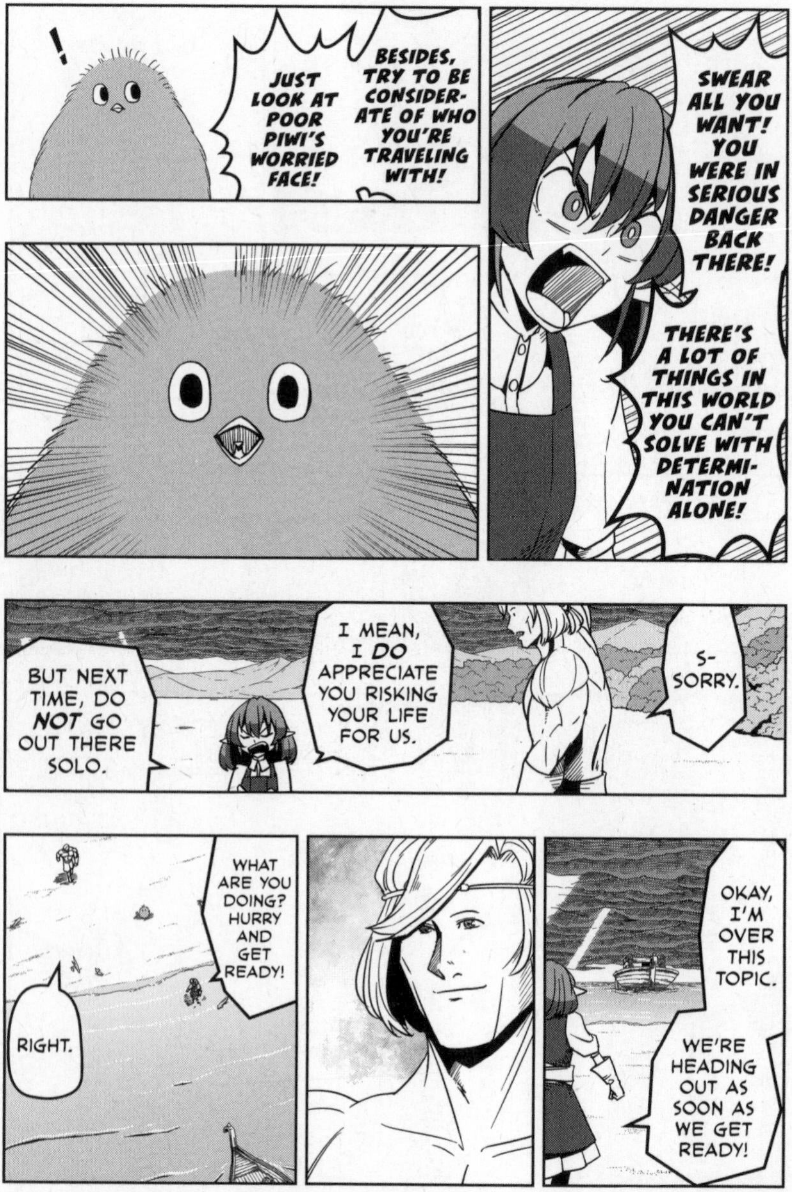
SWEAR ALL YOU WANT! YOU WERE IN SERIOUS DANGER BACK THERE!
THERE'S A LOT OF THINGS IN THIS WORLD YOU CAN'T SOLVE WITH DETERMINATION ALONE!
BESIDES, TRY TO BE CONSIDERATE OF WHO YOU'RE TRAVELING WITH!
JUST LOOK AT POOR PIWI'S WORRIED FACE!
!
S-SORRY.
I MEAN, I *DO* APPRECIATE YOU RISKING YOUR LIFE FOR US.
BUT NEXT TIME, DO *NOT* GO OUT THERE SOLO.
OKAY, I'M OVER THIS TOPIC.
WE'RE HEADING OUT AS SOON AS WE GET READY!
WHAT ARE YOU DOING? HURRY AND GET READY!
RIGHT.

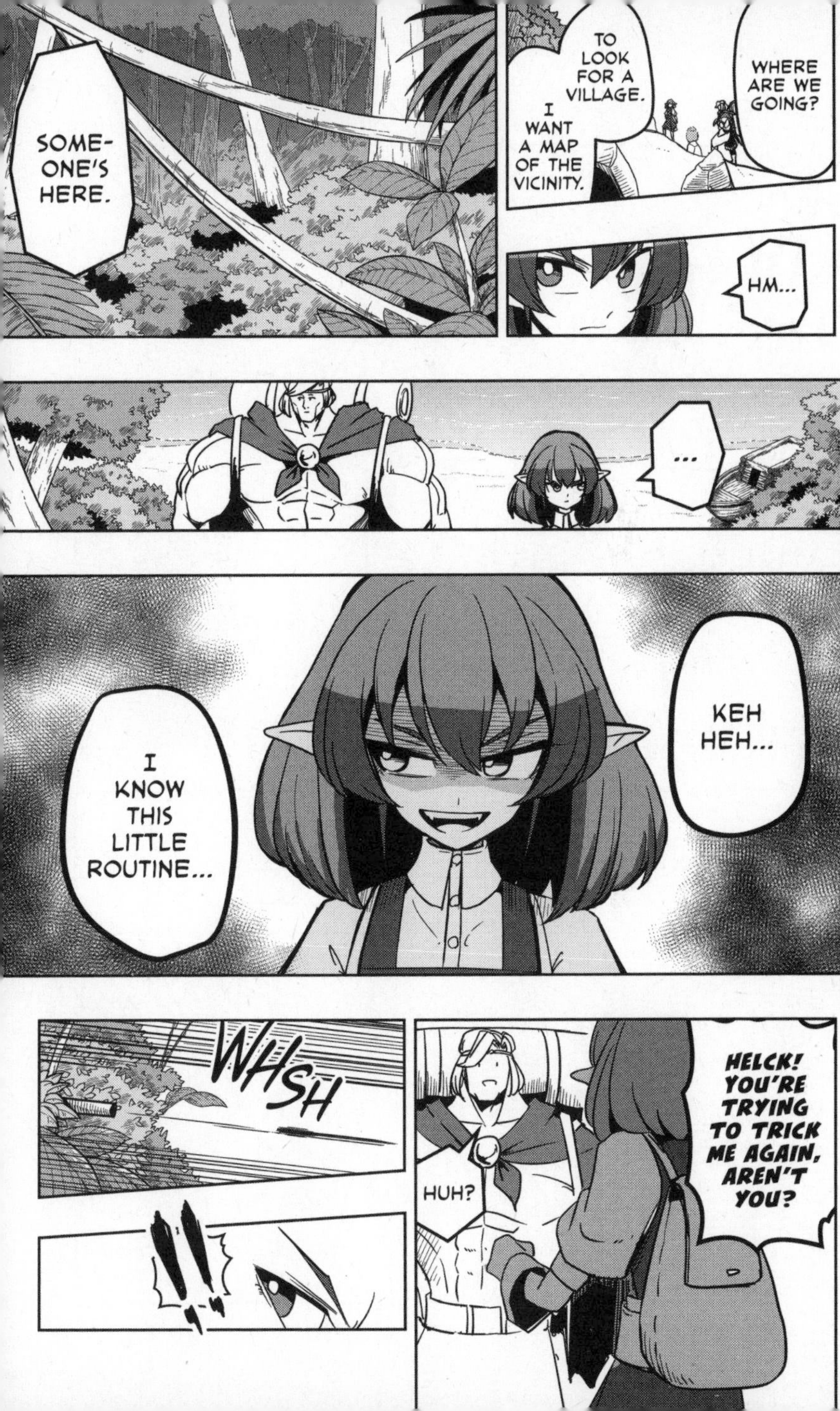
WHERE ARE WE GOING?
TO LOOK FOR A VILLAGE.
I WANT A MAP OF THE VICINITY.
HM...
SOME-ONE'S HERE.
...
KEH HEH...
I KNOW THIS LITTLE ROUTINE...
HELCK! YOU'RE TRYING TO TRICK ME AGAIN, AREN'T YOU?
HUH?
WHSH
!!

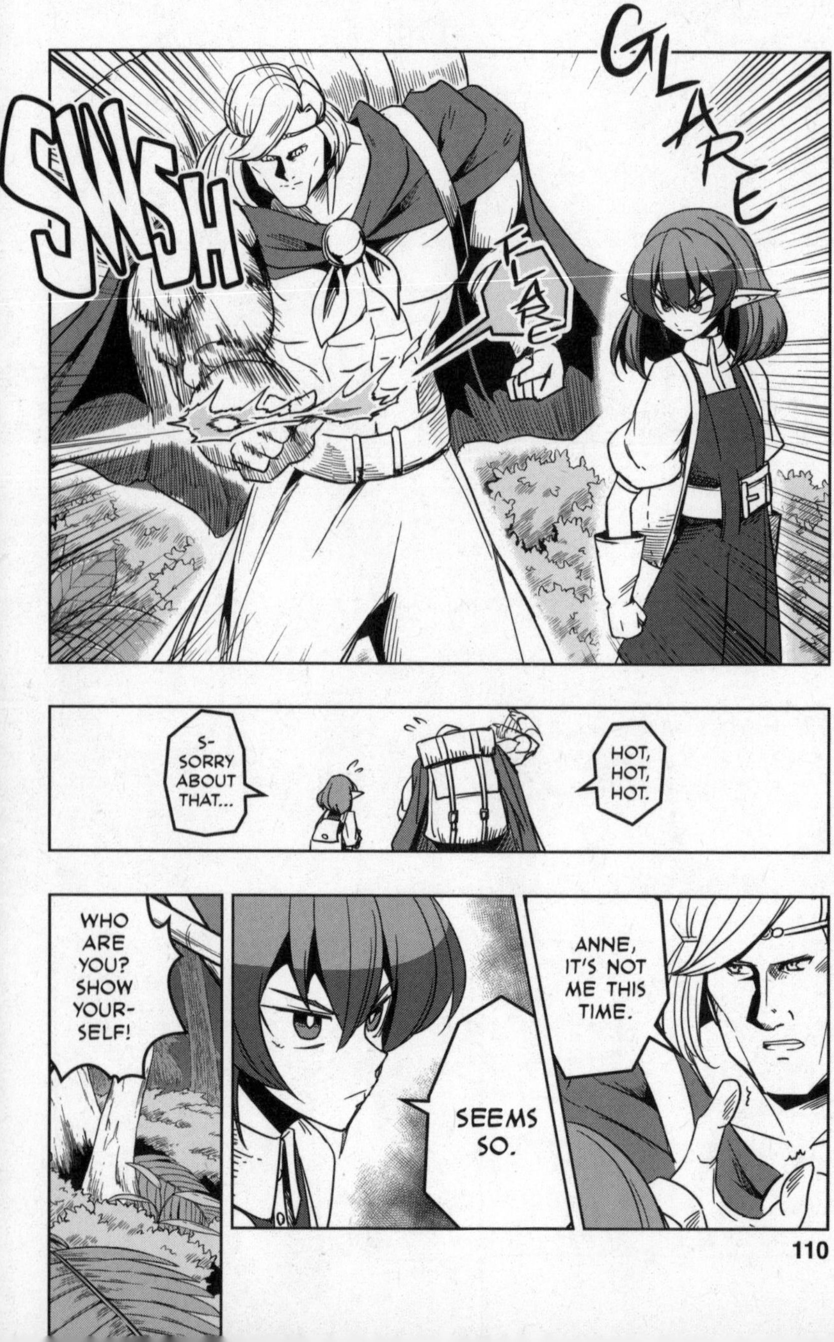
GLARE
FLARE
SWSH
HOT, HOT, HOT.
S-SORRY ABOUT THAT...
ANNE, IT'S NOT ME THIS TIME.
SEEMS SO.
WHO ARE YOU? SHOW YOUR-SELF!

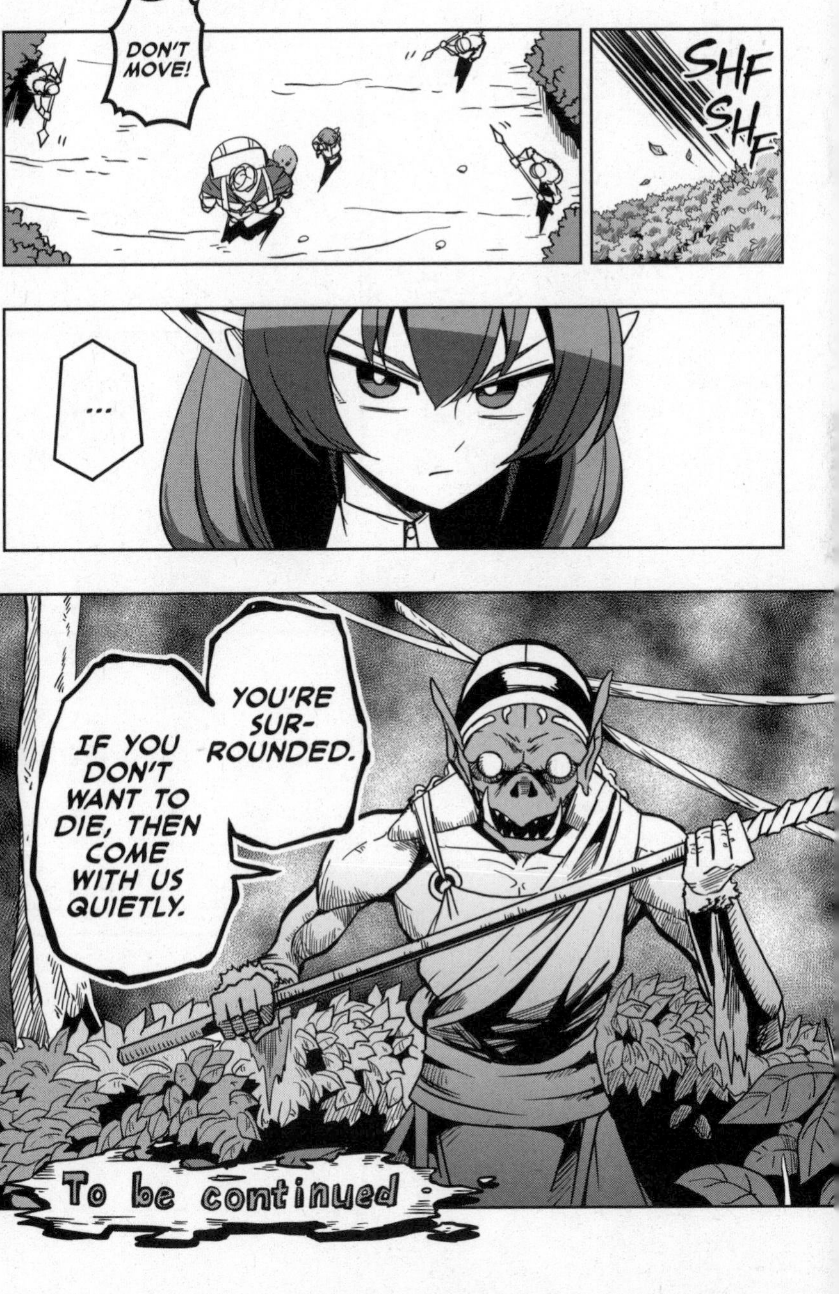
SHF SHF
DON'T MOVE!
...
YOU'RE SUR- ROUNDED.
IF YOU DON'T WANT TO DIE, THEN COME WITH US QUIETLY.
To be continued

I'M JUST FINE ②

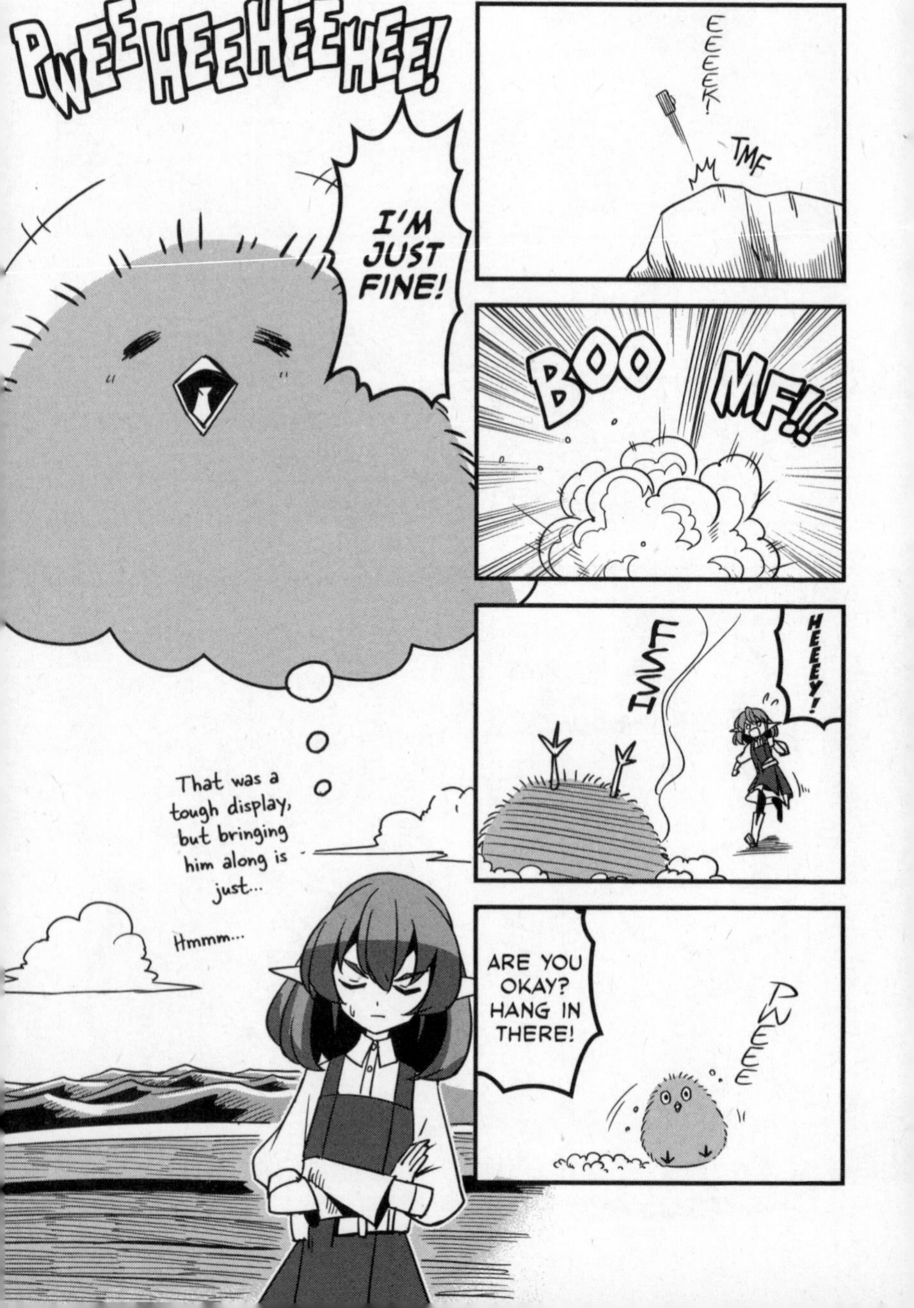
EEEEK!
TMF
BOOMF!!
FSSH
HEEEY!
ARE YOU OKAY? HANG IN THERE!
PWEEE
PWEEHEEHEEHEE!
I'M JUST FINE!
That was a tough display, but bringing him along is just...
Hmmm...

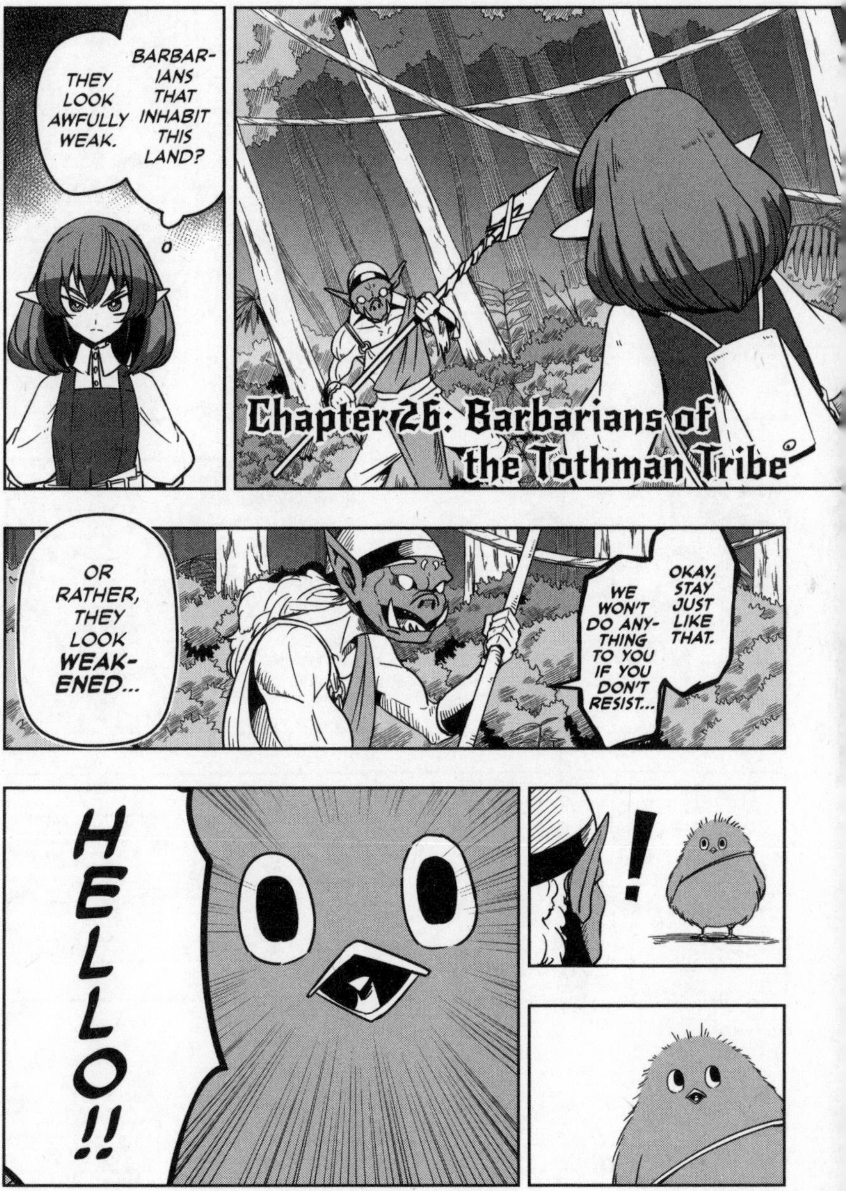
Chapter 26: Barbarians of the Tothman Tribe
BARBARIANS THAT INHABIT THIS LAND?
THEY LOOK AWFULLY WEAK.
OKAY, STAY JUST LIKE THAT.
WE WON'T DO ANYTHING TO YOU IF YOU DON'T RESIST...
OR RATHER, THEY LOOK **WEAKENED**...
!
HELLO!!

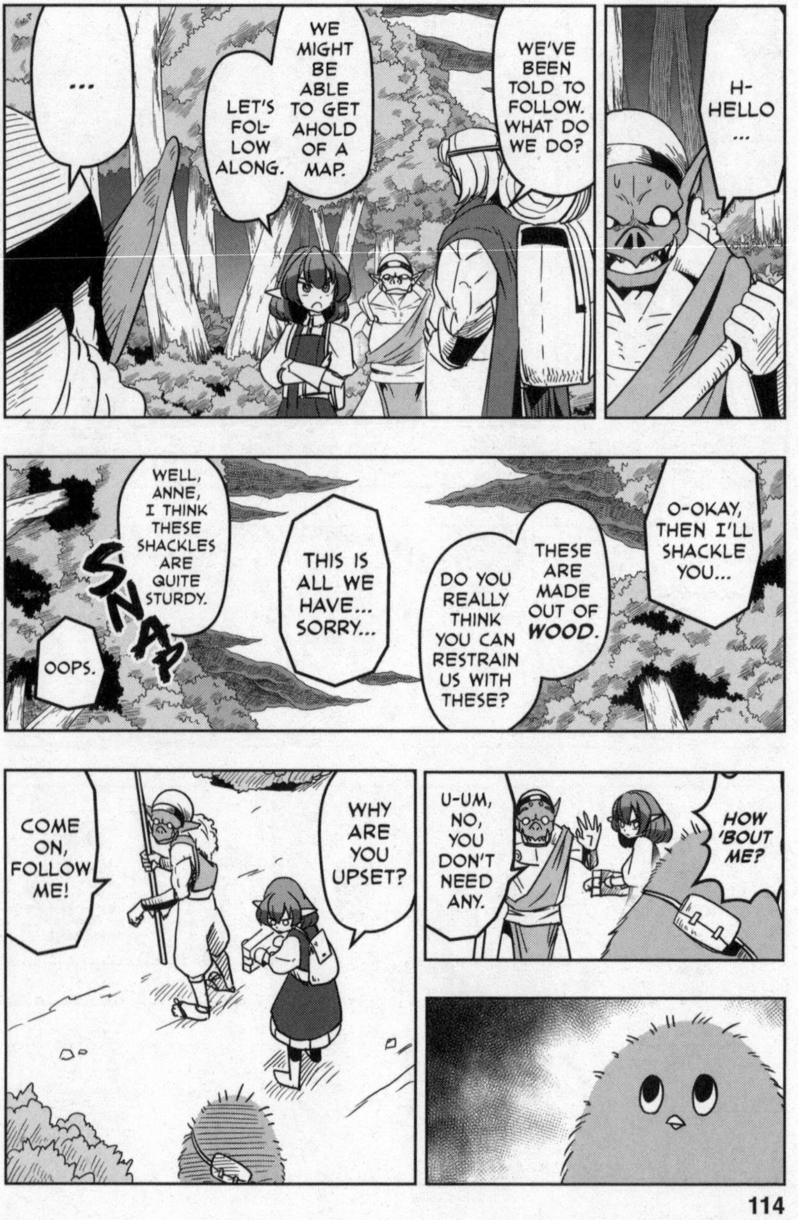
H-HELLO...
WE'VE BEEN TOLD TO FOLLOW. WHAT DO WE DO?
WE MIGHT BE ABLE TO GET AHOLD OF A MAP.
LET'S FOL-LOW ALONG.
...
O-OKAY, THEN I'LL SHACKLE YOU...
THESE ARE MADE OUT OF *WOOD*.
DO YOU REALLY THINK YOU CAN RESTRAIN US WITH THESE?
THIS IS ALL WE HAVE... SORRY...
WELL, ANNE, I THINK THESE SHACKLES ARE QUITE STURDY.
SNAP
OOPS.
HOW 'BOUT ME?
U-UM, NO, YOU DON'T NEED ANY.
WHY ARE YOU UPSET?
COME ON, FOLLOW ME!

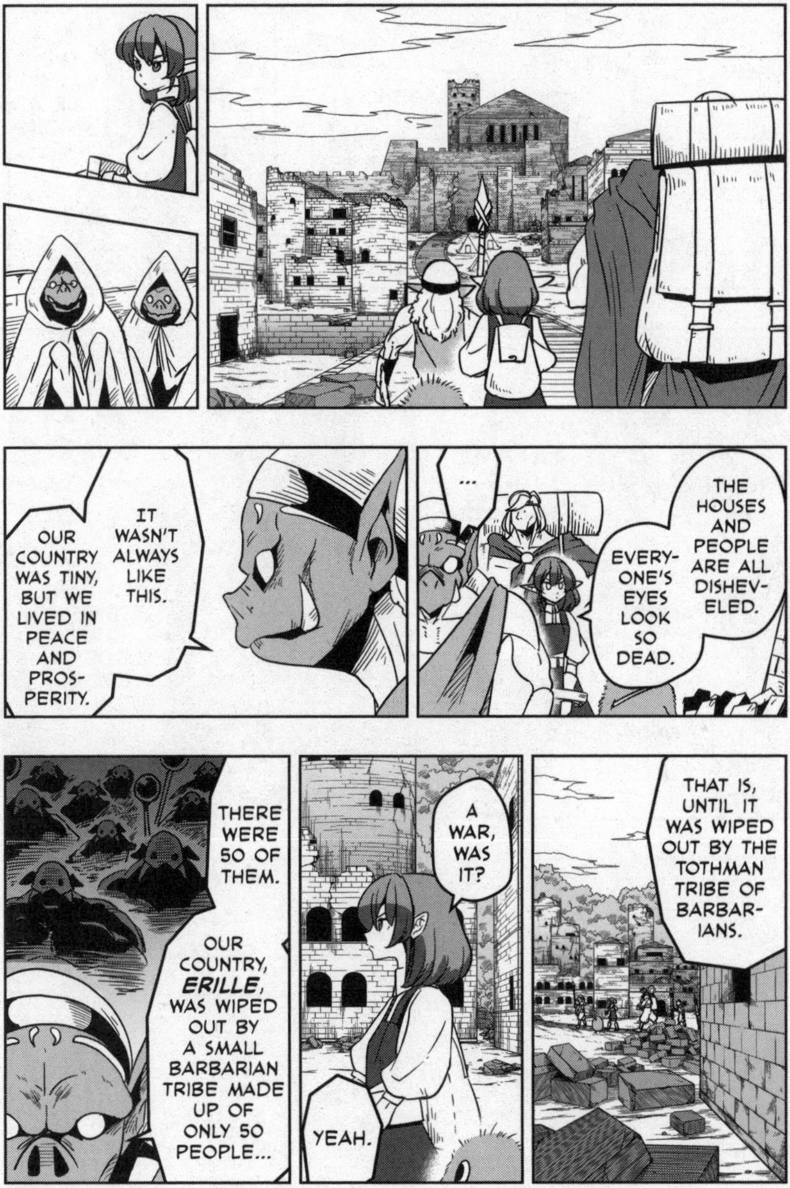
THE HOUSES AND PEOPLE ARE ALL DISHEVELED.
EVERYONE'S EYES LOOK SO DEAD.
...
IT WASN'T ALWAYS LIKE THIS.
OUR COUNTRY WAS TINY, BUT WE LIVED IN PEACE AND PROSPERITY.
THAT IS, UNTIL IT WAS WIPED OUT BY THE TOTHMAN TRIBE OF BARBARIANS.
A WAR, WAS IT?
YEAH.
THERE WERE 50 OF THEM.
OUR COUNTRY, *ERILLE*, WAS WIPED OUT BY A SMALL BARBARIAN TRIBE MADE UP OF ONLY 50 PEOPLE...

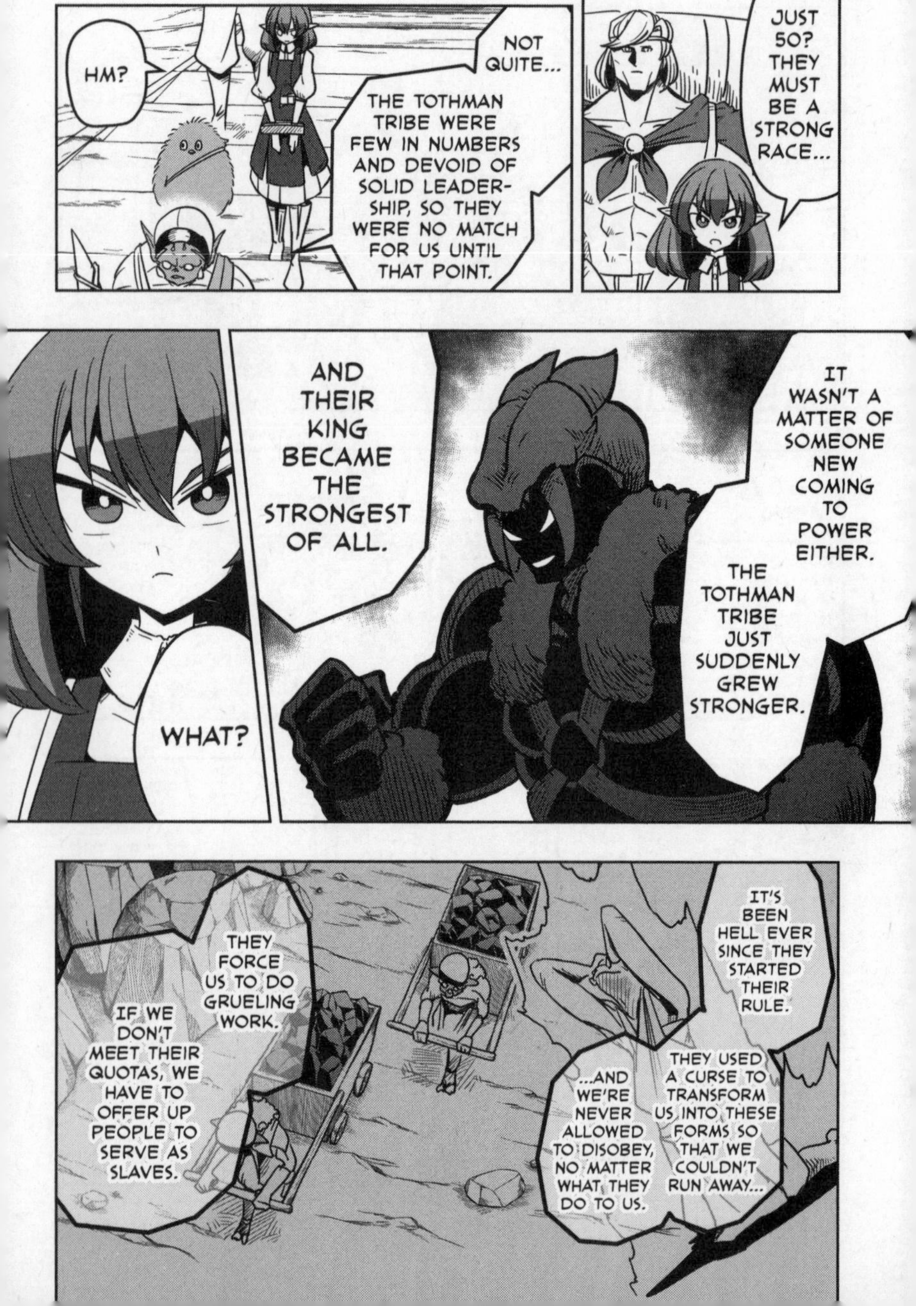
JUST 50? THEY MUST BE A STRONG RACE...
NOT QUITE...
HM?
THE TOTHMAN TRIBE WERE FEW IN NUMBERS AND DEVOID OF SOLID LEADER-SHIP, SO THEY WERE NO MATCH FOR US UNTIL THAT POINT.
IT WASN'T A MATTER OF SOMEONE NEW COMING TO POWER EITHER.
THE TOTHMAN TRIBE JUST SUDDENLY GREW STRONGER.
AND THEIR KING BECAME THE STRONGEST OF ALL.
WHAT?
IT'S BEEN HELL EVER SINCE THEY STARTED THEIR RULE.
THEY FORCE US TO DO GRUELING WORK.
IF WE DON'T MEET THEIR QUOTAS, WE HAVE TO OFFER UP PEOPLE TO SERVE AS SLAVES.
THEY USED A CURSE TO TRANSFORM US INTO THESE FORMS SO THAT WE COULDN'T RUN AWAY...
...AND WE'RE NEVER ALLOWED TO DISOBEY, NO MATTER WHAT THEY DO TO US.

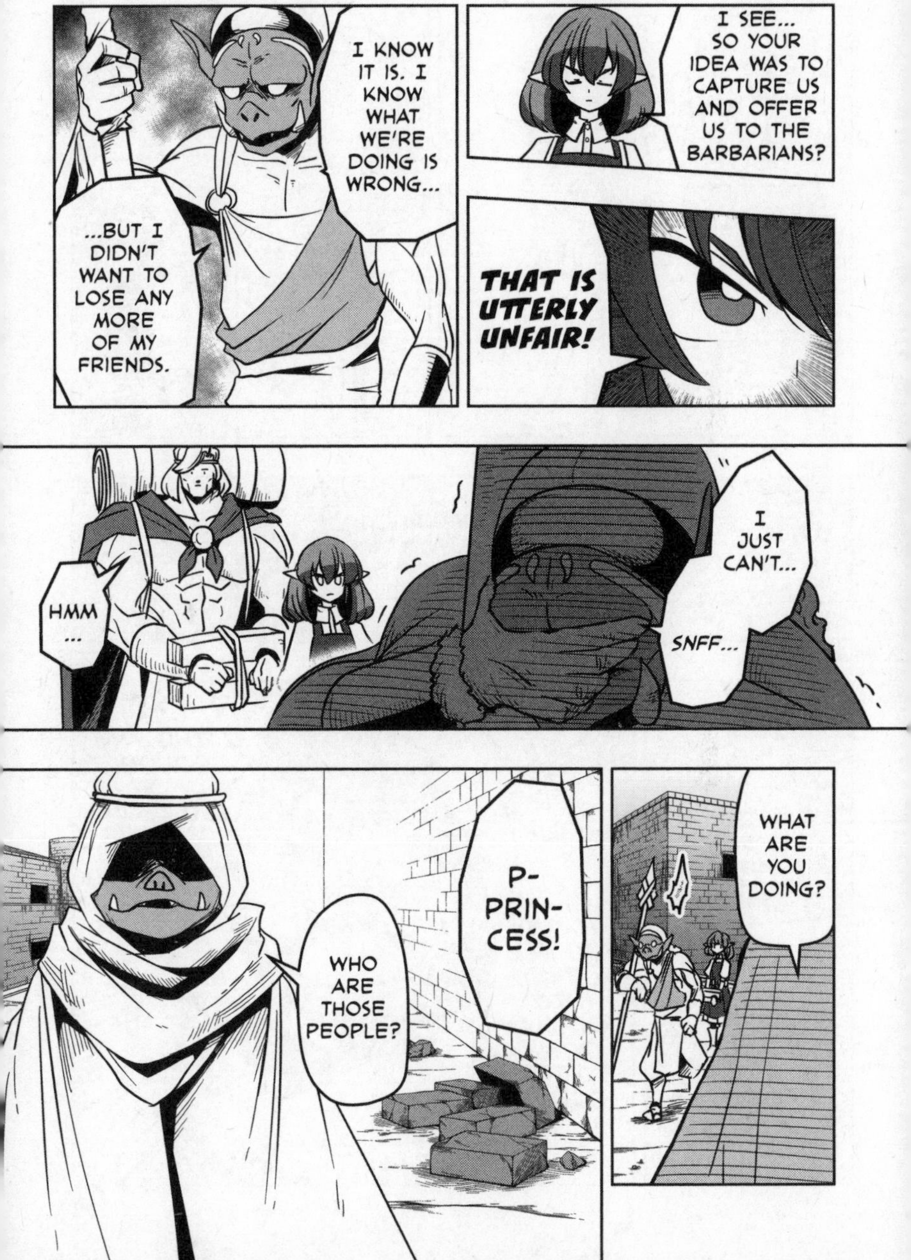
I SEE... SO YOUR IDEA WAS TO CAPTURE US AND OFFER US TO THE BARBARIANS?
THAT IS UTTERLY UNFAIR!
I KNOW IT IS. I KNOW WHAT WE'RE DOING IS WRONG...
...BUT I DIDN'T WANT TO LOSE ANY MORE OF MY FRIENDS.
I JUST CAN'T...
SNFF...
HMM...
WHAT ARE YOU DOING?
P-PRIN-CESS!
WHO ARE THOSE PEOPLE?

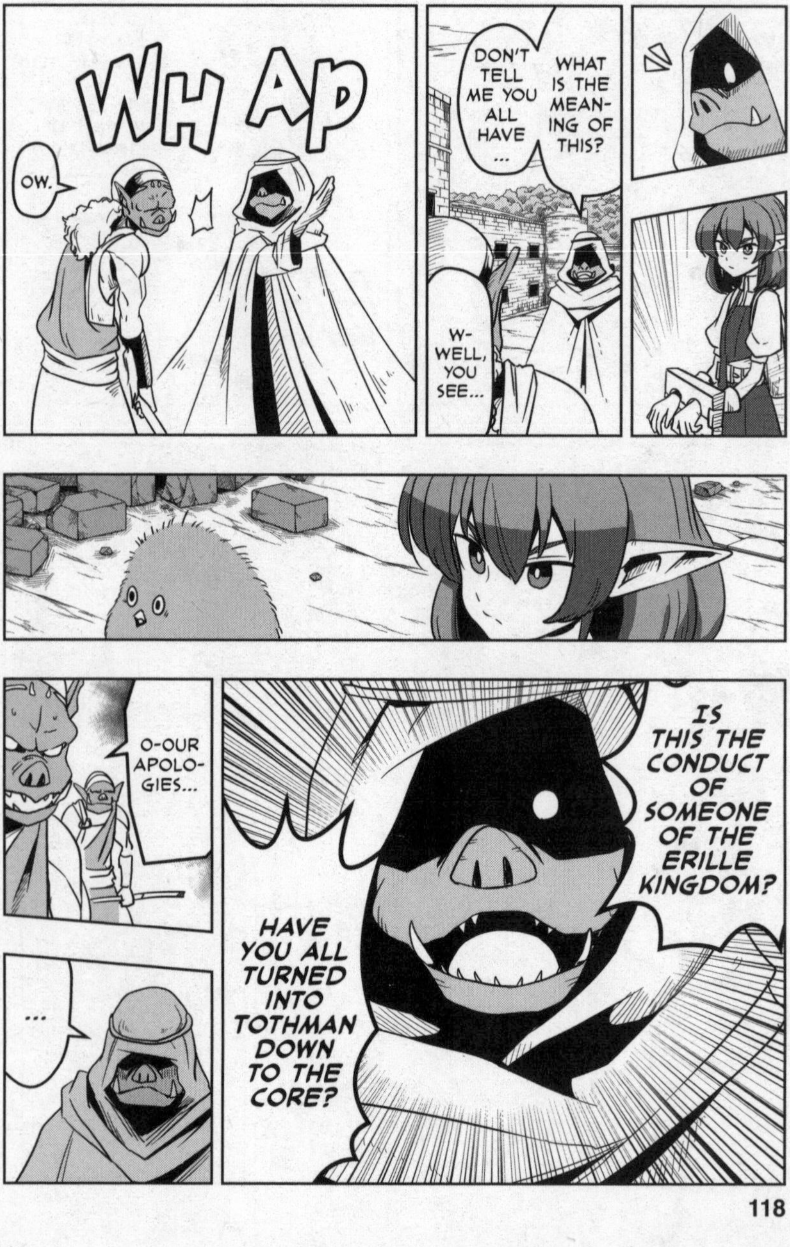
WHAT IS THE MEANING OF THIS?
DON'T TELL ME YOU ALL HAVE ...
W-WELL, YOU SEE...
WHAP
OW.
IS THIS THE CONDUCT OF SOMEONE OF THE ERILLE KINGDOM?
HAVE YOU ALL TURNED INTO TOTHMAN DOWN TO THE CORE?
O-OUR APOLOGIES...
...

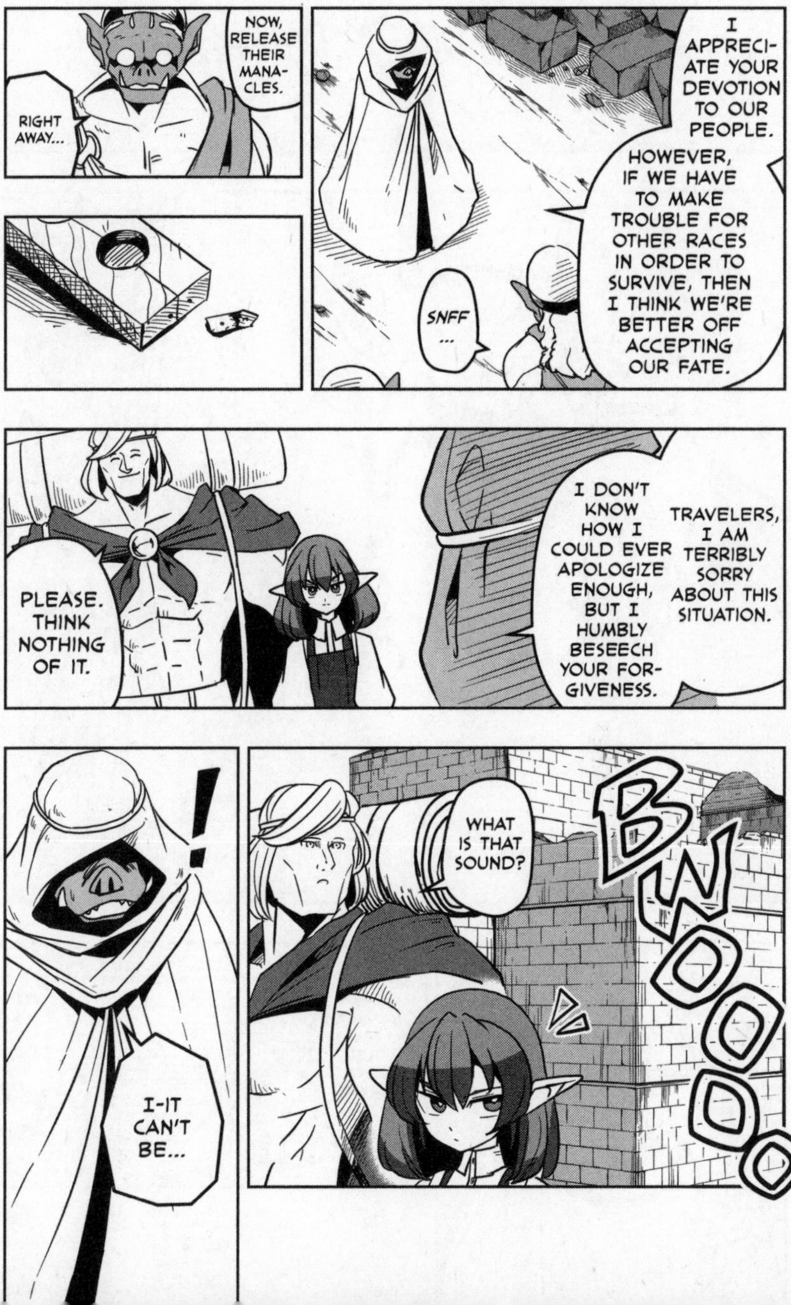
I APPRECIATE YOUR DEVOTION TO OUR PEOPLE.
HOWEVER, IF WE HAVE TO MAKE TROUBLE FOR OTHER RACES IN ORDER TO SURVIVE, THEN I THINK WE'RE BETTER OFF ACCEPTING OUR FATE.
SNFF...
NOW, RELEASE THEIR MANACLES.
RIGHT AWAY...
TRAVELERS, I AM TERRIBLY SORRY ABOUT THIS SITUATION.
I DON'T KNOW HOW I COULD EVER APOLOGIZE ENOUGH, BUT I HUMBLY BESEECH YOUR FORGIVENESS.
PLEASE. THINK NOTHING OF IT.
BWOOOO
WHAT IS THAT SOUND?
!
I-IT CAN'T BE...

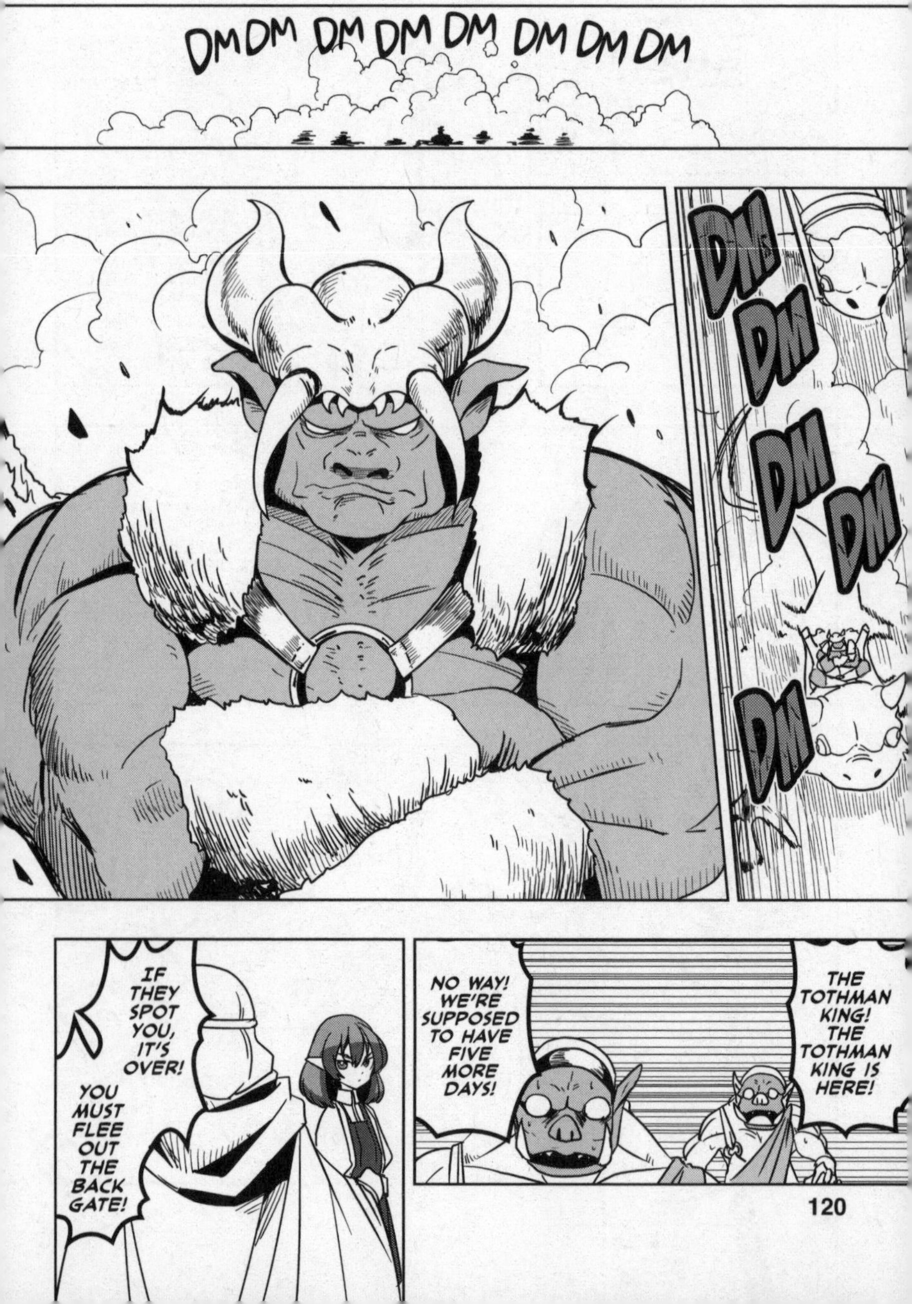
DMDM DM DM DM DM DM DM
DM DM DM DM DM
IF THEY SPOT YOU, IT'S OVER!
YOU MUST FLEE OUT THE BACK GATE!
THE TOTHMAN KING! THE TOTHMAN KING IS HERE!
NO WAY! WE'RE SUPPOSED TO HAVE FIVE MORE DAYS!

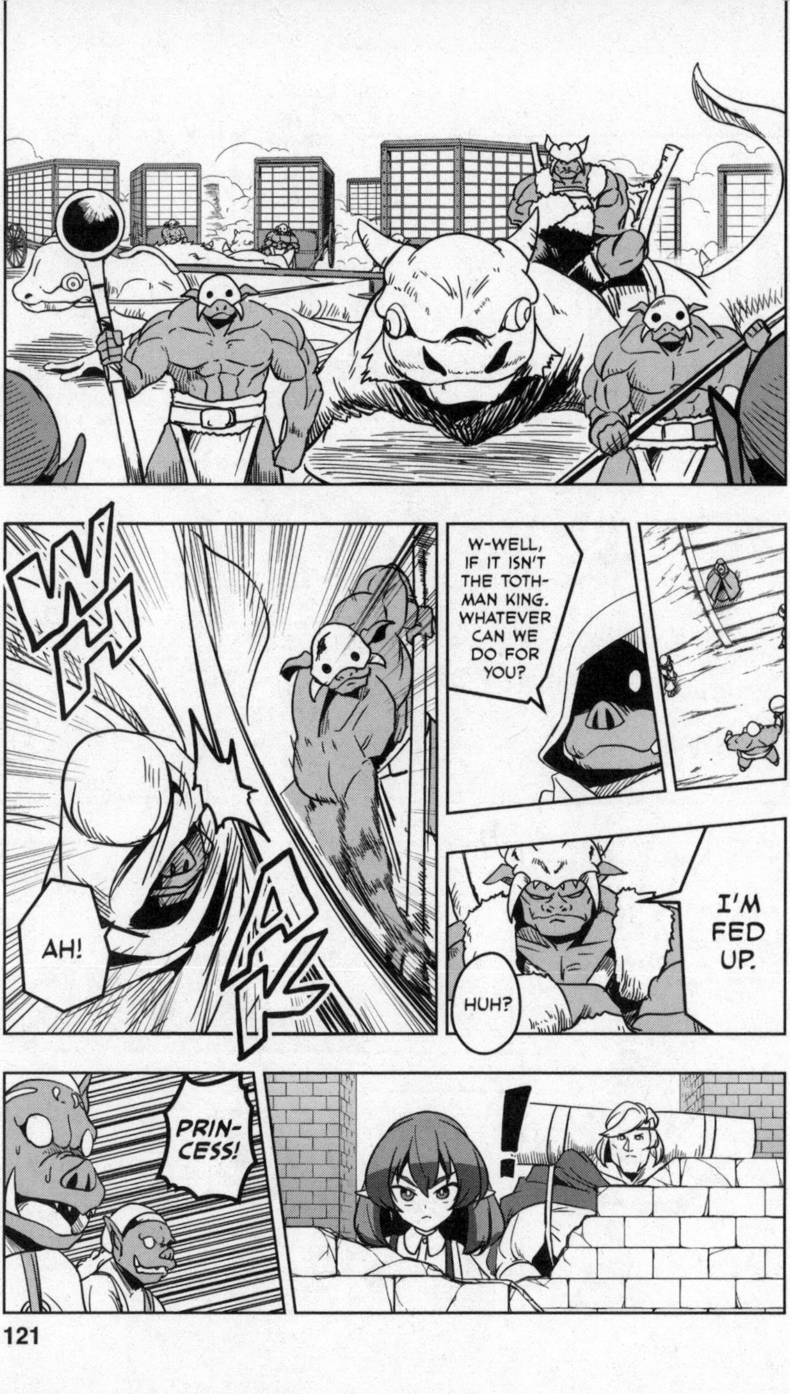
W-WELL, IF IT ISN'T THE TOTH-MAN KING. WHATEVER CAN WE DO FOR YOU?
I'M FED UP.
HUH?
WHAM
AH!
!
PRIN-CESS!

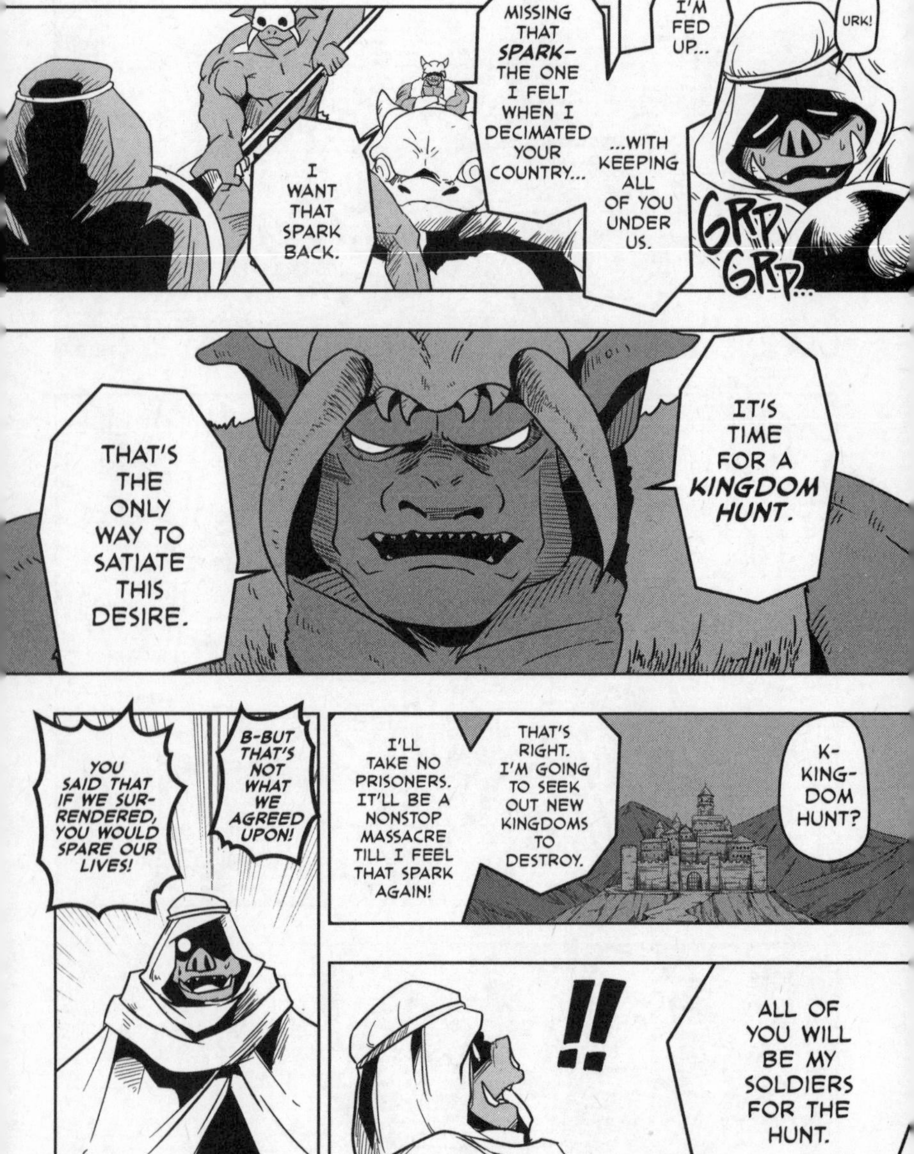
URK!
I'M FED UP...
...WITH KEEPING ALL OF YOU UNDER US.
GRP GRP...
I'M MISSING THAT SPARK—THE ONE I FELT WHEN I DECIMATED YOUR COUNTRY...
I WANT THAT SPARK BACK.
IT'S TIME FOR A KINGDOM HUNT.
THAT'S THE ONLY WAY TO SATIATE THIS DESIRE.
K-KINGDOM HUNT?
THAT'S RIGHT. I'M GOING TO SEEK OUT NEW KINGDOMS TO DESTROY.
I'LL TAKE NO PRISONERS. IT'LL BE A NONSTOP MASSACRE TILL I FEEL THAT SPARK AGAIN!
!!
ALL OF YOU WILL BE MY SOLDIERS FOR THE HUNT.
B-BUT THAT'S NOT WHAT WE AGREED UPON!
YOU SAID THAT IF WE SURRENDERED, YOU WOULD SPARE OUR LIVES!

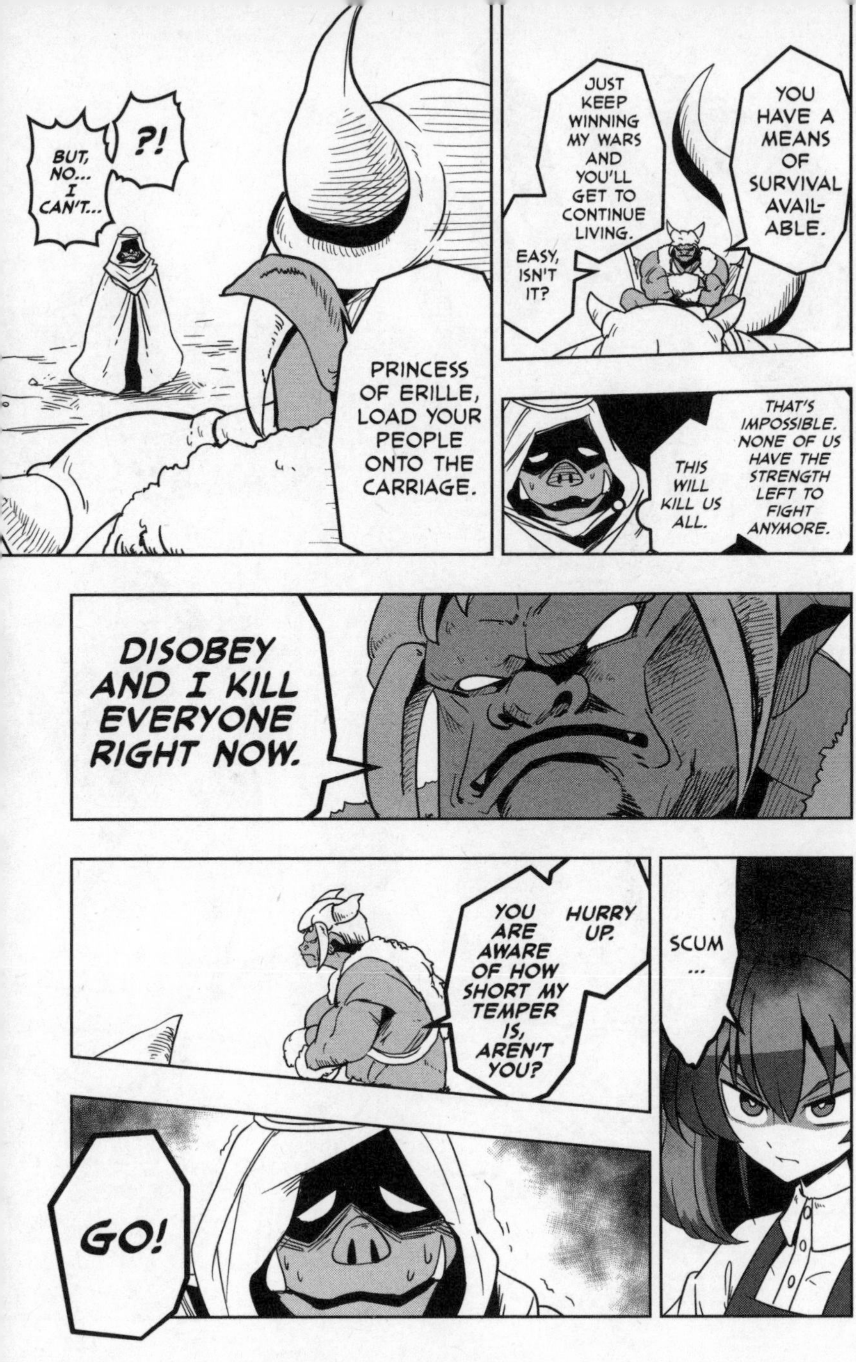
YOU HAVE A MEANS OF SURVIVAL AVAILABLE.
JUST KEEP WINNING MY WARS AND YOU'LL GET TO CONTINUE LIVING.
EASY, ISN'T IT?
THAT'S IMPOSSIBLE. NONE OF US HAVE THE STRENGTH LEFT TO FIGHT ANYMORE.
THIS WILL KILL US ALL.
PRINCESS OF ERILLE, LOAD YOUR PEOPLE ONTO THE CARRIAGE.
?!
BUT, NO... I CAN'T...
DISOBEY AND I KILL EVERYONE RIGHT NOW.
SCUM ...
HURRY UP.
YOU ARE AWARE OF HOW SHORT MY TEMPER IS, AREN'T YOU?
GO!

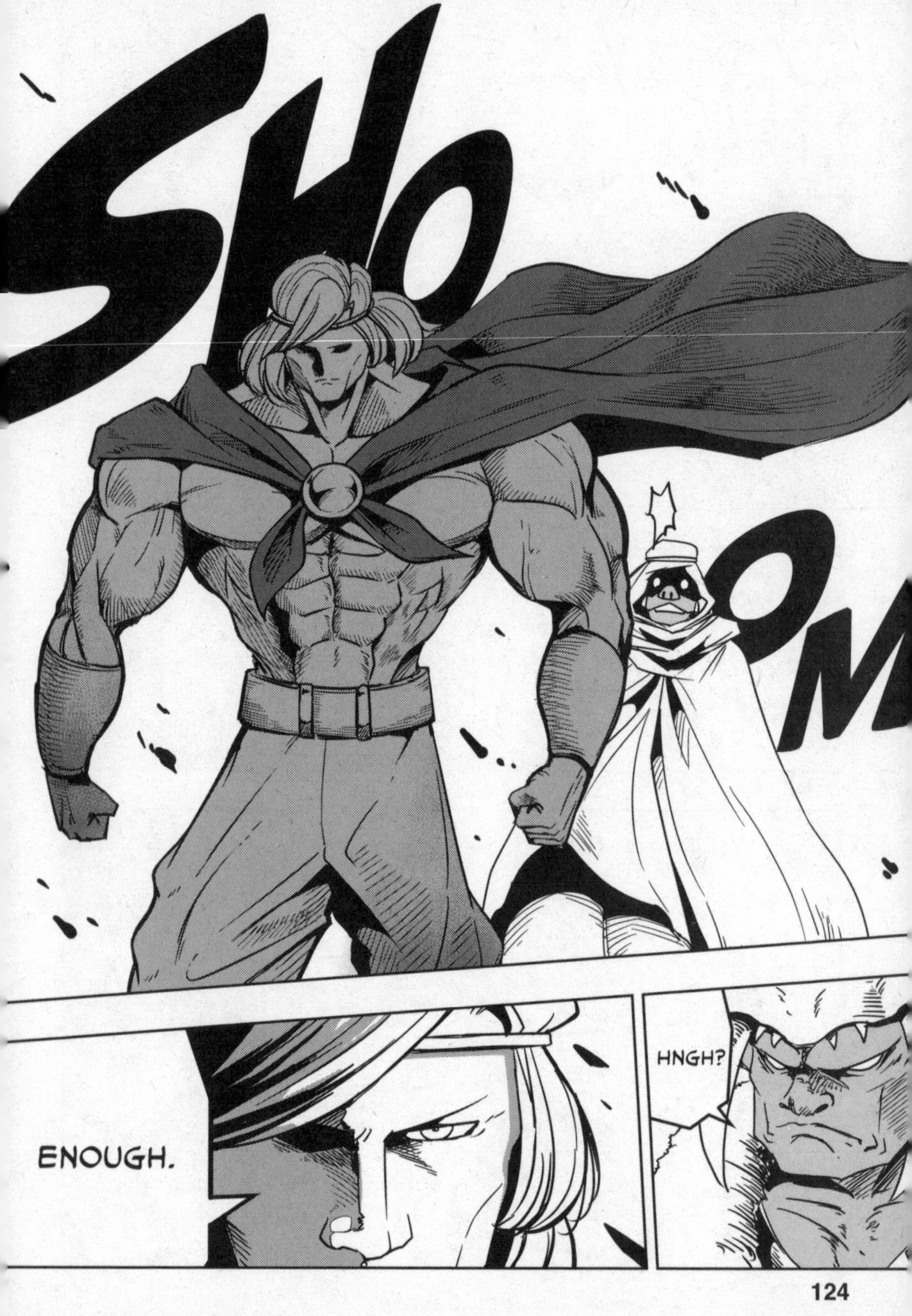
SHOOM
HNGH?
ENOUGH.

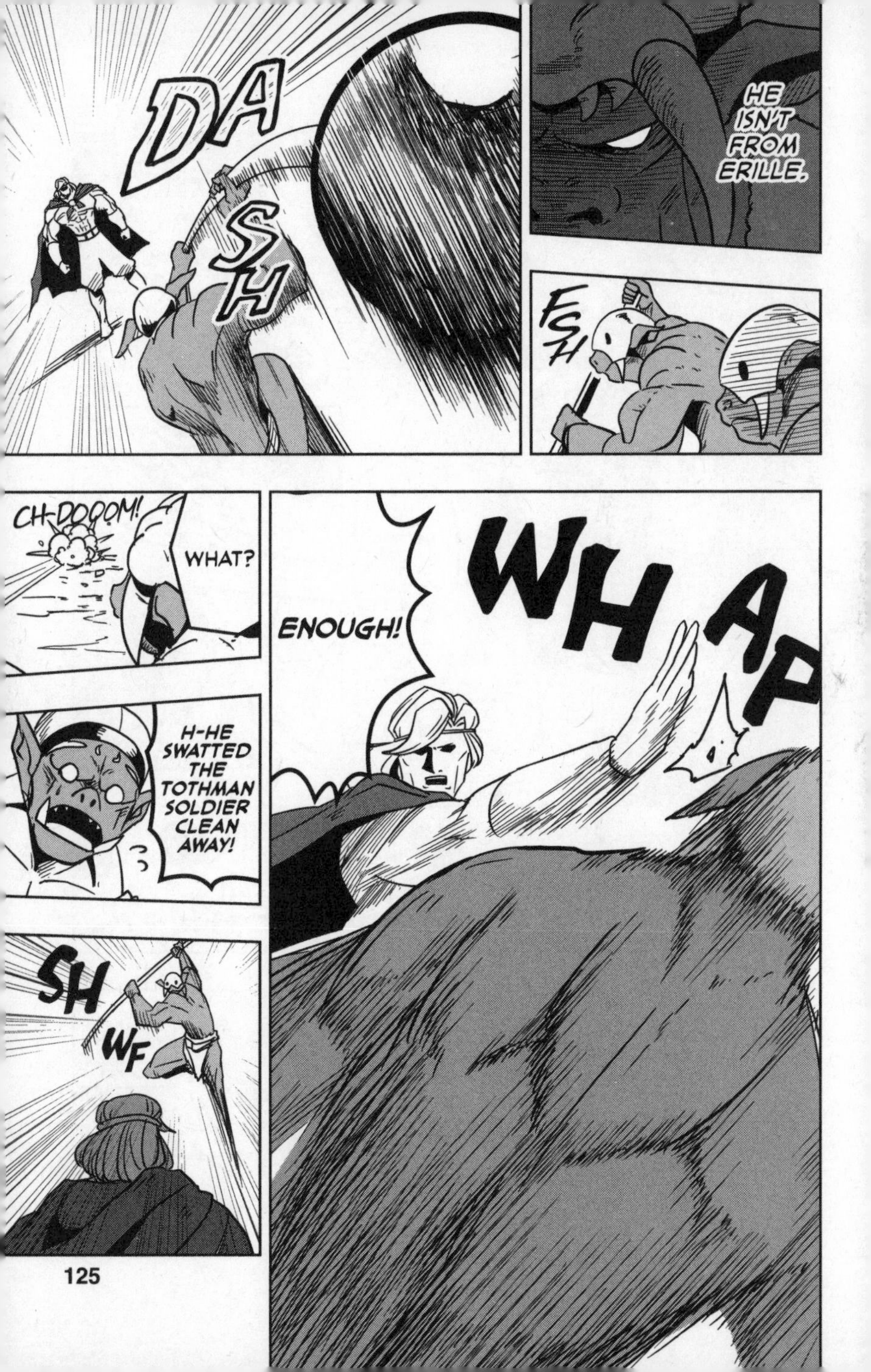
HE ISN'T FROM ERILLE.
FSH
DASH
ENOUGH!
WHAP
CH-DOOOM!
WHAT?
H-HE SWATTED THE TOTHMAN SOLDIER CLEAN AWAY!
SHWF

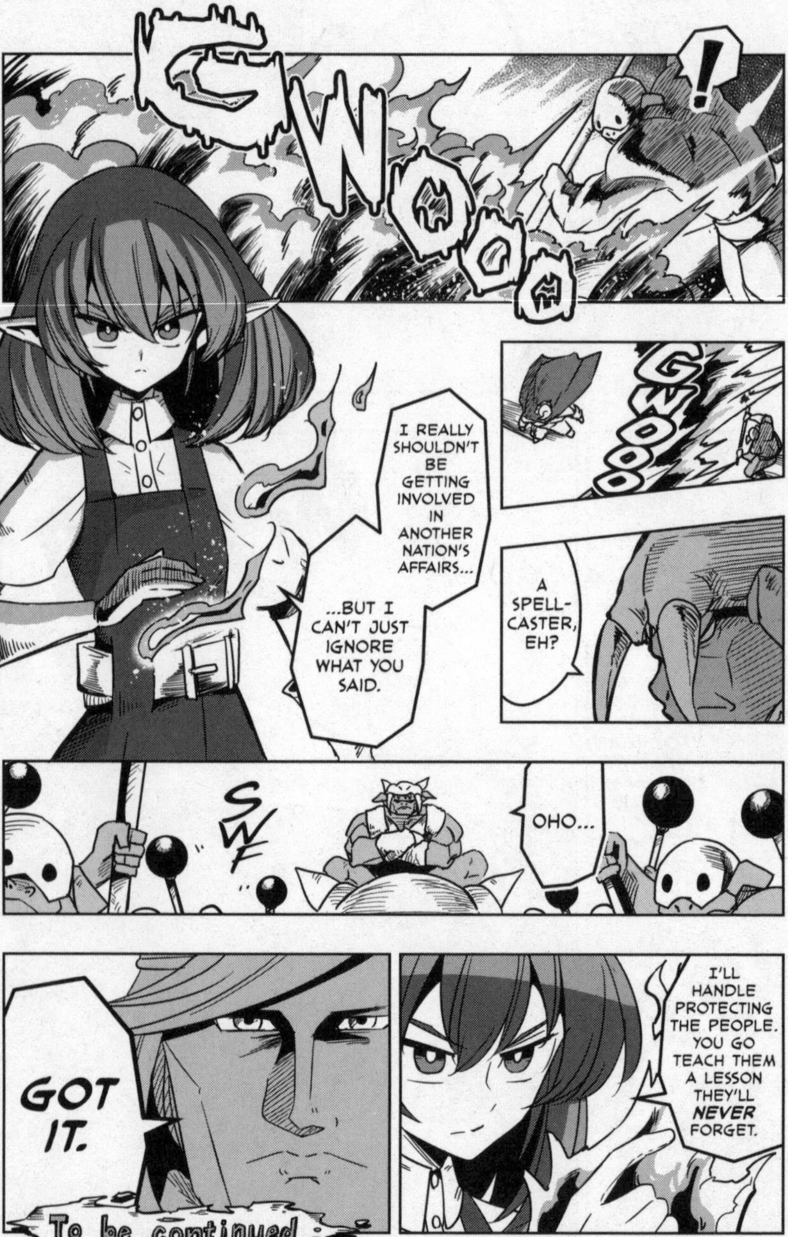
GWOOO
!
GWOOOO
A SPELL-CASTER, EH?
I REALLY SHOULDN'T BE GETTING INVOLVED IN ANOTHER NATION'S AFFAIRS...
...BUT I CAN'T JUST IGNORE WHAT YOU SAID.
OHO...
SWF
I'LL HANDLE PROTECTING THE PEOPLE. YOU GO TEACH THEM A LESSON THEY'LL NEVER FORGET.
GOT IT.
To be continued

Chapter 27: Power of the Tothman King

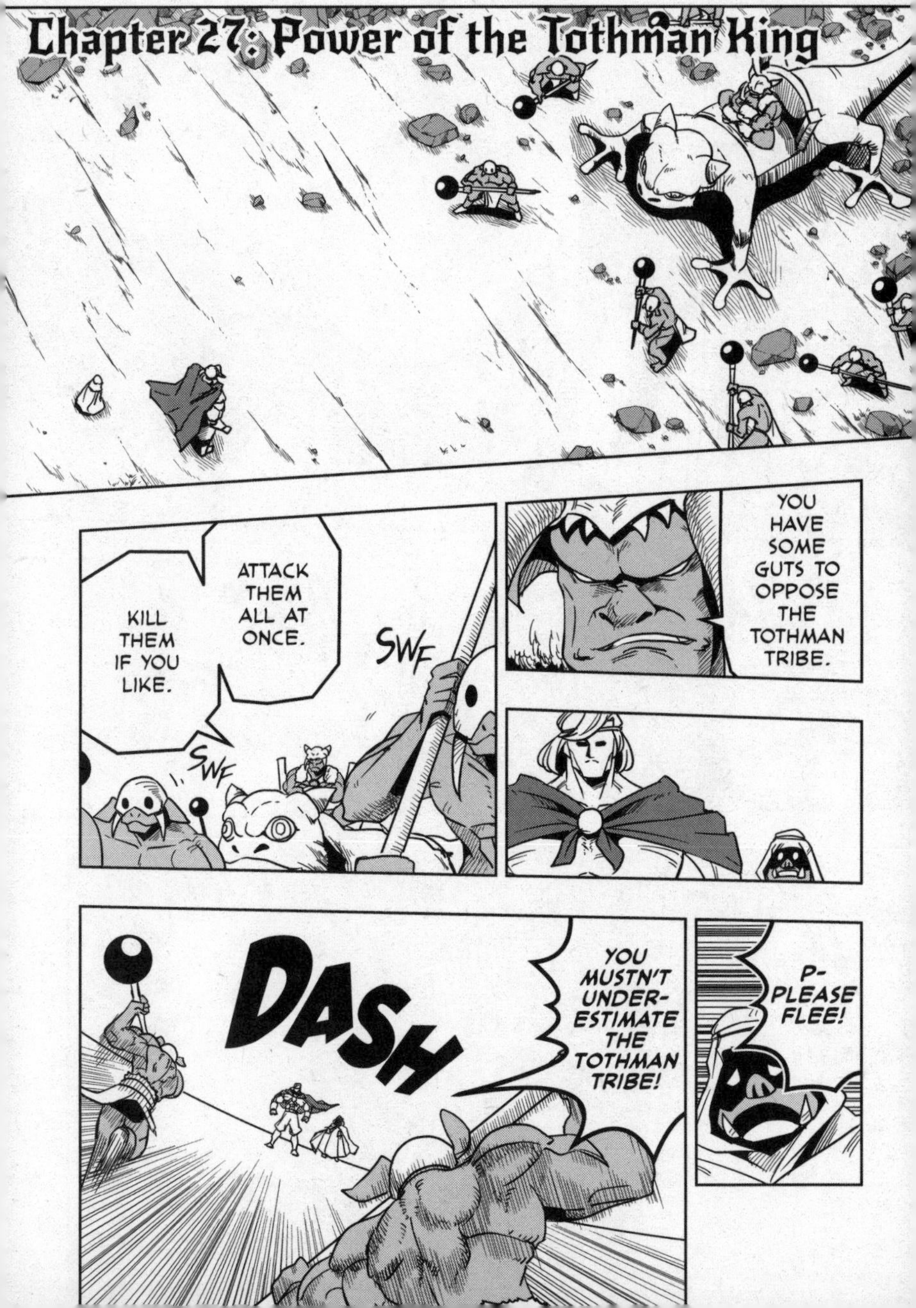
YOU HAVE SOME GUTS TO OPPOSE THE TOTHMAN TRIBE.
ATTACK THEM ALL AT ONCE.
KILL THEM IF YOU LIKE.
SWF
SWF
P-PLEASE FLEE!
YOU MUSTN'T UNDER-ESTIMATE THE TOTHMAN TRIBE!
DASH

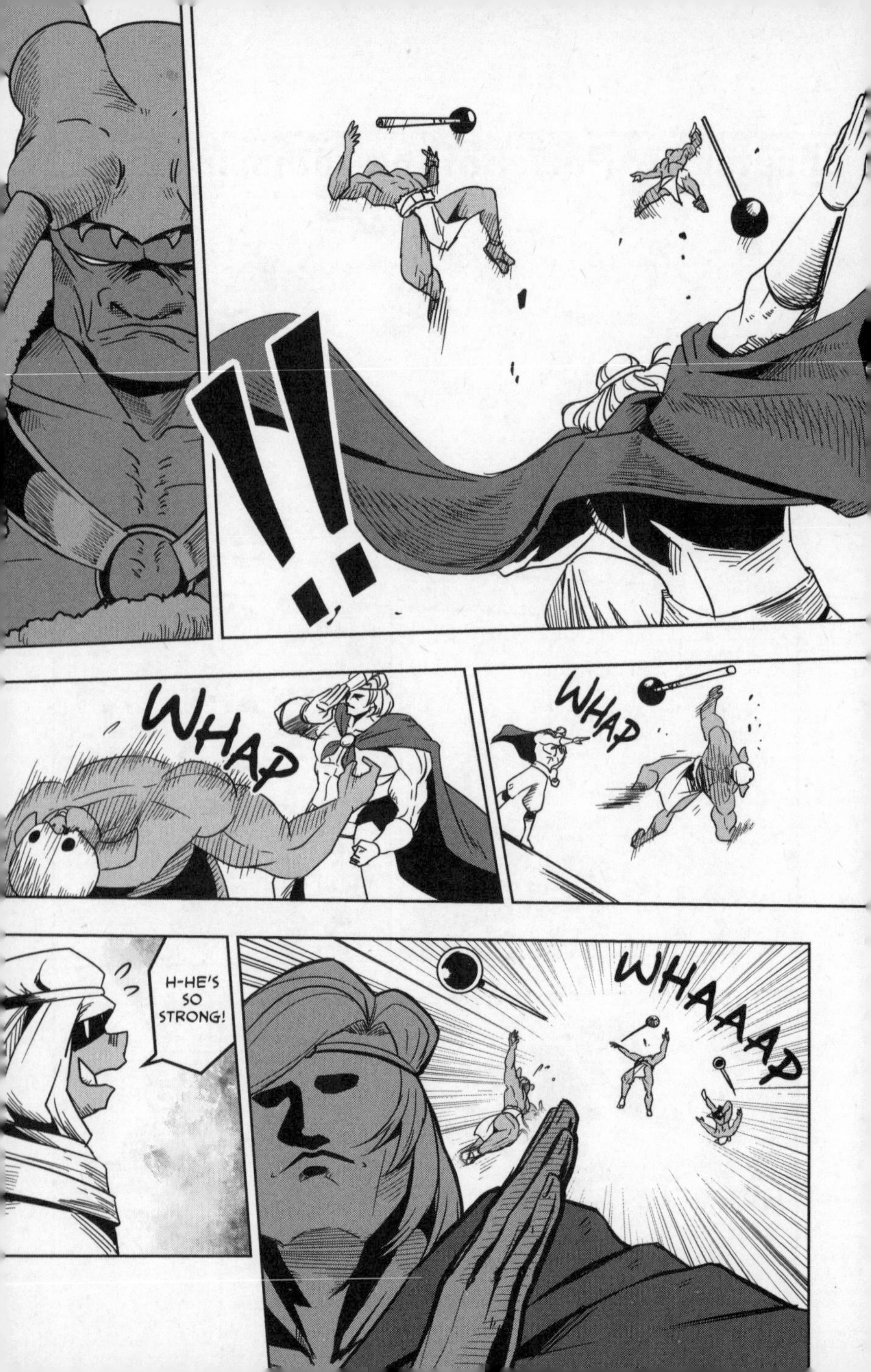
!!
WHAP
WHAP
WHAAAAP
H-HE'S SO STRONG!

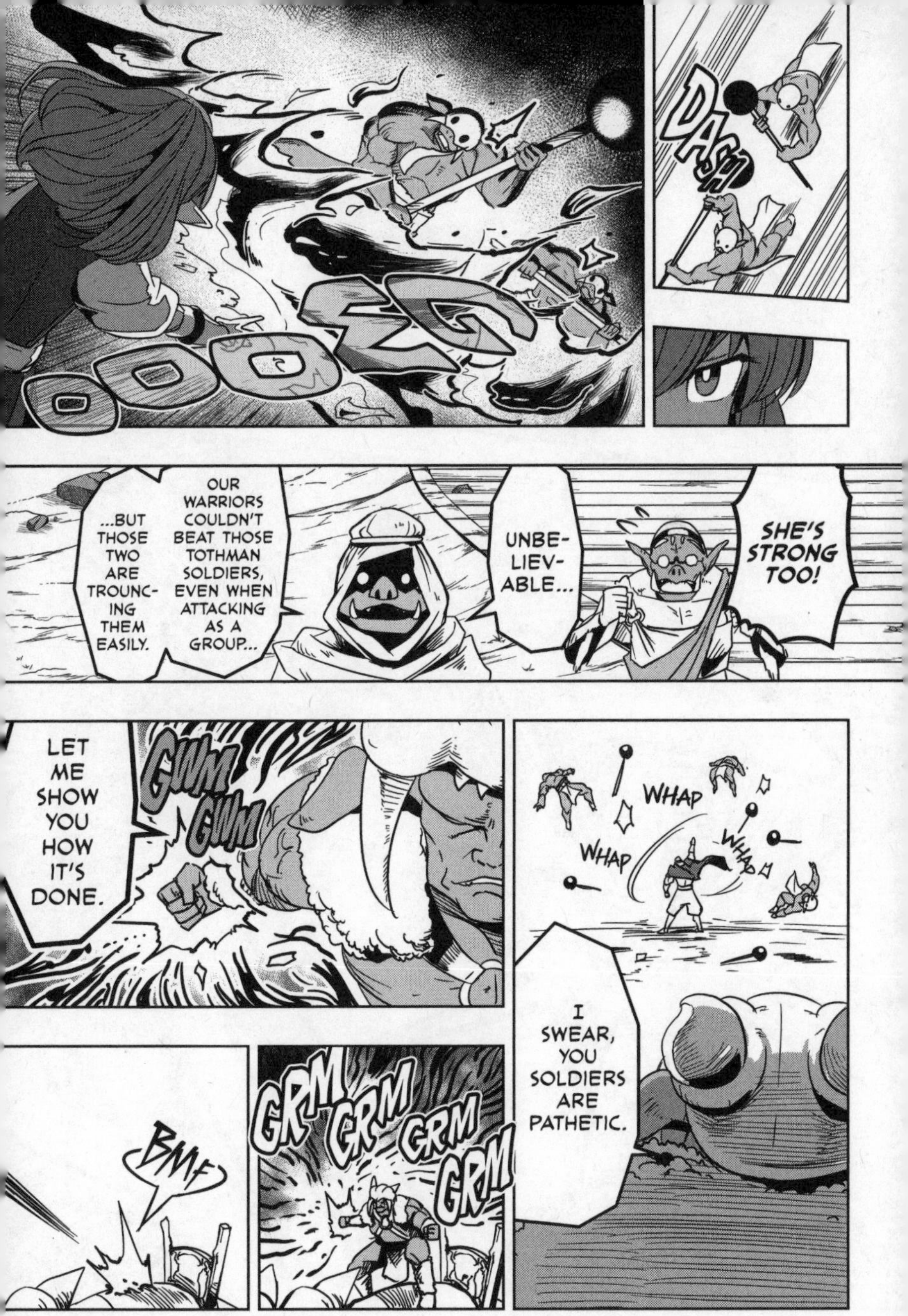
DASH
SHE'S STRONG TOO!
UNBE-LIEV-ABLE...
OUR WARRIORS COULDN'T BEAT THOSE TOTHMAN SOLDIERS, EVEN WHEN ATTACKING AS A GROUP...
...BUT THOSE TWO ARE TROUNC-ING THEM EASILY.
WHAP
WHAP
WHAP
I SWEAR, YOU SOLDIERS ARE PATHETIC.
GWM GWM
LET ME SHOW YOU HOW IT'S DONE.
GRM GRM GRM GRM
BMF

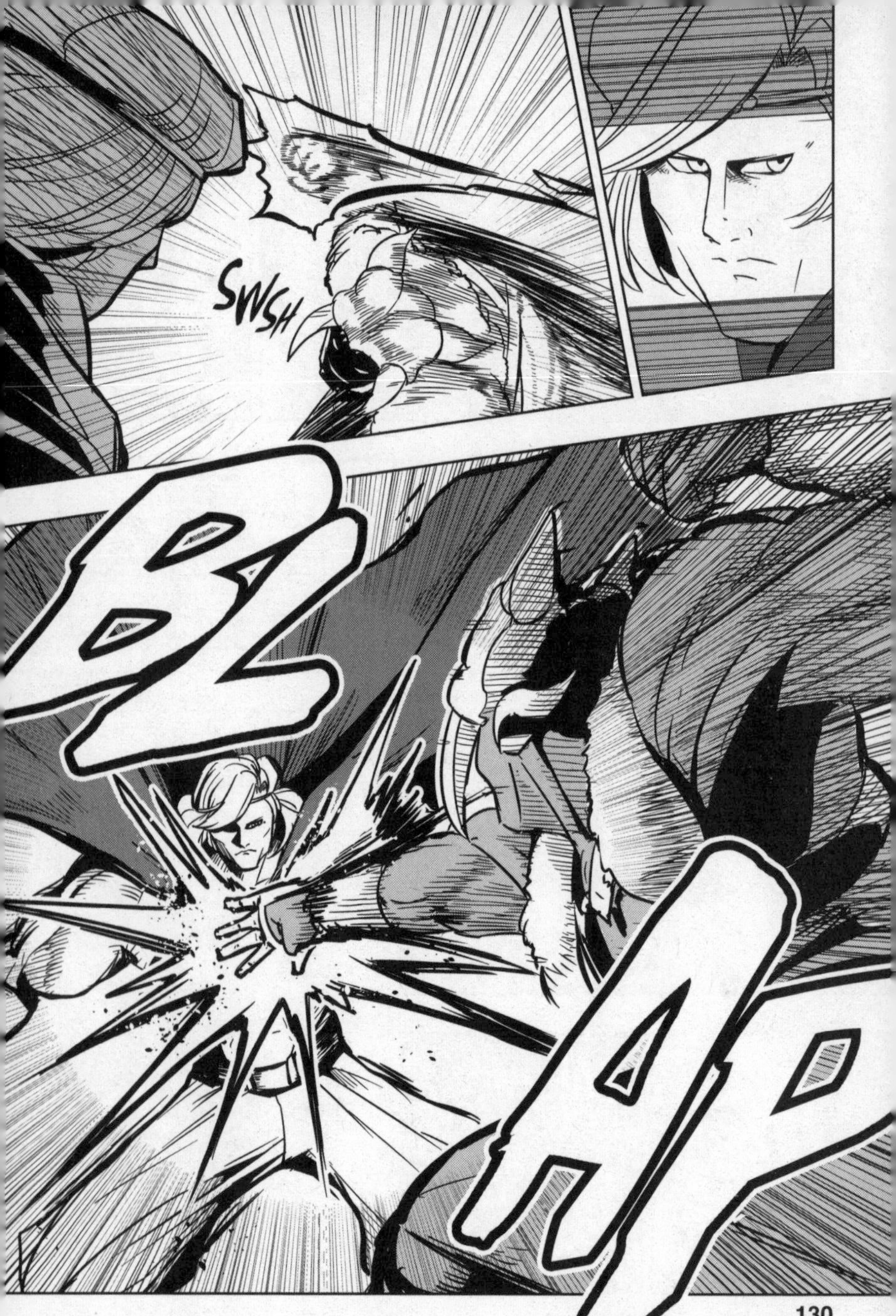
SWISH
BLAP

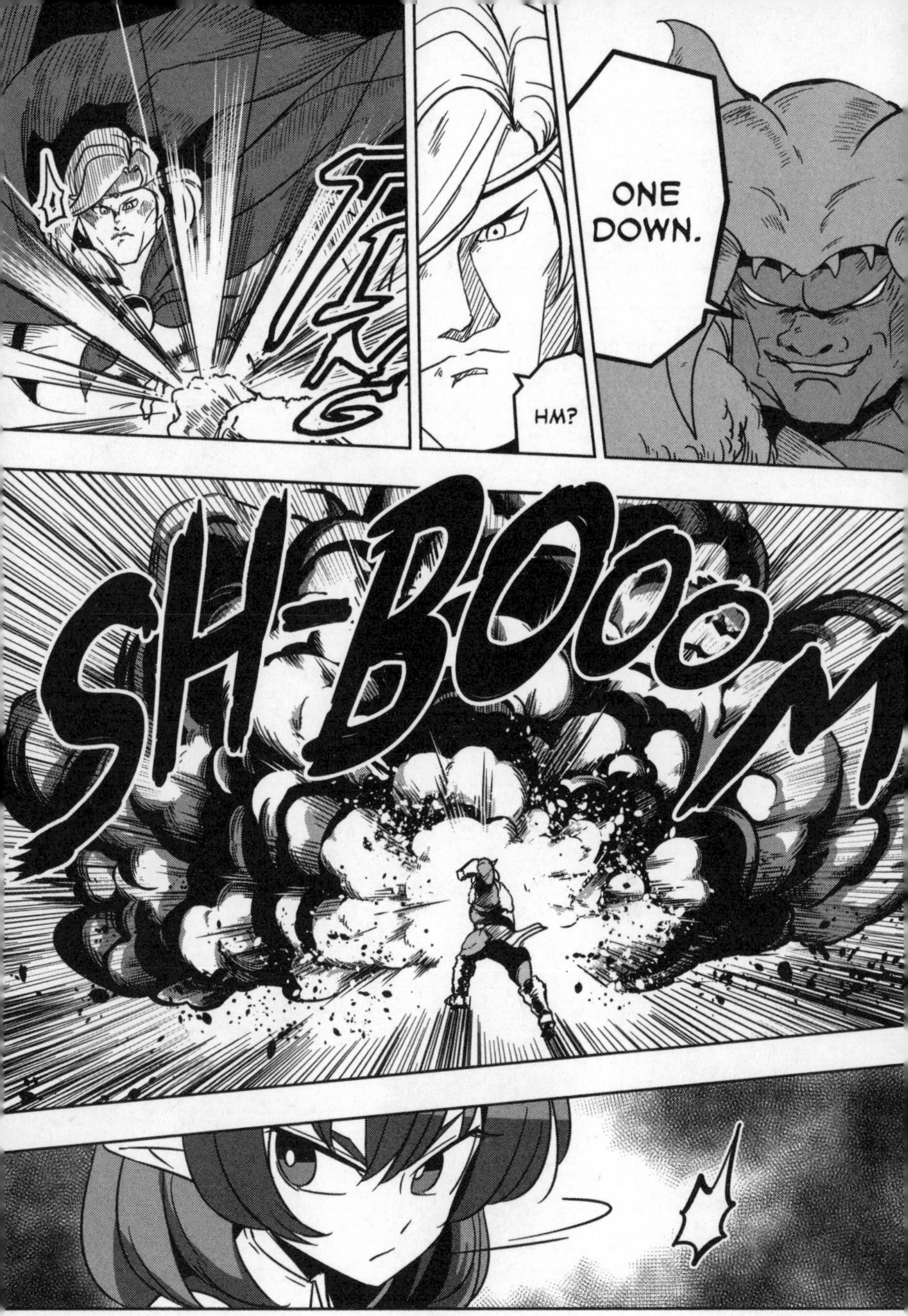
ONE DOWN.
HM?
SH-BOOOM

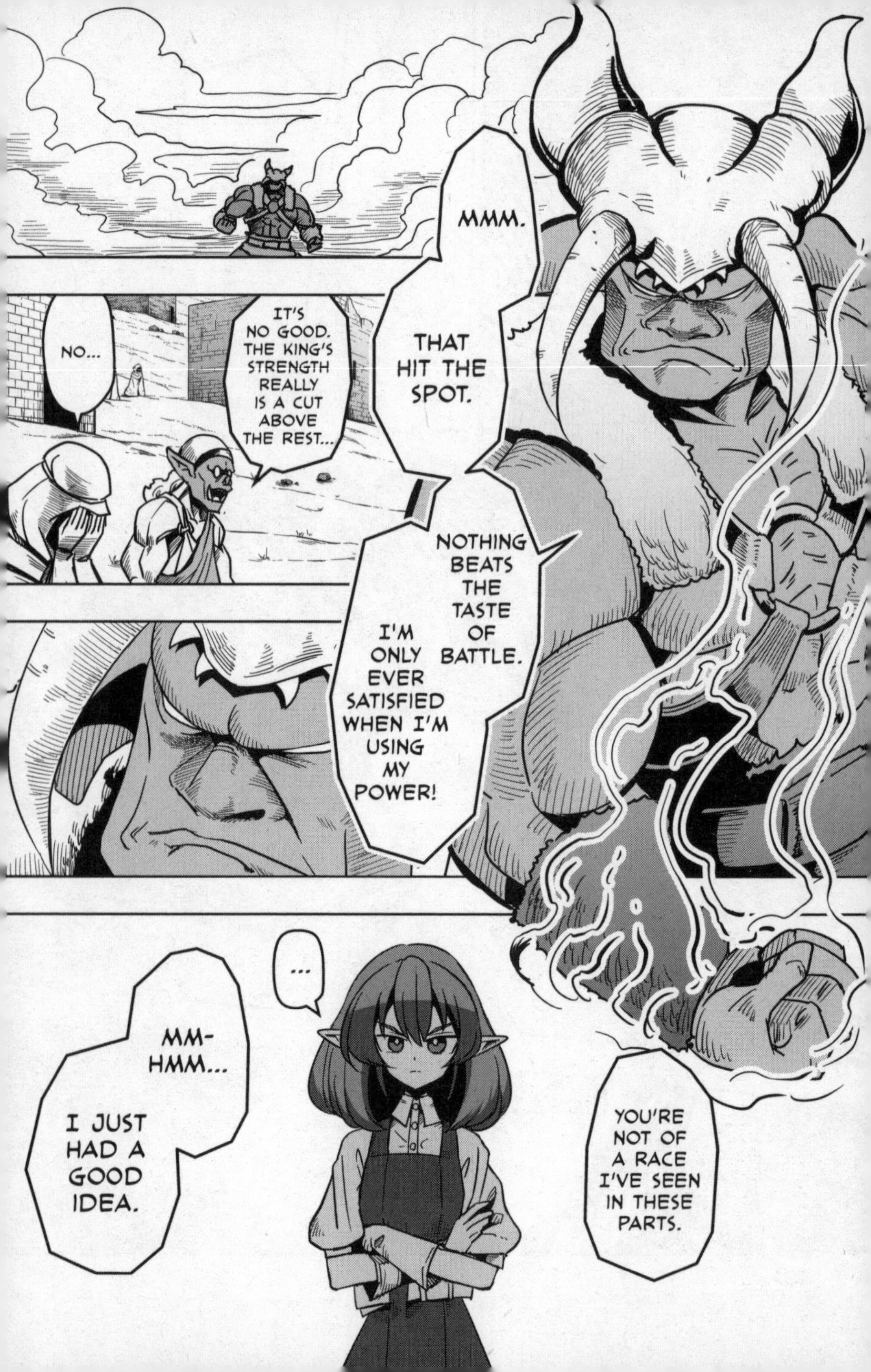
MMM.
THAT HIT THE SPOT.
NOTHING BEATS THE TASTE OF BATTLE.
IT'S NO GOOD. THE KING'S STRENGTH REALLY IS A CUT ABOVE THE REST...
NO...
I'M ONLY EVER SATISFIED WHEN I'M USING MY POWER!
YOU'RE NOT OF A RACE I'VE SEEN IN THESE PARTS.
...
MM-HMM...
I JUST HAD A GOOD IDEA.

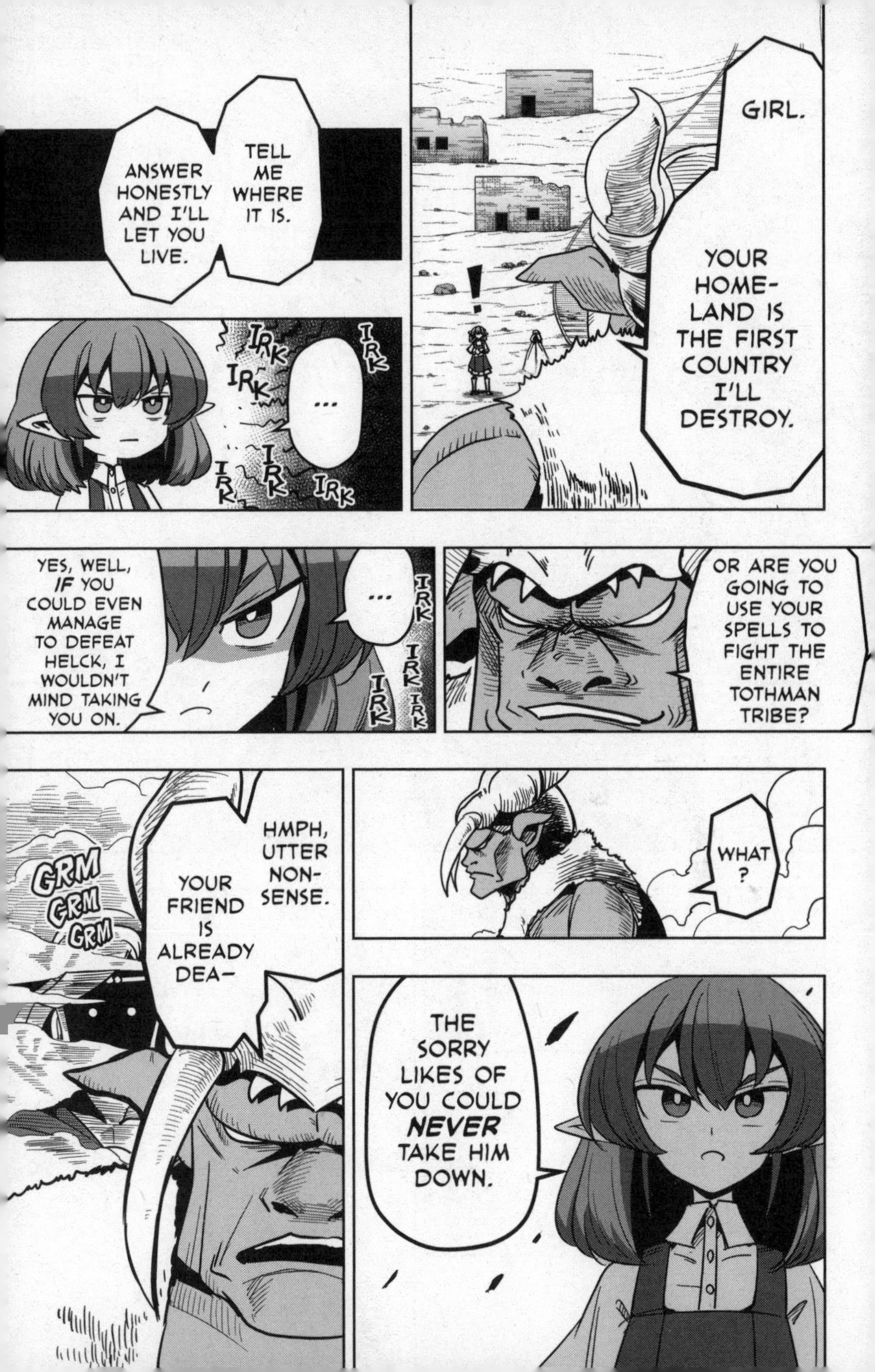
GIRL.
YOUR HOMELAND IS THE FIRST COUNTRY I'LL DESTROY.
TELL ME WHERE IT IS.
ANSWER HONESTLY AND I'LL LET YOU LIVE.
IRK
IRK
IRK
...
IRK
IRK
IRK
OR ARE YOU GOING TO USE YOUR SPELLS TO FIGHT THE ENTIRE TOTHMAN TRIBE?
IRK
IRK
IRK
IRK
...
YES, WELL, *IF* YOU COULD EVEN MANAGE TO DEFEAT HELCK, I WOULDN'T MIND TAKING YOU ON.
WHAT?
THE SORRY LIKES OF YOU COULD ***NEVER*** TAKE HIM DOWN.
HMPH, UTTER NONSENSE.
YOUR FRIEND IS ALREADY DEA—
GRM
GRM
GRM

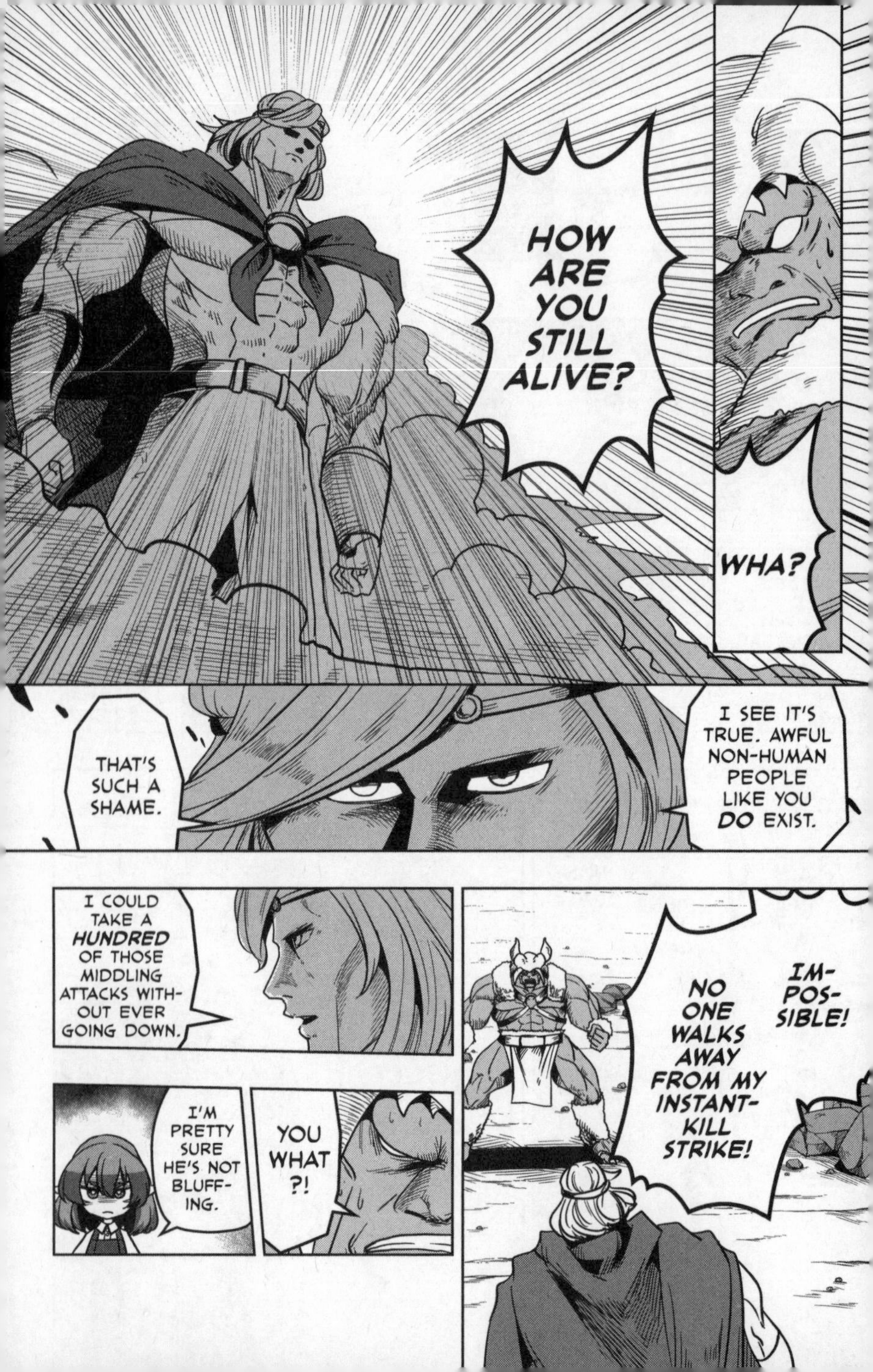
WHA?
HOW ARE YOU STILL ALIVE?
I SEE IT'S TRUE. AWFUL NON-HUMAN PEOPLE LIKE YOU *DO* EXIST.
THAT'S SUCH A SHAME.
IM-POS-SIBLE!
NO ONE WALKS AWAY FROM MY INSTANT-KILL STRIKE!
I COULD TAKE A ***HUNDRED*** OF THOSE MIDDLING ATTACKS WITH-OUT EVER GOING DOWN.
YOU WHAT?!
I'M PRETTY SURE HE'S NOT BLUFF-ING.

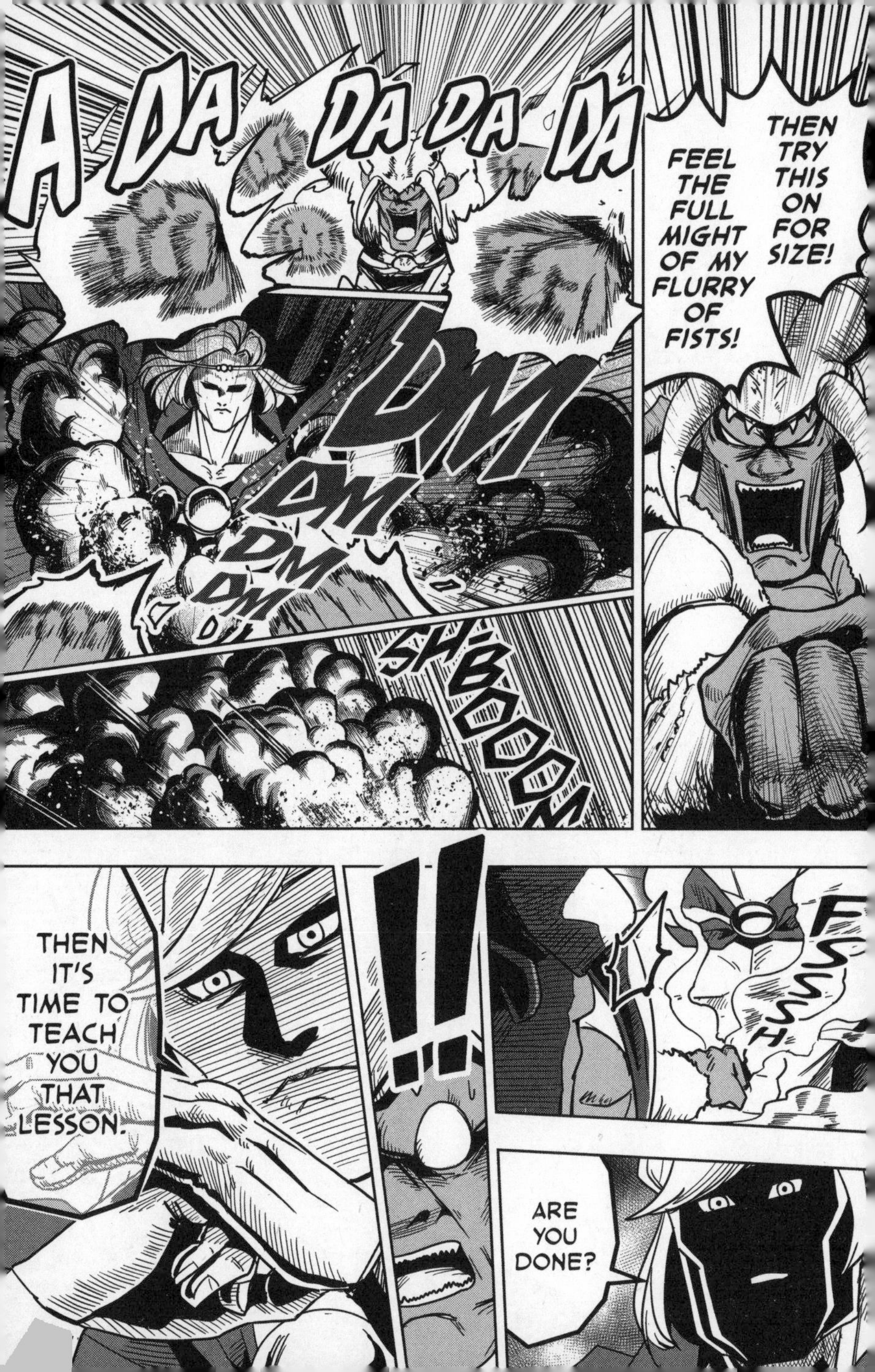
THEN TRY THIS ON FOR SIZE!
FEEL THE FULL MIGHT OF MY FLURRY OF FISTS!
A DA DA DA DA DA
DM DM DM DM D
SHBOOOM
FSSSH
ARE YOU DONE?
!!
THEN IT'S TIME TO TEACH YOU THAT LESSON.

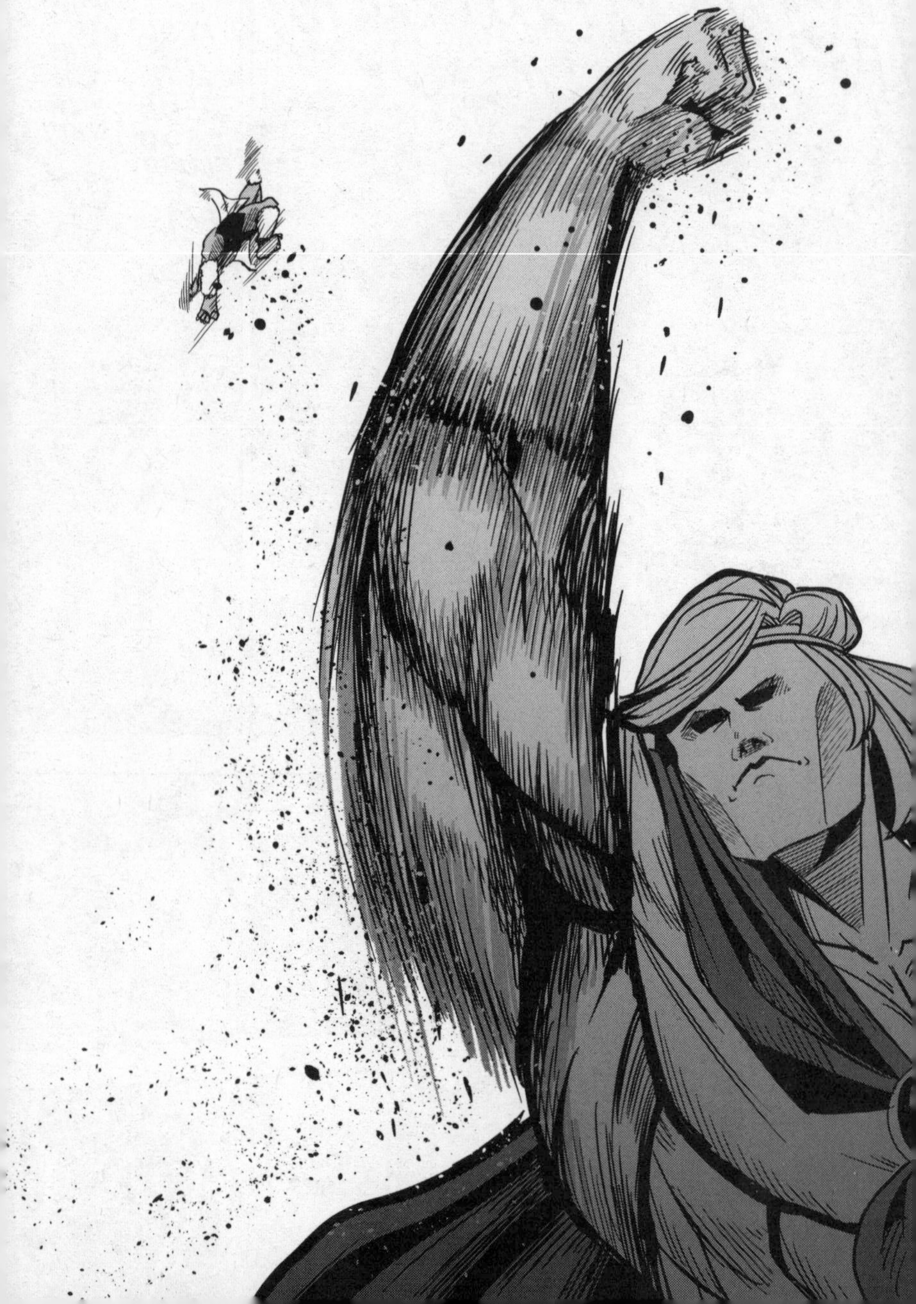

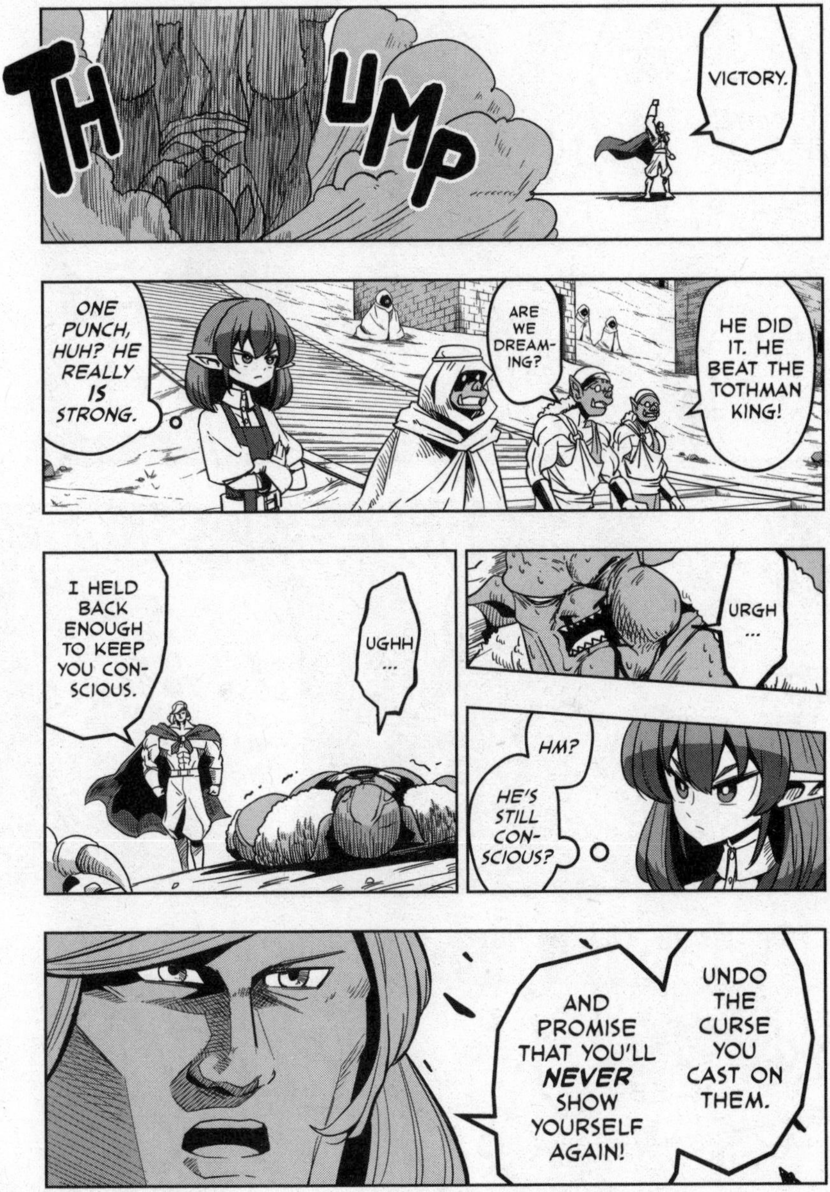

VICTORY.
THUMP
HE DID IT. HE BEAT THE TOTHMAN KING!
ARE WE DREAMING?
ONE PUNCH, HUH? HE REALLY *IS* STRONG.
URGH ...
HM?
HE'S STILL CONSCIOUS?
UGHH ...
I HELD BACK ENOUGH TO KEEP YOU CONSCIOUS.
UNDO THE CURSE YOU CAST ON THEM.
AND PROMISE THAT YOU'LL ***NEVER*** SHOW YOURSELF AGAIN!

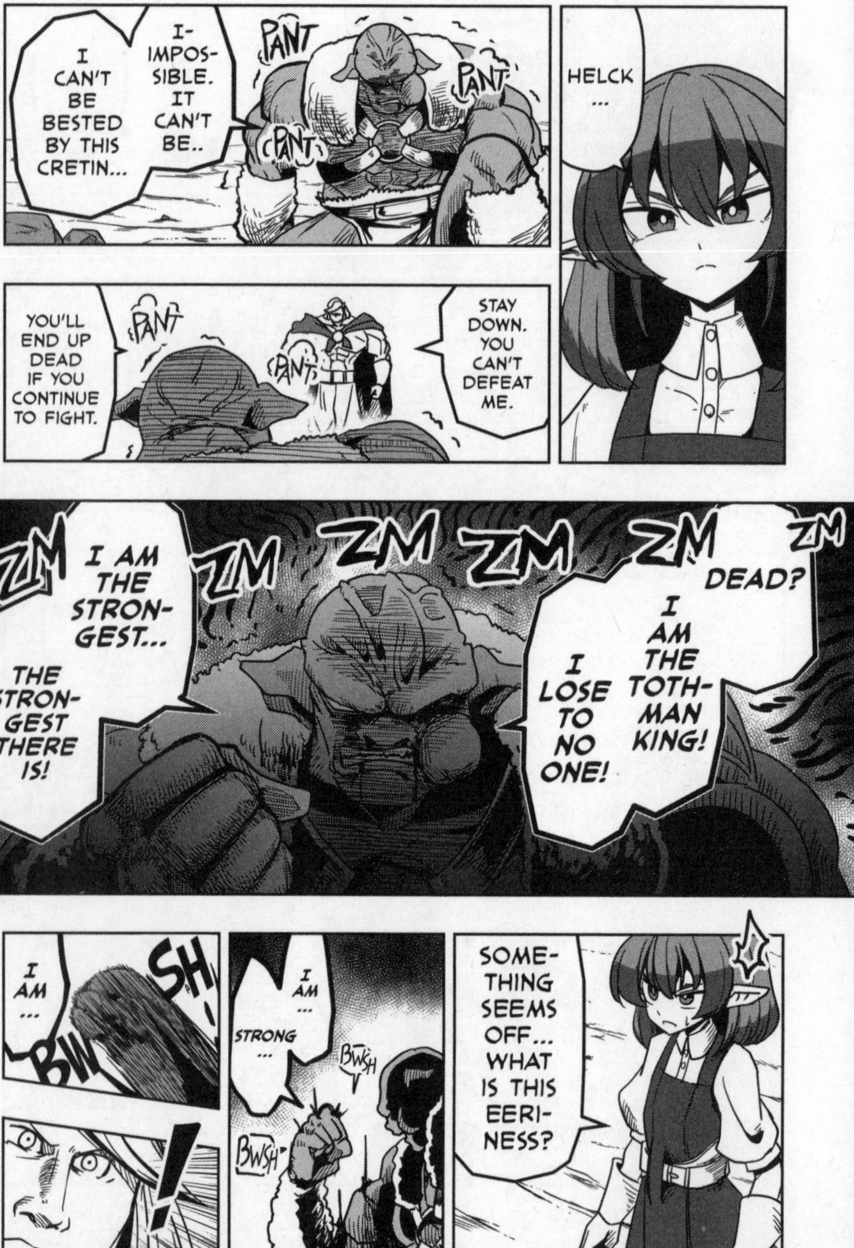
HELCK...
PANT
PANT
I-IMPOSSIBLE. IT CAN'T BE..
PANT
I CAN'T BE BESTED BY THIS CRETIN...
STAY DOWN. YOU CAN'T DEFEAT ME.
PANT
PANT
YOU'LL END UP DEAD IF YOU CONTINUE TO FIGHT.
ZM ZM ZM ZM ZM ZM
DEAD?
I AM THE TOTHMAN KING!
I LOSE TO NO ONE!
I AM THE STRONGEST...
THE STRONGEST THERE IS!
SOMETHING SEEMS OFF... WHAT IS THIS EERINESS?
I AM...
STRONG...
BWSH
BWSH
I AM...
SH
BW
!

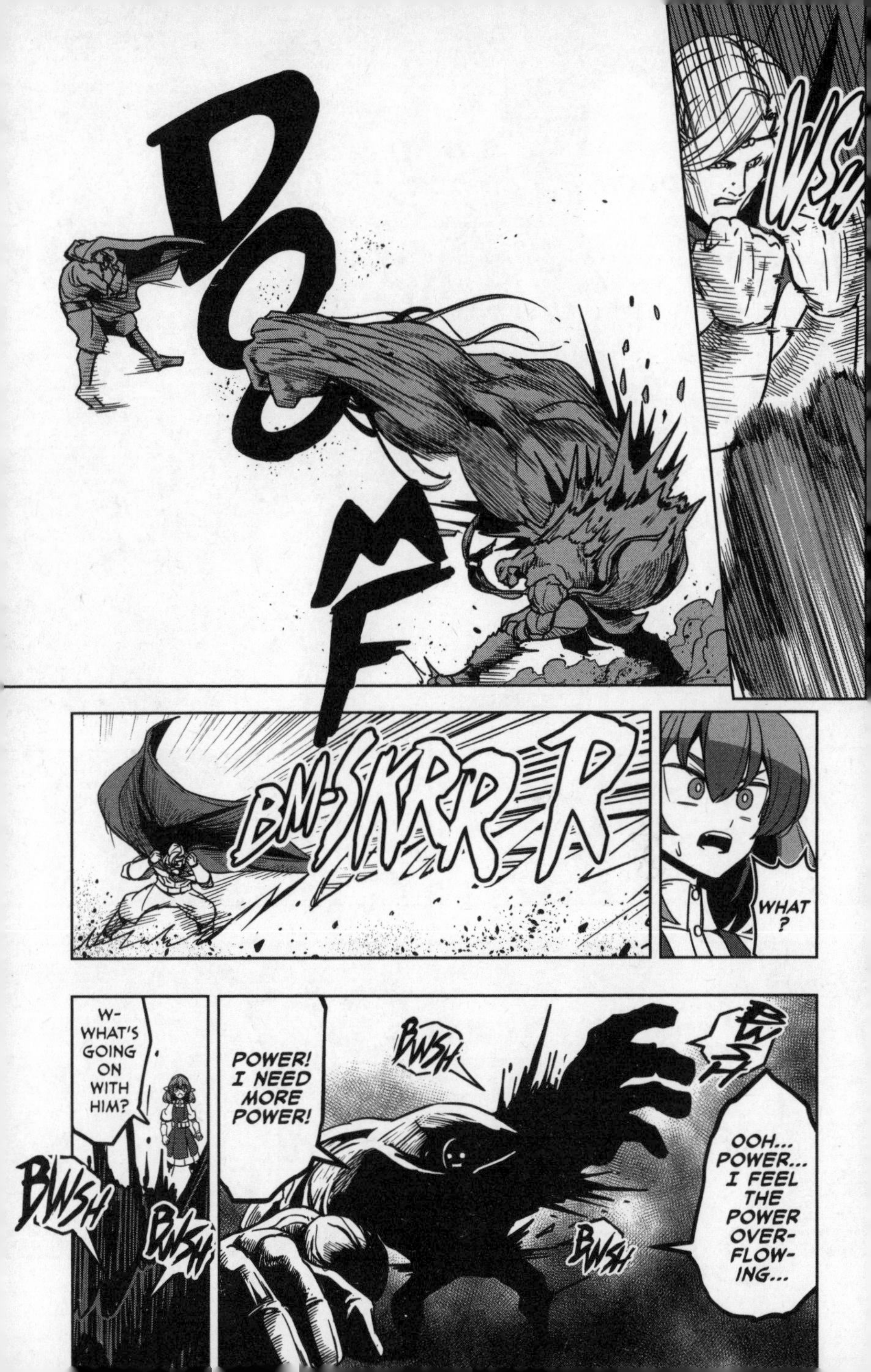
VSH
DOOMF
WHAT?
BM-SKRR-R
BWSH
OOH... POWER... I FEEL THE POWER OVER-FLOWING...
BWSH
POWER! I NEED MORE POWER!
BWSH
W-WHAT'S GOING ON WITH HIM?
BWSH
BWSH

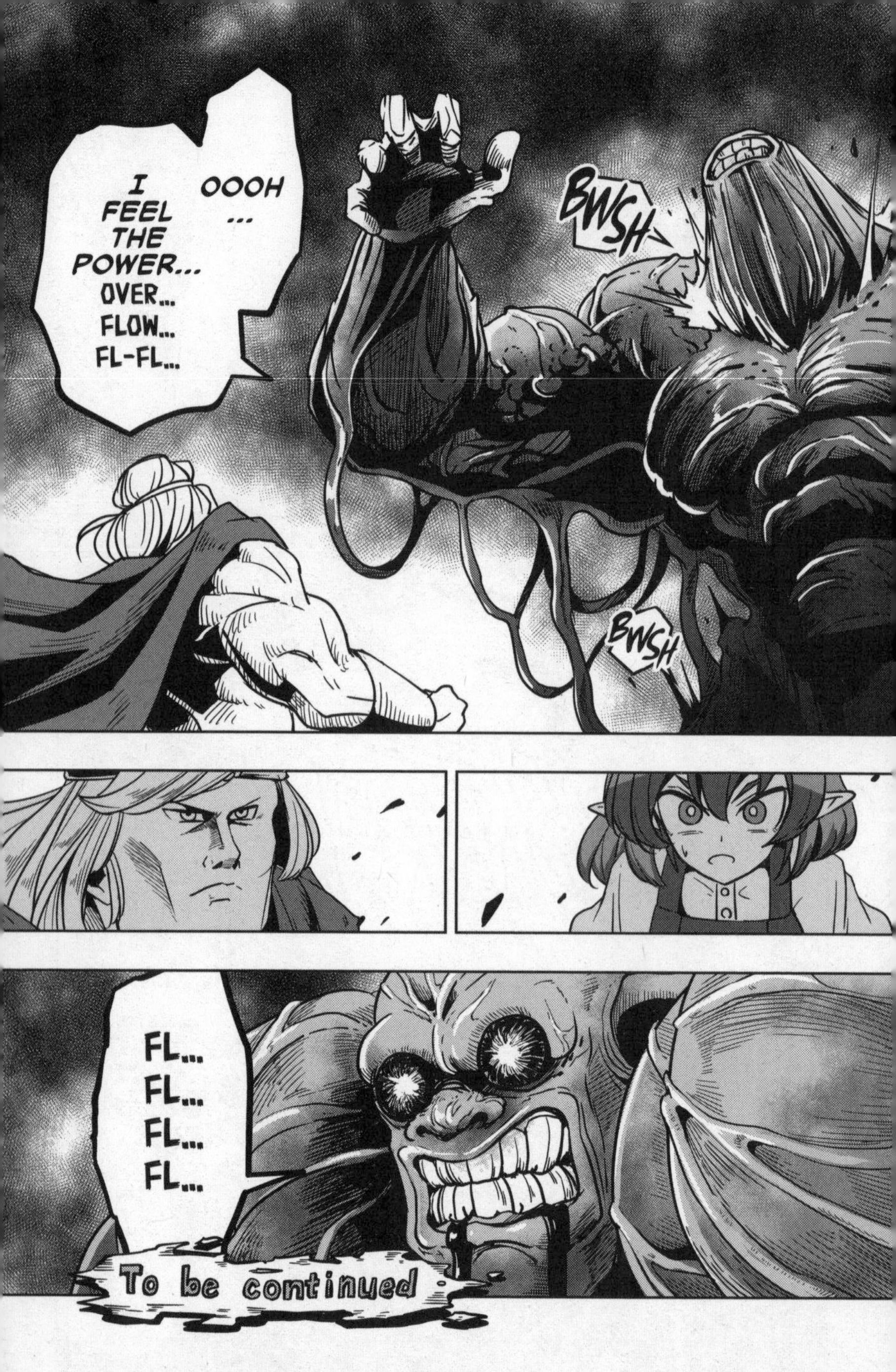
BWSH
OOOH ...
I FEEL THE POWER... OVER... FLOW... FL-FL...
BWSH
FL... FL... FL... FL...
To be continued

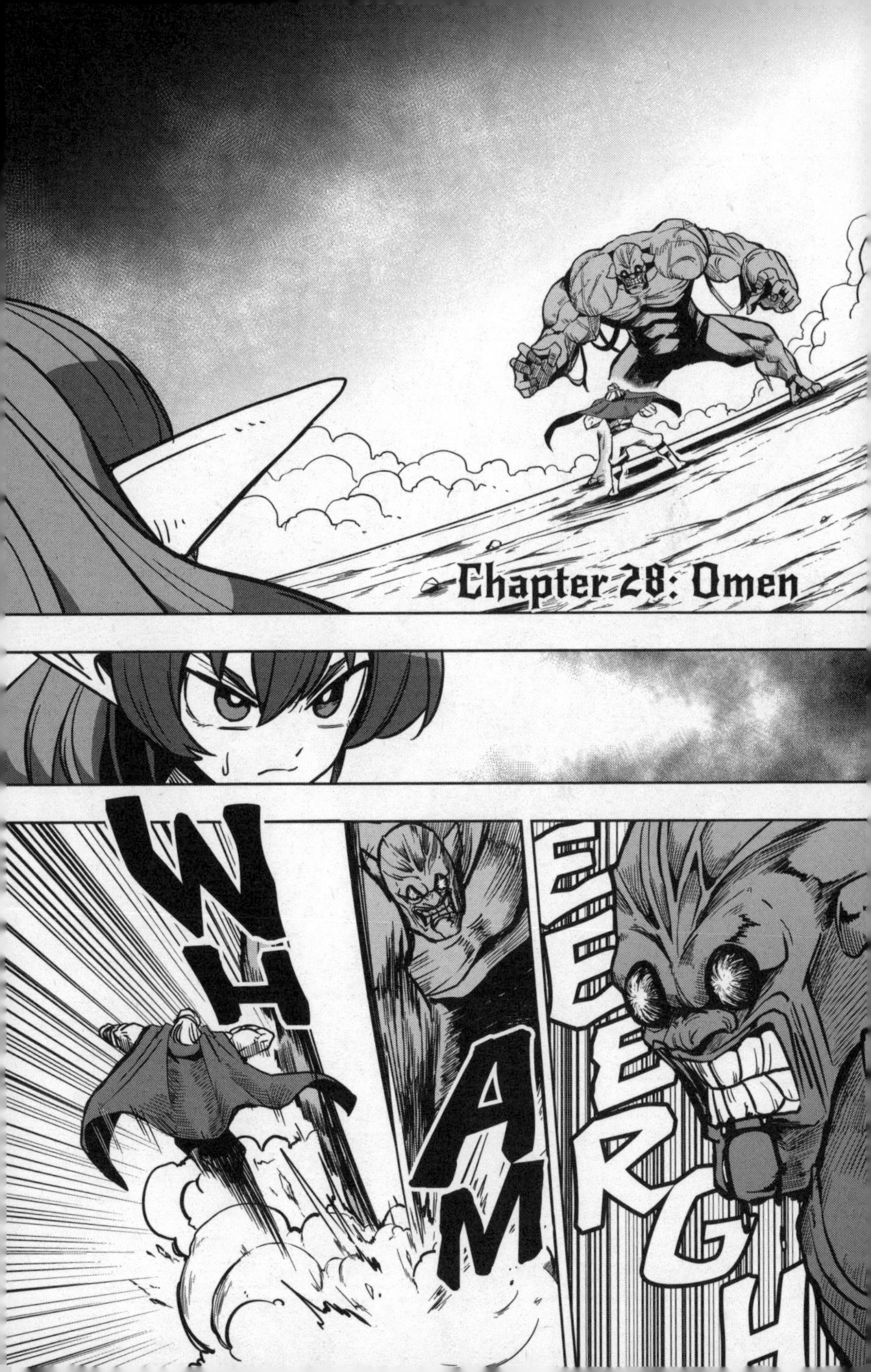
Chapter 28: Omen
WHAM
EEERGH

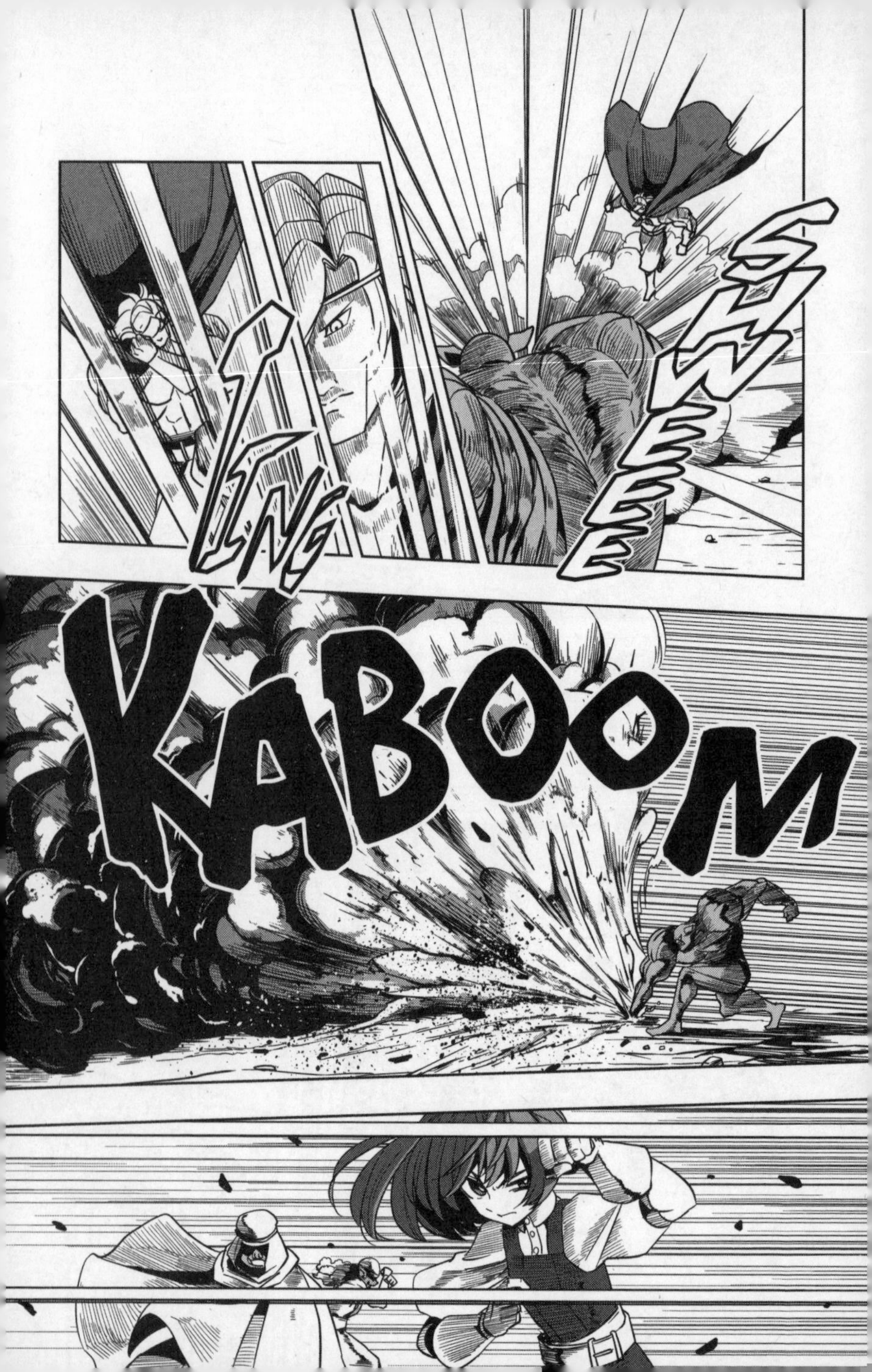
KABOOM

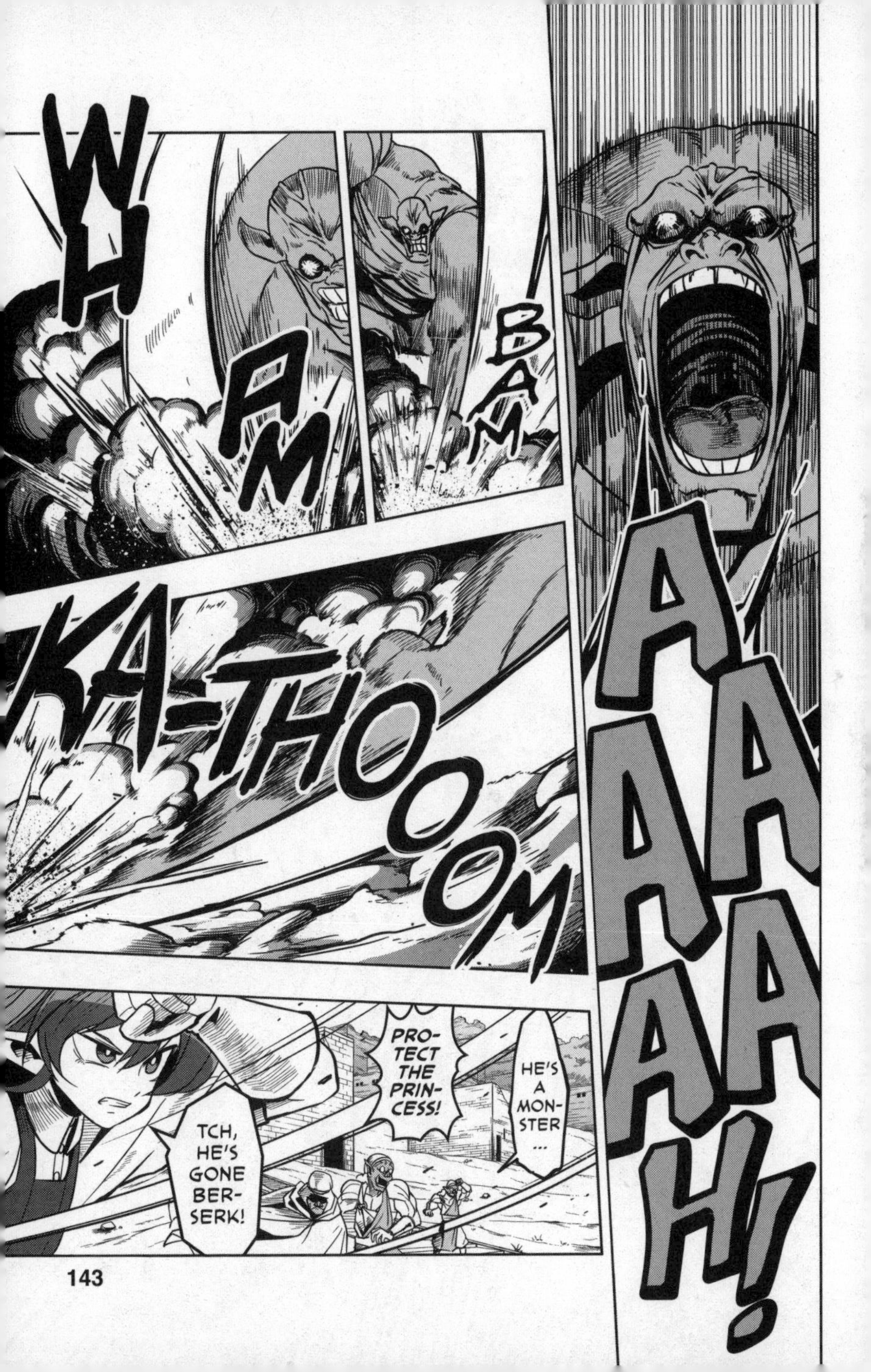
AAAAAAH!
BAM
WHAM
KA-THOOOM
HE'S A MON-STER...
PRO-TECT THE PRIN-CESS!
TCH, HE'S GONE BER-SERK!

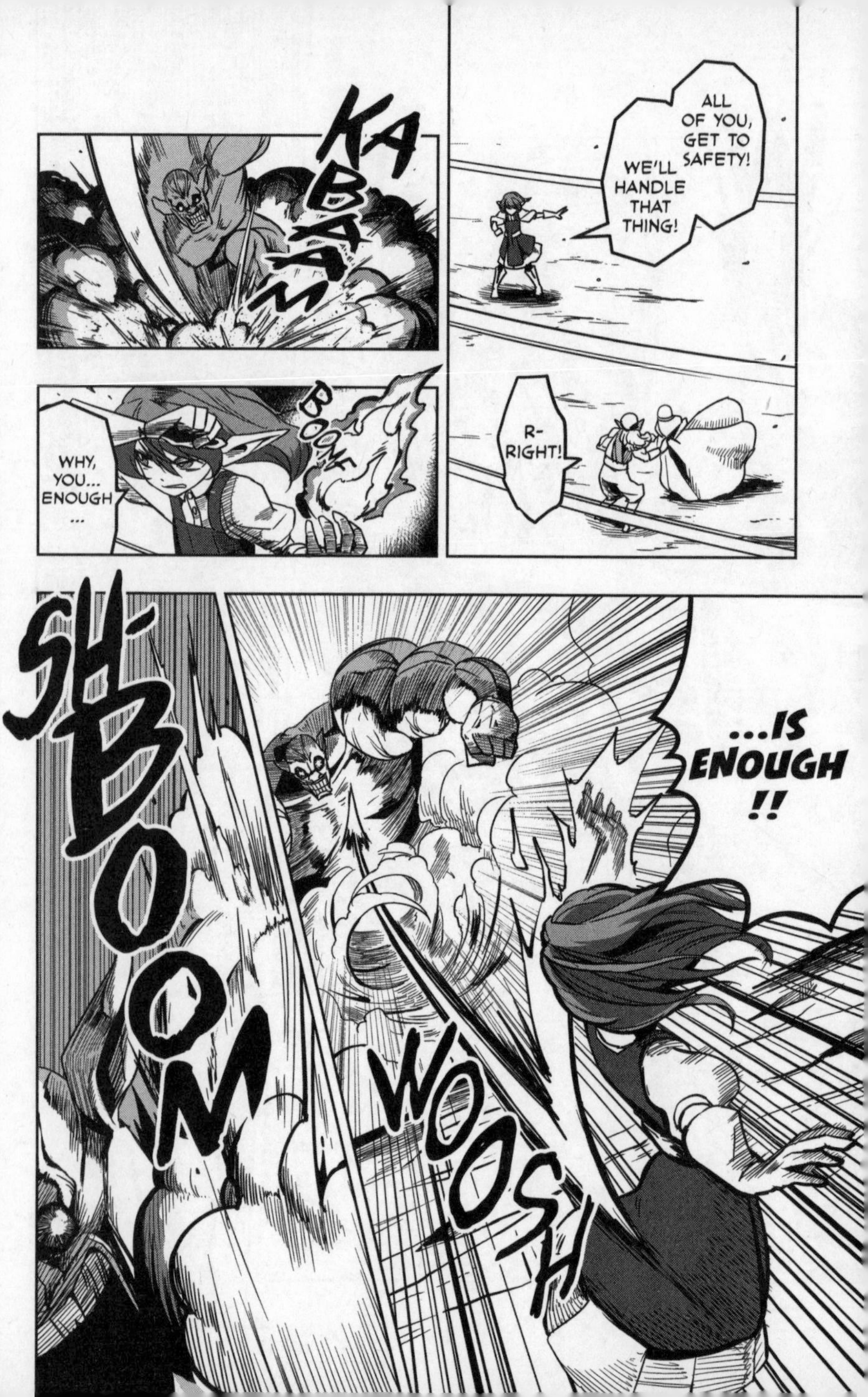
ALL OF YOU, GET TO SAFETY!
WE'LL HANDLE THAT THING!
KABAAM
R-RIGHT!
BOOM
WHY, YOU... ENOUGH ...
...IS ENOUGH !!
SH-BOOM
WOOSH

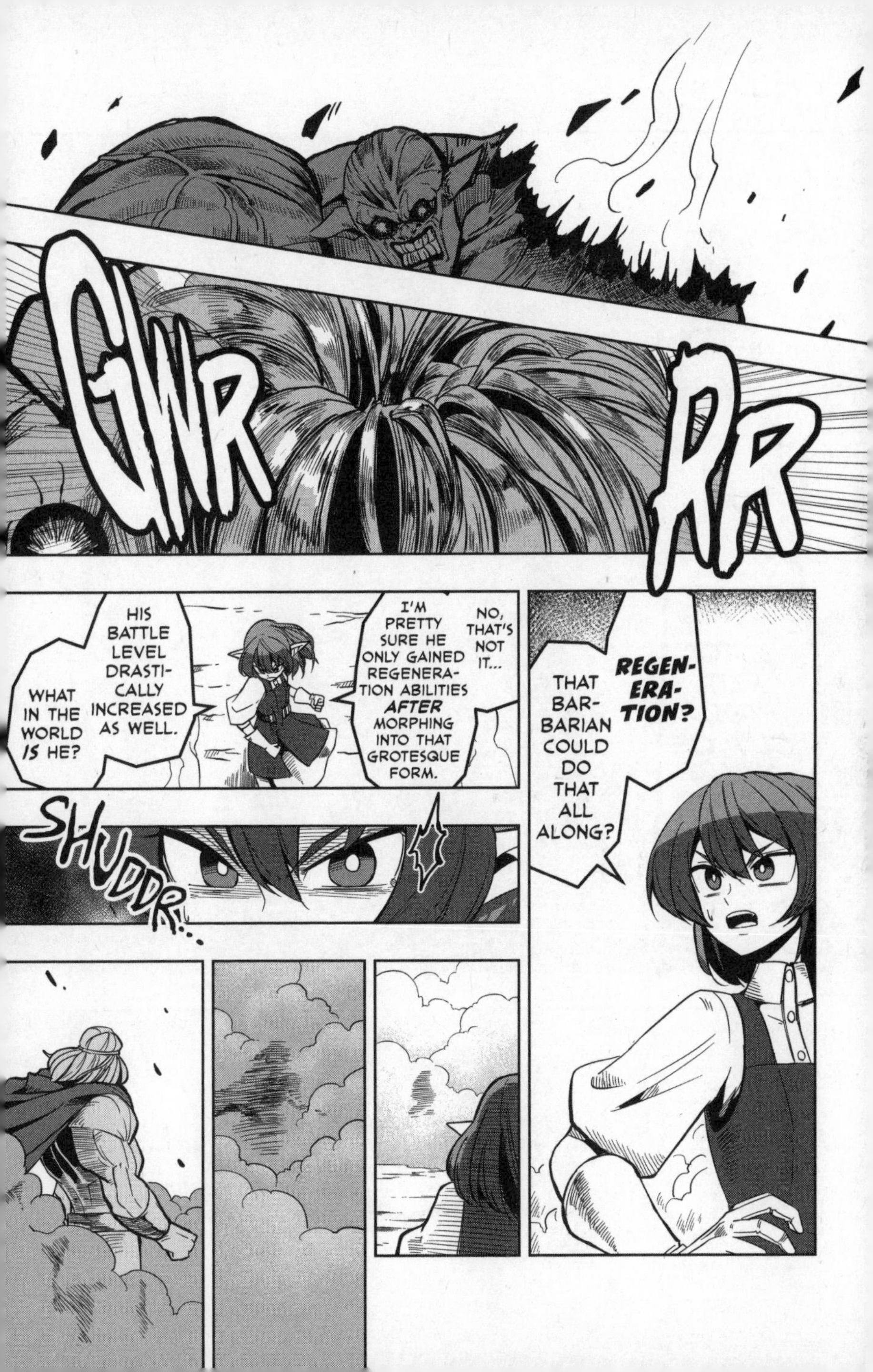
GWR RR
REGENERATION?
THAT BARBARIAN COULD DO THAT ALL ALONG?
NO, THAT'S NOT IT...
I'M PRETTY SURE HE ONLY GAINED REGENERATION ABILITIES *AFTER* MORPHING INTO THAT GROTESQUE FORM.
HIS BATTLE LEVEL DRASTICALLY INCREASED AS WELL.
WHAT IN THE WORLD *IS* HE?
SHUDDR...

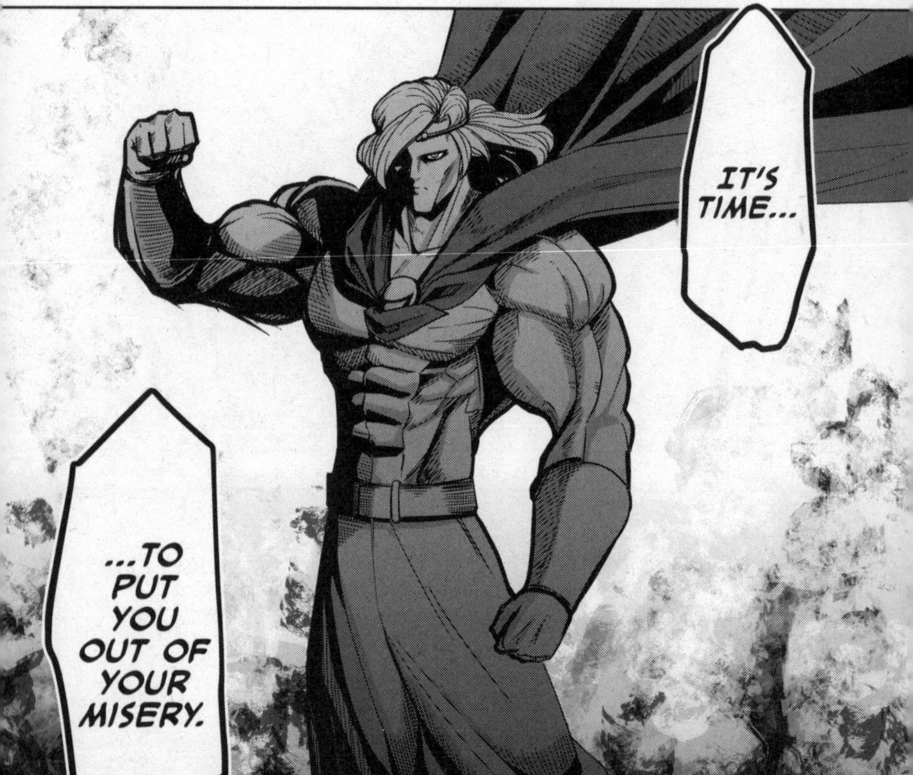
IT'S TIME...
...TO PUT YOU OUT OF YOUR MISERY.

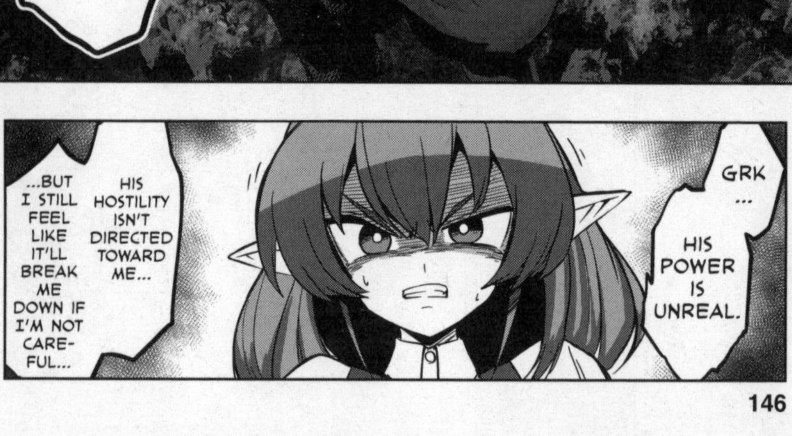
GRK ...
HIS POWER IS UNREAL.
HIS HOSTILITY ISN'T DIRECTED TOWARD ME...
...BUT I STILL FEEL LIKE IT'LL BREAK ME DOWN IF I'M NOT CARE-FUL...

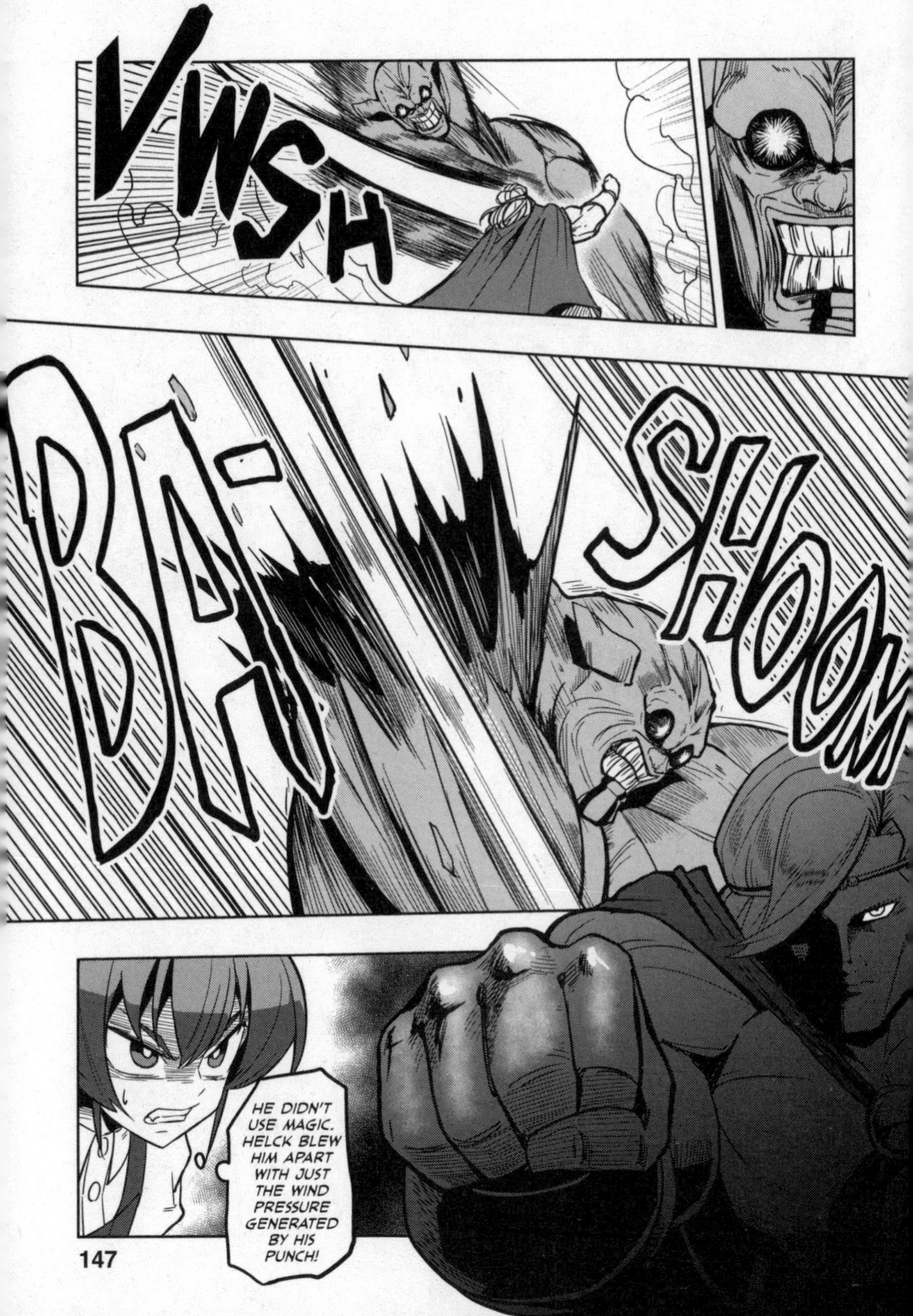
VWSH
BAM
SHOOM
HE DIDN'T USE MAGIC. HELCK BLEW HIM APART WITH JUST THE WIND PRESSURE GENERATED BY HIS PUNCH!

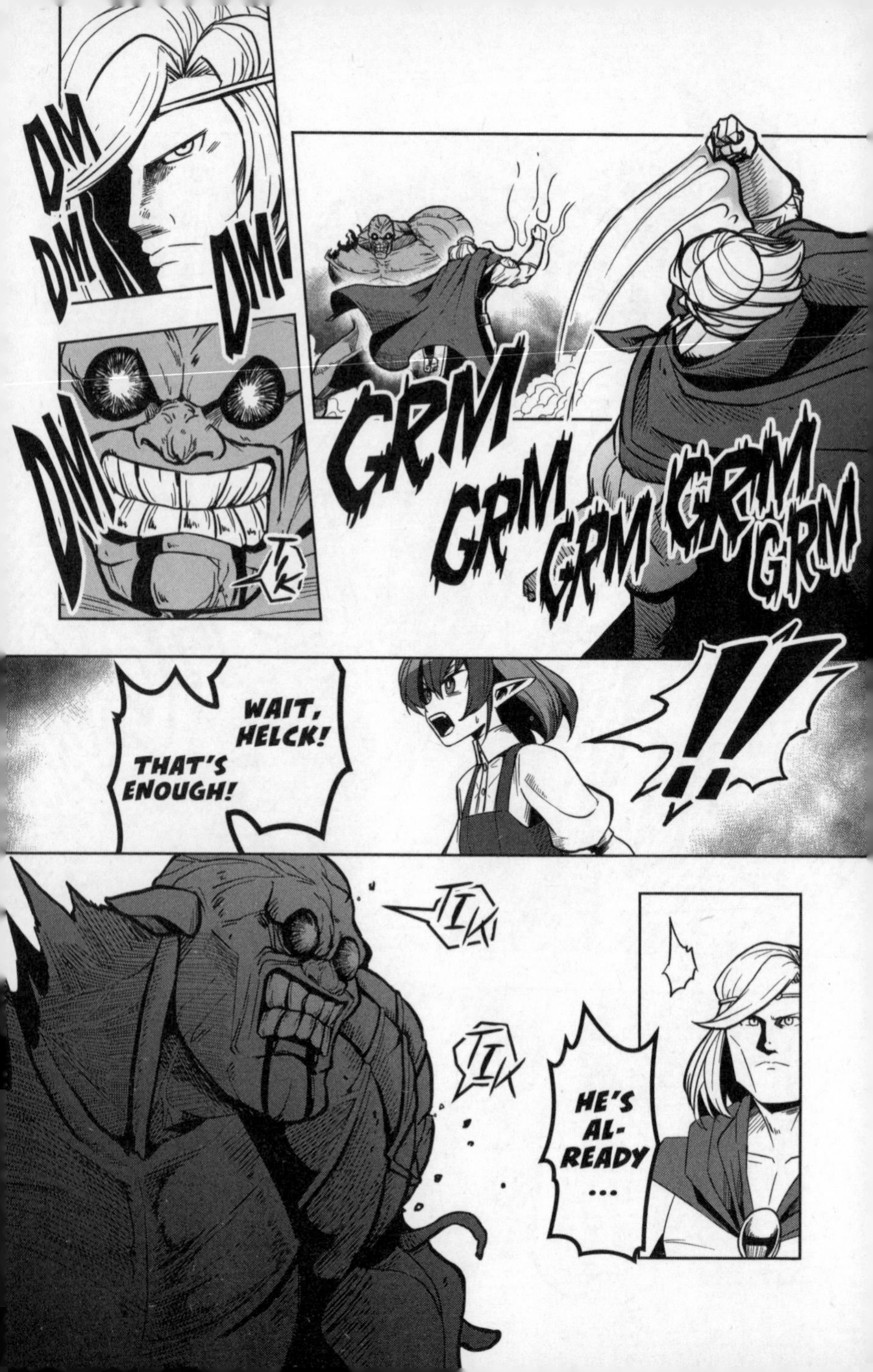
GRM GRM GRM GRM GRM GRM
DM DM DM
DM
TIK
!!
WAIT, HELCK! THAT'S ENOUGH!
HE'S AL-READY ...
TIK
TIK

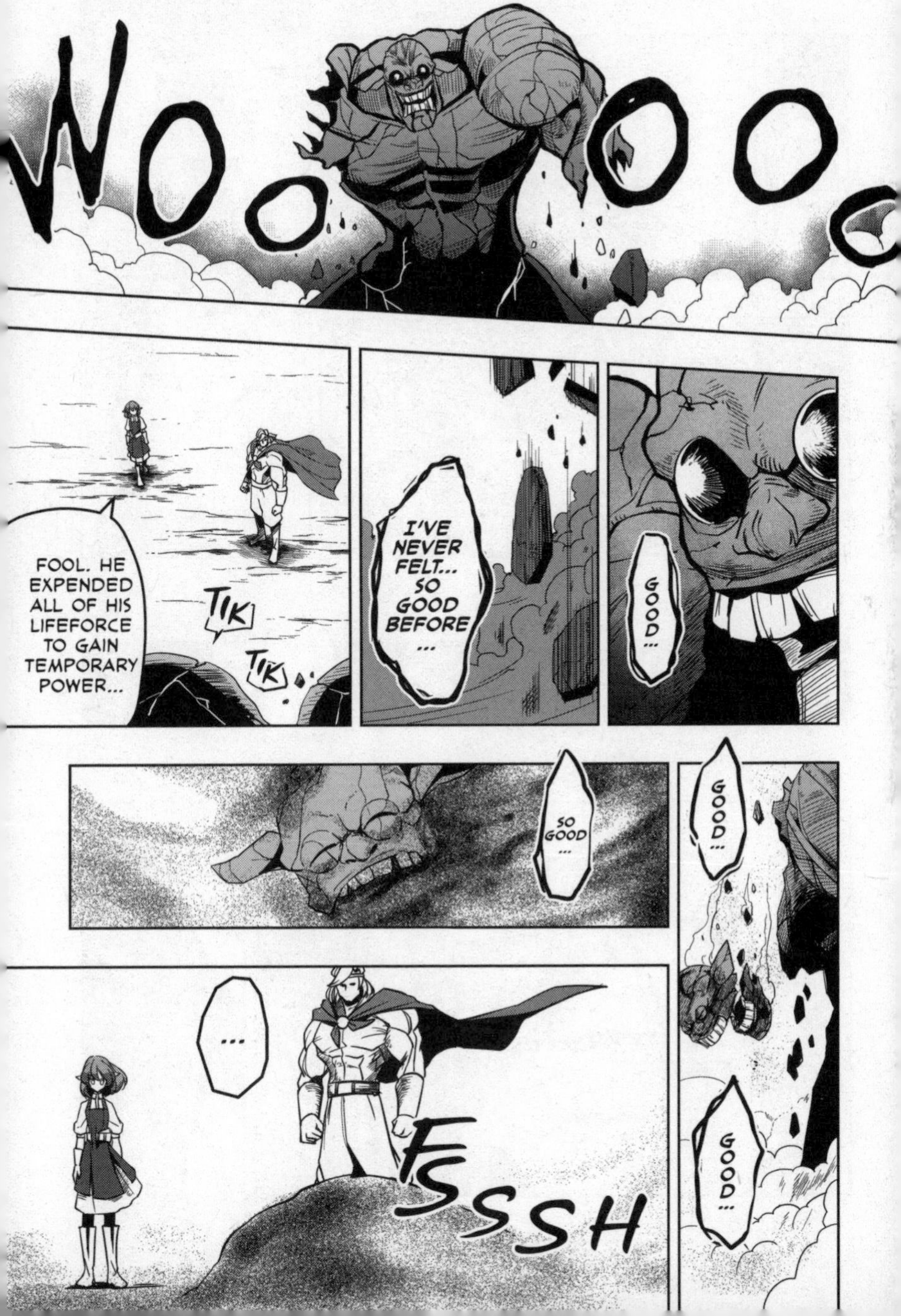
WOOOOO
GOOD...
I'VE NEVER FELT... SO GOOD BEFORE...
FOOL. HE EXPENDED ALL OF HIS LIFEFORCE TO GAIN TEMPORARY POWER...
TIK
TIK
GOOD...
GOOD...
SO GOOD...
...
FSSSH

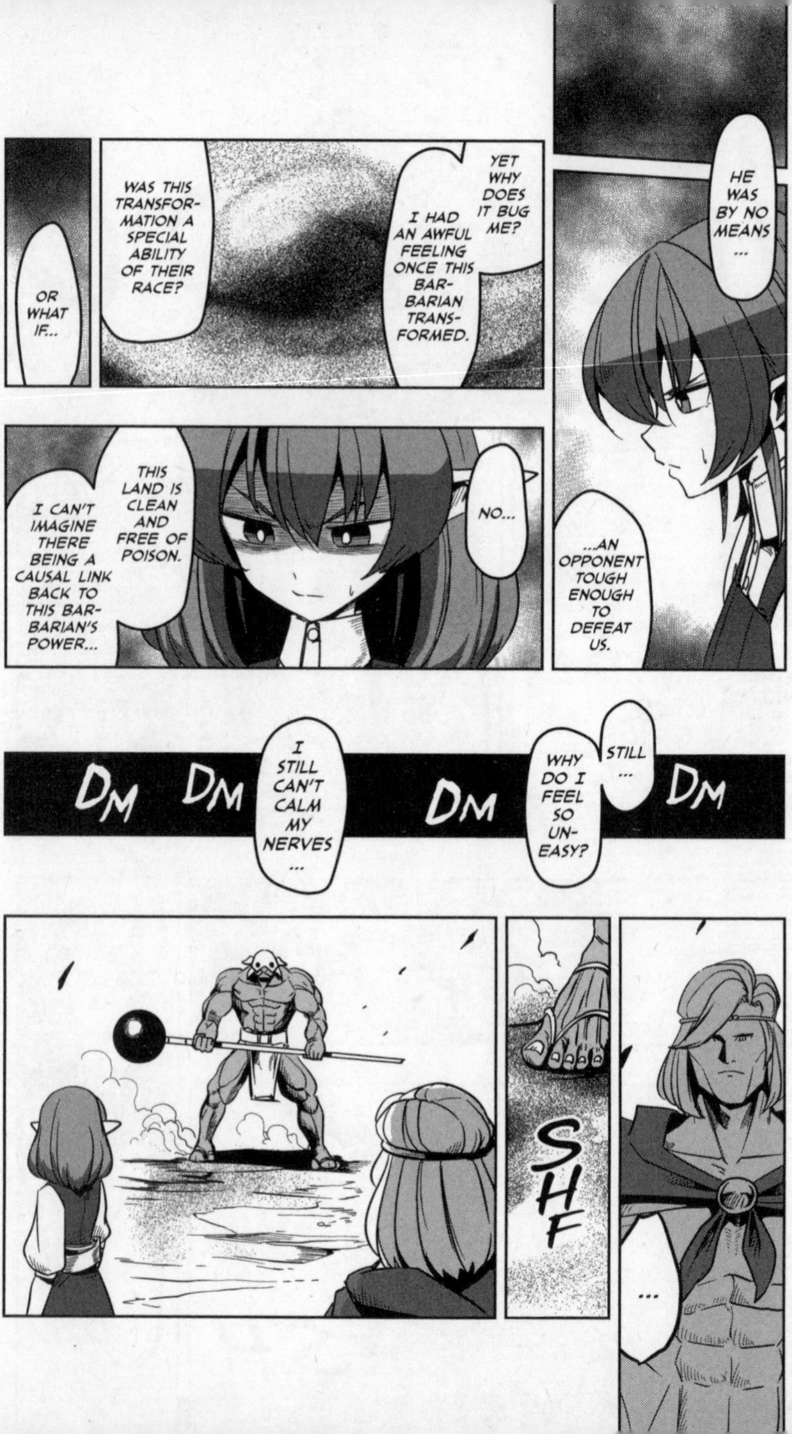
HE WAS BY NO MEANS...
...AN OPPONENT TOUGH ENOUGH TO DEFEAT US.
YET WHY DOES IT BUG ME?
I HAD AN AWFUL FEELING ONCE THIS BARBARIAN TRANSFORMED.
WAS THIS TRANSFORMATION A SPECIAL ABILITY OF THEIR RACE?
OR WHAT IF...
NO...
THIS LAND IS CLEAN AND FREE OF POISON.
I CAN'T IMAGINE THERE BEING A CAUSAL LINK BACK TO THIS BARBARIAN'S POWER...
DM
STILL...
WHY DO I FEEL SO UNEASY?
DM
I STILL CAN'T CALM MY NERVES...
DM
DM
...
SHF

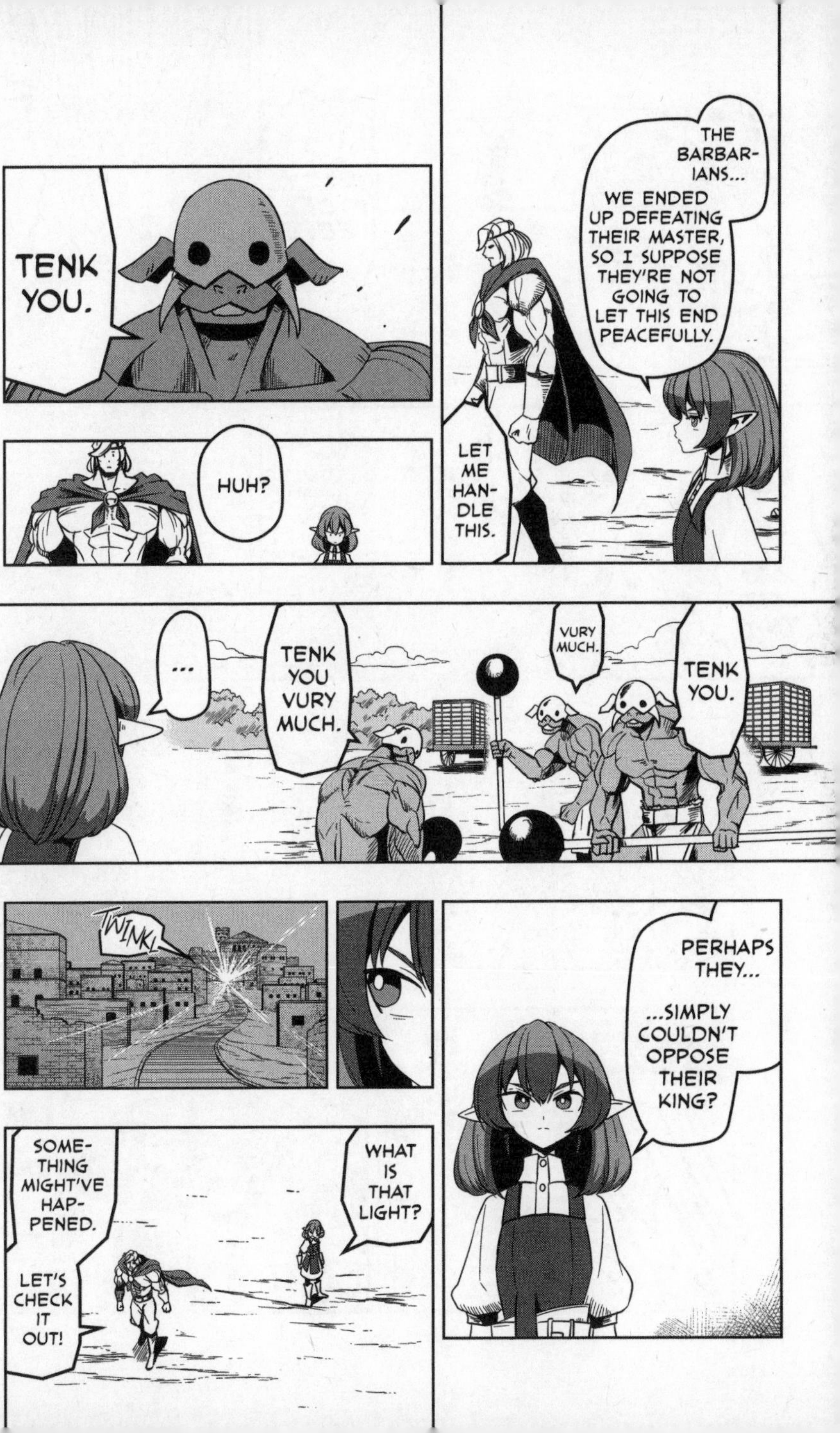
THE BARBARIANS...
WE ENDED UP DEFEATING THEIR MASTER, SO I SUPPOSE THEY'RE NOT GOING TO LET THIS END PEACEFULLY.
LET ME HANDLE THIS.
TENK YOU.
HUH?
TENK YOU.
VURY MUCH.
TENK YOU VURY MUCH.
...
PERHAPS THEY...
...SIMPLY COULDN'T OPPOSE THEIR KING?
TWINKL
WHAT IS THAT LIGHT?
SOMETHING MIGHT'VE HAPPENED.
LET'S CHECK IT OUT!

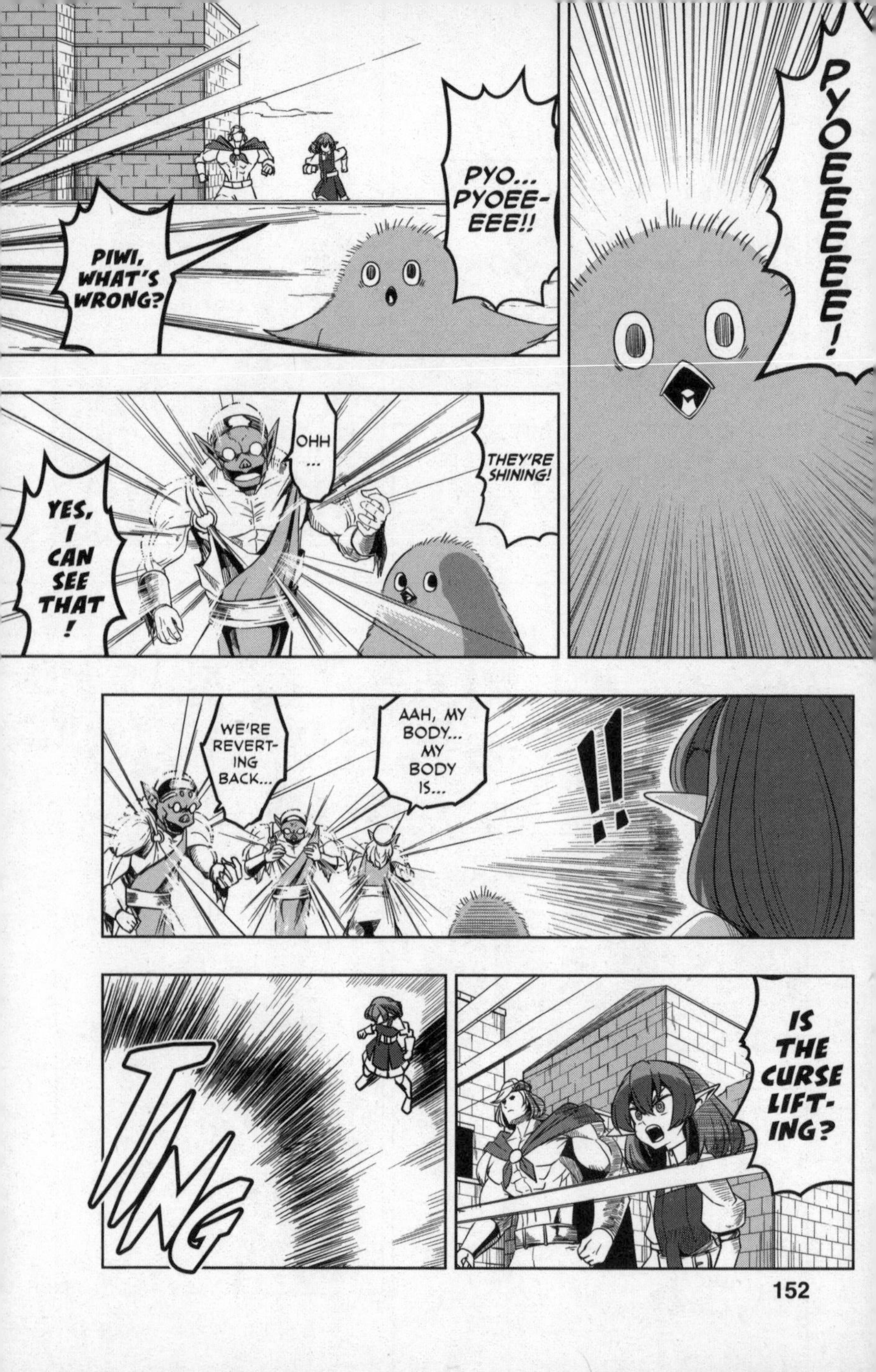
PYOEEEEEE!
PYO... PYOEE-EEE!!
PIWI, WHAT'S WRONG?
THEY'RE SHINING!
OHH...
YES, I CAN SEE THAT!
!!
AAH, MY BODY... MY BODY IS...
WE'RE REVERT-ING BACK...
IS THE CURSE LIFT-ING?
TING

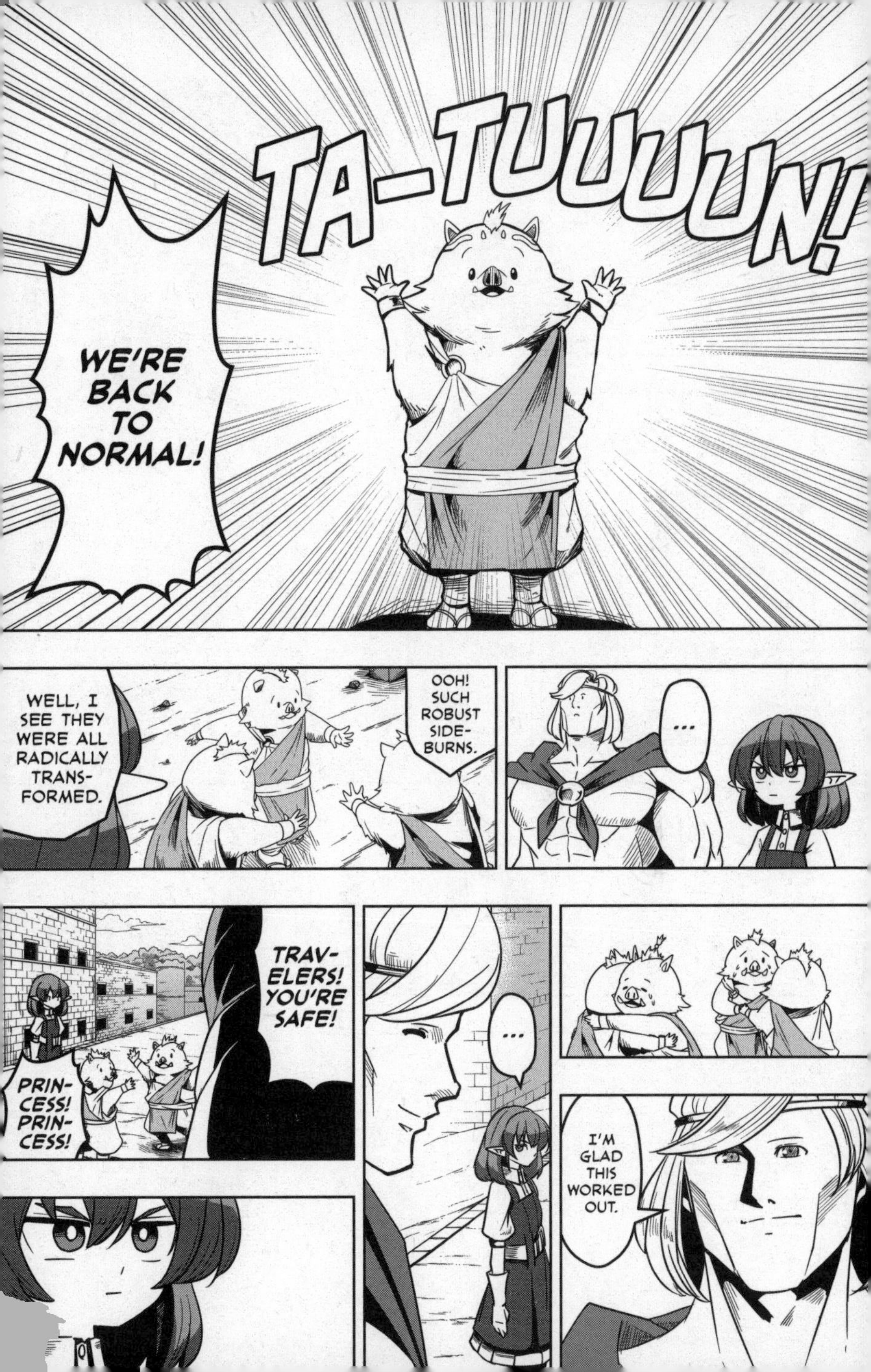
TA-TUUUUN!
WE'RE BACK TO NORMAL!
...
OOH! SUCH ROBUST SIDE-BURNS.
WELL, I SEE THEY WERE ALL RADICALLY TRANS-FORMED.
I'M GLAD THIS WORKED OUT.
...
TRAV-ELERS! YOU'RE SAFE!
PRIN-CESS! PRIN-CESS!

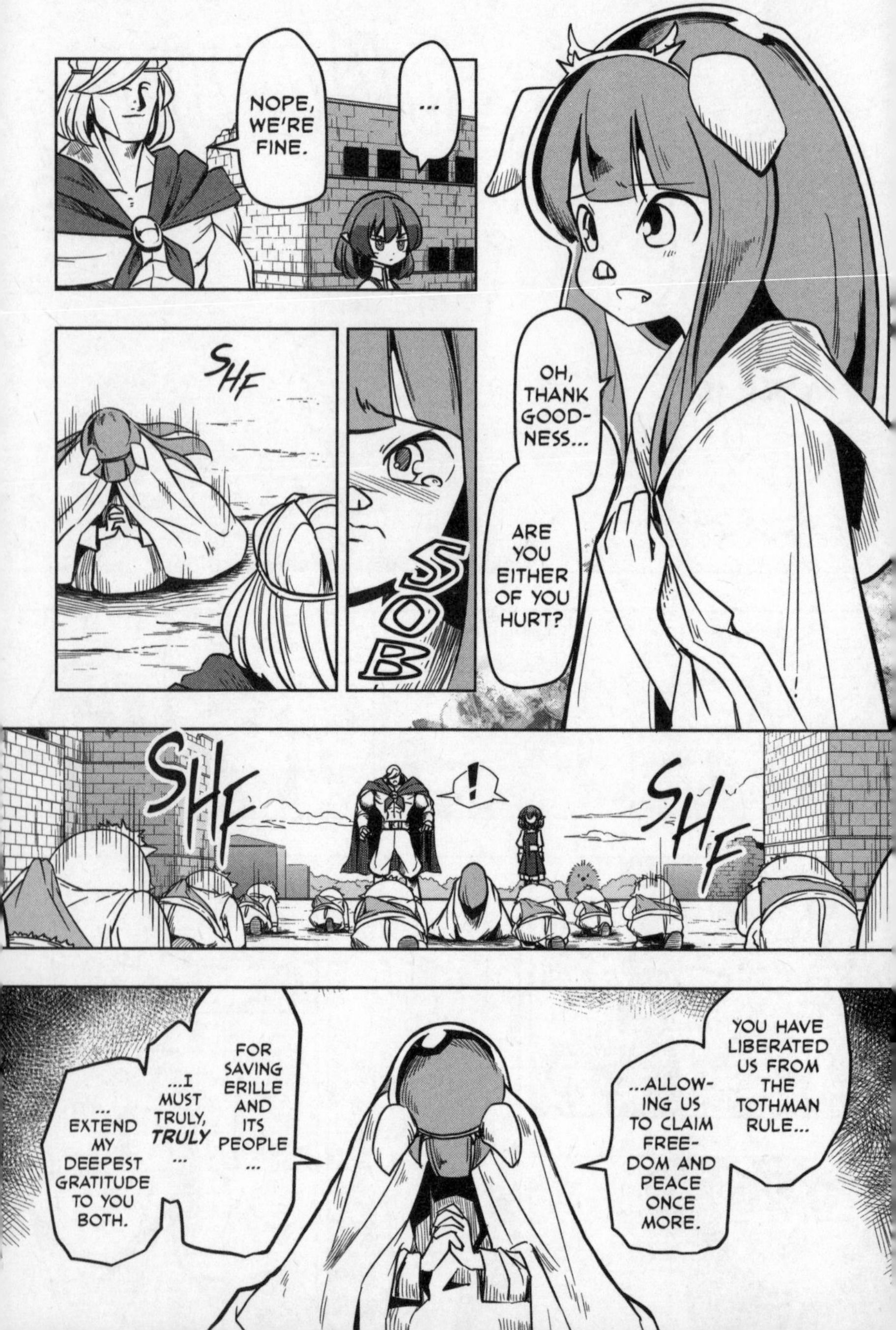
OH, THANK GOOD-NESS...
ARE YOU EITHER OF YOU HURT?
...
NOPE, WE'RE FINE.
SOB
SHF
SHF
!
SHF
YOU HAVE LIBERATED US FROM THE TOTHMAN RULE...
...ALLOW-ING US TO CLAIM FREE-DOM AND PEACE ONCE MORE.
FOR SAVING ERILLE AND ITS PEOPLE...
...I MUST TRULY, *TRULY*...
...EXTEND MY DEEPEST GRATITUDE TO YOU BOTH.

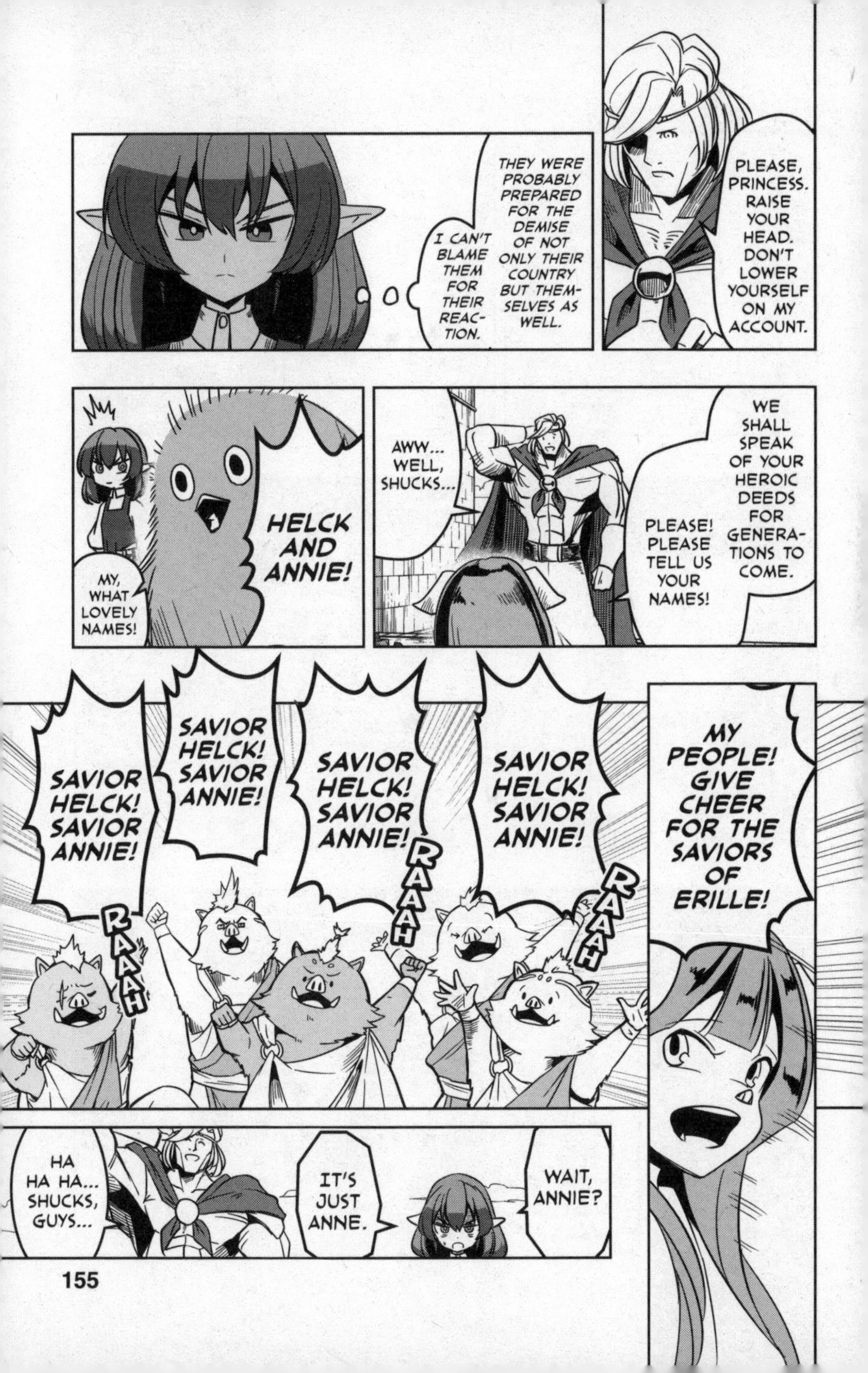
PLEASE, PRINCESS. RAISE YOUR HEAD. DON'T LOWER YOURSELF ON MY ACCOUNT.
THEY WERE PROBABLY PREPARED FOR THE DEMISE OF NOT ONLY THEIR COUNTRY BUT THEMSELVES AS WELL.
I CAN'T BLAME THEM FOR THEIR REACTION.
WE SHALL SPEAK OF YOUR HEROIC DEEDS FOR GENERATIONS TO COME.
PLEASE! PLEASE TELL US YOUR NAMES!
AWW... WELL, SHUCKS...
HELCK AND ANNIE!
MY, WHAT LOVELY NAMES!
MY PEOPLE! GIVE CHEER FOR THE SAVIORS OF ERILLE!
SAVIOR HELCK! SAVIOR ANNIE!
RAAAH
SAVIOR HELCK! SAVIOR ANNIE!
RAAAH
SAVIOR HELCK! SAVIOR ANNIE!
SAVIOR HELCK! SAVIOR ANNIE!
RAAAH
WAIT, ANNIE?
IT'S JUST ANNE.
HA HA HA... SHUCKS, GUYS...

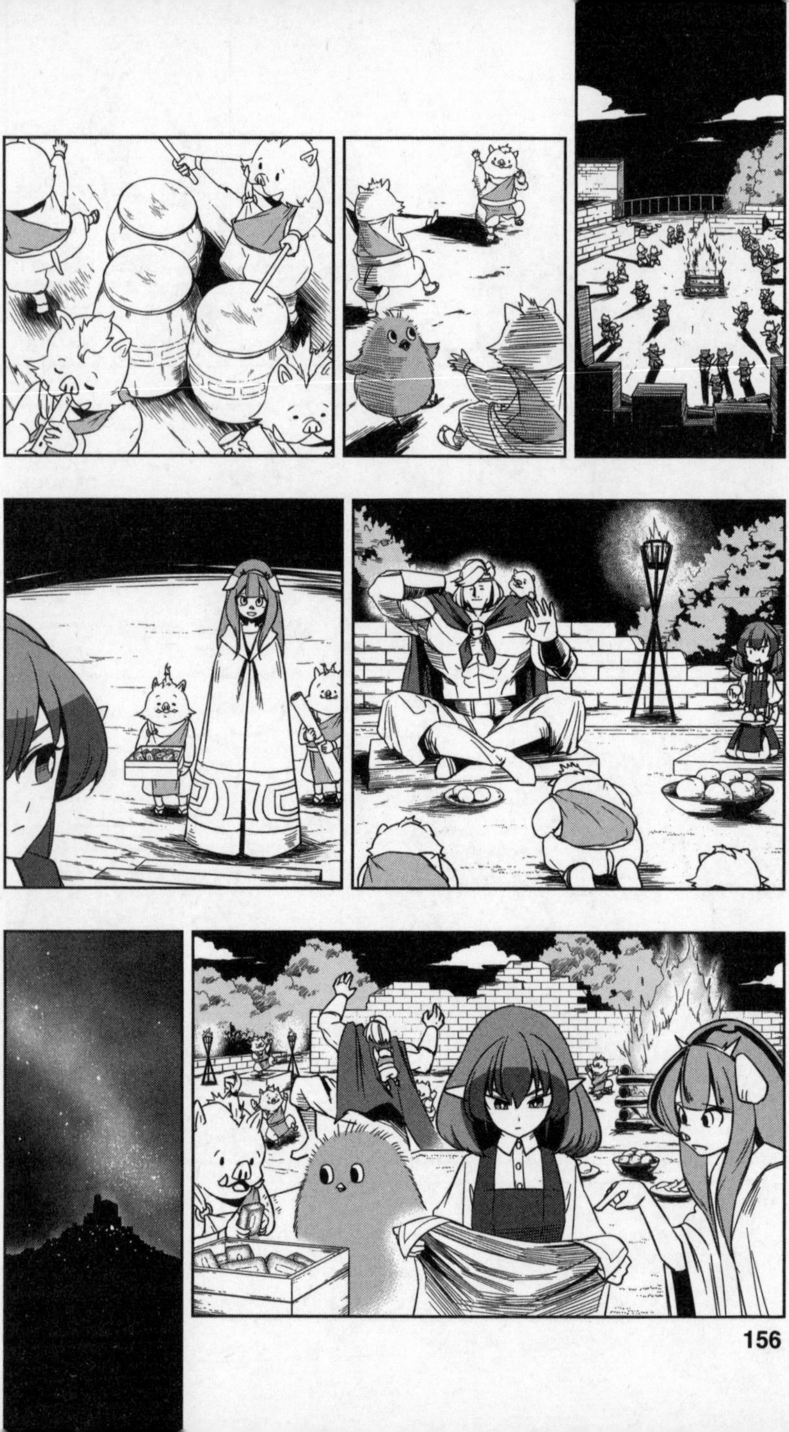

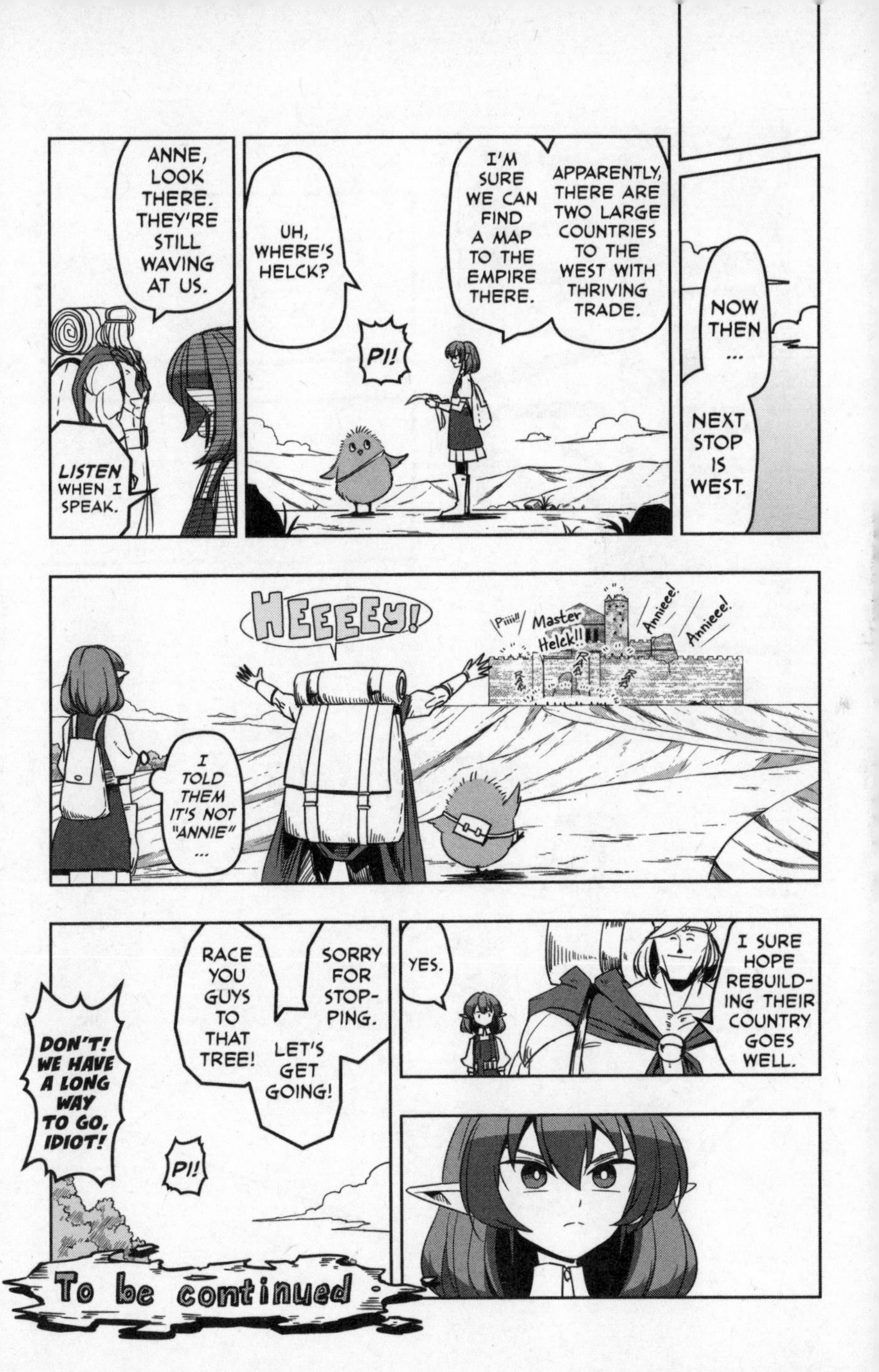
NOW THEN ...
NEXT STOP IS WEST.
APPARENTLY, THERE ARE TWO LARGE COUNTRIES TO THE WEST WITH THRIVING TRADE.
I'M SURE WE CAN FIND A MAP TO THE EMPIRE THERE.
UH, WHERE'S HELCK?
PI!
ANNE, LOOK THERE. THEY'RE STILL WAVING AT US.
LISTEN WHEN I SPEAK.
HEEEEY!
Annieee!
Annieee!
Master Helck!!
Piiii!!
I TOLD THEM IT'S NOT "ANNIE" ...
I SURE HOPE REBUILDING THEIR COUNTRY GOES WELL.
YES.
SORRY FOR STOPPING.
LET'S GET GOING!
RACE YOU GUYS TO THAT TREE!
DON'T! WE HAVE A LONG WAY TO GO, IDIOT!
PI!
To be continued

PIWI'S LUGGAGE

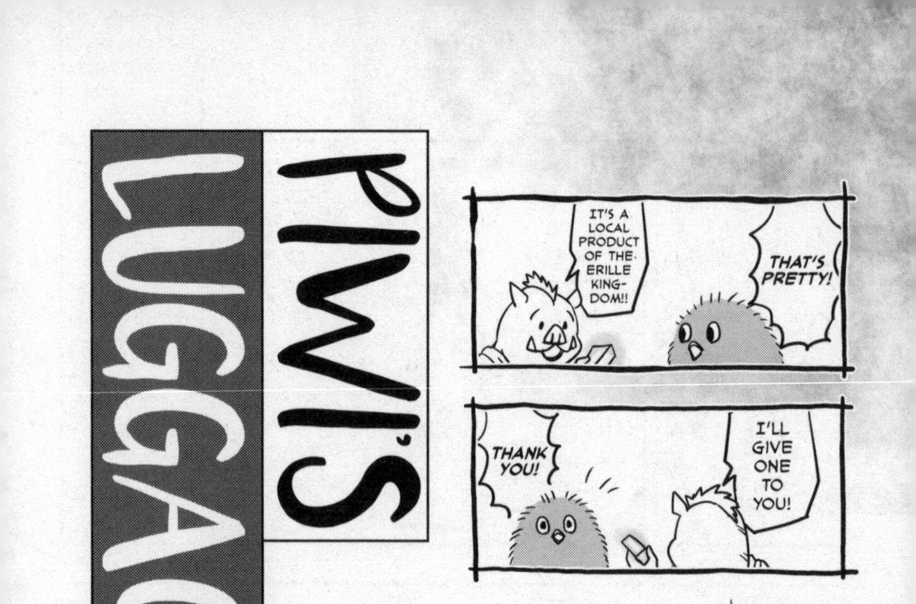
THAT'S PRETTY!
IT'S A LOCAL PRODUCT OF THE ERILLE KINGDOM!!
I'LL GIVE ONE TO YOU!
THANK YOU!

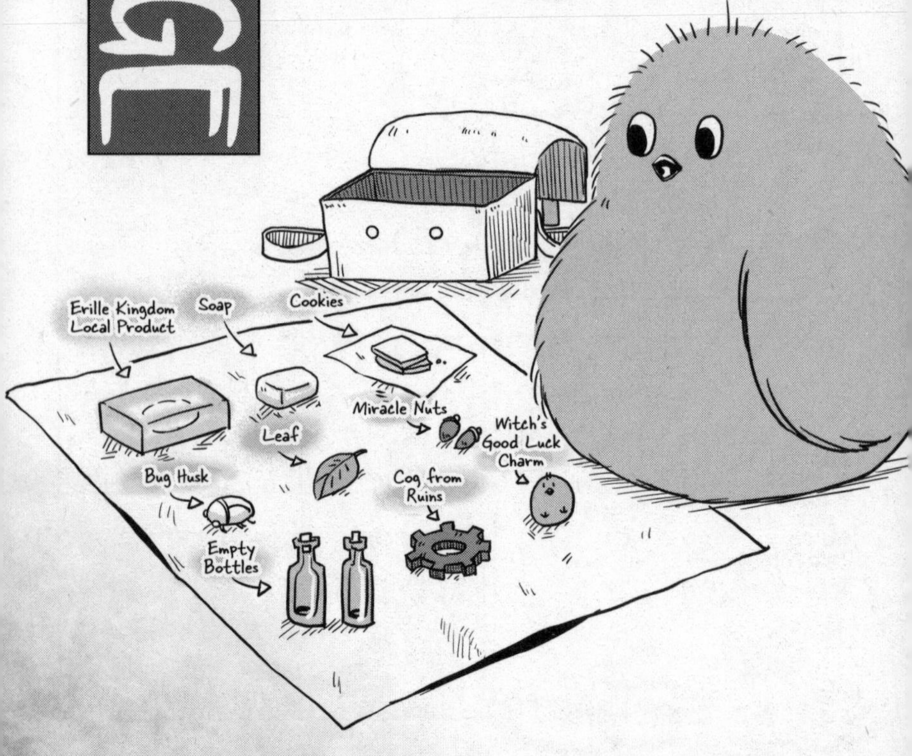
Cookies
Soap
Erille Kingdom Local Product
Miracle Nuts
Witch's Good Luck Charm
Leaf
Cog from Ruins
Bug Husk
Empty Bottles

Chapter 29: In Service of a Map

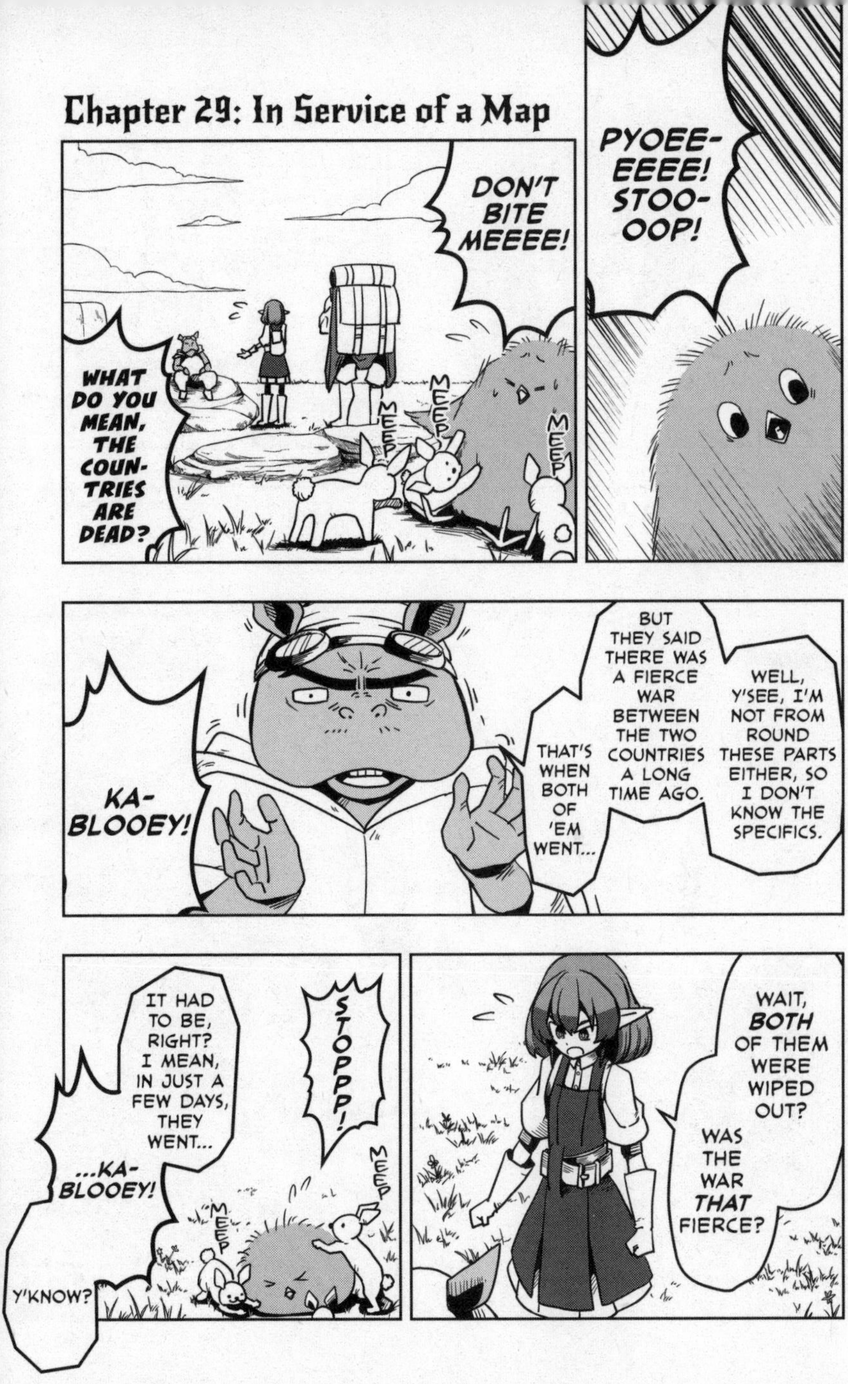
PYOEE-EEEE! STOO-OOP!
DON'T BITE MEEEE!
WHAT DO YOU MEAN, THE COUNTRIES ARE DEAD?
MEEP
MEEP
MEEP
WELL, Y'SEE, I'M NOT FROM ROUND THESE PARTS EITHER, SO I DON'T KNOW THE SPECIFICS.
BUT THEY SAID THERE WAS A FIERCE WAR BETWEEN THE TWO COUNTRIES A LONG TIME AGO.
THAT'S WHEN BOTH OF 'EM WENT...
KA-BLOOEY!
WAIT, BOTH OF THEM WERE WIPED OUT?
WAS THE WAR THAT FIERCE?
STOPPP!
IT HAD TO BE, RIGHT? I MEAN, IN JUST A FEW DAYS, THEY WENT...
...KA-BLOOEY!
MEEP
MEEP
Y'KNOW?

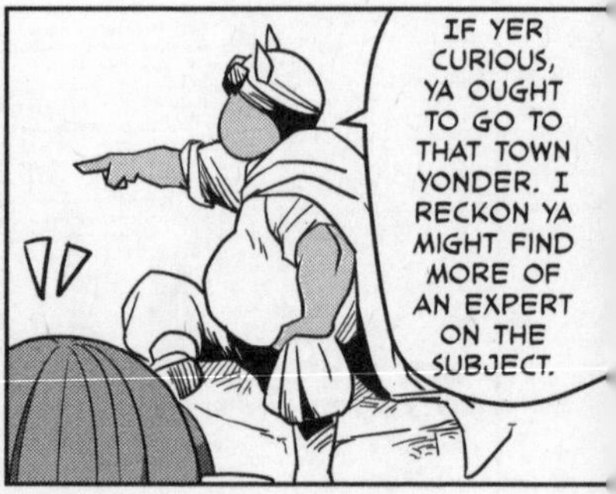
IF YER CURIOUS, YA OUGHT TO GO TO THAT TOWN YONDER. I RECKON YA MIGHT FIND MORE OF AN EXPERT ON THE SUBJECT.

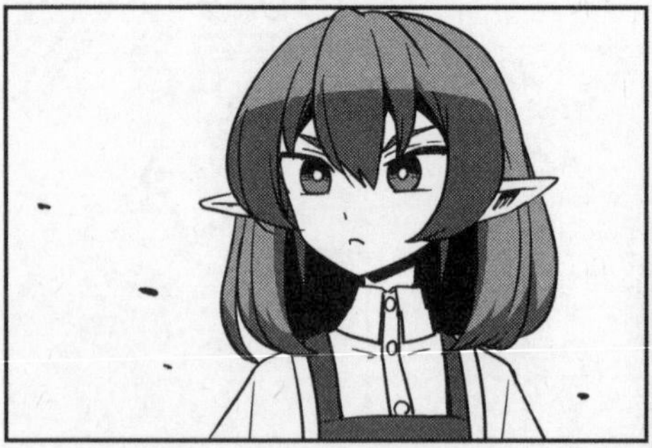

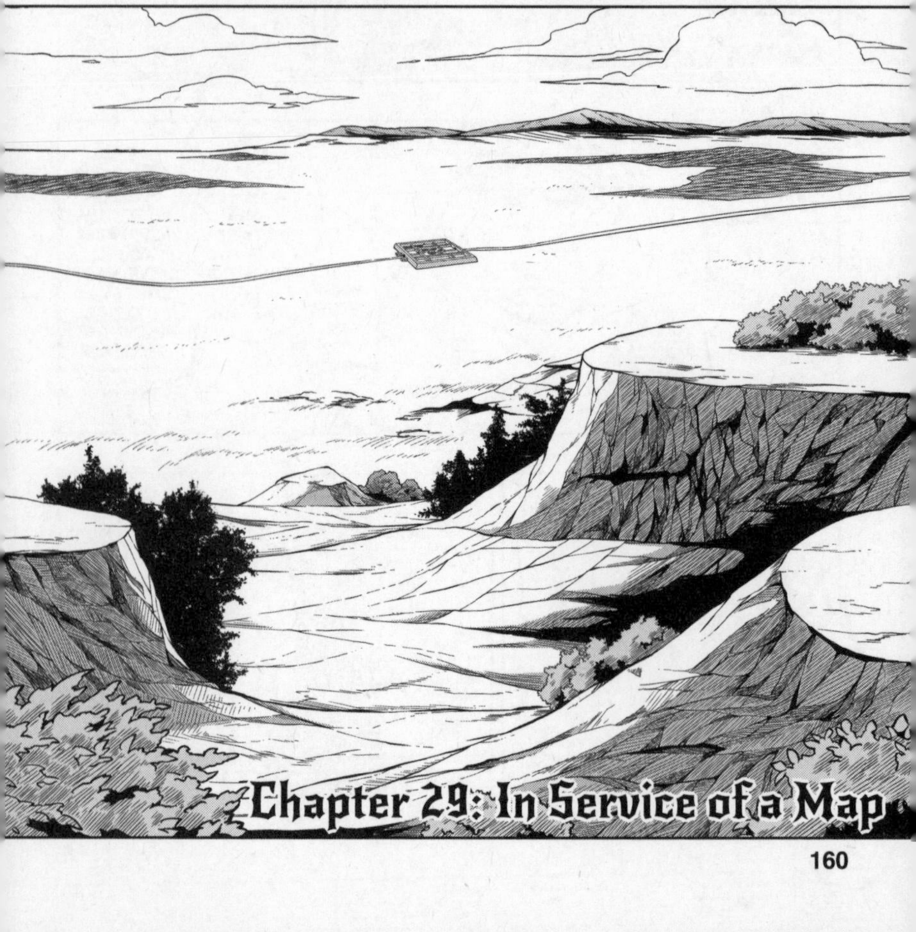
Chapter 29: In Service of a Map

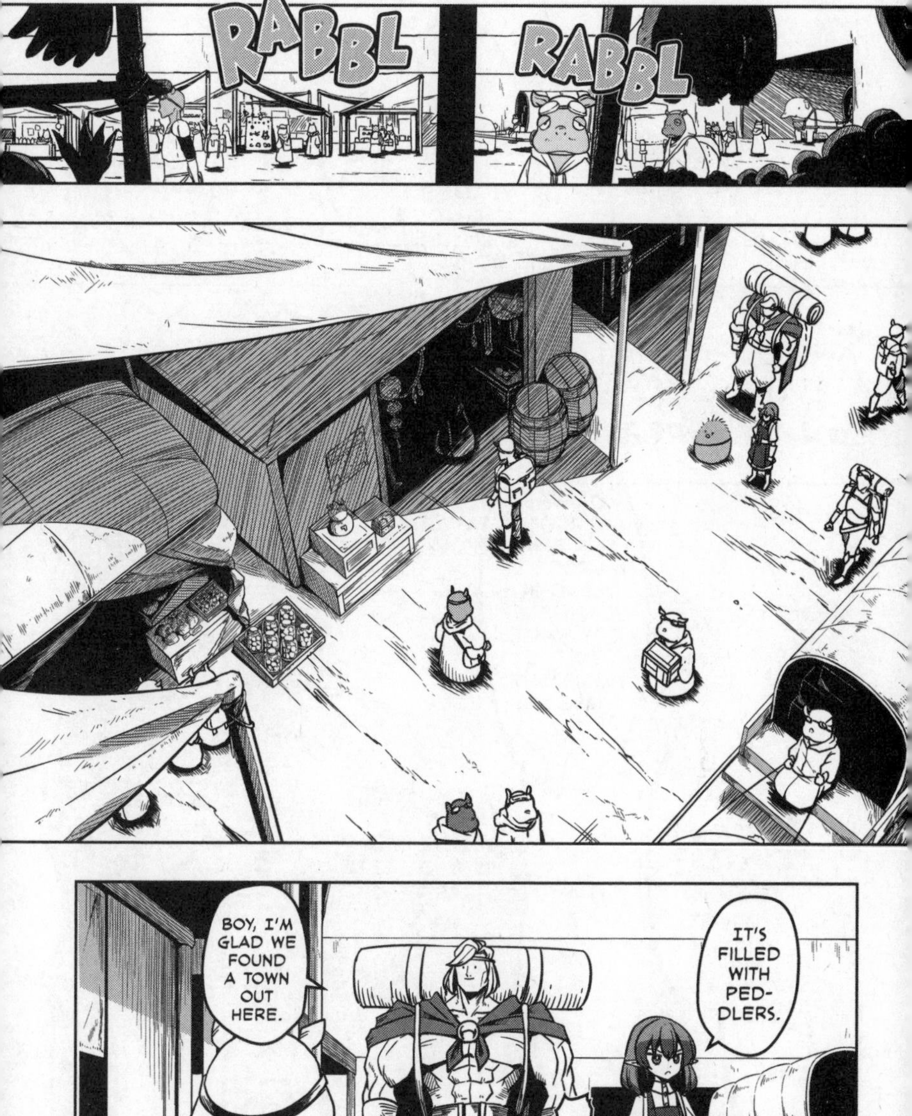
RABBL
RABBL
IT'S FILLED WITH PED-DLERS.
BOY, I'M GLAD WE FOUND A TOWN OUT HERE.

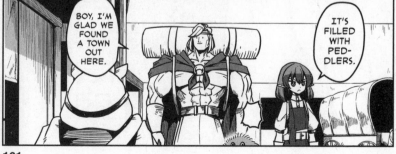

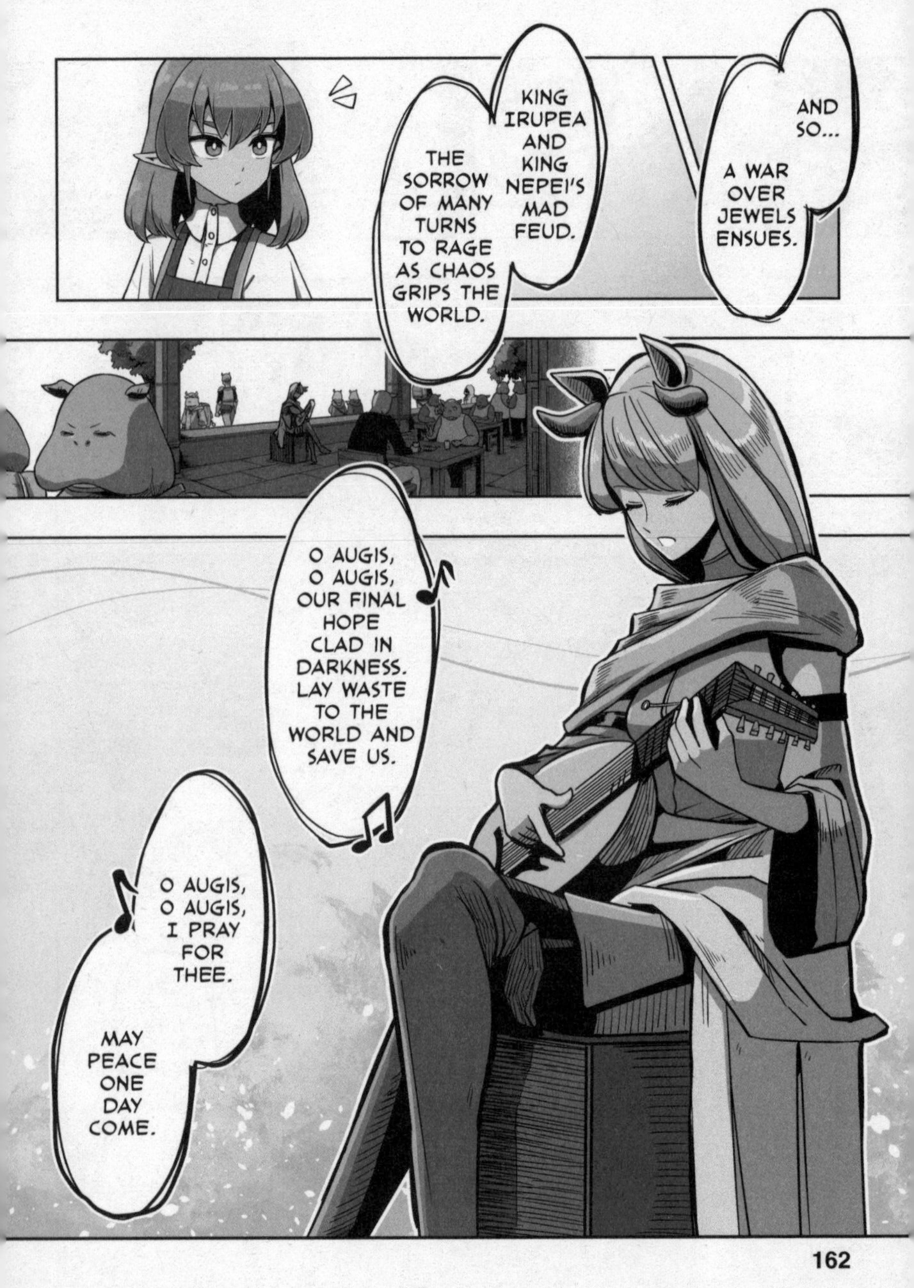
AND SO...
A WAR OVER JEWELS ENSUES.
KING IRUPEA AND KING NEPEI'S MAD FEUD.
THE SORROW OF MANY TURNS TO RAGE AS CHAOS GRIPS THE WORLD.
O AUGIS, O AUGIS, OUR FINAL HOPE CLAD IN DARKNESS. LAY WASTE TO THE WORLD AND SAVE US.
O AUGIS, O AUGIS, I PRAY FOR THEE.
MAY PEACE ONE DAY COME.

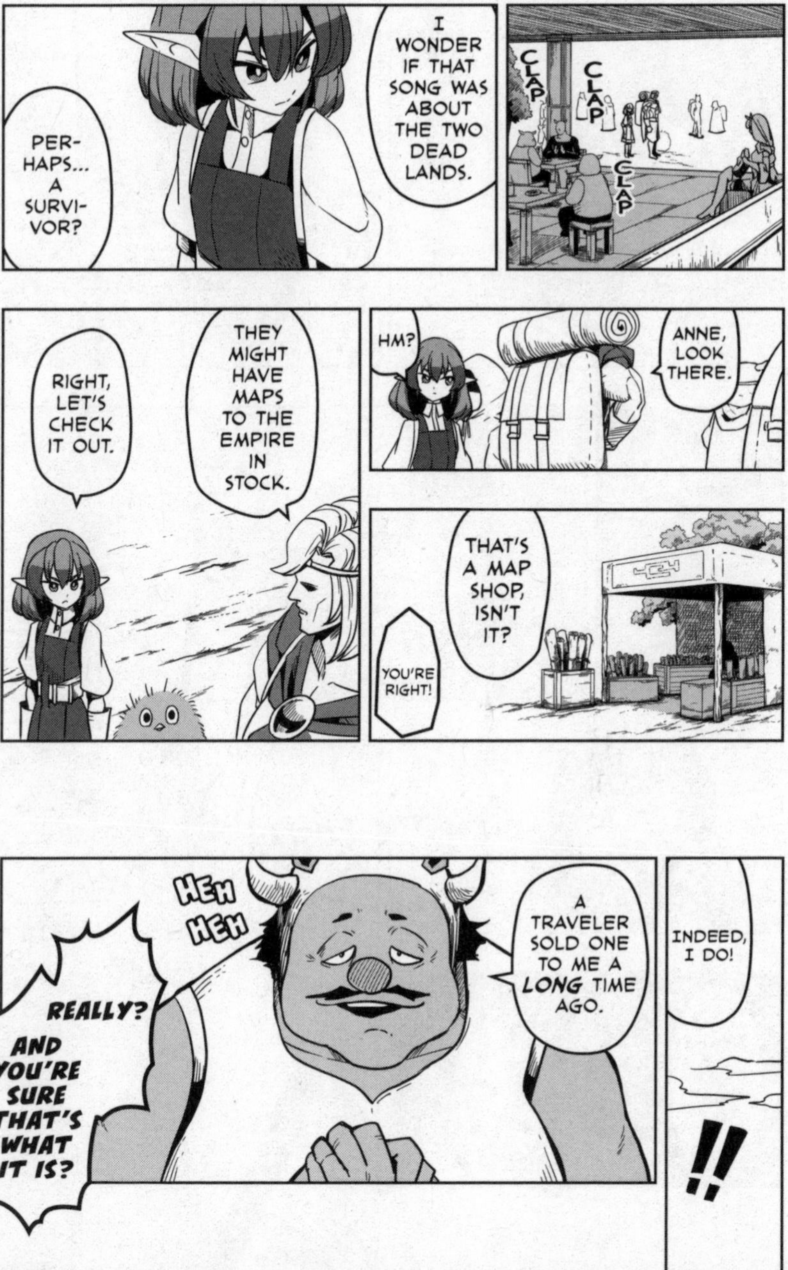
CLAP
CLAP
CLAP
I WONDER IF THAT SONG WAS ABOUT THE TWO DEAD LANDS.
PER-HAPS... A SURVI-VOR?
ANNE, LOOK THERE.
HM?
THAT'S A MAP SHOP, ISN'T IT?
YOU'RE RIGHT!
THEY MIGHT HAVE MAPS TO THE EMPIRE IN STOCK.
RIGHT, LET'S CHECK IT OUT.
INDEED, I DO!
!!
A TRAVELER SOLD ONE TO ME A LONG TIME AGO.
HEH HEH
REALLY? AND YOU'RE SURE THAT'S WHAT IT IS?

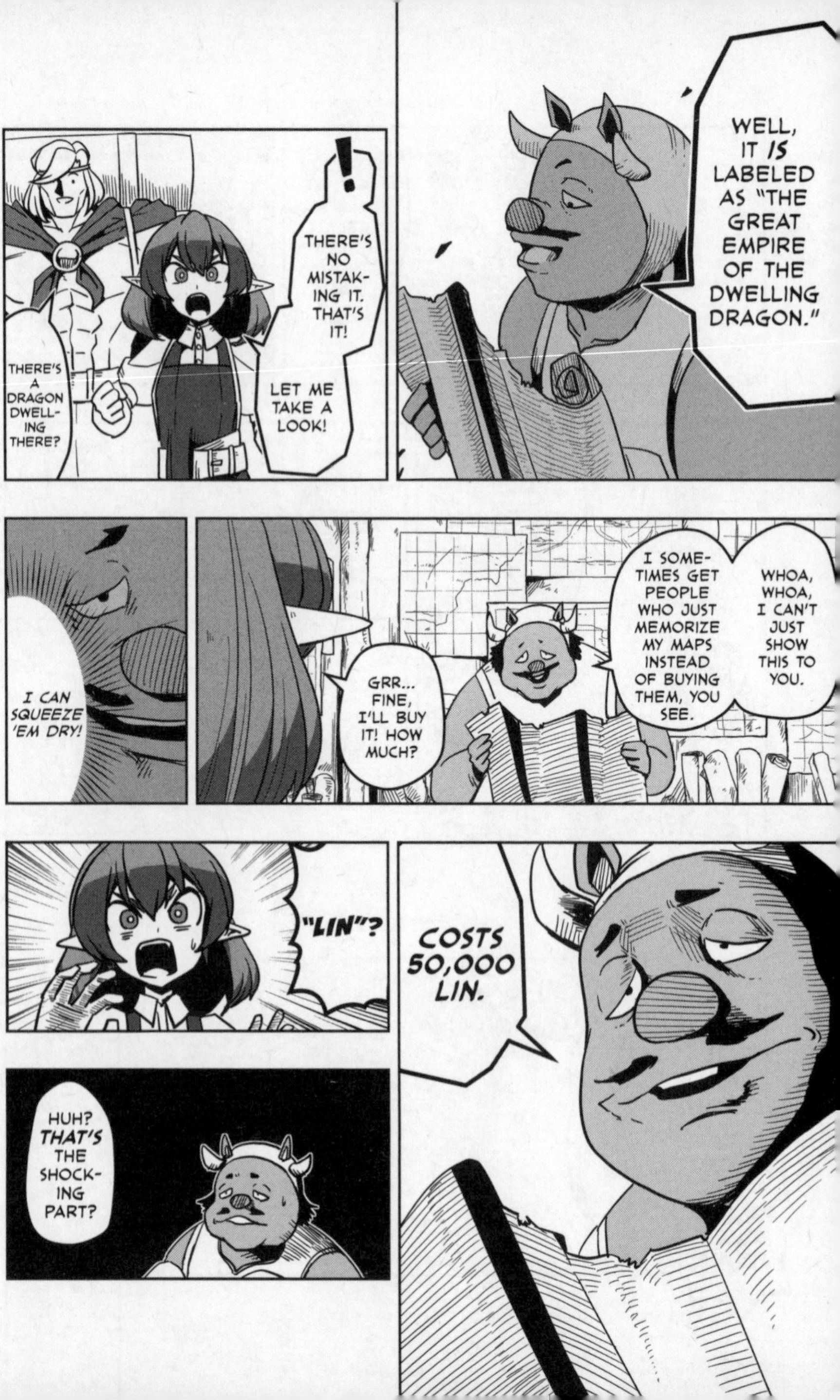
WELL, IT IS LABELED AS "THE GREAT EMPIRE OF THE DWELLING DRAGON."
!
THERE'S NO MISTAK-ING IT. THAT'S IT!
LET ME TAKE A LOOK!
THERE'S A DRAGON DWELL-ING THERE?
WHOA, WHOA, I CAN'T JUST SHOW THIS TO YOU.
I SOME-TIMES GET PEOPLE WHO JUST MEMORIZE MY MAPS INSTEAD OF BUYING THEM, YOU SEE.
GRR... FINE, I'LL BUY IT! HOW MUCH?
I CAN SQUEEZE 'EM DRY!
COSTS 50,000 LIN.
"LIN"?
HUH? THAT'S THE SHOCK-ING PART?

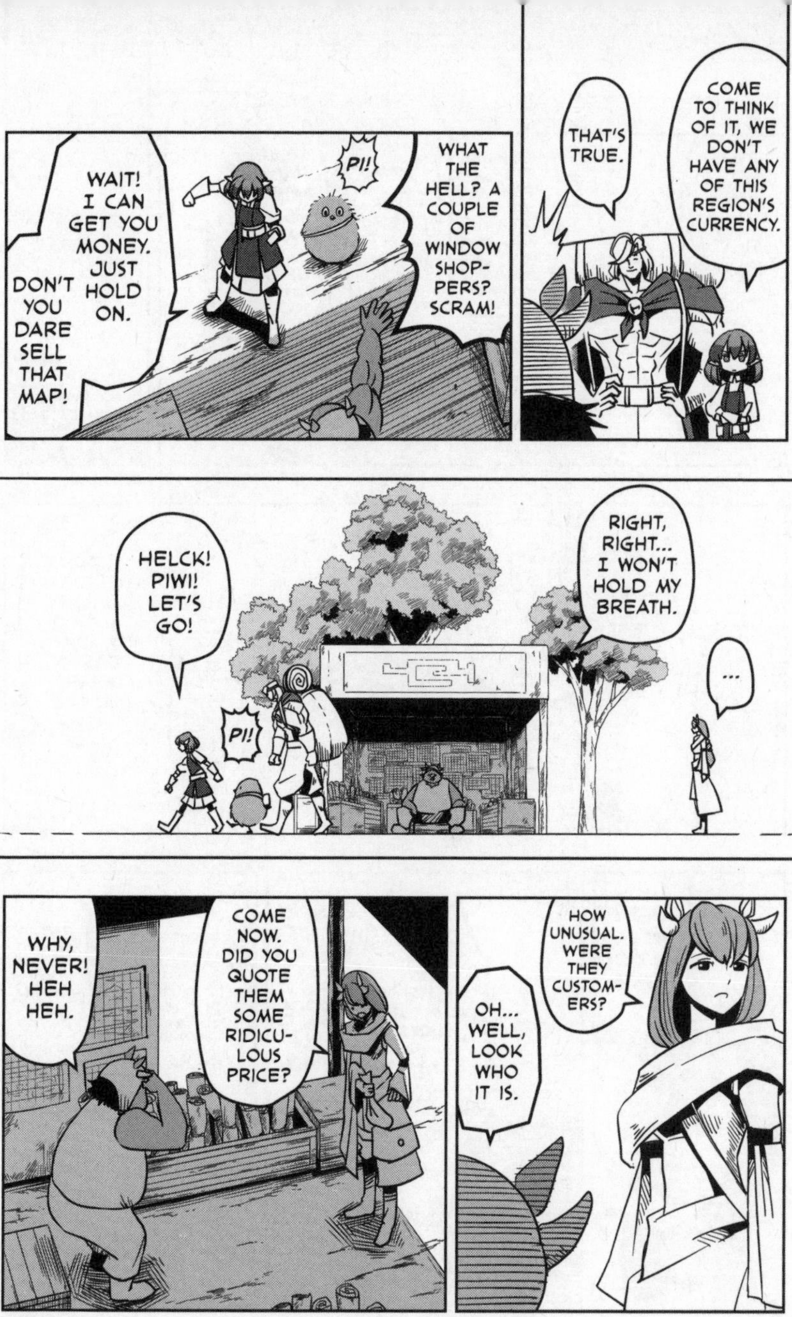
COME TO THINK OF IT, WE DON'T HAVE ANY OF THIS REGION'S CURRENCY.
THAT'S TRUE.
WHAT THE HELL? A COUPLE OF WINDOW SHOP-PERS? SCRAM!
PI!
WAIT! I CAN GET YOU MONEY. JUST HOLD ON.
DON'T YOU DARE SELL THAT MAP!
RIGHT, RIGHT... I WON'T HOLD MY BREATH.
...
HELCK! PIWI! LET'S GO!
PI!
HOW UNUSUAL. WERE THEY CUSTOM-ERS?
OH... WELL, LOOK WHO IT IS.
COME NOW. DID YOU QUOTE THEM SOME RIDICU-LOUS PRICE?
WHY, NEVER! HEH HEH.

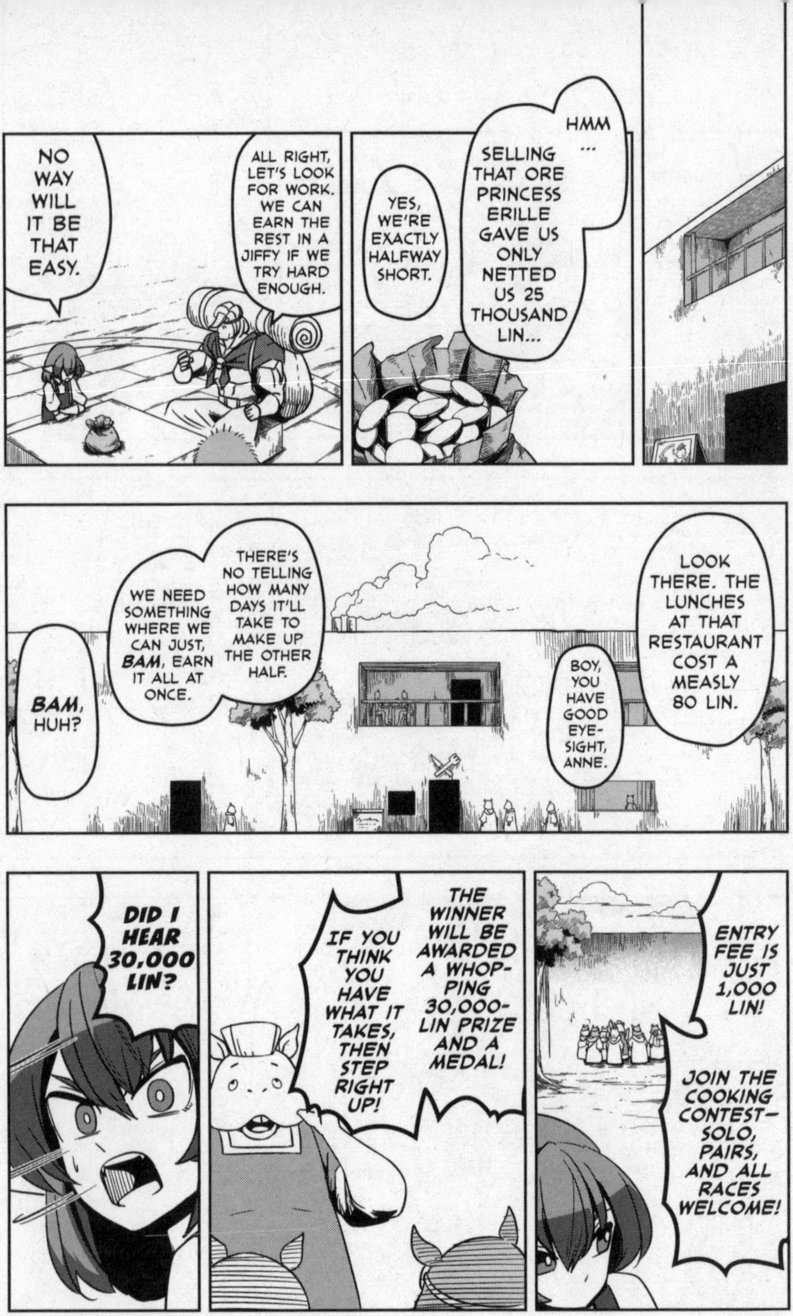
HMM...
SELLING THAT ORE PRINCESS ERILLE GAVE US ONLY NETTED US 25 THOUSAND LIN...
YES, WE'RE EXACTLY HALFWAY SHORT.
ALL RIGHT, LET'S LOOK FOR WORK. WE CAN EARN THE REST IN A JIFFY IF WE TRY HARD ENOUGH.
NO WAY WILL IT BE THAT EASY.
LOOK THERE. THE LUNCHES AT THAT RESTAURANT COST A MEASLY 80 LIN.
BOY, YOU HAVE GOOD EYE-SIGHT, ANNE.
THERE'S NO TELLING HOW MANY DAYS IT'LL TAKE TO MAKE UP THE OTHER HALF.
WE NEED SOMETHING WHERE WE CAN JUST, *BAM*, EARN IT ALL AT ONCE.
BAM, HUH?
ENTRY FEE IS JUST 1,000 LIN!
JOIN THE COOKING CONTEST— SOLO, PAIRS, AND ALL RACES WELCOME!
THE WINNER WILL BE AWARDED A WHOP-PING 30,000-LIN PRIZE AND A MEDAL!
IF YOU THINK YOU HAVE WHAT IT TAKES, THEN STEP RIGHT UP!
DID I HEAR 30,000 LIN?

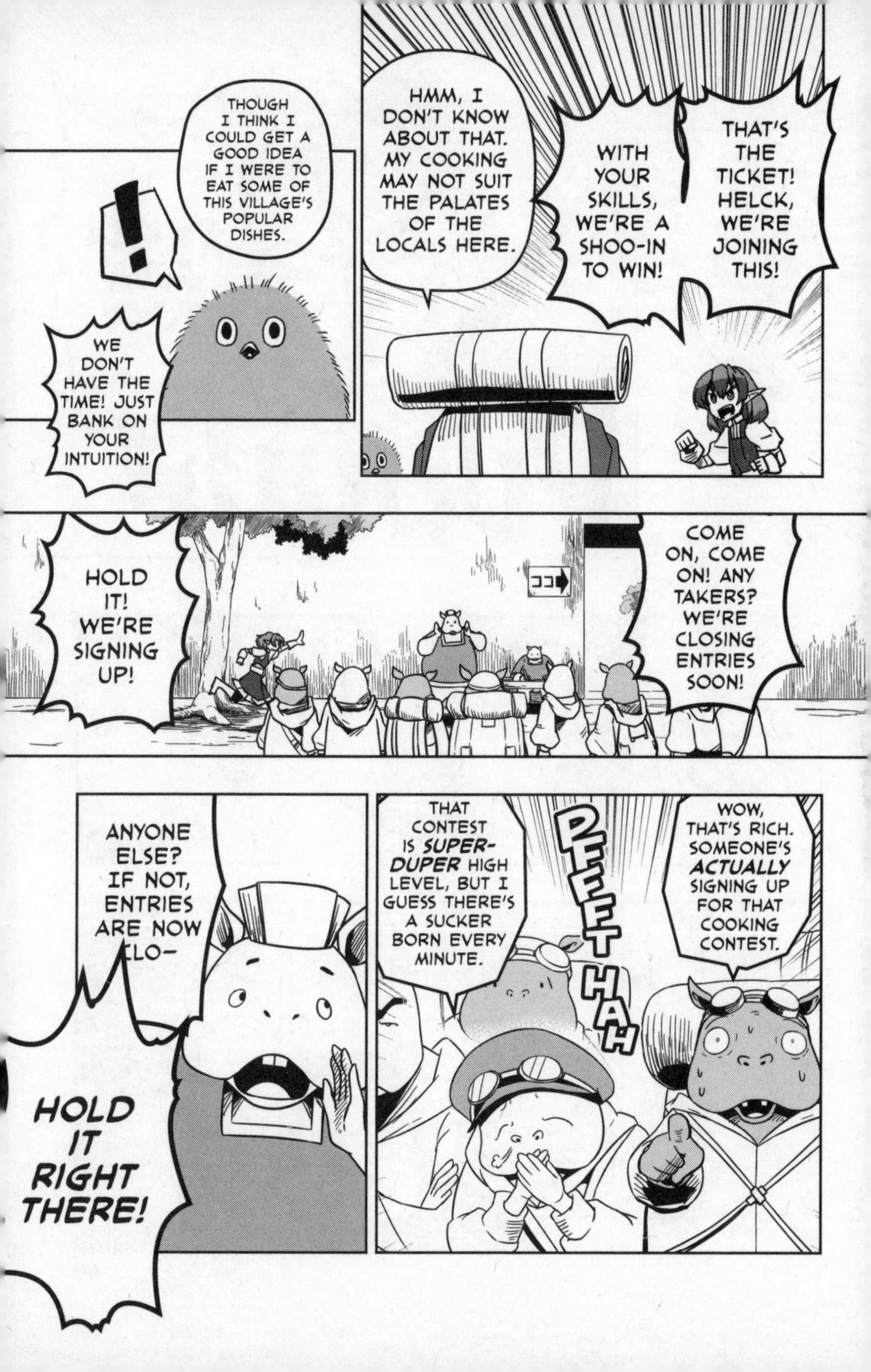
THAT'S THE TICKET! HELCK, WE'RE JOINING THIS!
WITH YOUR SKILLS, WE'RE A SHOO-IN TO WIN!
HMM, I DON'T KNOW ABOUT THAT. MY COOKING MAY NOT SUIT THE PALATES OF THE LOCALS HERE.
THOUGH I THINK I COULD GET A GOOD IDEA IF I WERE TO EAT SOME OF THIS VILLAGE'S POPULAR DISHES.
!
WE DON'T HAVE THE TIME! JUST BANK ON YOUR INTUITION!
COME ON, COME ON! ANY TAKERS? WE'RE CLOSING ENTRIES SOON!
ココ
HOLD IT! WE'RE SIGNING UP!
WOW, THAT'S RICH. SOMEONE'S *ACTUALLY* SIGNING UP FOR THAT COOKING CONTEST.
PFFFT HAH
THAT CONTEST IS *SUPER-DUPER* HIGH LEVEL, BUT I GUESS THERE'S A SUCKER BORN EVERY MINUTE.
ANYONE ELSE? IF NOT, ENTRIES ARE NOW CLO—
HOLD IT RIGHT THERE!

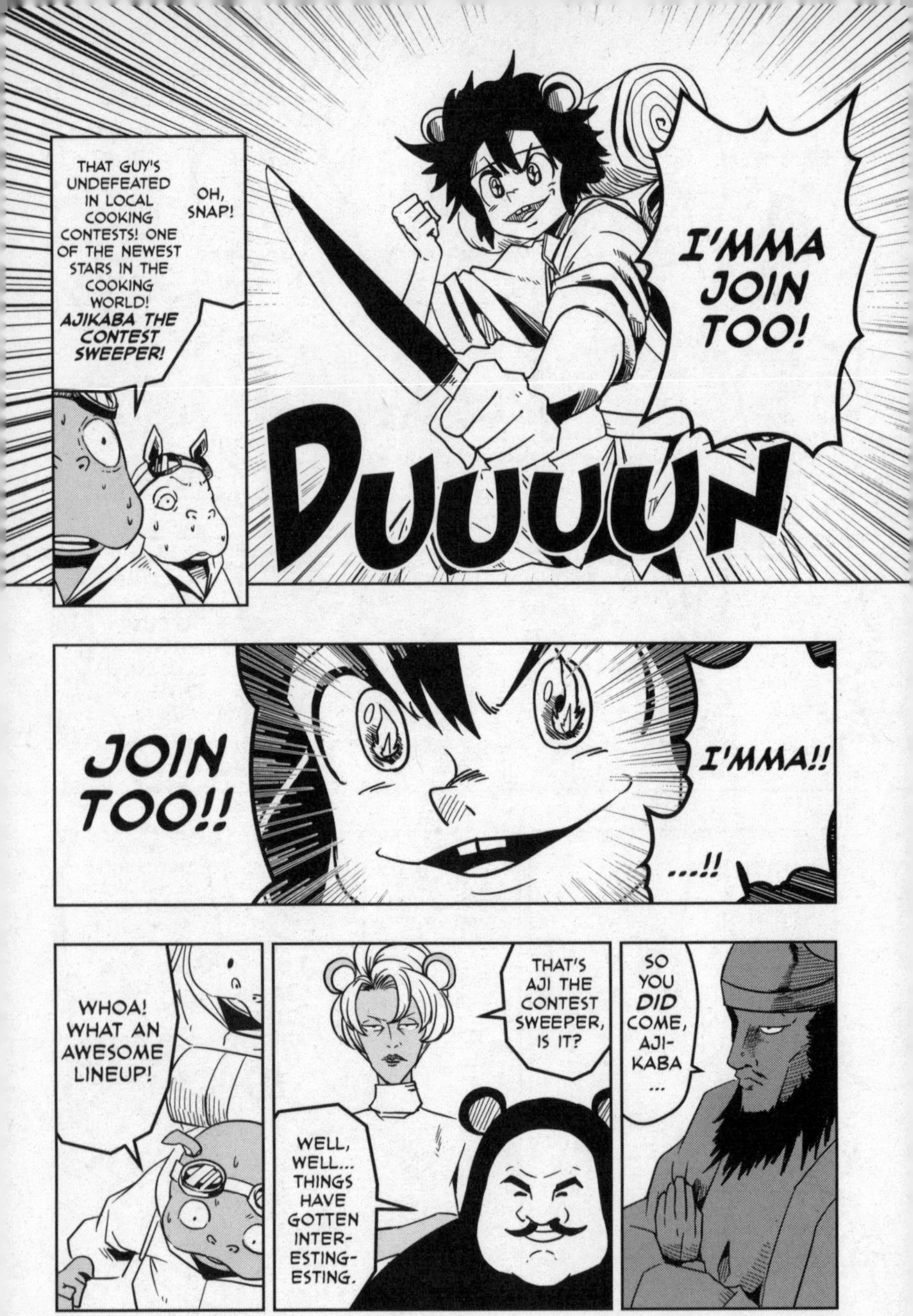
I'MMA JOIN TOO!
DUUUUUN
OH, SNAP!
THAT GUY'S UNDEFEATED IN LOCAL COOKING CONTESTS! ONE OF THE NEWEST STARS IN THE COOKING WORLD! *AJIKABA THE CONTEST SWEEPER!*
I'MMA!!
JOIN TOO!!
...!!
SO YOU *DID* COME, AJI-KABA...
THAT'S AJI THE CONTEST SWEEPER, IS IT?
WELL, WELL... THINGS HAVE GOTTEN INTER-ESTING-ESTING.
WHOA! WHAT AN AWESOME LINEUP!

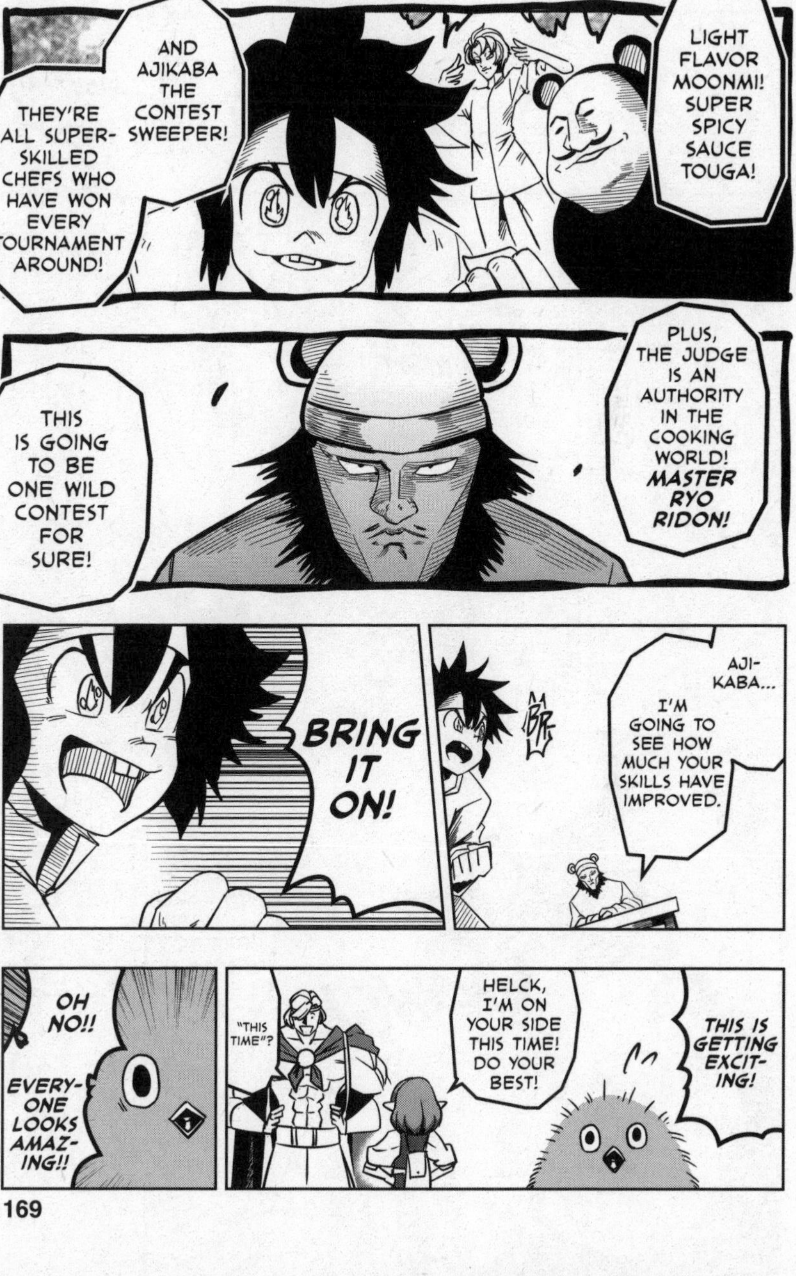
LIGHT FLAVOR MOONMI! SUPER SPICY SAUCE TOUGA!
AND AJIKABA THE CONTEST SWEEPER!
THEY'RE ALL SUPER-SKILLED CHEFS WHO HAVE WON EVERY TOURNAMENT AROUND!
PLUS, THE JUDGE IS AN AUTHORITY IN THE COOKING WORLD! MASTER RYO RIDON!
THIS IS GOING TO BE ONE WILD CONTEST FOR SURE!
AJI-KABA...
I'M GOING TO SEE HOW MUCH YOUR SKILLS HAVE IMPROVED.
BRING IT ON!
THIS IS GETTING EXCIT-ING!
HELCK, I'M ON YOUR SIDE THIS TIME! DO YOUR BEST!
"THIS TIME"?
OH NO!!
EVERY-ONE LOOKS AMAZ-ING!!

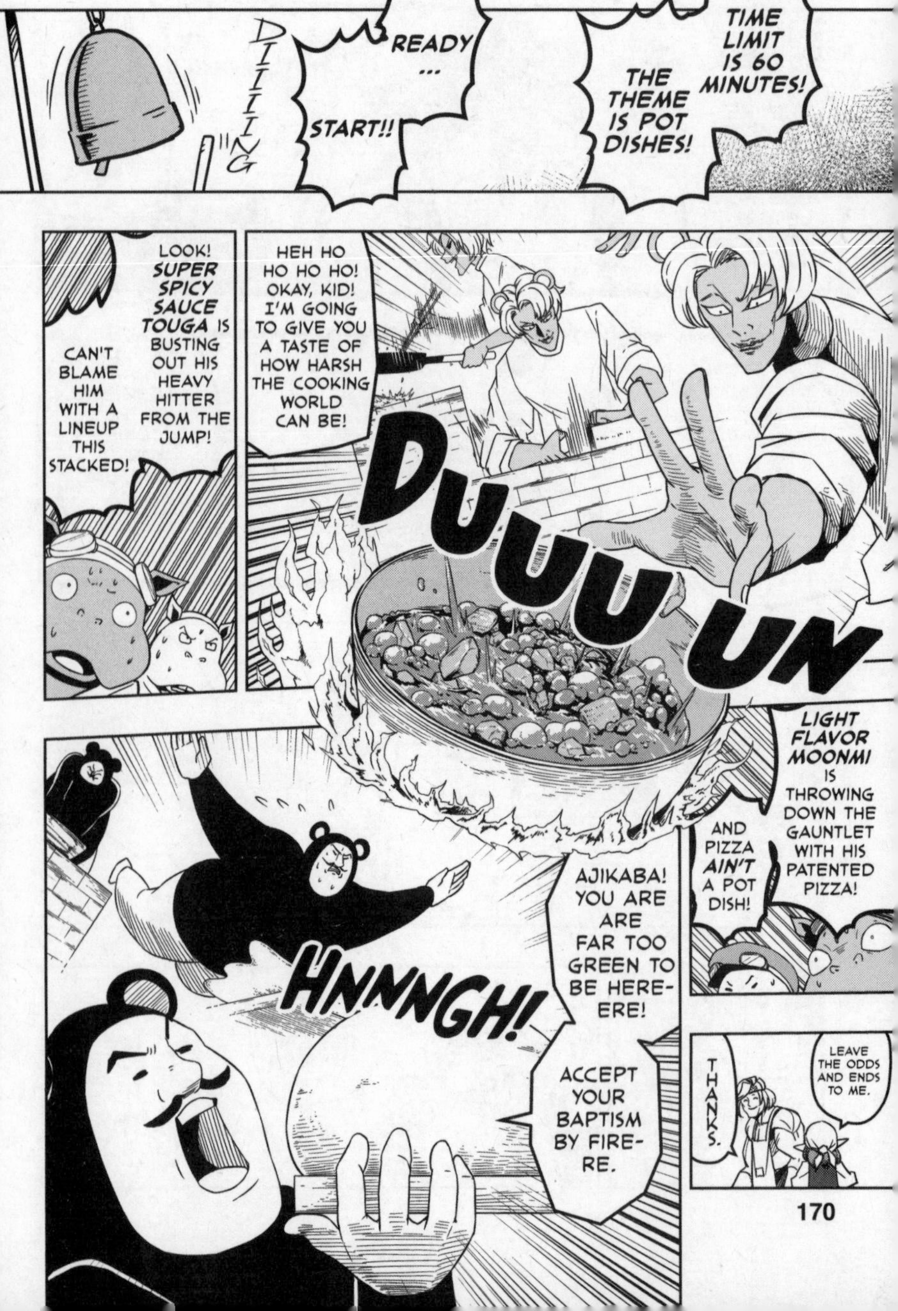
TIME LIMIT IS 60 MINUTES!
THE THEME IS POT DISHES!
READY... START!!
DIIIIING
HEH HO HO HO HO! OKAY, KID! I'M GOING TO GIVE YOU A TASTE OF HOW HARSH THE COOKING WORLD CAN BE!
DUUUUUN
LOOK! *SUPER SPICY SAUCE TOUGA* IS BUSTING OUT HIS HEAVY HITTER FROM THE JUMP!
CAN'T BLAME HIM WITH A LINEUP THIS STACKED!
LIGHT FLAVOR MOONMI IS THROWING DOWN THE GAUNTLET WITH HIS PATENTED PIZZA!
AND PIZZA *AIN'T* A POT DISH!
LEAVE THE ODDS AND ENDS TO ME.
THANKS.
AJIKABA! YOU ARE ARE FAR TOO GREEN TO BE HERE-ERE!
HNNNGH!
ACCEPT YOUR BAPTISM BY FIRE-RE.

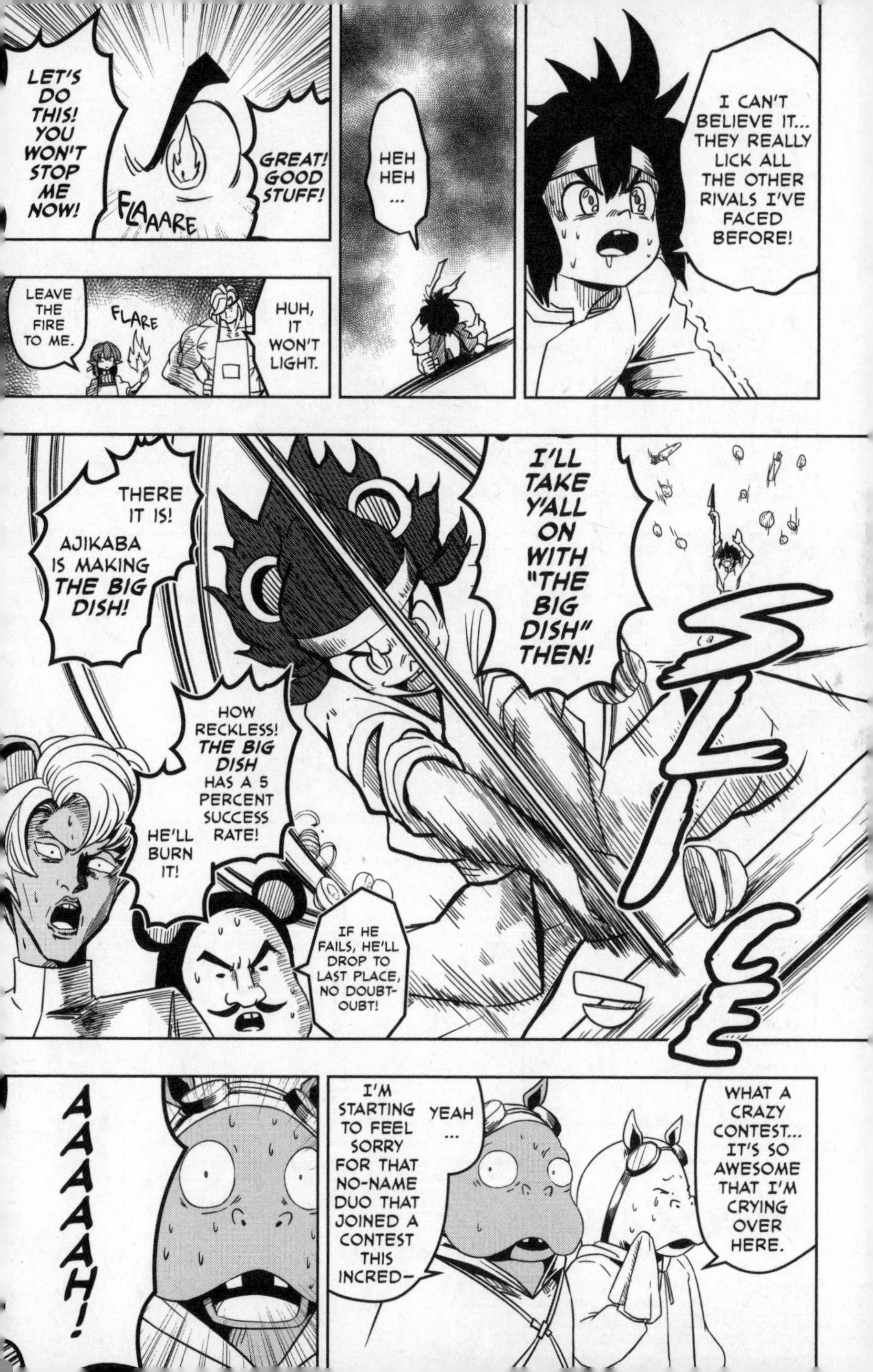
I CAN'T BELIEVE IT... THEY REALLY LICK ALL THE OTHER RIVALS I'VE FACED BEFORE!
HEH HEH ...
GREAT! GOOD STUFF!
LET'S DO THIS! YOU WON'T STOP ME NOW!
FLAAARE
HUH, IT WON'T LIGHT.
FLARE
LEAVE THE FIRE TO ME.
I'LL TAKE Y'ALL ON WITH "THE BIG DISH" THEN!
SLICE
THERE IT IS! AJIKABA IS MAKING THE BIG DISH!
HOW RECKLESS! THE BIG DISH HAS A 5 PERCENT SUCCESS RATE!
HE'LL BURN IT!
IF HE FAILS, HE'LL DROP TO LAST PLACE, NO DOUBT-OUBT!
WHAT A CRAZY CONTEST... IT'S SO AWESOME THAT I'M CRYING OVER HERE.
YEAH ...
I'M STARTING TO FEEL SORRY FOR THAT NO-NAME DUO THAT JOINED A CONTEST THIS INCRED–
AAAAAAH!

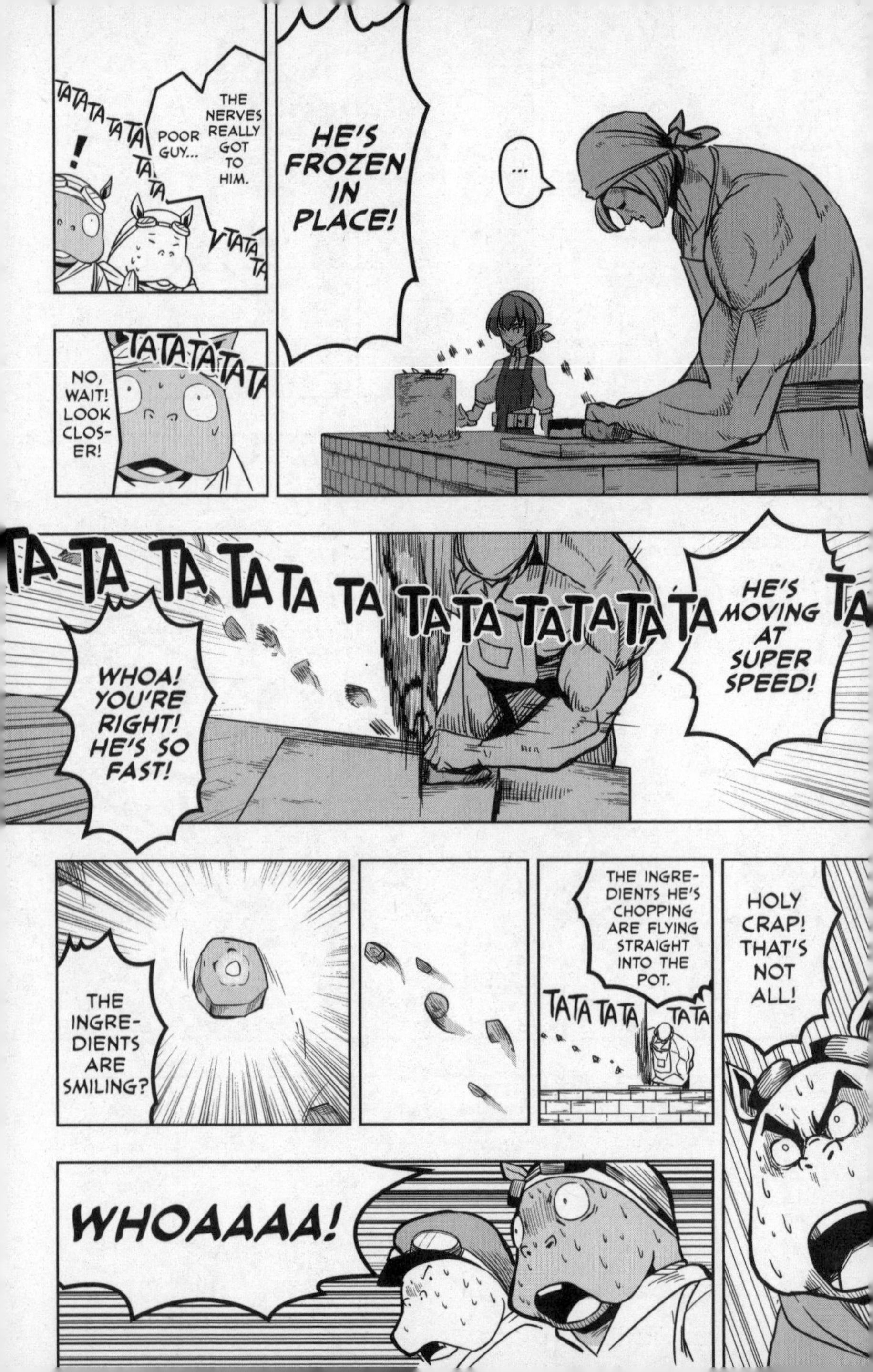

...
HE'S FROZEN IN PLACE!
THE NERVES REALLY GOT TO HIM.
POOR GUY...
TATATATATA TA TA
!
TATATA
TATATATATATA
NO, WAIT! LOOK CLOS- ER!
HE'S MOVING AT SUPER SPEED!
TA TA TA TA TATA TA TATA TATATATATA TA
WHOA! YOU'RE RIGHT! HE'S SO FAST!
HOLY CRAP! THAT'S NOT ALL!
THE INGRE- DIENTS HE'S CHOPPING ARE FLYING STRAIGHT INTO THE POT.
TATATATA TATA
THE INGRE- DIENTS ARE SMILING?
WHOAAAA!

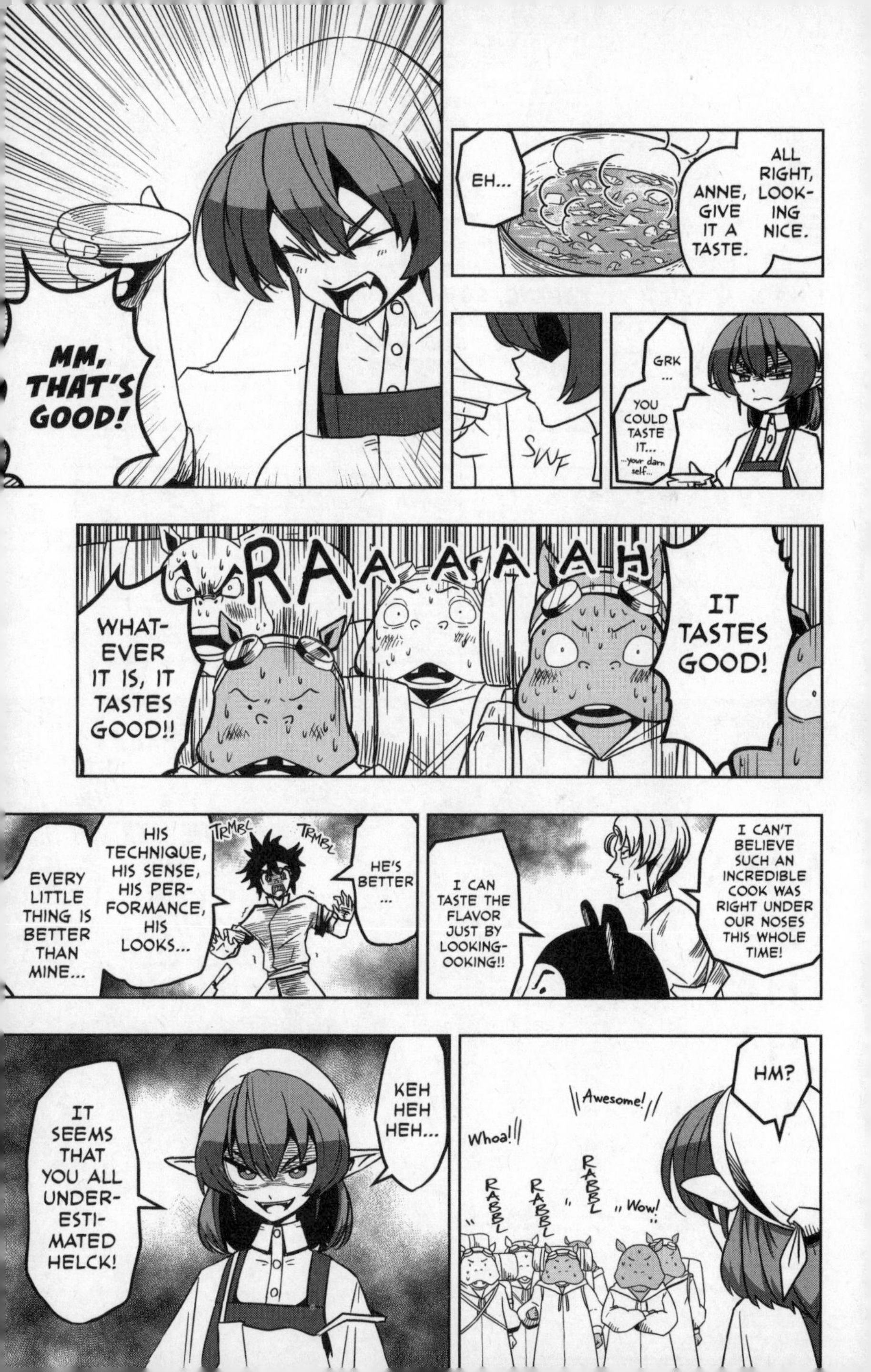
ALL RIGHT, LOOKING NICE.
ANNE, GIVE IT A TASTE.
EH...
MM, THAT'S GOOD!
GRK ...
YOU COULD TASTE IT...
...your darn self...
SWF
RAAAAAH
IT TASTES GOOD!
WHATEVER IT IS, IT TASTES GOOD!!
I CAN'T BELIEVE SUCH AN INCREDIBLE COOK WAS RIGHT UNDER OUR NOSES THIS WHOLE TIME!
I CAN TASTE THE FLAVOR JUST BY LOOKING-OOKING!!
HE'S BETTER ...
TRMBL
TRMBL
HIS TECHNIQUE, HIS SENSE, HIS PERFORMANCE, HIS LOOKS...
EVERY LITTLE THING IS BETTER THAN MINE...
HM?
Awesome!
Whoa!
RABBL
RABBL
RABBL
Wow!
KEH HEH HEH...
IT SEEMS THAT YOU ALL UNDERESTIMATED HELCK!

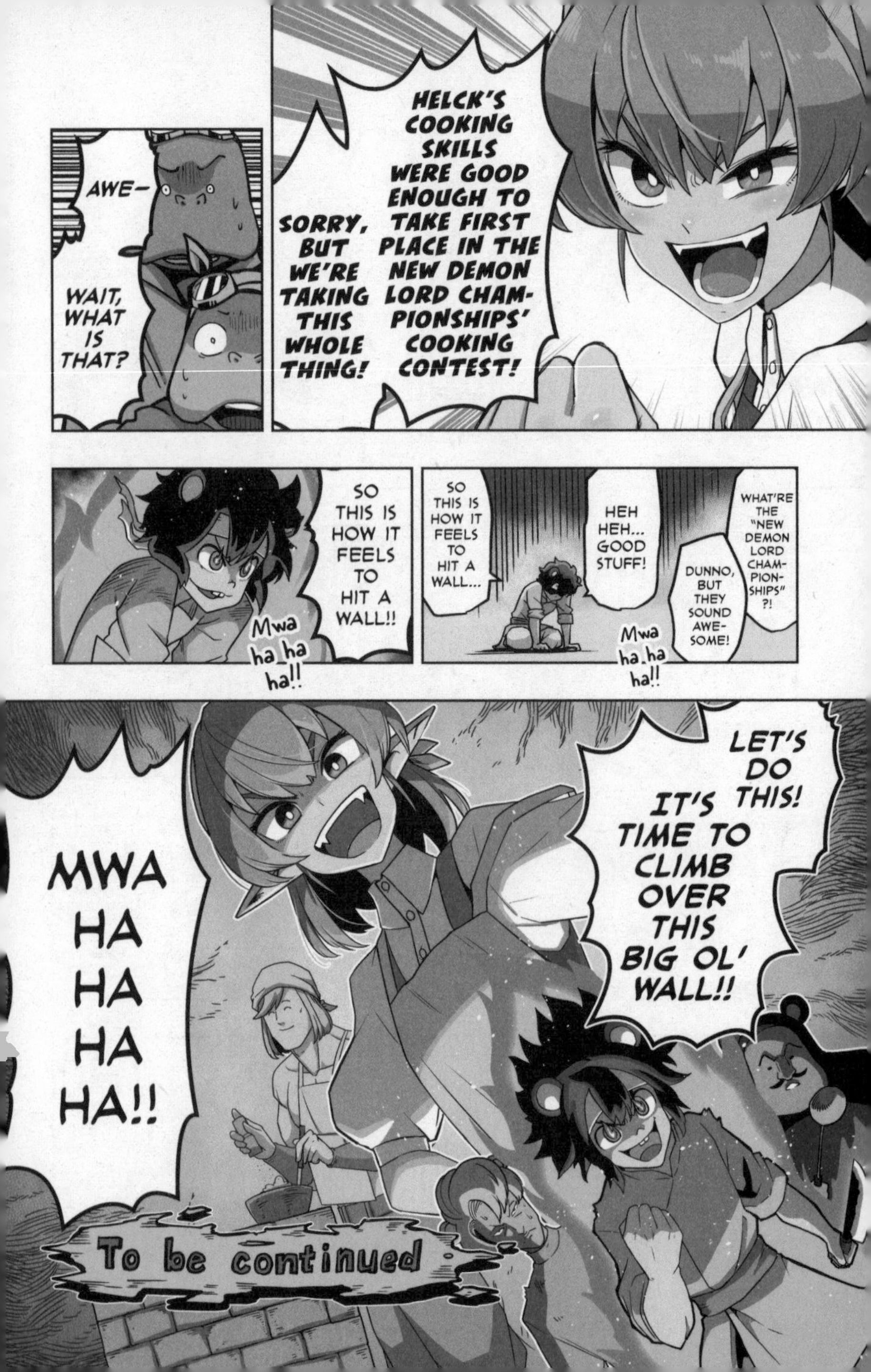
HELCK'S COOKING SKILLS WERE GOOD ENOUGH TO TAKE FIRST PLACE IN THE NEW DEMON LORD CHAMPIONSHIPS' COOKING CONTEST!
SORRY, BUT WE'RE TAKING THIS WHOLE THING!
AWE—
WAIT, WHAT IS THAT?
WHAT'RE THE "NEW DEMON LORD CHAMPIONSHIPS"?!
DUNNO, BUT THEY SOUND AWESOME!
HEH HEH... GOOD STUFF!
SO THIS IS HOW IT FEELS TO HIT A WALL...
Mwa ha ha ha!!
SO THIS IS HOW IT FEELS TO HIT A WALL!!
Mwa ha ha ha!!
LET'S DO THIS!
IT'S TIME TO CLIMB OVER THIS BIG OL' WALL!!
MWA HA HA HA HA!!
To be continued

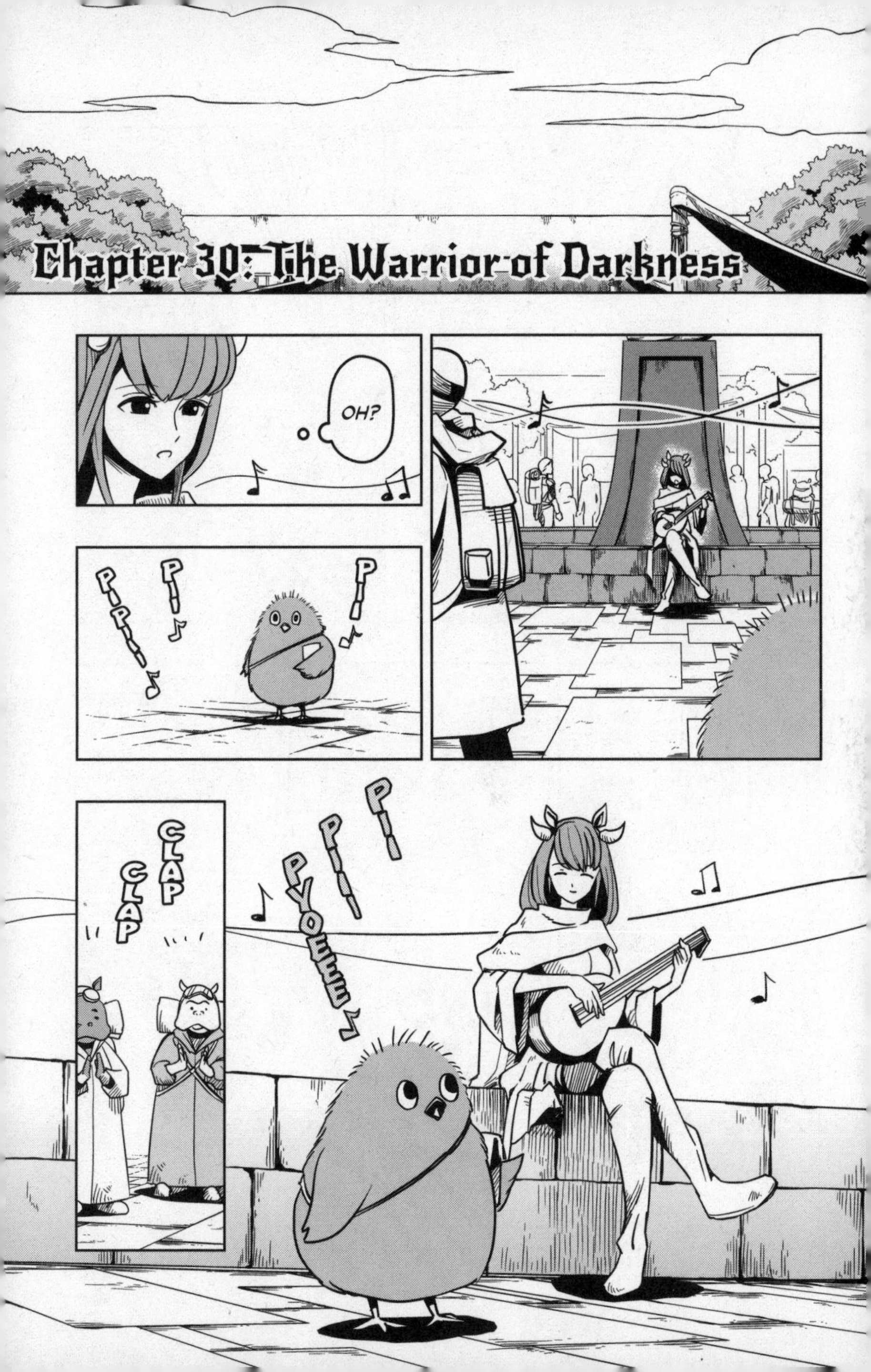
Chapter 30: The Warrior of Darkness
OH?
PI♪
PI♪
PIPIII♪
PI
PI
PYOEEE♪
CLAP
CLAP

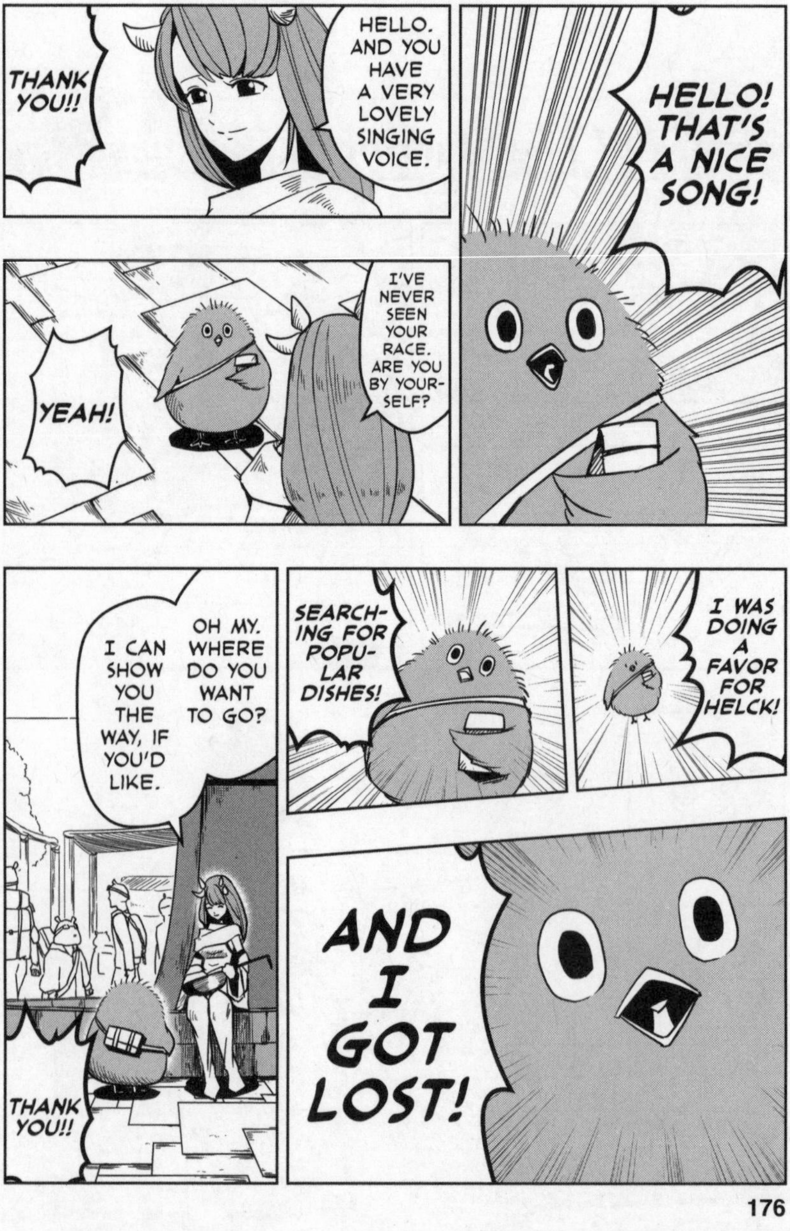
HELLO! THAT'S A NICE SONG!
HELLO. AND YOU HAVE A VERY LOVELY SINGING VOICE.
THANK YOU!!
I'VE NEVER SEEN YOUR RACE. ARE YOU BY YOURSELF?
YEAH!
I WAS DOING A FAVOR FOR HELCK!
SEARCHING FOR POPULAR DISHES!
AND I GOT LOST!
OH MY. WHERE DO YOU WANT TO GO?
I CAN SHOW YOU THE WAY, IF YOU'D LIKE.
THANK YOU!!

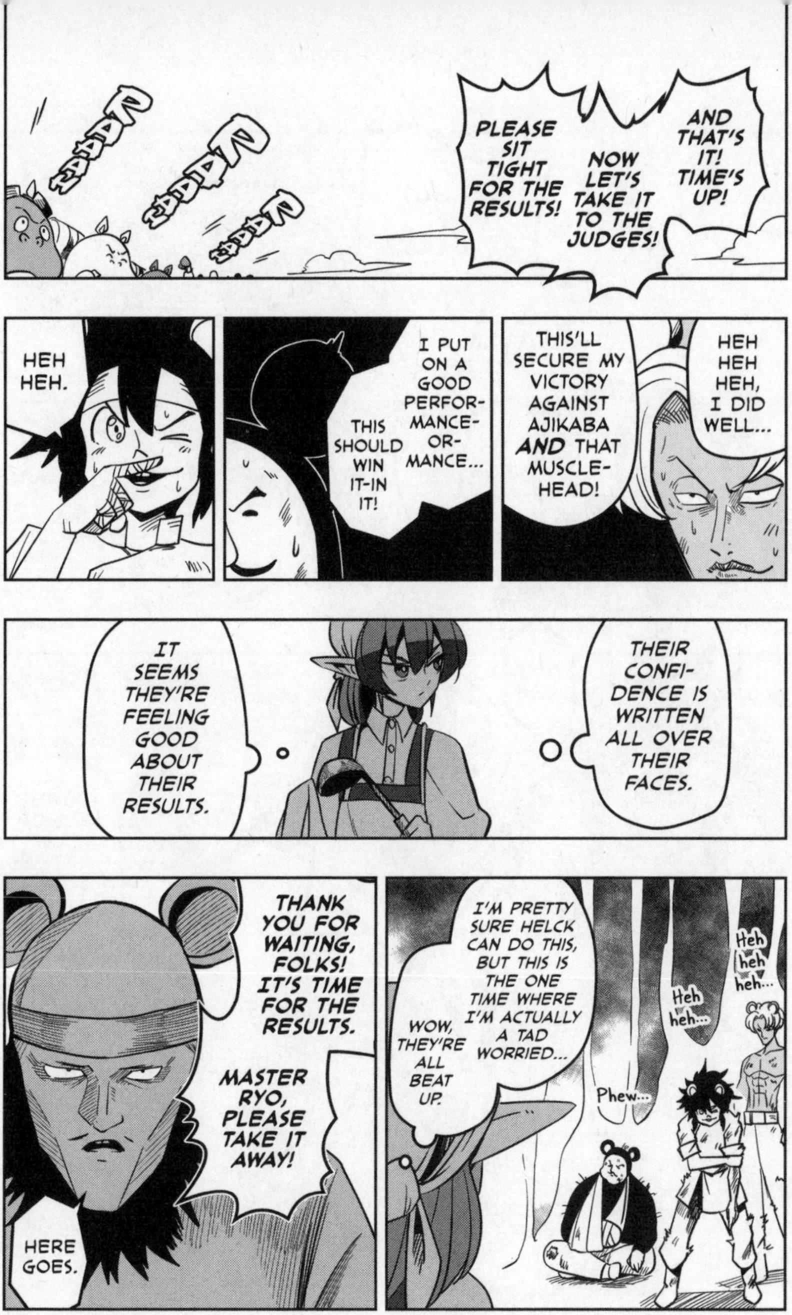
AND THAT'S IT! TIME'S UP!
NOW LET'S TAKE IT TO THE JUDGES!
PLEASE SIT TIGHT FOR THE RESULTS!
RAAAH
RAAAAH
RAAH
HEH HEH HEH, I DID WELL...
THIS'LL SECURE MY VICTORY AGAINST AJIKABA AND THAT MUSCLE-HEAD!
I PUT ON A GOOD PERFOR-MANCE-OR-MANCE...
THIS SHOULD WIN IT-IN IT!
HEH HEH.
THEIR CONFI-DENCE IS WRITTEN ALL OVER THEIR FACES.
IT SEEMS THEY'RE FEELING GOOD ABOUT THEIR RESULTS.
Heh heh heh...
Heh heh...
I'M PRETTY SURE HELCK CAN DO THIS, BUT THIS IS THE ONE TIME WHERE I'M ACTUALLY A TAD WORRIED...
Phew...
WOW, THEY'RE ALL BEAT UP.
THANK YOU FOR WAITING, FOLKS! IT'S TIME FOR THE RESULTS.
MASTER RYO, PLEASE TAKE IT AWAY!
HERE GOES.

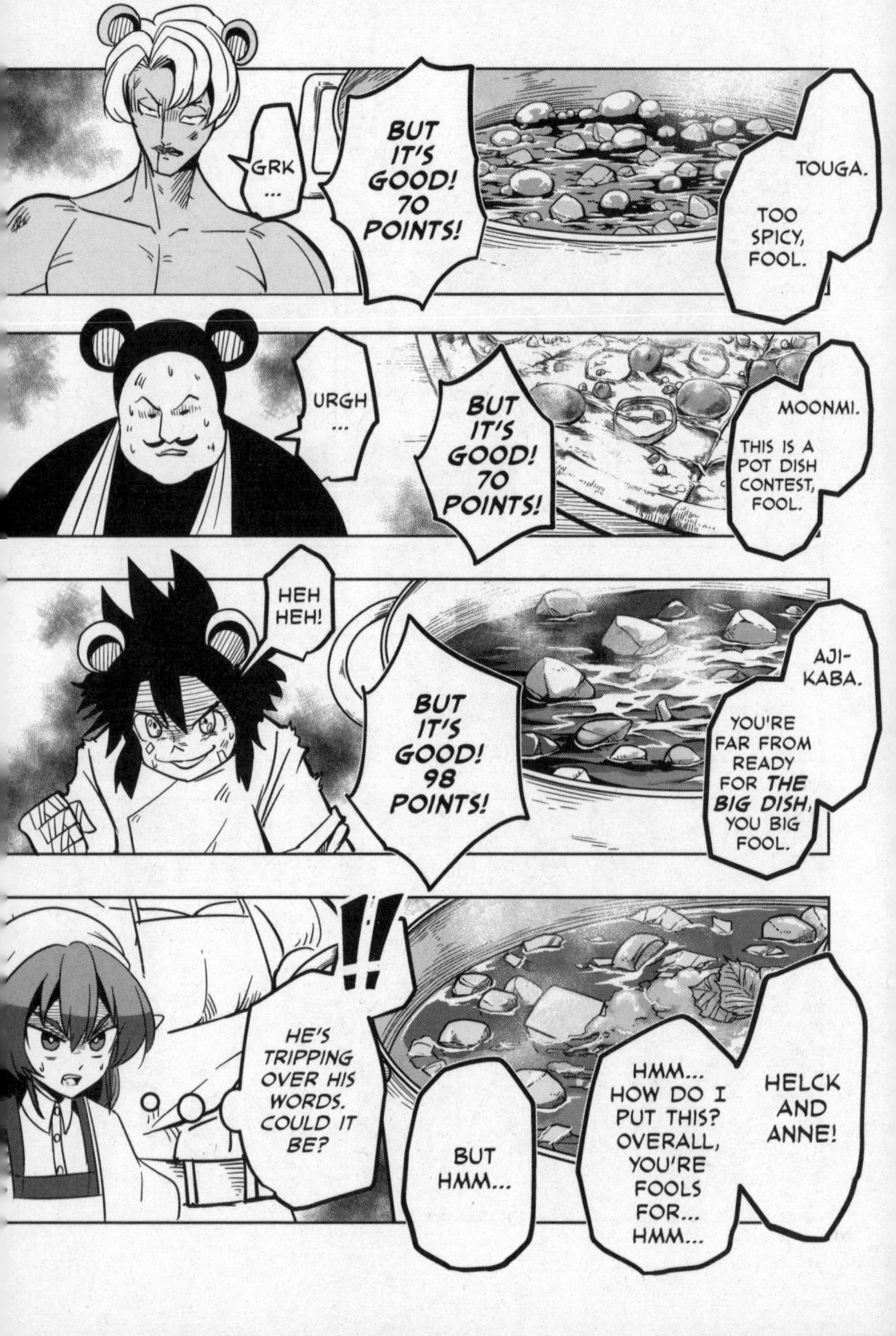
TOUGA. TOO SPICY, FOOL.
BUT IT'S GOOD! 70 POINTS!
GRK ...
MOONMI. THIS IS A POT DISH CONTEST, FOOL.
BUT IT'S GOOD! 70 POINTS!
URGH ...
AJI-KABA. YOU'RE FAR FROM READY FOR *THE BIG DISH*, YOU BIG FOOL.
BUT IT'S GOOD! 98 POINTS!
HEH HEH!
HELCK AND ANNE!
HMM... HOW DO I PUT THIS? OVERALL, YOU'RE FOOLS FOR... HMM...
BUT HMM...
!!
HE'S TRIPPING OVER HIS WORDS. COULD IT BE?

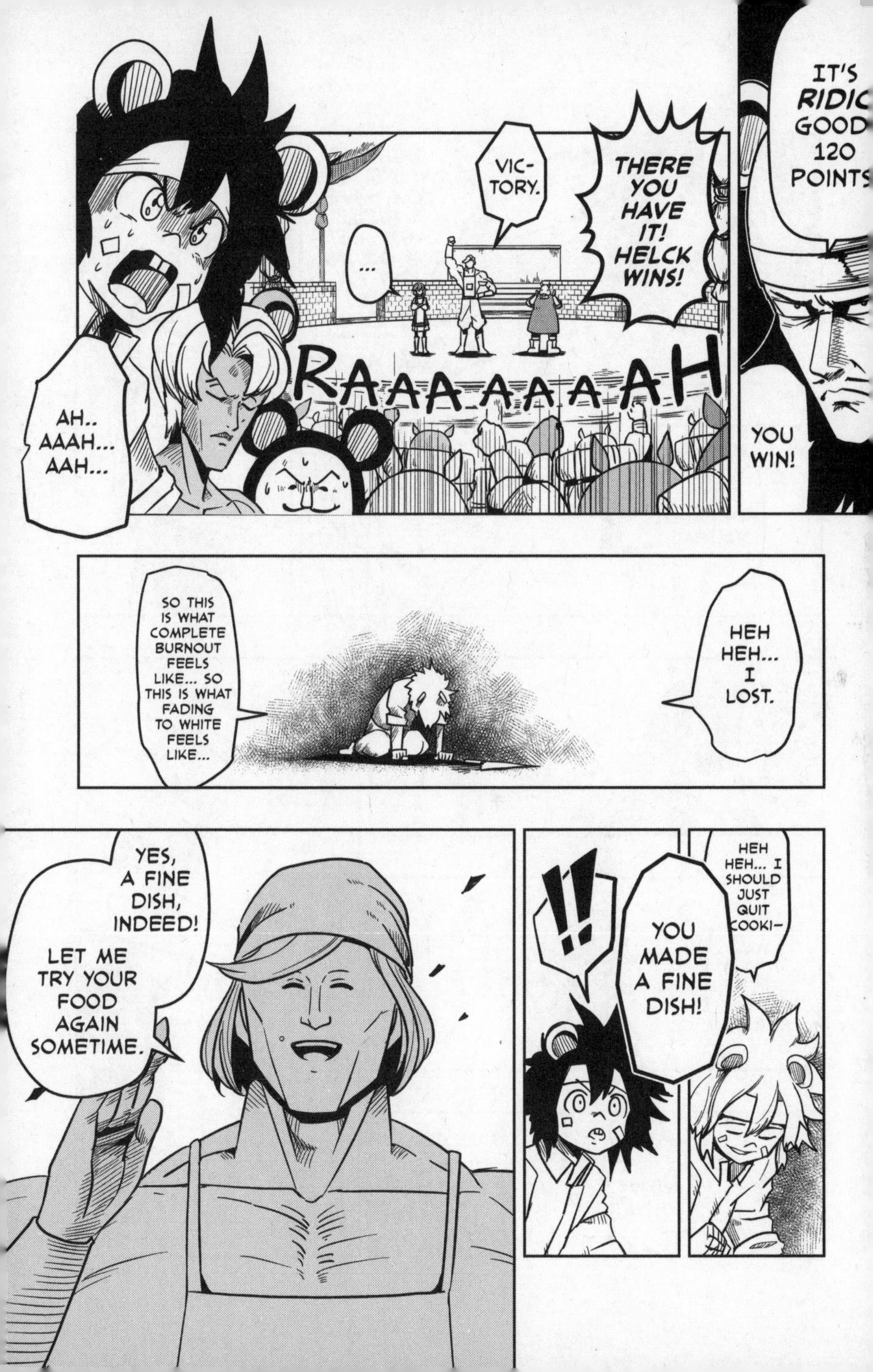
IT'S RIDIC GOOD 120 POINTS
YOU WIN!
THERE YOU HAVE IT! HELCK WINS!
VIC-TORY.
...
RAAAAAAAH
AH.. AAAH... AAH...
HEH HEH... I LOST.
SO THIS IS WHAT COMPLETE BURNOUT FEELS LIKE... SO THIS IS WHAT FADING TO WHITE FEELS LIKE...
HEH HEH... I SHOULD JUST QUIT COOKI-
YOU MADE A FINE DISH!
!!
YES, A FINE DISH, INDEED!
LET ME TRY YOUR FOOD AGAIN SOMETIME.

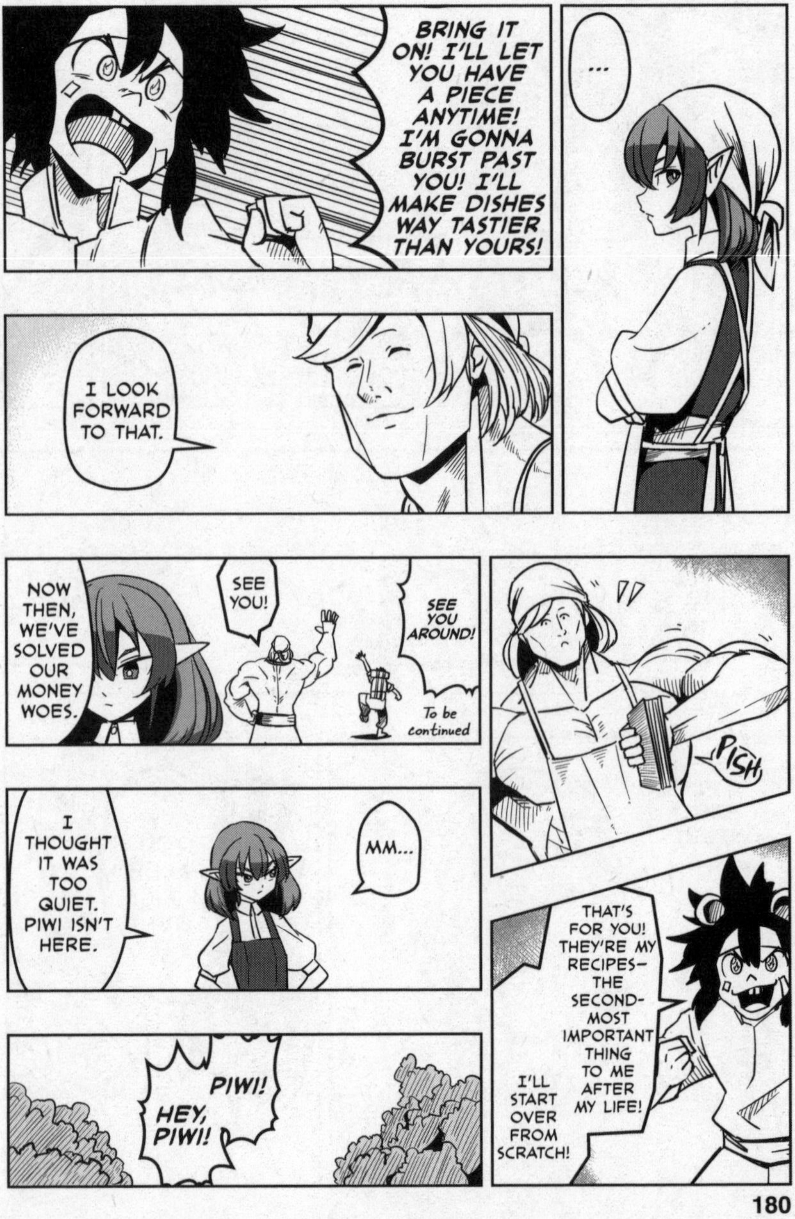
...
BRING IT ON! I'LL LET YOU HAVE A PIECE ANYTIME! I'M GONNA BURST PAST YOU! I'LL MAKE DISHES WAY TASTIER THAN YOURS!
I LOOK FORWARD TO THAT.
PISH
THAT'S FOR YOU! THEY'RE MY RECIPES—THE SECOND-MOST IMPORTANT THING TO ME AFTER MY LIFE!
I'LL START OVER FROM SCRATCH!
SEE YOU AROUND!
SEE YOU!
NOW THEN, WE'VE SOLVED OUR MONEY WOES.
To be continued
MM...
I THOUGHT IT WAS TOO QUIET. PIWI ISN'T HERE.
PIWI!
HEY, PIWI!

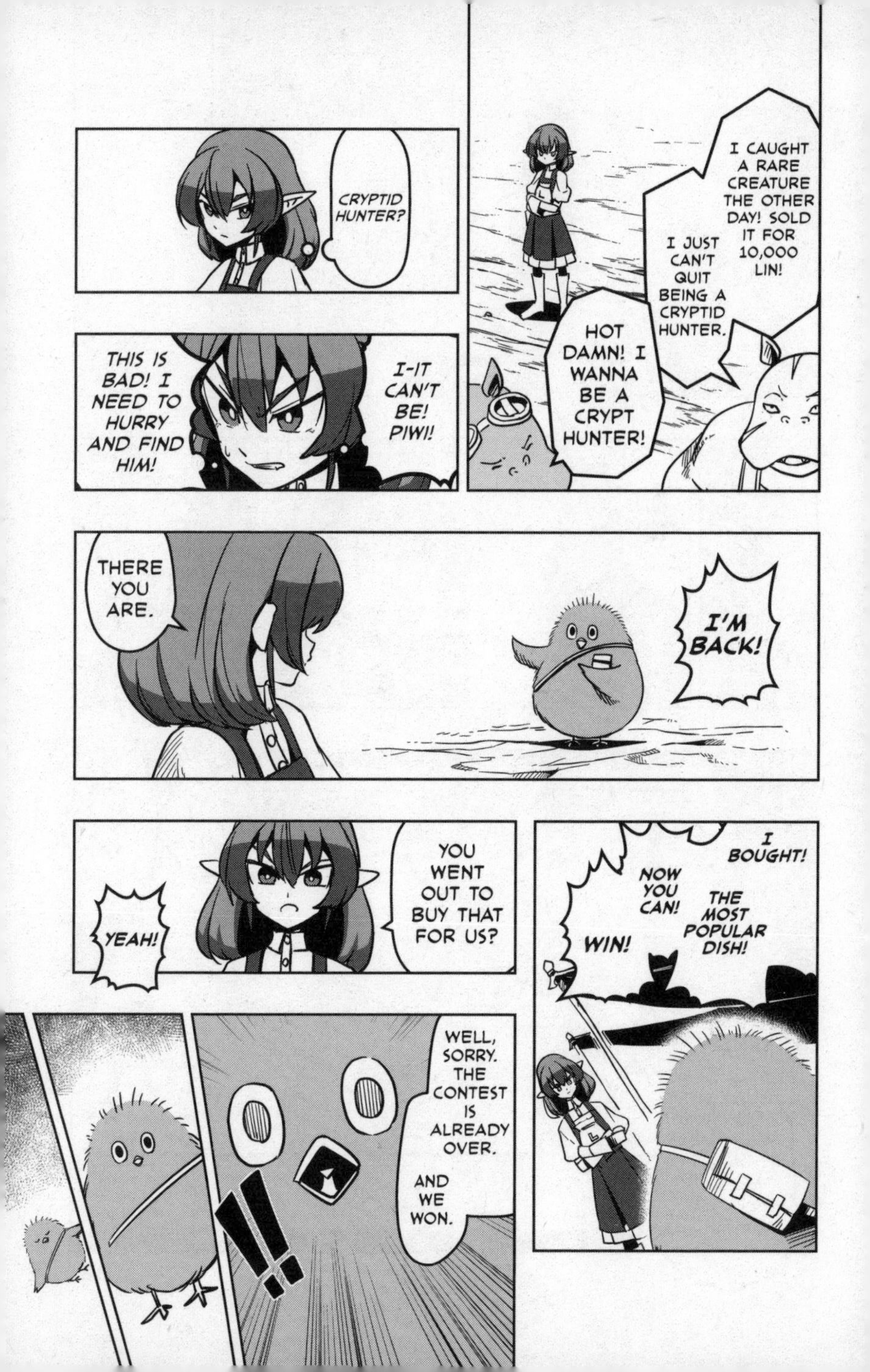
I CAUGHT A RARE CREATURE THE OTHER DAY! SOLD IT FOR 10,000 LIN!
I JUST CAN'T QUIT BEING A CRYPTID HUNTER.
HOT DAMN! I WANNA BE A CRYPT HUNTER!
CRYPTID HUNTER?
I-IT CAN'T BE! PIWI!
THIS IS BAD! I NEED TO HURRY AND FIND HIM!
I'M BACK!
THERE YOU ARE.
I BOUGHT!
THE MOST POPULAR DISH!
NOW YOU CAN!
WIN!
YOU WENT OUT TO BUY THAT FOR US?
YEAH!
WELL, SORRY. THE CONTEST IS ALREADY OVER.
AND WE WON.
!!

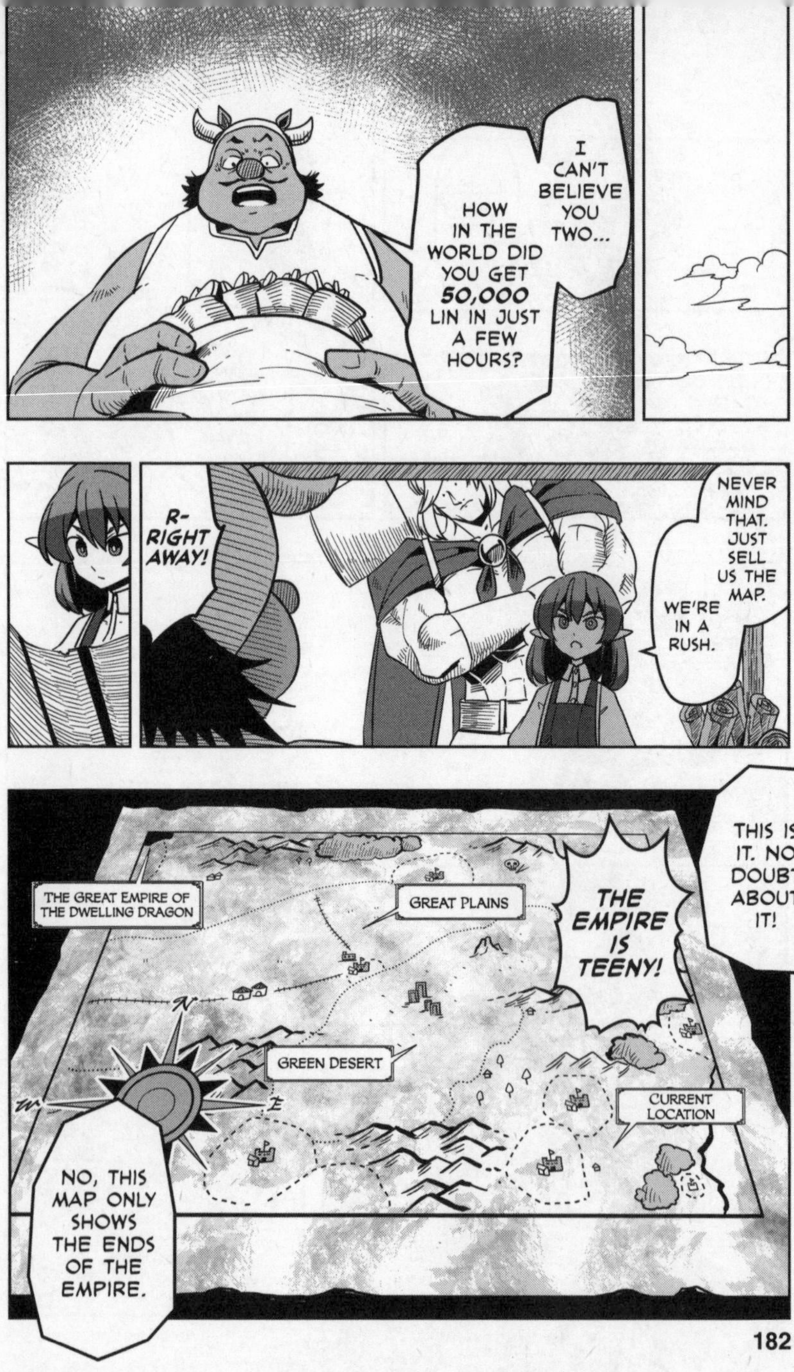
I CAN'T BELIEVE YOU TWO...
HOW IN THE WORLD DID YOU GET **50,000** LIN IN JUST A FEW HOURS?
NEVER MIND THAT. JUST SELL US THE MAP.
WE'RE IN A RUSH.
R-RIGHT AWAY!
THIS IS IT. NO DOUBT ABOUT IT!
THE EMPIRE IS TEENY!
THE GREAT EMPIRE OF THE DWELLING DRAGON
GREAT PLAINS
GREEN DESERT
CURRENT LOCATION
NO, THIS MAP ONLY SHOWS THE ENDS OF THE EMPIRE.

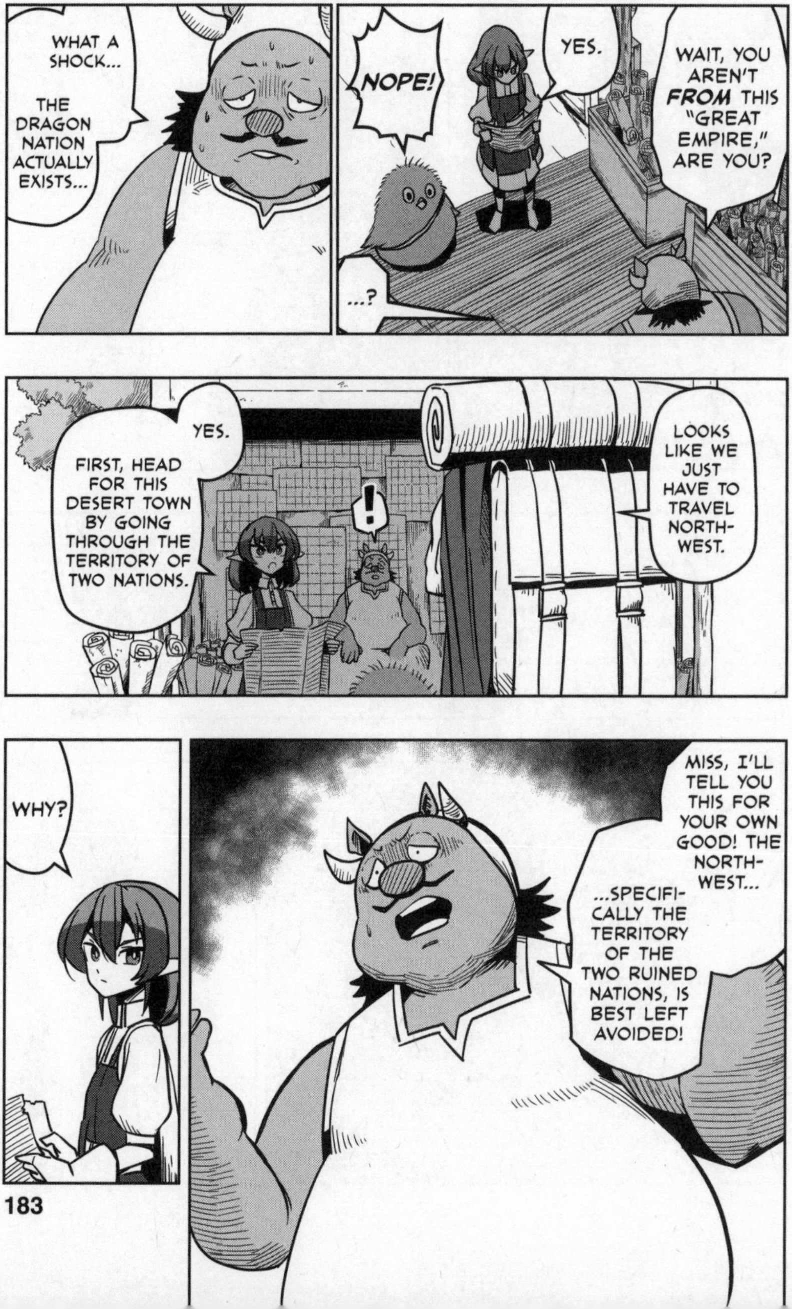
WAIT, YOU AREN'T *FROM* THIS "GREAT EMPIRE," ARE YOU?
YES.
NOPE!
...?
WHAT A SHOCK...
THE DRAGON NATION ACTUALLY EXISTS...
LOOKS LIKE WE JUST HAVE TO TRAVEL NORTH-WEST.
YES.
FIRST, HEAD FOR THIS DESERT TOWN BY GOING THROUGH THE TERRITORY OF TWO NATIONS.
!
MISS, I'LL TELL YOU THIS FOR YOUR OWN GOOD! THE NORTH-WEST...
...SPECIFI-CALLY THE TERRITORY OF THE TWO RUINED NATIONS, IS BEST LEFT AVOIDED!
WHY?

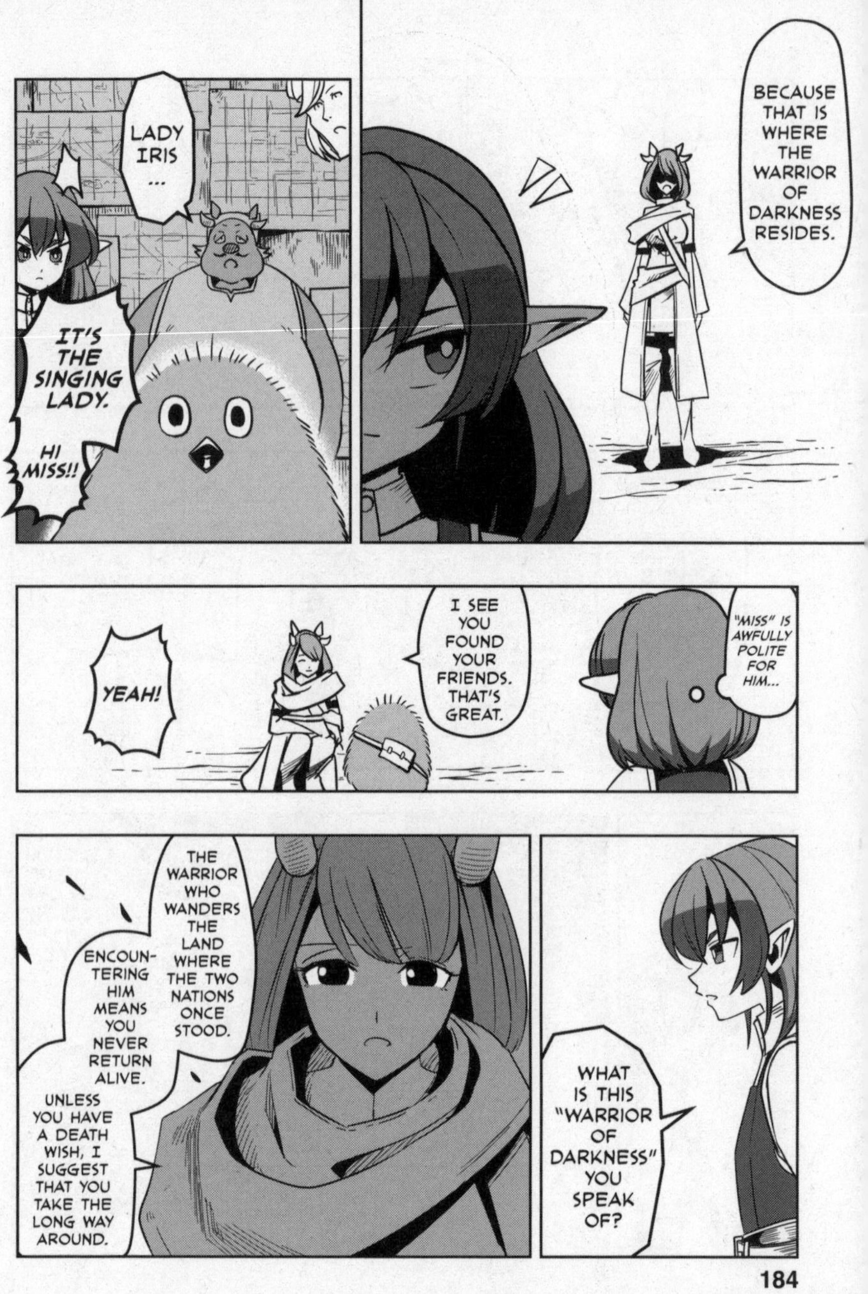
BECAUSE THAT IS WHERE THE WARRIOR OF DARKNESS RESIDES.
LADY IRIS ...
IT'S THE SINGING LADY.
HI MISS!!
"MISS" IS AWFULLY POLITE FOR HIM...
I SEE YOU FOUND YOUR FRIENDS. THAT'S GREAT.
YEAH!
WHAT IS THIS "WARRIOR OF DARKNESS" YOU SPEAK OF?
THE WARRIOR WHO WANDERS THE LAND WHERE THE TWO NATIONS ONCE STOOD.
ENCOUN-TERING HIM MEANS YOU NEVER RETURN ALIVE.
UNLESS YOU HAVE A DEATH WISH, I SUGGEST THAT YOU TAKE THE LONG WAY AROUND.

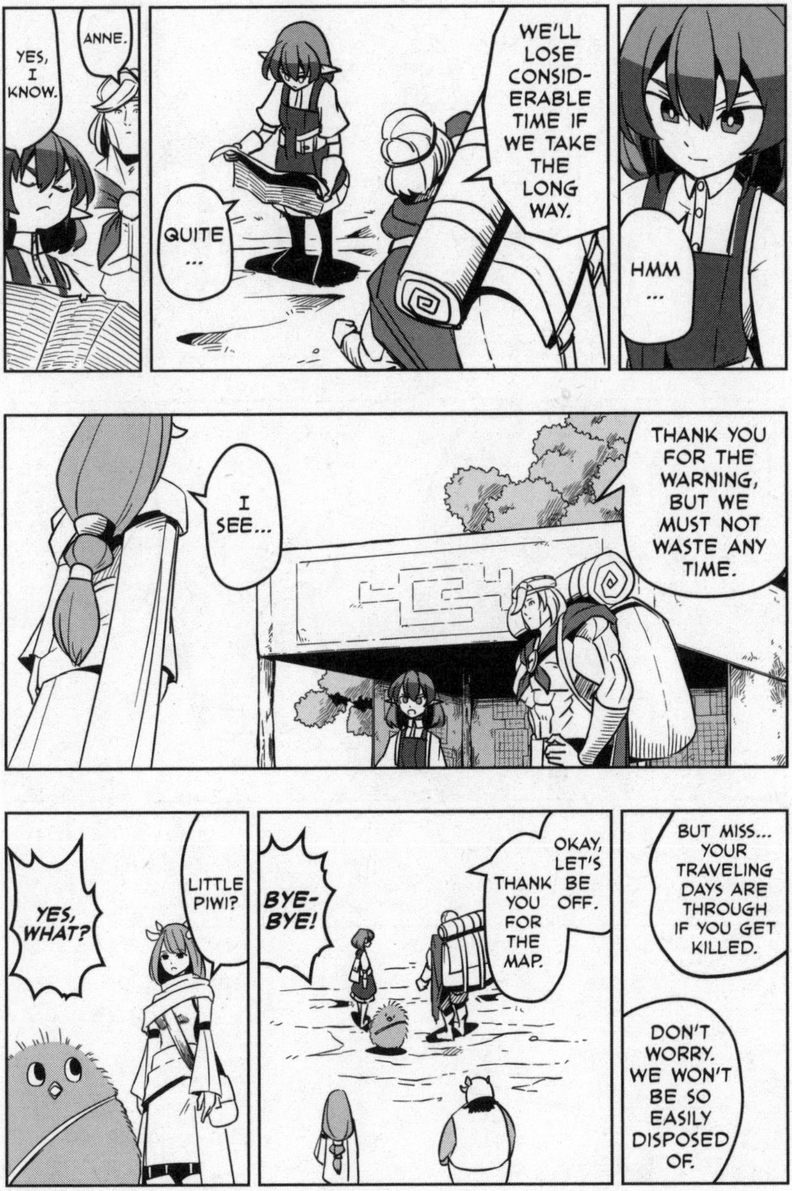
HMM...
WE'LL LOSE CONSID-ERABLE TIME IF WE TAKE THE LONG WAY.
QUITE...
ANNE.
YES, I KNOW.
THANK YOU FOR THE WARNING, BUT WE MUST NOT WASTE ANY TIME.
I SEE...
BUT MISS... YOUR TRAVELING DAYS ARE THROUGH IF YOU GET KILLED.
DON'T WORRY. WE WON'T BE SO EASILY DISPOSED OF.
OKAY, LET'S BE OFF.
THANK YOU FOR THE MAP.
BYE-BYE!
LITTLE PIWI?
YES, WHAT?

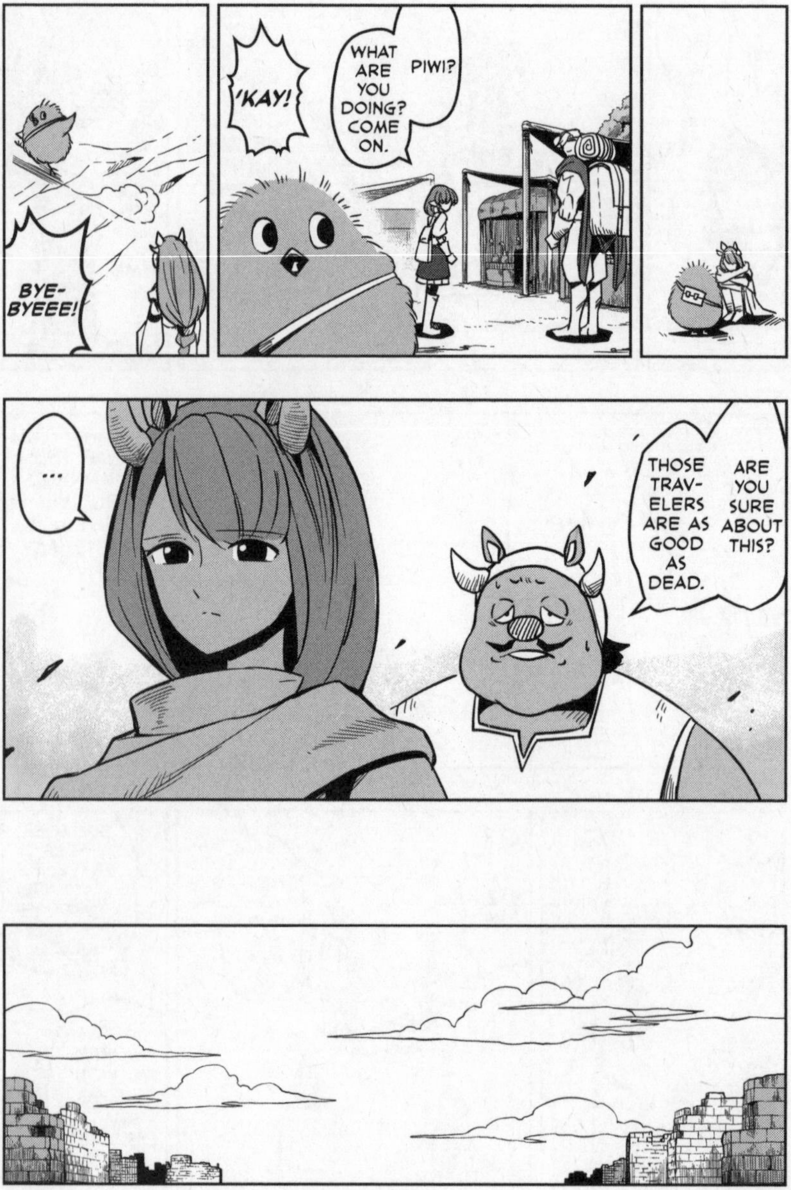
PIWI?
WHAT ARE YOU DOING? COME ON.
'KAY!
BYE-BYEEE!
ARE YOU SURE ABOUT THIS?
THOSE TRAV-ELERS ARE AS GOOD AS DEAD.
...

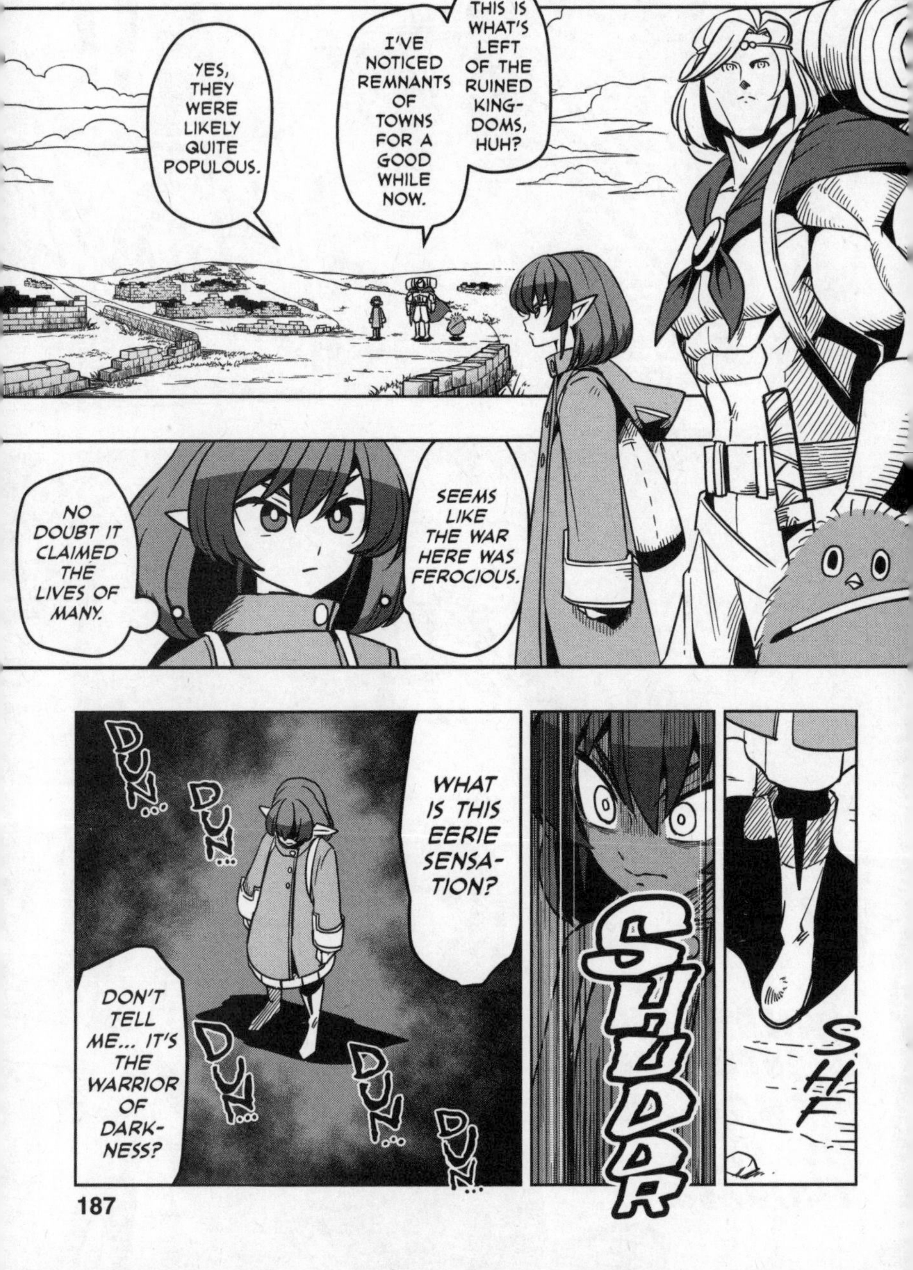
THIS IS WHAT'S LEFT OF THE RUINED KING-DOMS, HUH?
I'VE NOTICED REMNANTS OF TOWNS FOR A GOOD WHILE NOW.
YES, THEY WERE LIKELY QUITE POPULOUS.
SEEMS LIKE THE WAR HERE WAS FEROCIOUS.
NO DOUBT IT CLAIMED THE LIVES OF MANY.
SHF
SHUDDR
WHAT IS THIS EERIE SENSA-TION?
DUN... DUN... DUN... DUN... DUN...
DON'T TELL ME... IT'S THE WARRIOR OF DARK-NESS?

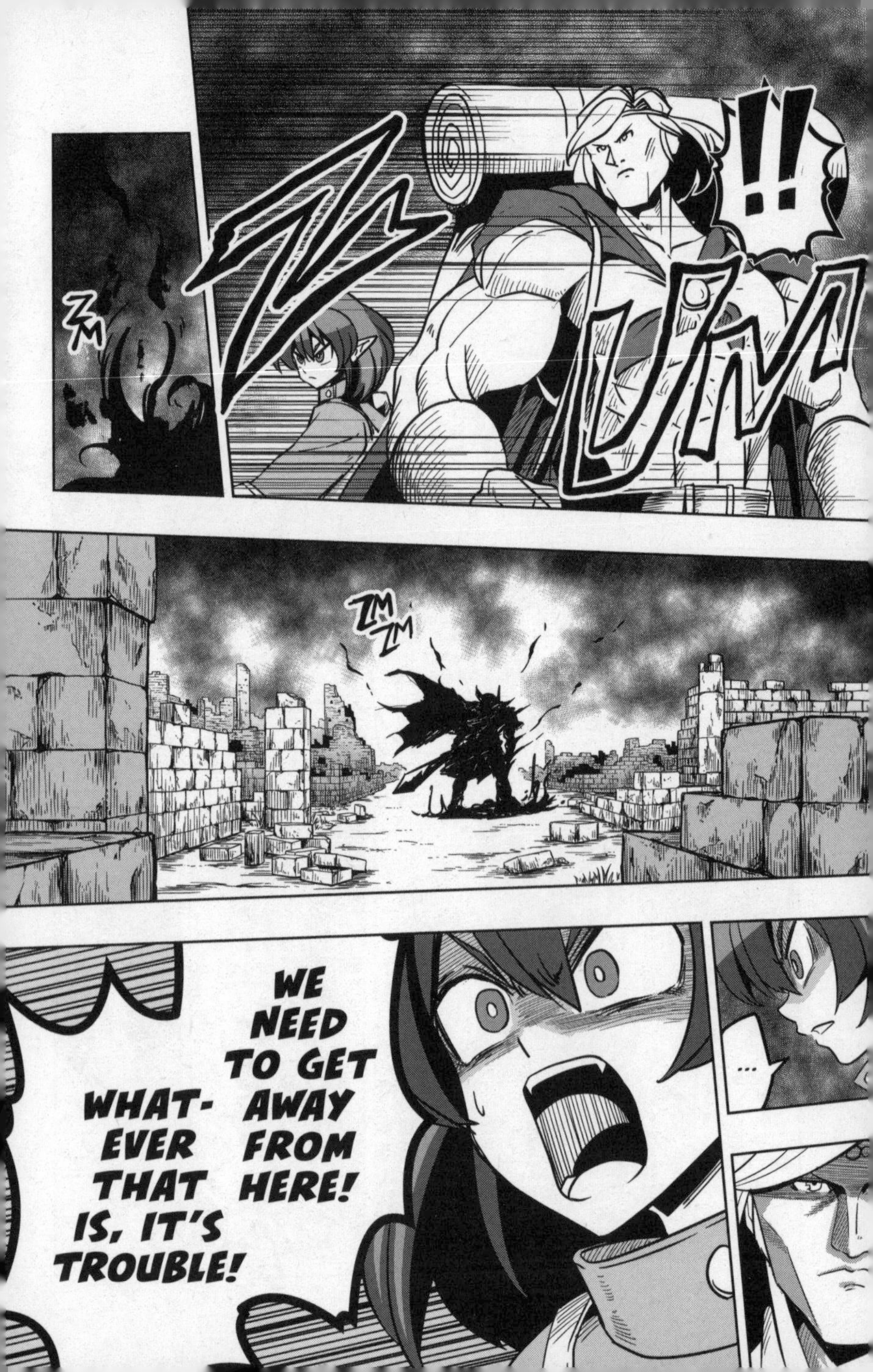
ZUM!!
ZM
ZM ZM
...
WHAT-EVER THAT IS, IT'S TROUBLE! WE NEED TO GET AWAY FROM HERE!

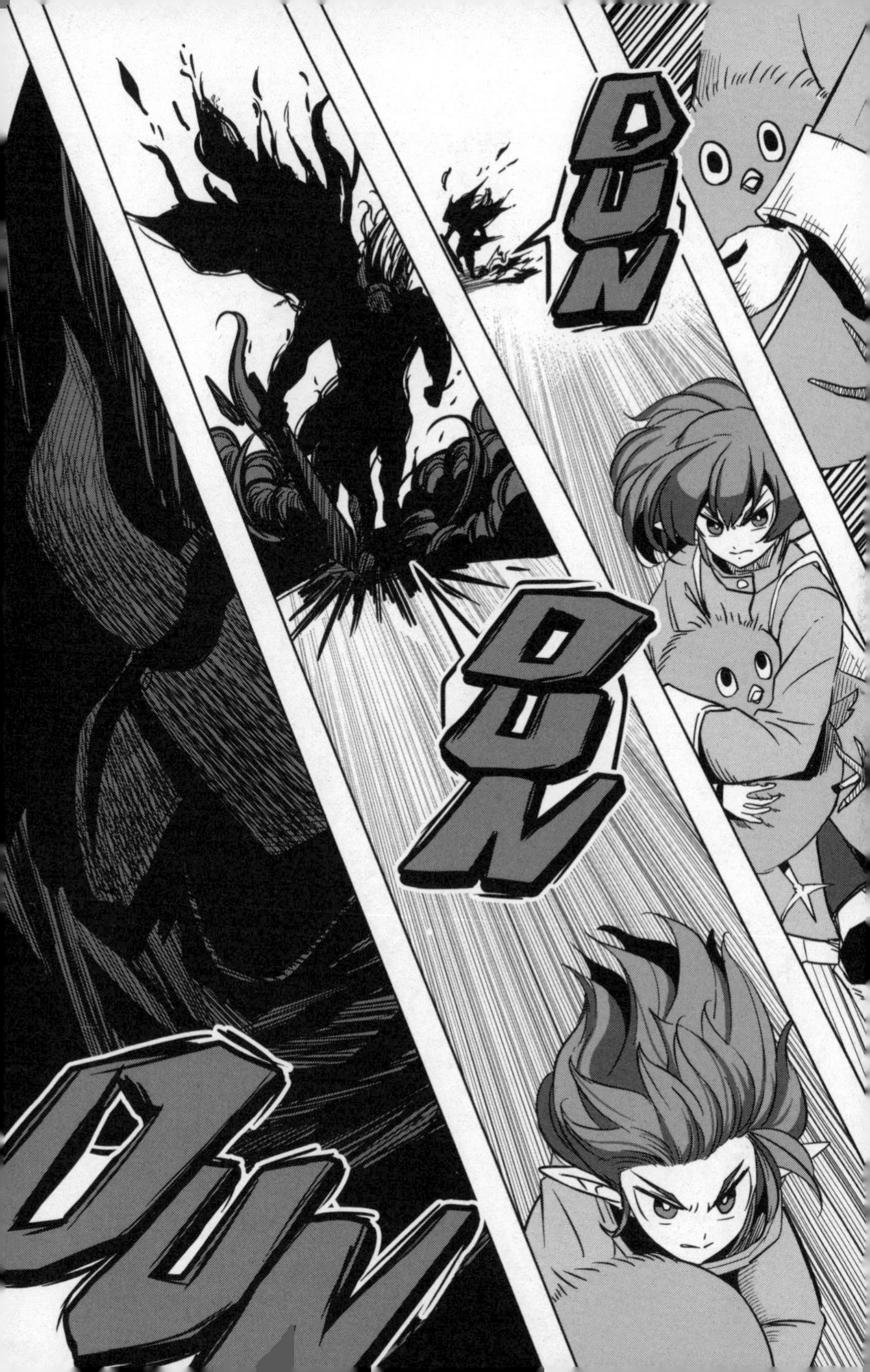
DON
DON
DO

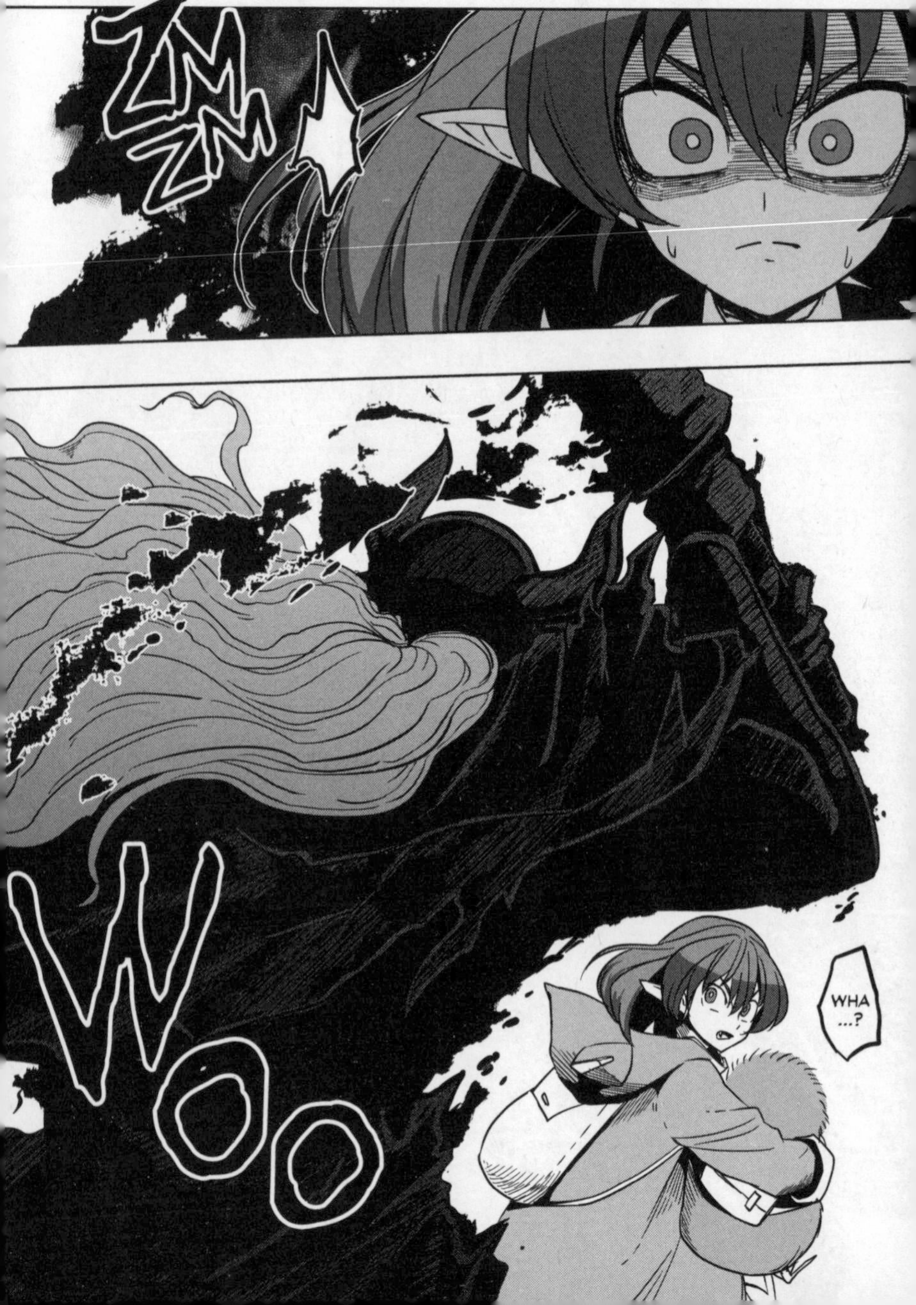
ZM ZM
WHA ...?
WOOO

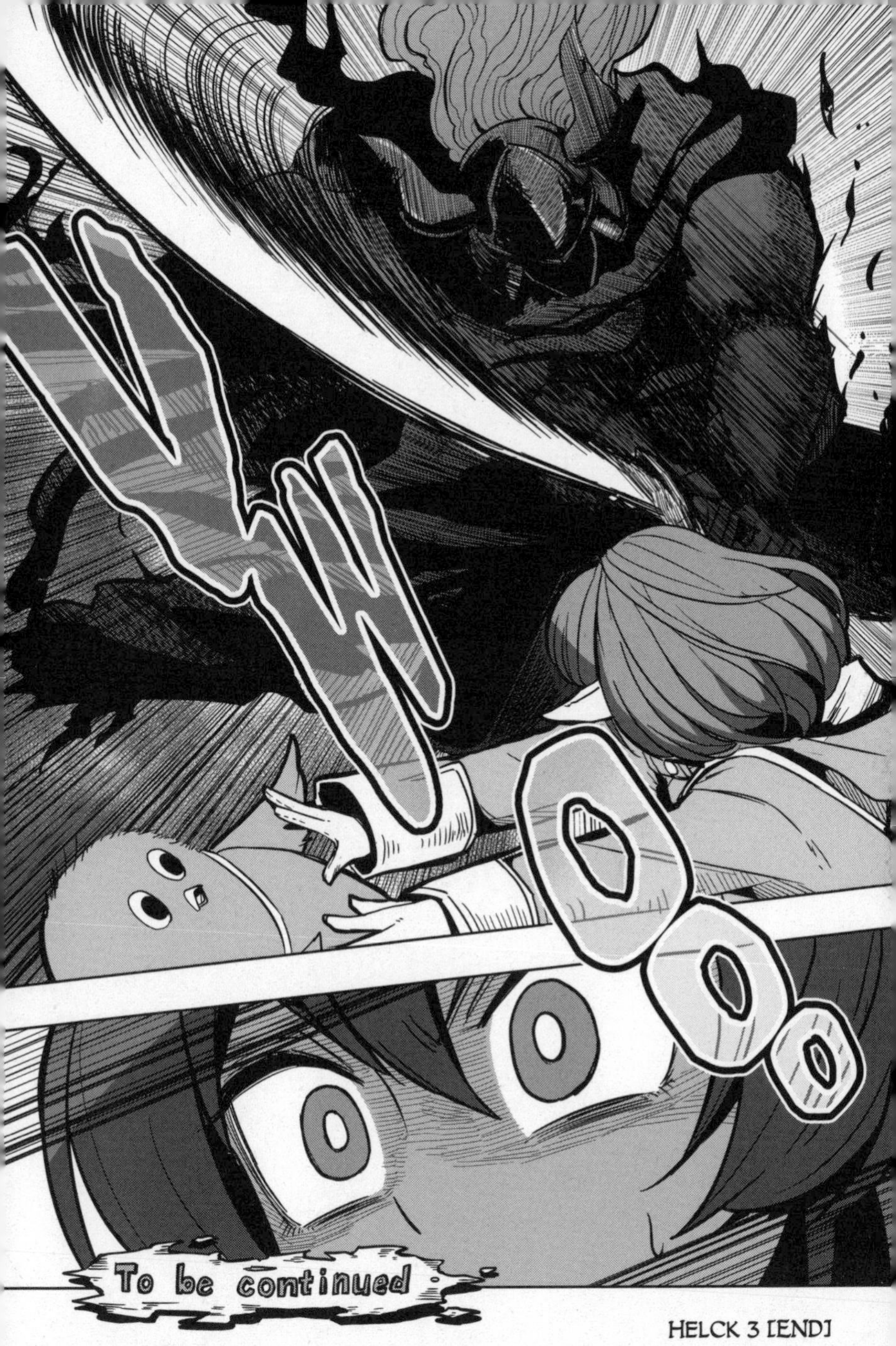
WHOOO
To be continued

HELCK 3 [END]

BONUS COMIC

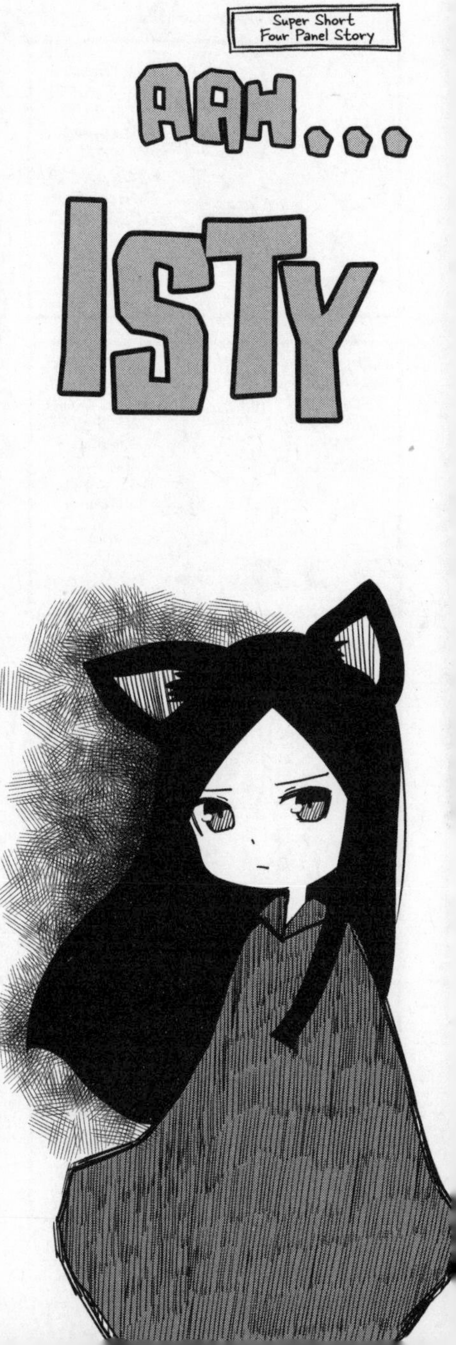
Super Short Four Panel Story
AAH...
ISTY

ASTA

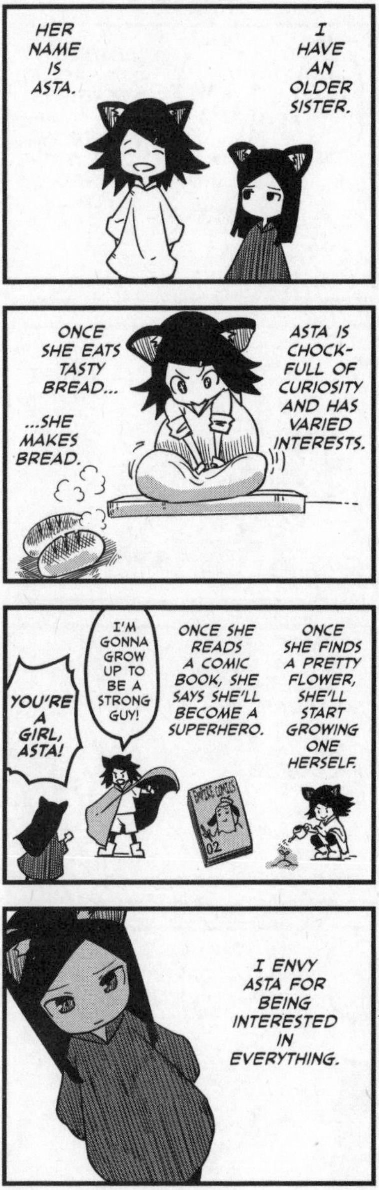
I HAVE AN OLDER SISTER.
HER NAME IS ASTA.
ASTA IS CHOCK-FULL OF CURIOSITY AND HAS VARIED INTERESTS.
ONCE SHE EATS TASTY BREAD...
...SHE MAKES BREAD.
ONCE SHE FINDS A PRETTY FLOWER, SHE'LL START GROWING ONE HERSELF.
ONCE SHE READS A COMIC BOOK, SHE SAYS SHE'LL BECOME A SUPERHERO.
I'M GONNA GROW UP TO BE A STRONG GUY!
YOU'RE A GIRL, ASTA!
I ENVY ASTA FOR BEING INTERESTED IN EVERYTHING.

HYURAN

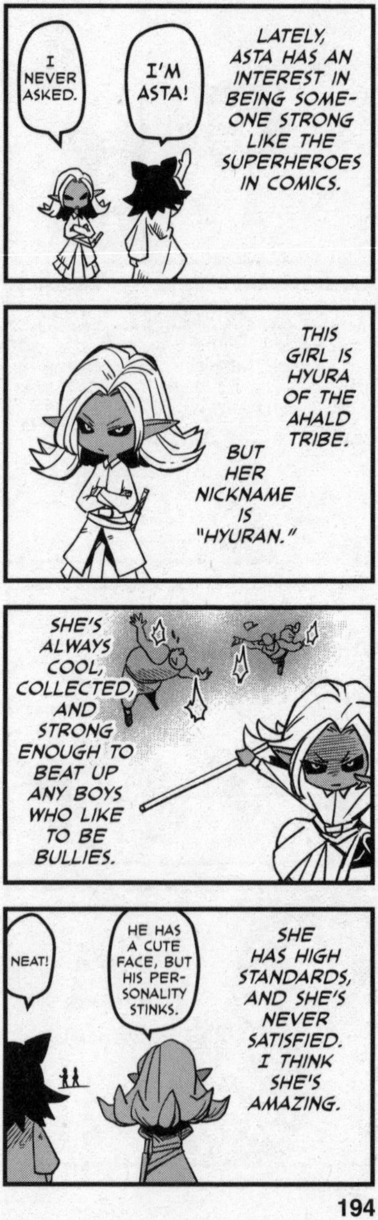
LATELY, ASTA HAS AN INTEREST IN BEING SOMEONE STRONG LIKE THE SUPERHEROES IN COMICS.
I'M ASTA!
I NEVER ASKED.
THIS GIRL IS HYURA OF THE AHALD TRIBE.
BUT HER NICKNAME IS "HYURAN."
SHE'S ALWAYS COOL, COLLECTED, AND STRONG ENOUGH TO BEAT UP ANY BOYS WHO LIKE TO BE BULLIES.
SHE HAS HIGH STANDARDS, AND SHE'S NEVER SATISFIED. I THINK SHE'S AMAZING.
HE HAS A CUTE FACE, BUT HIS PERSONALITY STINKS.
NEAT!

COMPLAIN

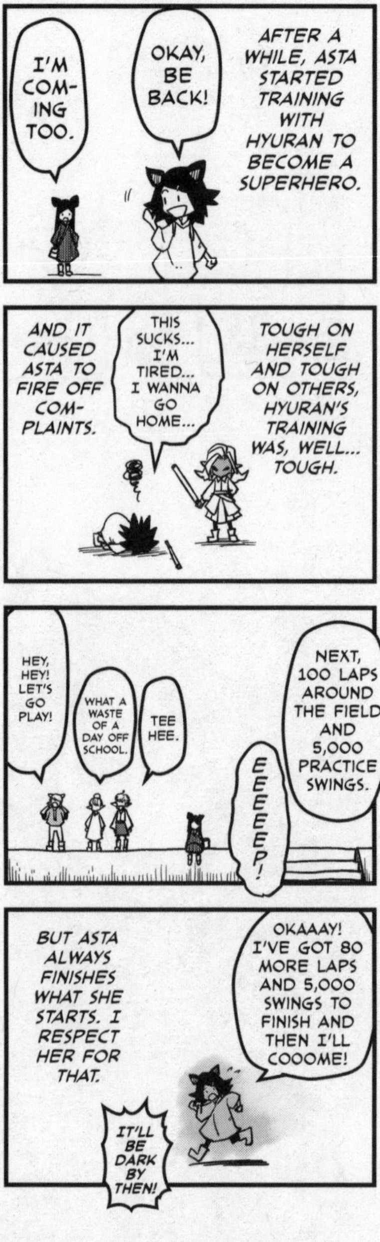
AFTER A WHILE, ASTA STARTED TRAINING WITH HYURAN TO BECOME A SUPERHERO.
OKAY, BE BACK!
I'M COMING TOO.
TOUGH ON HERSELF AND TOUGH ON OTHERS, HYURAN'S TRAINING WAS, WELL... TOUGH.
THIS SUCKS... I'M TIRED... I WANNA GO HOME...
AND IT CAUSED ASTA TO FIRE OFF COMPLAINTS.
NEXT, 100 LAPS AROUND THE FIELD AND 5,000 PRACTICE SWINGS.
EEEEEEP!
TEE HEE.
WHAT A WASTE OF A DAY OFF SCHOOL.
HEY, HEY! LET'S GO PLAY!
OKAAAY! I'VE GOT 80 MORE LAPS AND 5,000 SWINGS TO FINISH AND THEN I'LL COOOME!
BUT ASTA ALWAYS FINISHES WHAT SHE STARTS. I RESPECT HER FOR THAT.
IT'LL BE DARK BY THEN!

TACTICS

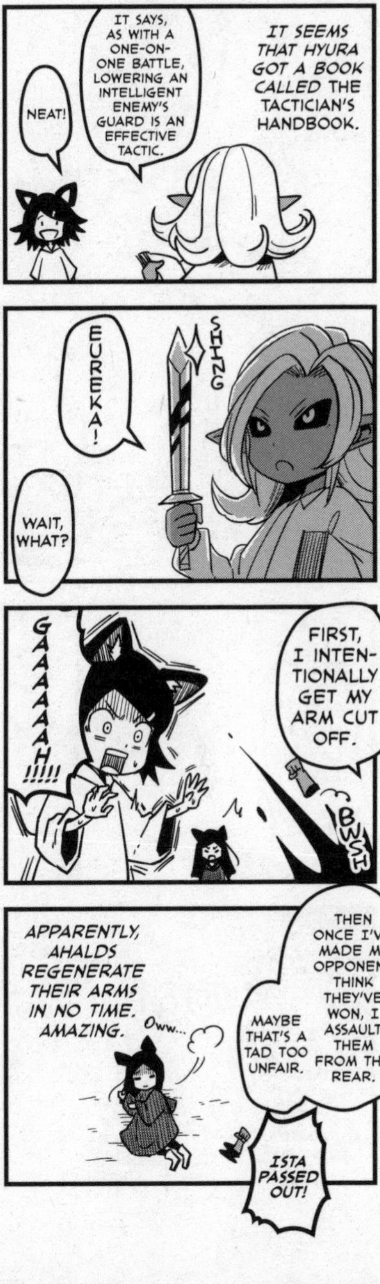
IT SEEMS THAT HYURA GOT A BOOK CALLED THE TACTICIAN'S HANDBOOK.
IT SAYS, AS WITH A ONE-ON-ONE BATTLE, LOWERING AN INTELLIGENT ENEMY'S GUARD IS AN EFFECTIVE TACTIC.
NEAT!
SHING
EUREKA!
WAIT, WHAT?
FIRST, I INTENTIONALLY GET MY ARM CUT OFF.
BWSH
GAAAAAAAH!!!!!
THEN ONCE I'VE MADE MY OPPONENT THINK THEY'VE WON, I ASSAULT THEM FROM THE REAR.
MAYBE THAT'S A TAD TOO UNFAIR.
APPARENTLY, AHALDS REGENERATE THEIR ARMS IN NO TIME. AMAZING.
Oww...
ISTA PASSED OUT!

QUIT

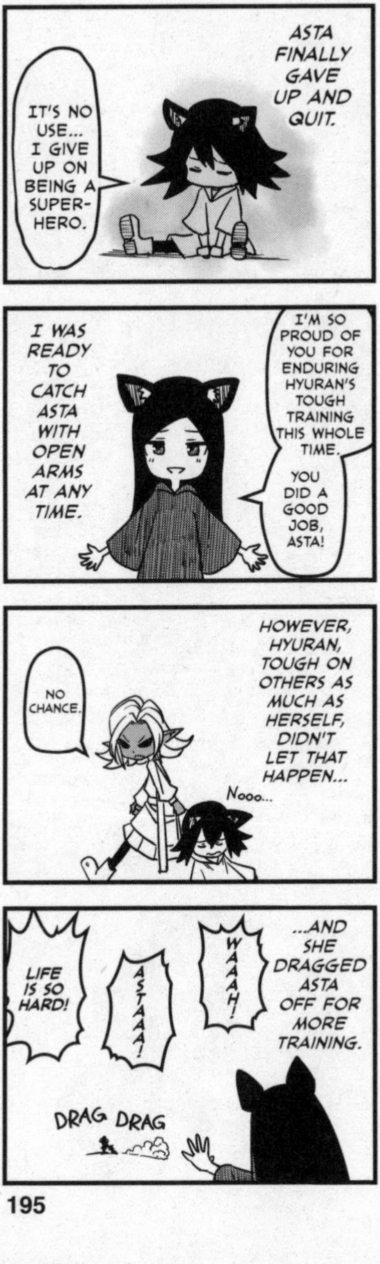
ASTA FINALLY GAVE UP AND QUIT.
IT'S NO USE... I GIVE UP ON BEING A SUPER-HERO.
I'M SO PROUD OF YOU FOR ENDURING HYURAN'S TOUGH TRAINING THIS WHOLE TIME.
YOU DID A GOOD JOB, ASTA!
I WAS READY TO CATCH ASTA WITH OPEN ARMS AT ANY TIME.
HOWEVER, HYURAN, TOUGH ON OTHERS AS MUCH AS HERSELF, DIDN'T LET THAT HAPPEN...
NO CHANCE.
Nooo...
...AND SHE DRAGGED ASTA OFF FOR MORE TRAINING.
WAAAH!
ASTAAA!
LIFE IS SO HARD!
DRAG DRAG

TROUBLE

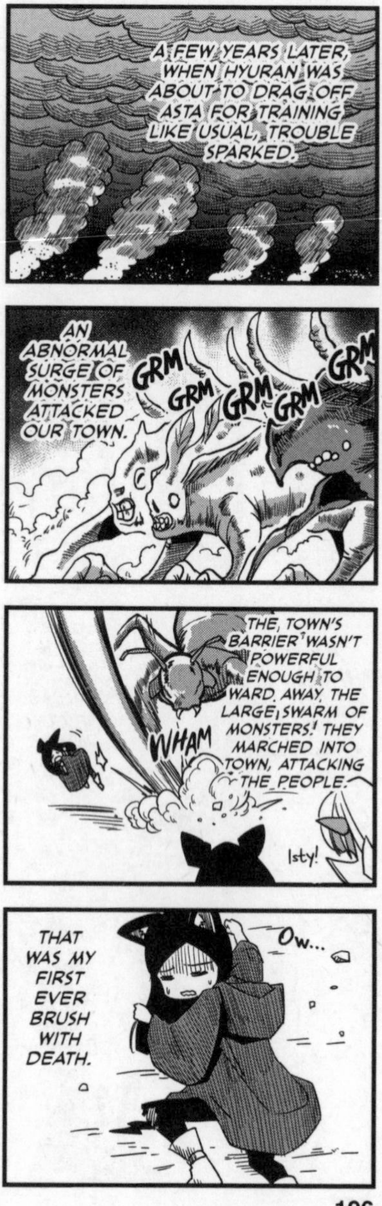
A FEW YEARS LATER, WHEN HYURAN WAS ABOUT TO DRAG OFF ASTA FOR TRAINING LIKE USUAL, TROUBLE SPARKED.
AN ABNORMAL SURGE OF MONSTERS ATTACKED OUR TOWN.
GRM
GRM
GRM
GRM
GRM
THE TOWN'S BARRIER WASN'T POWERFUL ENOUGH TO WARD AWAY THE LARGE SWARM OF MONSTERS! THEY MARCHED INTO TOWN, ATTACKING THE PEOPLE.
WHAM
Isty!
Ow...
THAT WAS MY FIRST EVER BRUSH WITH DEATH.

FLAMES

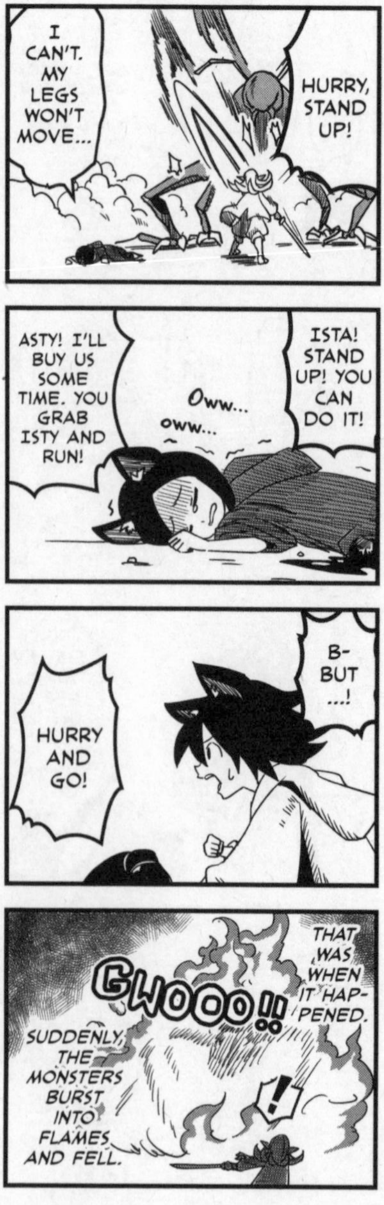
HURRY, STAND UP!
I CAN'T. MY LEGS WON'T MOVE...
ISTA! STAND UP! YOU CAN DO IT!
Oww... oww...
ASTY! I'LL BUY US SOME TIME. YOU GRAB ISTY AND RUN!
B-BUT ...!
HURRY AND GO!
THAT WAS WHEN IT HAPPENED.
GWOOO!!
SUDDENLY, THE MONSTERS BURST INTO FLAMES AND FELL.

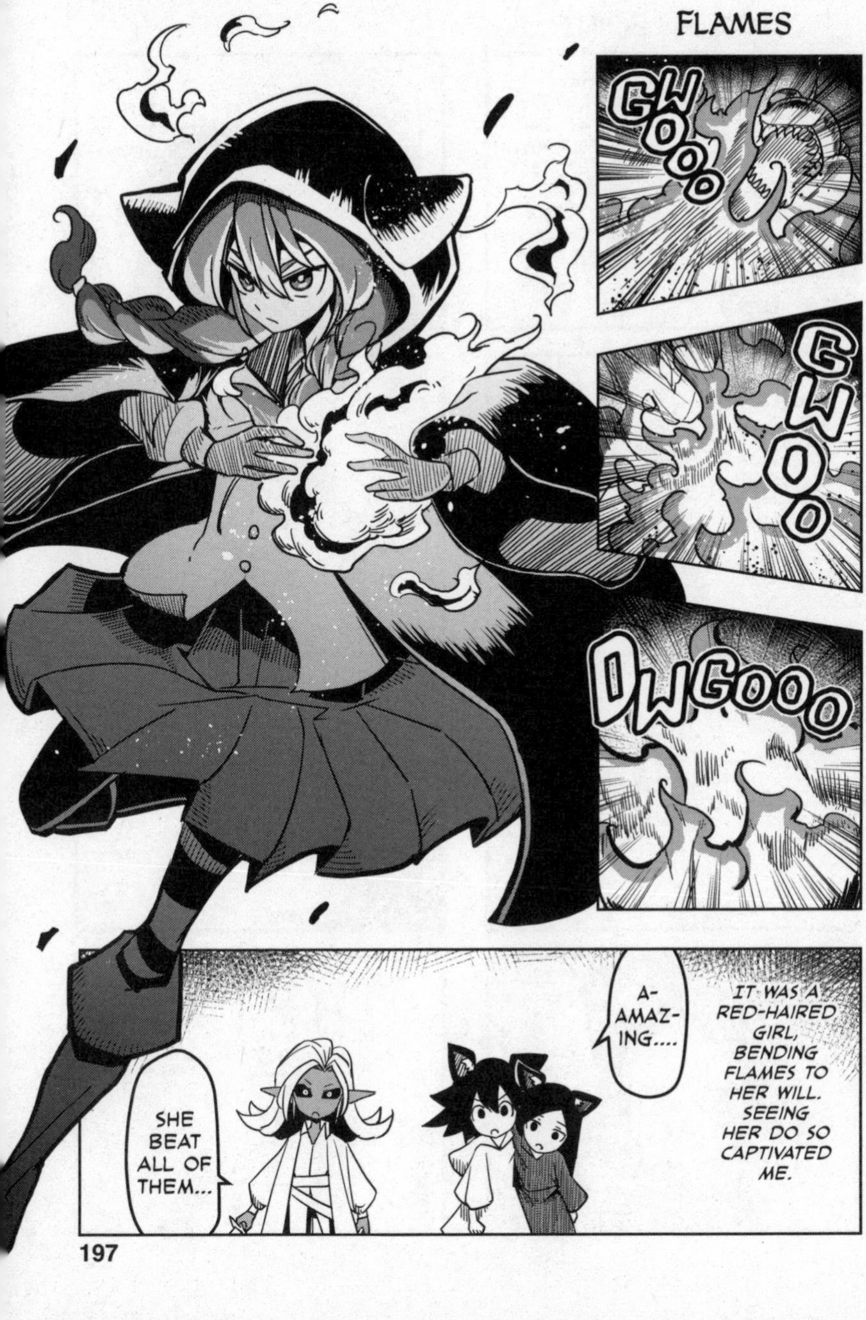
FLAMES
GWOOO
GWOO
DWGOOO
IT WAS A RED-HAIRED GIRL, BENDING FLAMES TO HER WILL. SEEING HER DO SO CAPTIVATED ME.
A-AMAZ-ING....
SHE BEAT ALL OF THEM...

?!

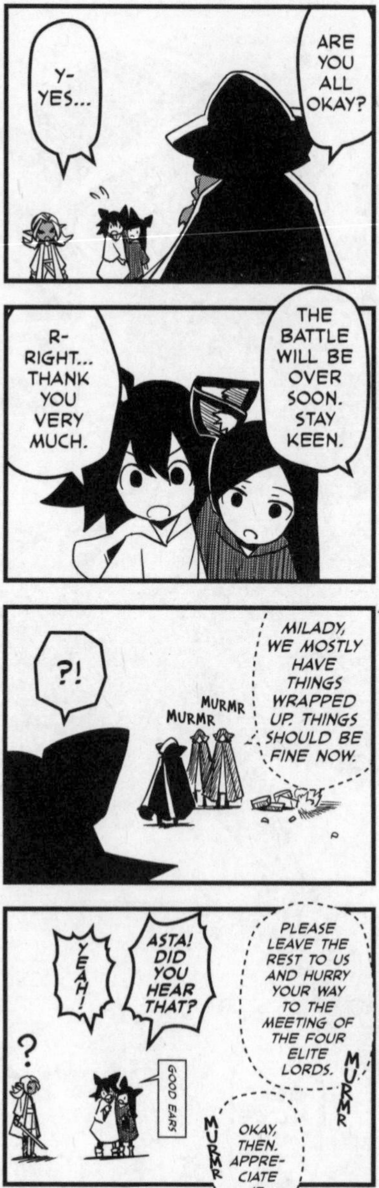
ARE YOU ALL OKAY?
Y-YES...
THE BATTLE WILL BE OVER SOON. STAY KEEN.
R-RIGHT... THANK YOU VERY MUCH.
MILADY, WE MOSTLY HAVE THINGS WRAPPED UP. THINGS SHOULD BE FINE NOW.
MURMR
MURMR
?!
PLEASE LEAVE THE REST TO US AND HURRY YOUR WAY TO THE MEETING OF THE FOUR ELITE LORDS.
MURMR
ASTA! DID YOU HEAR THAT?
YEAH!
GOOD EARS
?
MURMR
OKAY, THEN. APPRECIATE IT.

TURNING POINT

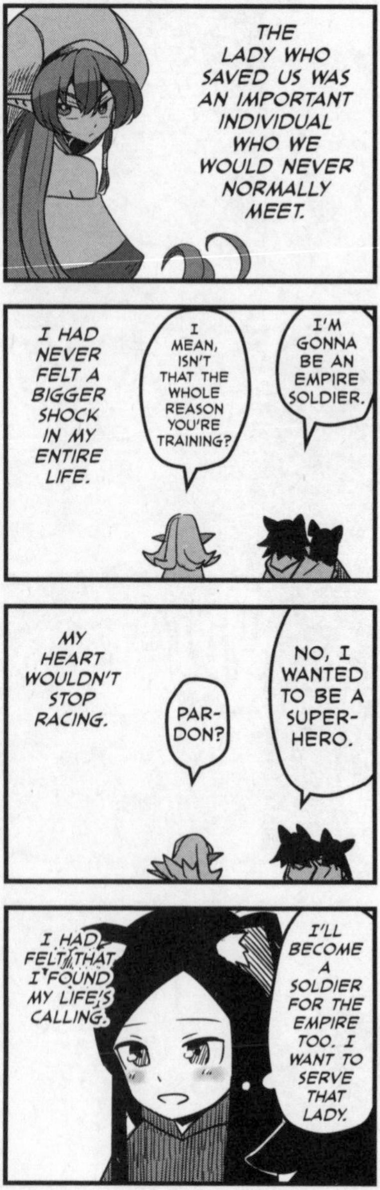
THE LADY WHO SAVED US WAS AN IMPORTANT INDIVIDUAL WHO WE WOULD NEVER NORMALLY MEET.
I'M GONNA BE AN EMPIRE SOLDIER.
I MEAN, ISN'T THAT THE WHOLE REASON YOU'RE TRAINING?
I HAD NEVER FELT A BIGGER SHOCK IN MY ENTIRE LIFE.
NO, I WANTED TO BE A SUPER-HERO.
PAR-DON?
MY HEART WOULDN'T STOP RACING.
I'LL BECOME A SOLDIER FOR THE EMPIRE TOO. I WANT TO SERVE THAT LADY.
I HAD FELT THAT I FOUND MY LIFE'S CALLING.

VILE CANDY

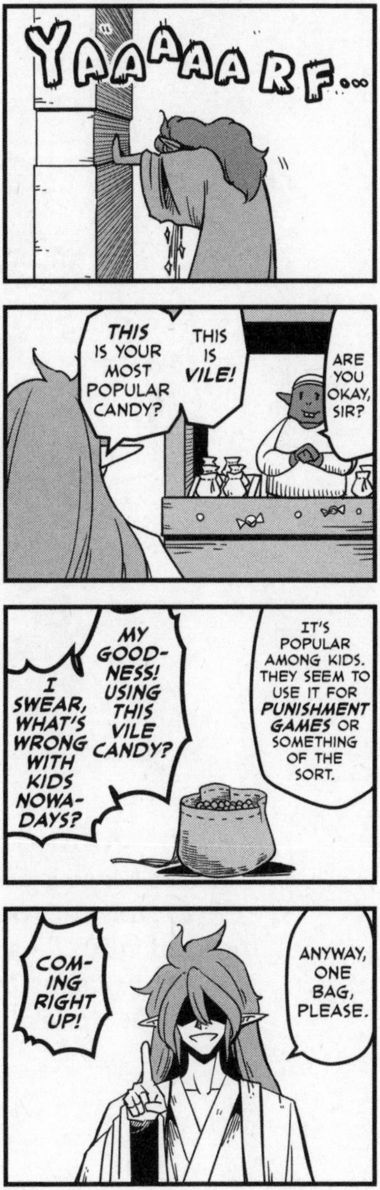
YAAAAARF...
ARE YOU OKAY, SIR?
THIS IS VILE!
THIS IS YOUR MOST POPULAR CANDY?
IT'S POPULAR AMONG KIDS. THEY SEEM TO USE IT FOR PUNISHMENT GAMES OR SOMETHING OF THE SORT.
MY GOODNESS! USING THIS VILE CANDY?
I SWEAR, WHAT'S WRONG WITH KIDS NOWADAYS?
ANYWAY, ONE BAG, PLEASE.
COMING RIGHT UP!

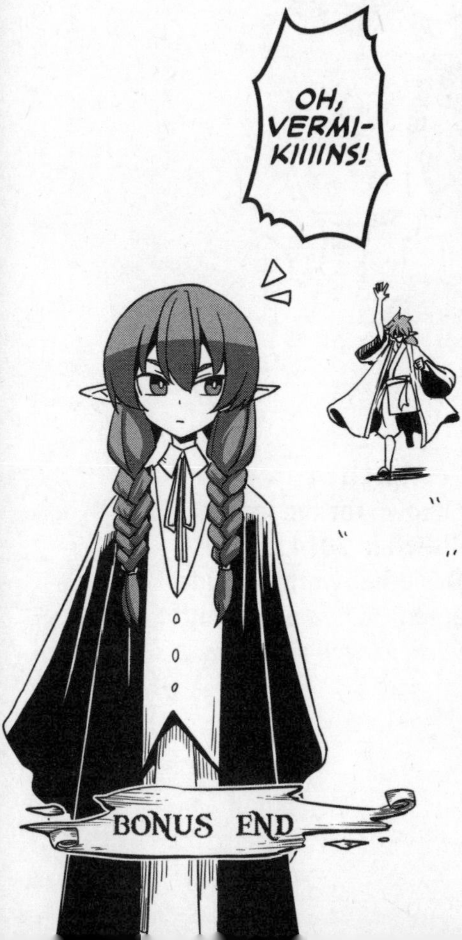
OH, VERMIKIIIINS!
BONUS END

About the Author

Nanaki Nanao is best known for the manga
Helck, originally published in 2014 and re-
released in 2022. Nanao's other works include
Piwi and *Völundo: Divergent Sword Saga*, both
set in the world of *Helck*, as well as *Acaria*.

Helck

3

Story and Art by NANAKI NANAO

Translation: **DAVID EVELYN**
Touch-Up Art & Lettering: **ANNALIESE "ACE" CHRISTMAN**
Design: **KAM LI**
Editor: **JACK CARRILLO CONCORDIA**

HELCK SHINSOBAN Vol. 3
by Nanaki NANAO
© 2022 Nanaki NANAO
All rights reserved.
Original Japanese edition published by SHOGAKUKAN.
English translation rights in the United States of America, Canada, the
United Kingdom, Ireland, Australia and New Zealand arranged with
SHOGAKUKAN.

Original Cover Design: Masato ISHIZAWA + Bay Bridge Studio

The stories, characters, and incidents mentioned in this publication are
entirely fictional.

Printed in the U.S.A.

Published by VIZ Media, LLC
P.O. Box 77010
San Francisco, CA 94107

10 9 8 7 6 5 4 3 2 1
First printing, May 2023

viz.com

shonensunday.com

PARENTAL ADVISORY
HELCK is rated T for Teen and is recom-
mended for ages 13 and up. This volume
contains fantasy violence.

A new feudal fairytale begins!

YASHAHIME

— PRINCESS HALF-DEMON —

Story and Art
Takashi Shiina

Main Character Design
Rumiko Takahashi

Script Cooperation Katsuyuki Sumisawa

Can the three teenage daughters of demon dog half-brothers Inuyasha and Sesshomaru save their parents, themselves, and both realms from the menace of the seven mystical Rainbow Pearls?

RATED T TEEN VIZ

The adventure is over but life goes on for an elf mage just beginning to learn what living is all about.

Frieren

Beyond Journey's End

Decades after their victory, the funeral of one of her friends confronts Frieren with her own near immortality. Frieren sets out to fulfill the last wishes of her comrades and finds herself beginning a new adventure...

Story by **Kanehito Yamada**
Art by **Tsukasa Abe**

Kidnapped by the Demon King and imprisoned in his castle, Princess Syalis is...bored.

Sleepy Princess in the Demon Castle

Story & Art by
KAGIJI KUMANOMATA

Captured princess Syalis decides to while away her hours in the Demon Castle by sleeping, but getting a good night's rest turns out to be a lot of work! She begins by fashioning a DIY pillow out of the fur of her Teddy Demon guards and an "air mattress" from the magical Shield of the Wind. Things go from bad to worse—for her captors—when some of Princess Syalis's schemes end in her untimely—if temporary—demise and she chooses the Forbidden Grimoire for her bedtime reading...

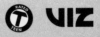

Komi Can't Communicate

Story & Art by Tomohito Oda

The journey to a hundred friends begins with a single conversation.

Socially anxious high school student Shoko Komi's greatest dream is to make some friends, but everyone at school mistakes her crippling social anxiety for cool reserve. With the whole student body keeping its distance and Komi unable to utter a single word, friendship might be forever beyond her reach.

VIZ   ⓣ

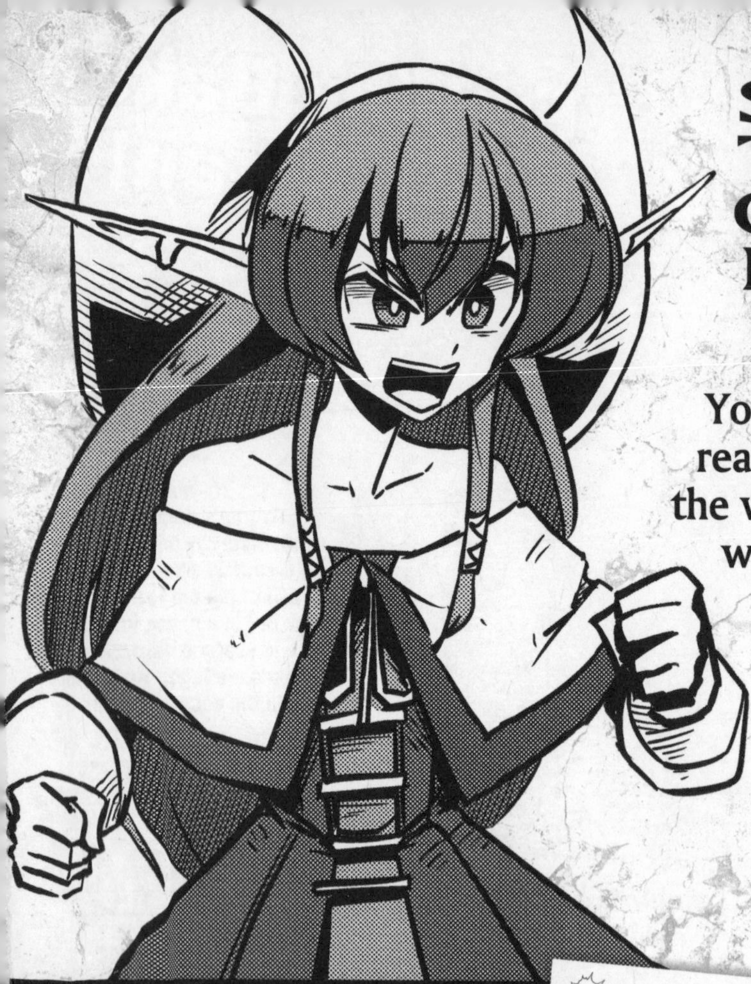

STOP!

You're reading the wrong way!

In keeping with the original Japanese comic format, this book reads from right to left—so action, sound effects and word balloons are completely reversed to preserve the orientation of the original artwork.

Check out the diagram shown here to get the hang of things, and then turn to the other side of the book to get started!

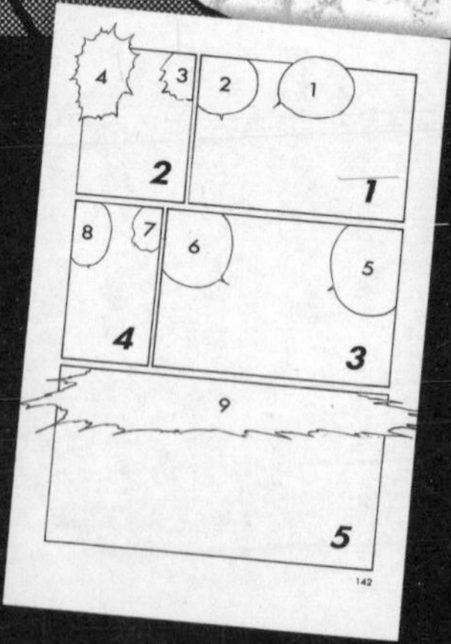
1
2
3
4
1
2
5
6
7
8
3
4
9
5
142